NEW YORK REVIEW
CLASSICS

M000211159

STONES OF ARAN: PILGRIMAGE

TIM ROBINSON was born in 1935 and brought up in Yorkshire. He studied mathematics at Cambridge and worked as a teacher and artist in Istanbul, Vienna, and London. In 1972 he moved to the Aran Islands to write and make maps. He now lives in Roundstone, County Galway. He is also the author of *Mapping South Connemara* (1985) and *Setting Foot on the Shores of Connemara and Other Writings* (1996). His *Folding Landscape Project*, which won a major European Conservation Award in 1987, has produced radically new maps of the Burren in County Clare, the Aran Islands, and Connemara.

ROBERT MACFARLANE is the author of *Mountains of the Mind: A History of a Fascination* (2003), which won the Somerset Maugham Award, and *The Wild Places* (2007), which won the Boardman-Tasker Prize for Mountain Literature. He is a Fellow of Emmanuel College, Cambridge.

Stones of Aran
PILGRIMAGE

TIM ROBINSON

Introduction by
ROBERT MACFARLANE

NEW YORK REVIEW BOOKS

New York

THIS IS A NEW YORK REVIEW BOOK
PUBLISHED BY THE NEW YORK REVIEW OF BOOKS
435 Hudson Street, New York, NY 10014
www.nyrb.com

Copyright © 1986 by Tim Robinson
Introduction copyright © 2008 by Robert Macfarlane

Library of Congress Cataloging-in-Publication Data
Robinson, Tim, 1935–
  Stones of Aran : pilgrimage / by Tim Robinson ; introduction by Robert
Macfarlane.
      p. cm. — (New York Review Books classics)
  Reprint. Originally published: Mullingar, Co. Westmeath, Ireland :
Lilliput Press, 1986 (With new introd.)
  Includes bibliographical references and index.
  ISBN 978-1-59017-277-3 (alk. paper)
  1. Aran Islands (Ireland)—Description and travel. 2. Robinson, Tim,
1935- —Travel—Ireland—Aran Islands. 3. Walking—Ireland—Aran
Islands. I. Title.
  DA990.A8R62 2008
  941.7'48—dc22

                                    2007052585
ISBN 978-1-59017-277-3

Printed in the United States of America on acid-free paper.
10 9 8 7 6 5

CONTENTS

II. EXCURSION ·

III. NORTH ·

INTRODUCTION

In County Clare on the west coast of Ireland, between the granite of Galway and the sandstone of Liscannor, rises a vast limestone escarpment—pewter in color on a dull day, and silver in sunshine. The limestone begins in the area of Clare known as the Burren, from the Gaelic *boireann*, meaning "rocky place." It extends in a northwesterly direction, dipping beneath the Atlantic, to resurge thirty miles offshore as three islands: Árainn, Inis Meáin, and Inis Oírr—or the Aran Islands, as they are also called.

Limestone has been blessed with two exceptional English writers. The first of these is W. H. Auden, who loved the high karst shires of England's Pennines. What most moved Auden about limestone was the way it eroded. Limestone is soluble in water, which means that any weaknesses in the original rock get slowly deepened by a process of liquid wear. Thus the form into which limestone grows over time is determined by its first flaws. For Auden, this was a human as well as a mineral quality: he found in limestone a version of the truth that we are defined by our faults as much as by our substance.

The second of the great limestone writers is Tim Robinson. In the summer of 1972, Robinson and his wife—to whom he refers in his writing only as "M"—moved from London to Aran, the largest of the islands. Their first winter was difficult: big Atlantic storms, brief days, and "an unprecedented sequence of deaths [among the islanders], mainly by drowning or by falls and exposure on the crags," all challenged their resolve to continue living there. But they did stay, and Robinson—a mathematician by training and an artist by vocation—began to consider how he might respond creatively to his adopted landscape.

So began one of the most sustained, intensive, and imaginative studies of a place that has ever been carried out. Robinson conceived of a local epic: a two-volume prose study of Aran, accompanied by a new map of all three islands (which he would survey and draw). He decided that he would not write a "diary of intoxication" about Aran, for enough of these already existed, penned by J. M. Synge, W. B. Yeats, and Lady Gregory among others. Instead the first volume, *Pilgrimage*, would describe a circumambulation of the island's coast. Robinson would walk the coastline clockwise, sunwise—"the circuit that blesses"—and he would walk not at "a penitential trudge but at an inquiring, digressive and wondering pace." The features of the coast would be the stations of this offbeat pilgrimage, and close attention would be its method of devotion. The landscape itself would improvise the narrative. Once this ritual beating of the island's bounds was completed, he would then delve into Aran's intricate interior for the second volume, *Labyrinth*.

Long before psycho-geography became a modish term, Robinson was out on the *dérive*: walking the rimrock, surveying, measuring, talking to the "custodians of local lore," watching, dreaming, and recording. In bad weather—of which there is plenty on Aran—he would hold his notebook and pencil inside a clear plastic bag, tied shut at his wrists, and proceed in this manner. He must have looked, to those who encountered him, like a deranged dowser or pilgrim, wandering through the mists and the storm spray, hands locked together in mania or prayer.

For years, Robinson walked, and as he did the sentences began to come: beautiful, dense, paced. *Pilgrimage* was published in 1986, fourteen years after his arrival on Aran. As with all great landscape works (of which there are very few), it is at once territorially specific and utterly mythic. The one island becomes in Robinson's view both a fragment of "broken, blessed, Pangaea" (a version of the world on which we all live, and whose materiality we differently adore and resist) and also a terrain with its own intricate and indigenous histories. He wanted, as he put it, to remain attentive to "the subtle actualities of Aran life," but also to "the immensities in which this little place is wrapped." This continual vibration between the particular and the universal is one of the book's most distinctive actions.

The opening chapter, "Timescape with Signpost," offers a creation myth for Aran: its geological birth out of the ur-continent of Pangaea and from "its unbounded encircling ocean was Panthalassa, all-sea." The writing here is fabulous in the old sense of that word: a localized version of Genesis, in which can distantly be heard the thunder of Old Testament rhythms. It places Aran and its people in the context of what John McPhee has called "deep time": the geological perspective of past and future that can make human presence, "all our lore and our nightmares," seem irrelevant. "Unless vaster earth-processes intervene," writes Robinson, "Aran will ultimately dwindle to a little reef and disappear. It seems unlikely that any creatures we would recognize as our descendants will be here to chart that rock in whatever shape of sea succeeds to Galway Bay." Such timescales make a nonsense of most human behavior and all human prejudices—especially that of nationalism. The idea that you can belong to a defined area of land, or even that a defined area of land can belong to you? Lunacy, says Robinson. Seen within the perspective of deep time, "the geographies over which we are so suicidally passionate are...fleeting expressions of the earth's face."

But after this opening vision of "immensity," Robinson focuses tightly down upon Aran's "actualities": the habits of its birds, animals, and plants; its present human customs and pasts. Aran has been inhabited for more than four thousand years, and such prolonged human activity on such a limited area of land means that history exists thickly there. Each era has left its marks, usually in the form of stone (a substance that "may fall, but still endures"): cairns, walls, tombs, cashels, megaliths, cells, chapels...Robinson treats each of these structures as a historical puzzle, whose origins and name might—with luck and diligence—be fathomed.

He brings this fierce curiosity to bear on all the phenomena that he encounters on his pilgrimage. How was the storm beach of Gort na gCapall formed? Why does the wren flourish on one side of Aran, and the raven on the other? Why is Cockle Strand so called? How were the puffins of Poll an Iomair, the trough-like cliff, harvested? What ceremonies surrounded the firing of the kelp kiln of Mainistir? Robinson investigates these questions, and thousands more. He is interested, to borrow a phrase from Les Murray, in only everything. Reading *Pilgrimage*, you are astonished at the density of the cultural strata that have settled over this landscape, and at the care and precision with which Robinson excavates them.

Many landscape writers have striven to give their prose the characteristics of the terrain they are describing. Few have succeeded as fully as Robinson. The erosive habits of limestone means that it is rich with clandestine places: runnels, crevasses, hollows, and gulleys. So too is Robinson's style, the polished surfaces of which contain an enormous complexity of thought. Like limestone, his books are broken up into irregular sections. "Chapters" is not quite the word for these sections: better, perhaps, to call them "blocks," or even "clints"—the exact term for the surface of a weathered slab of limestone.

Robinson's writing also shares with limestone a concern for historical record. Limestone's solubility, as he brilliantly observes, makes it "a uniquely tender and memorious ground. Every shower sends rivulets wandering across its surface, deepening the ways of their predecessors and gradually engraving their initial caprices as law into the stone." The "memorious" properties of limestone are matched by the ancient oral culture of the Aran Islands; a collective "folk-mind" that is tenacious in its recall of story and its connection to place. This oral culture has, though, become increasingly vulnerable over the twentieth and twenty-first centuries, as the islands have opened up to the outside world and what

Robinson anxiously calls "the material destructiveness of modern life." So *Pilgrimage* can be understood as Robinson's transcription and ordering of the island's folk-mind—a memory-map. It is an attempt to safeguard perishable knowledge, and to slow the evaporation of Gaelic from the islands.

There is no plot to *Pilgrimage*, as there is no plot to a landscape. Robinson repeats himself with variation, because this is what his chosen terrain does. His narrative proceeds by the ancient contingencies of geology and the immediate contingencies of footfall, and by pattern, affinity, and form. Early in *Pilgrimage*, for instance, in a section called "Arguments from Weakness," Robinson is remarking on the "schema of fissure-planes and strata-partings" that is visible in the sea cliffs and certain stone fields near An Aill Bhán, the White Cliff. Suddenly his imagination turns skyward, and he recalls seeing the contrails left by transatlantic airplanes flying from Shannon airport:

> slow silver darts [that] rise one by one far in the south-east, arc silently across the dazzling heights and sink to the western horizon while their murmurous voices are still lagging past the zenith; I have seen their departures follow on so closely that three or four are glinting in the sky at once and their vapour-trails entwine and merge and are scored into the blue as if the sky itself were weakened, fissured and veined, along an invisible line of predestined fall.

It is a beautiful and layered movement; from the fissured stone to the fissured sky, from the "memorious" rock to the "murmurous" machines, and from the prehistoric to the present. A movement, too, from the aesthetic to the moral. For the implication emerges that these miraculous airplanes, with their fouling vapor trails, represent all that will eventually bring us down. That poised final phrase, "predestined fall," refers simultaneously to the trajectory of each airplane and to humanity's own parabola toward self-destruction.

While he is never a prescriptive writer, Robinson is a committed writer, and his commitment is to the idea of what might loosely be termed living well upon the earth. All of Robinson's works—his maps, his essays, his two-volume study of Connemara, and both books of *Stones of Aran*—fold into a visionary attempt to find "our way back to the world." He speaks, in his austerely passionate manner, of wanting in his art to forge the contradictions of modernity "into a state of consciousness even fleetingly worthy of its ground." He knows this to be an impossible task: too great for a single person, a single lifetime. But he attempts it nonetheless, for the west of Ireland is "*the* exemplary terrain upon which to dream of that work"—and because such an attempt must be made, if our line of predestined fall is to be overstepped.

—ROBERT MACFARLANE

Stones of Aran
PILGRIMAGE

ACKNOWLEDGEMENTS

Maura Scannell of the National Botanic Gardens, Conor Mac-Dermot of the Geological Survey, Professor Etienne Rynne and Dr. John Waddell of the Archaeological Department, UCG, Professor T. S. Ó Máille, Dr. Angela Burke of Roinn na Nua-Ghaeilge, UCD, and the library staff of UCG—to these and to many others who backed me with learning, and to the several hundred Aran men, women and children who shared their lore with me, I owe the possibility of this book.

Do mo chairde Árannacha

TIMESCAPE WITH SIGNPOST

Cosmologists now say that Time began ten or fifteen thousand million years ago, and that the horizon of the visible universe is therefore the same number of light-years distant from us. Appeals are pending, of course, and this sentence of retrospective finitude may be varied, so that in a few years' time the figure mentioned could look as quaintly crabbed as the dating of Creation at 4004 BC by an arithmetical theologian of the seventeenth century does today. But for the moment let it stand as the context, the ultimate context, of other spans of time and space mentioned throughout this book (320 million years, a century, a quarter of a mile, a couple of paces, are measures that recur, I note, on thumbing through my manuscript) and so of my writing and your reading of these words, that arise like an inwardly directed signpost at one particular little crossroads of reality, the coincidence of a period of my life with a spell of Aran's existence. And let it stand as excuse for such a number of words based on so inadequate an experiencing of such a tiny patch of land, for a natural reaction to the sentence is to immerse oneself in the intense implication of the whole in the particular, if only to make the most out of every square foot of allotted ground.

If it is true that Time began, it is clear that nothing else has begun since, that every apparent origin is a stage in an elder process. Those three hundred and twenty million years are the time elapsed since the limestone of which Aran is formed was being laid down as layer upon layer of sediment in a tropical sea. But that sea was already ancient and full of intricate lives, the heirs of a previous three thousand million years of evolution. The sediment itself was the fallout of microscopic skeletons from those cloud-like generations of drifting lives, while the shells of bigger, more elaborate organisms buried with and by the rest now form another substantial and visible fraction of Aran's substance.

This genesis of Aran is not to be distinguished from that of the whole limestone area of central Ireland, or indeed from that of other limestones farther afield in Europe and America that date from this same Carboniferous period. It was another fifty million years before the old sea-bed was brought up into the air so that erosion could begin slowly to carve out the local sea-ways that guarantee Aran a measure of separate destiny. And in another way it is misleading to talk of Aran coming to birth in a tropical sea, as if to imply that the climate here, at this latitude and longitude of the globe, was then tropical. That over-simplification is no longer acceptable even in a layman's summary of the past, since the wonderful speculation of "continental drift" has become the sober science of "plate tectonics." For it is now known that the earth's crust is made up of fifteen or so contiguous plates, like those of a tortoise shell but more various in size and shape, and that these plates are in continuous motion, at rates like an inch a year, bearing the continents and ocean beds with them as comparatively minor irregularities of their surfaces. Where two plates are moving away from one another molten rock wells up into the gap from the interior of the earth and consolidates to supplement their margins; this is happening along the centre of the Atlantic at present, as America and Europe drift apart. What happens at the other edges where plates are in collision depends on whether they carry the lighter rocks that form continents or the heavier ones that underlie ocean beds. Two continents driven together may crumple and pile up into mountain chains, as in the Himalayas which represent the impaction of India and Asia. Or an oceanic plate may be forced downwards under a continental mass, giving rise to earthquakes and volcanoes as it remelts in the depths of the earth; the unrest of the Andes is an effect of South America's slow overriding of the Pacific plate. So the geographies over which we are so suicidally passionate are, on this scale of events, fleeting expressions of the earth's face. Two hundred million years ago the Atlantic did not exist and all the land-masses of today were clasped together in one continuity, in pre-Adamite innocence of the fact that one day scientists inhabiting its scattered fragments would give it the lovely name of Pangaea, all-earth, and that its unbounded encircling ocean was Panthalassa, all-sea.

But even great Pangaea is not the beginning; it is no more than a half-way house, inadequate but indispensable, for the mind travelling back in search of Eden. The rocks of Aran, for instance, predate it, as do many others. Although the previous migrations of the continental bits and pieces that came together to form that one huge and quickly fading image of wholeness are not well understood, it seems that the portion of the earth's crust carrying the sea in which Aran's limestone was being deposited was at that time in the tropics and south of the equator. The detailed history of that sea, its slow changes in depth, temperature and turbidity, together with that of the life-forms it nurtured, is preserved in the variations of the rock-layers themselves, and through its influence on the land-forms carved out of those rocks, with which human developments have had to come to terms, impresses a characteristic series of textures—the ground of this book—on one's experience of the islands today. That history of deposition ended some two hundred and seventy million years ago when in the coming together of the provinces of Pangaea mountains were forced up, which would be those of southern Europe, and as a side-effect the bed of this local sea was raised above the waters. Then began the converse process of the breaking down and washing away of highland by heat and frost, wind and rain, a crumb-by-crumb degradation picking away at every weakness in the rocks, until among innumerable oddities of topography it gave us Aran, at the same time as the wider earth-movements were opening Atlantics, elevating Alps and scattering the transitory unity of Pangaea across the face of the globe.

I use the term "Aran" as shorthand for the three Aran Islands, or perhaps for that unsummable totality of human perspectives upon them which is my real subject. But since the islands are a principal part of the Irish language's last precarious foothold on the world, I will call them individually by their correct names, Inis Oírr, Inis Meáin and Árainn, rather than the anglicisms Inisheer, Inishmaan and Inishmore. (This last was apparently concocted by the Ordnance Survey for its map of 1839, as a rendering in English phonetic values of the Irish "Inis Mór," big island, a name which did not exist previously but is now replacing "Árainn" even in the island's own speech.) The islands lie in a line across the mouth of Galway Bay: Inis Oírr, the smallest, has much to do with County Clare five miles away to the south-east; Inis Meáin (which means "middle island') is the most barren, least visited and until very recently the least open to this century's goods and ills; Árainn, the largest (about eight miles long and two miles across at its widest), exchanges views with the Connemara coast of County Galway six or eight miles to the north.

The name "Árainn," like the collective "Oileáin Árann," the Islands of Aran, derives from the word *ára,* a kidney, the sense of which has spread to include the loins and the back in general, and so come to be applied to the back of a rise of land. This last meaning has long been forgotten in speech, but it persists in sundry names of places with the appearance of a long ridge. And in fact the three Aran Islands are fragments of a single, long, low escarpment, a broken arm of the limestone uplands known as the Burren on the mainland to the east. They had been blocked out and given their individual existences by the forces described above long before the onset of the Ice Ages two hundred thousand years ago, but it was the glaciers creeping across and around them from the north that gave them their fineness of finish, polishing them like lenses for the clearer reading of the past. By the time the last of the ice-sheets had melted away about fifteen thousand years ago, large areas of the islands had been stripped of soil and all other debris of previous ages of erosion and left blank for the inscription of subsequent time.

This bare, soluble limestone is a uniquely tender and memorious ground. Every shower sends rivulets wandering across its surface, deepening the ways of their predecessors and gradually engraving their initial caprices as law into the stone. This recording of the weather of the ages also revivifies much more ancient fossils, which are precisely etched by the rain's delicate acids, so that now when a rising or setting sun shadows them forth, prehistory is as urgent underfoot as last night's graffiti in city streets. And every hairline fracture the rock has sustained throughout its geological troubles is eventually found out by the rain and dissolved into a noticeable cleft, so that the surface is divided up in a fashion that has been decisive for the development of field boundaries and paths, which have been obliged to follow and so reinscribe like visible scars the old invisible wounds. Further, this land has provided its inhabitants—the Neolithic tomb-builders, the Celtic cashelor, the monastic architect, the fence-making grazier of all ages—with one material only, stone, which may fall, but still endures. To this retentive nature of the terrain itself must be added the conservative effect of its situation just beyond the farthest reach of Europe, wrapped in a turn or two of ocean. The material destructiveness of modern life is only now beginning to impinge on Aran, and until very recently the sole custodian of this land of total recall has been a folk-mind of matching tenacity, focused by the limitations of island life and with the powers of memory of an ancient oral culture.

The record in stone of the human presence here covers nearly four thousand years. On each island are tombs and other structures dating from the end of the Stone Age, built by a people who probably had migrated up the Atlantic coast from Iberia. They were farmers, in search of land easily cleared with stone axes, and whether or not Aran had at that time rather more soil and tree cover than it does now, it, like its mainland relative, the Burren, was a more attractive terrain to these settlers than the heavily forested or boggy interior of the country. The Bronze Age too left burials here; a mound containing urn-burials was exposed by shifting sand-dunes in Inis Oírr in the last century, and various standing stones and uninvestigated cairns in obscure nooks of the other islands may date from the same period. But the grandest antiquities are the huge stone "cashels," dating from perhaps AD 100 or 200, that dominate the uplands of all three islands, and the two coastal forts, which may be a few centuries earlier, Dúchathair and famous Dún Aonghasa, on the Atlantic cliffs of Árainn. These are among the most impressive prehistoric remains of Celtic Europe, and they crown the heights of Aran like inexhaustible reservoirs of mystery and legend.

Aran may have little soil, but what it has is holy. Towards the end of the fifth century the pioneers of the great monastic movement sought out a retreat from the world here, and the fame of their sanctity and learning brought flocks of disciples, so that it has been written that "In this island a multitude of holy men resided, and innumerable saints unknown to all except Almighty God are here interred." The future founders of Clonmacnoise, Kilmacduach, Iona and other great monasteries studied at St. Enda's foundation in *Ára na Naomh*, Aran of the Saints. These monks established a pattern of settlement that still prevails, building their cells and chapels in the lee of the low inland cliffs that terrace the north-facing scarp-slope of the island chain, where the good wells are. None of the extant churches goes back quite to this heroic age of sanctity, but there are several tiny oratories from perhaps the eighth century, while some of the later, largely Romanesque and mediaeval churches have a nucleus of massive masonry from that period.

In mediaeval times the islands were under the sway of the Munster sept, the O'Briens, who built a fortified tower-house within the old walls of a Celtic cashel in Inis Oírr, and probably had a stronghold by the harbour at the monastic site of Cill

Éinne, the church of Enda, in Árainn. But given the islands' position stretched between the two provinces, it is not surprising that they were also claimed by the "Ferocious O'Flahertys" of Connacht, who eventually ousted the O'Briens. The merchants of Galway city, who regarded the O'Flahertys as mere pirates and smugglers against whom the Aran O'Briens had given a measure of naval protection, sought to advance the claims of the latter by referring the dispute to Queen Elizabeth. But the even-handed finding of her commission was that, as monastic lands, and the monasteries having been declared dissolved, the islands belonged to neither O'Flahertys nor O'Briens but to the Crown itself. In 1587 the Queen then granted them to an Englishman on condition that he keep a force of twenty English foot-soldiers there, and a castle was built at Cill Éinne. Aran, guarding the approaches to the rich port of Galway, was henceforward a pawn in a European strategy.

The garrison waxed and waned over the next three and a half centuries with the fear of continental invasion and Irish insurrection. At the time of the Cromwellian civil war the castle was manned by the Royalists, surrendered when Galway did, was retaken by an Irish expedition from Inishbofin, and was finally reduced by a large force of Parliamentarians, who rebuilt and enlarged it using stone from the plundered churches nearby. Their previous owner having been declared a "forfeiting traitor," the islands were now made over to one of the London "Adventurers" in return for his financial services to Parliament.

By degrees the islands then dropped out of history again. The landlords (the Digby family of Kildare, from about 1744 and throughout the famines of the nineteenth century) were absentees who took their two or three thousand pounds a year of rent and cared nothing for the place; in island folklore they are unreal and remote figures, not held responsible for the bitter oppressions worked by their local agents. More immediate and comprehensible were the principal tenant-farmers, middlemen and Justices of the Peace, the O'Flahertys of Cill Mhuirbhigh in the west of

Árainn. In the first half of the nineteenth century Patrick O'Flaherty "ruled like a King in Aran," summoning offenders to appear before him in his cattle-yard "on the first fine day," and if necessary ordering them to take themselves off to Galway gaol. His son and successor James was hated as a "landgrabber," one who would take over the leases of land from which another had been evicted, and he and his bailiffs were the principal targets of the sporadic terrorism of the islands' Fenians and Land Leaguers. The "Land War" in Aran culminated in the driving of the O'Flahertys' cattle, blindfolded, over the highest of the Atlantic cliffs. By that time the O'Flaherty estate included much of the best land in Árainn, and even today, although much of it has changed hands as the family fortunes were squandered, and some has been redistributed among smallholders, the contrast between those areas and the rest is striking; on one side of the old boundaries are the broad acres of one who could command the carrying-off of countless tons of stone, and on the other the incredible jigsaw puzzle of little fields of those who could only clear their stony patches and mark the ever-increasing subdivision of their holdings by building walls. These crooked dry-stone walls, about a thousand miles of them, are of all the islands' monuments the most moving, an image, in their wearisome repetitiousness and tireless spontaneity, of the labour of those disregarded generations.

Aran shared in the rent reductions and other benefits won nationally by the Land League agitations, and though hunger, fever, evictions and emigration were persistent curses on life even into this century, the islands' dark ages began to draw to a close. The old fort had long been in ruins and Cill Éinne had dwindled into a poverty-stricken village of landless fishermen, while nearby Cill Rónáin had grown into the islands' administrative capital and the home of its little Protestant community, triangulated by the barracks, the coastguard station and the Episcopalian church of St. Thomas. A steamer service from Galway was inaugurated in 1891, and the Congested Districts Board (the government agency set over those western districts in which the disproportion between population and resources was particularly dire) began to develop the fishing industry. Cill Rónáin became the port of a fleet of trawlers that has grown, with occasional setbacks, into a sizeable industry today. It became usual for those who came here in search of the residual essences of old Gaelic ways to throw up their hands at this raw, anglicized, profit-making Cill Rónáin and retire to Inis Meáin, which being less accessible had not suffered the same "corruption." But now that the old barracks is shared between the post office and a bar, and the coastguard station between the telephone exchange and a couple of *gardaí*, while the Protestant church is roofless and its potential congregation nil, that turn-of-the-century gombeen-town of Cill Rónáin has acquired a patina of interest and defers to the bright young world of mini-supermarkets, discos and craft boutiques with a certain frowsty charm. The Seventies, a decade of relative prosperity based on fishing and tourism, slowed but could not reverse a population decline that had come to seem inevitable. (In 1841 the population of the three islands was at its maximum, 3521; in 1971 it was 1496, while the figure for 1981 was 1386.) However, in that decade the building of bungalows has linked the villages into an almost continuous band along the north-facing slopes. Nevertheless little has changed as soon as one steps off the main road. The Congested Districts Board bought out the Digby estate (which by marriages had passed into the hands of the Guinnesses) in 1921, so the Aran farmer now owns the field of his labours, but holdings are still small, broken up into numerous separated parcels, and unproductive. In fact, as land-use falls off, some areas are becoming wonderfully overgrown with brambles and hazel scrub, outriders of the coming wilderness.

As with the fields and paths, so with the language; there are ominous signs of disuse and decay. Irish, the irreplaceable distillate of over two thousand years' experience of this country, which has been poured down the drains in the rest of Ireland but which was carried unspilt even through the famine century in those few little cups, the western *Gaeltachtaí* of Aran, Connemara and parts of Donegal and Kerry, is now evaporating even here (as if a word or two disappears every day, the name of a field becomes unintelligible overnight, an old saying decides that its wisdom or foolishness is henceforth inexpressible), while what remains is splashed with the torrents of English. Many in Aran, as elsewhere, stake heavily on the future of Irish (and it is an awesome choice for parents to entrust their children's mental development, or a writer a life's work, to an endangered language), but the cruel twists of history have put the survival of Irish in the hands of English; at least as essential as the dedication of Irish speakers would be a tolerance, indeed a positive welcoming, among English speakers, of cultural diversity, an awakening to the sanity of differences—and such wisdom is contrary to the stupefying mainstreams of our time. However, at present Irish is a vigorous reality in Aran, and is now as it has been for over a century one of the reasons for the outside world's fascination with this bare little place.

The history of this interest in Aran and its accumulated marvels is a rich series of footnotes to that of the Romantic Movement. These words from the earliest modern account of the islands, by John T. O'Flaherty writing in the *Transactions of the Royal Irish Academy* in 1825, give the flavour of that typical enterprise of contemporary scholarship, the reconquest of ancient Ireland, which would be followed by the reinstallation of its long-dispossessed but uncorrupted heir, the peasant:

> The Isles of Aran abound with the remains of Druidism— open temples, altars, stone pillars, sacred mounts of fire-worship, miraculous fountains, and evident vestiges of oak groves. . . . The Aranites, in their simplicity, consider these remains of Druidism still sacred and inviolable; being, as they imagine, the inchanted haunts and property of aerial beings, whose powers of doing mischief they greatly dread and studiously propitiate. For entertaining this kind of religious respect, they have another powerful motive: they believe that the cairns, or circular mounts, are the sepulchres, and some of them really are, of native chiefs and warriors of

antiquity, of whose military fame and wondrous achieve-
ments they have abundance of legendary stories....Indeed,
the solitude and romantic wildness of their "seagirt" abode,
and the venerable memorials of Christian piety and Celtic
worship, so numerously scattered over the surface of the
Aran Isles, fairly account for the enthusiasm, credulity, and
second-sight of these islanders.

For over a hundred years Rousseauistic nostalgia and the com-
plexes of nationalist emotions were wonder-working ingredients
in the Aran spell, interacting strangely with academic objectivity
and personal vision. Celticists of every specialism made the pilgrimage to Aran. After the antiquarians came the linguists, ethnographers and folklorists, and then the writers, poets, film-makers
and journalists. George Petrie, whose work was to wean Irish archaeology from a century of baseless speculation about druidical
fire-temples and the like, had made his first visit to Aran's monuments in 1822. John O'Donovan wrote the first careful description
of them and collected the relevant literary references and lore in
1839 for the first Ordnance Survey, which was among other things
a stock-taking of Ireland's richness in antiquities. In 1857 William
Wilde led an excursion of the Ethnological Section of the British
Association to Aran; a banquet for seventy was held within Dún
Aonghasa itself (the natives looked on from its ramparts) and
among the eminent diners were Petrie, O'Donovan, MacDonnell
the Provost of Trinity College, the historian Eugene O'Curry, the
poet and antiquarian Samuel Ferguson and the painter Frederick
Burton. Subsequent visitors of note included Lady Gregory looking for folklore, W. B. Yeats looking for magic, Douglas Hyde,
Eoin MacNeill and the young Patrick Pearse all looking for Ireland in Inis Meáin, Father O'Growney the apostle of language revival, and most memorably the playwright J. M. Synge, because of
his peerless report, *The Aran Islands*, of 1905. One could write an
intellectual history of renascent Ireland out of fireside encounters
in those hungry but hospitable Aran cabins, as well as a comic serial

out of the confrontation of dream and reality (without prejudging the question of which was which, or in what proportions) when the Araner and those who had come to save and be saved by him groped towards each other over the cultural rifts. And at last Aran began to speak for itself to the world. Even this briefest of surveys must name two of the islands' half-dozen authors: Liam O'Flaherty, 1896–1984, well known as a novelist in English and writer of short stories in both his languages, and Máirtín Ó Direáin, born in 1910, one of the chiefs in the poetic re-establishment of Irish.

The noble file of discoverers of Aran by degrees was absorbed into the ever-increasing summer traffic of visitors that is bringing such changes to the islands today. A decisive moment in the formulation of the Aran myth was the making of the film *Man of Aran* by the famous American director Robert Flaherty in 1932, which featured as if it were contemporary reality a long-abandoned aspect of island life, the harpooning of the gigantic "basking shark" from frail-looking "currachs," Aran's famous canoes of lath and canvas. The images Flaherty dealt us, of Man as subduer of sea-monsters, of Wife anxiously looking out for his return while rocking Babe-in-the-Cradle, and of Son eager to follow him into manhood—the perfect primal family in unmediated conflict with a world of towering waves and barren rocks, as if eternally in silhouette against the storm—remain like grand, sombre court-cards on the table of the mind, and will not be brushed aside by subsequent knowledge of the subtle actualities of Aran life.

As with thousands of others, it was a mild curiosity engendered by Flaherty's film that first brought us (my wife and myself) to Aran, in the summer of 1972. On the day of our arrival we met an old man who explained the basic geography: "The ocean," he told us, "goes all around the island." We let the remark direct our rambles on that brief holiday, and found indeed that the ocean encircles Aran like the rim of a magnifying glass, focusing attention to the point of obsession. A few months later we determined to leave London and the career in the visual arts I was pursuing there, and act on my belief in the virtue of an occasional brusque and even arbitrary change in mode of life. (I mention these personal details only as being the minimum necessary for the definition of the moment on which this narrative will converge, the point in physical and cultural space from which this timescape is observed and on which this book stands.) On that previous summer holiday Aran had presented itself, not at all as Flaherty's pedestal of rock on which to strike a heroic stance, but rather as a bed of flower-scented sunlight and breezes on which one might flirt delectably with alternative futures. But on our definitive arrival in November we found that bed canopied with hailstorms and full of all the damps of the Atlantic. The closing-in of that winter, until the days seemed like brief and gloomy dreams interrupting ever intenser nights, was accompanied by an unprecedented sequence of deaths, mainly by drowning or by falls and exposure on the crags, that perturbed and depressed the island, quite extinguished the glow of Christmas, and ceased only with the turn of the year, the prayers of the priest and the sinister total of seven. It was a severe induction but it left us with a knowledge of the dark side of this moon that has controlled the tides of our life ever since.

For my part (M's being her own story), what captivated me in that long winter were the immensities in which this little place is wrapped: the processions of grey squalls that stride in from the Atlantic horizon, briefly lash us with hail and go sailing off towards the mainland trailing rainbows; the breakers that continue to arch up, foam and fall across the shoals for days after a storm has abated; the long, wind-rattled nights, untamed then by electricity below, wildly starry above. Then I was dazzled by the minutiae of spring, the appearance each in its season of the flowers, starting with the tiny, white whitlow-grass blossoms hardly distinguishable from the last of the hailstones in the scant February pastures, and culminating by late May in paradisal tapestry-work across every meadow and around every rock. The summer had me exploring the honeysuckled boreens and the breezy clifftops; autumn proposed the Irish language, the blacksmith's quarter-comprehended tales, the intriguing gossip of the shops, and the discovery that there existed yet another literature it would take four or five years to begin to make one's own. This cycle could have spun on, the writings I had come here to do having narrowed themselves into a diary of intoxication with Aran, but that some way of contributing to this society and of surviving financially had to be found.

A suggestion from the post mistress in the western village of Cill Mhuirbhigh gave me the form of this contribution: since I seemed to have a hand for the drawing, an ear for the placenames and legs for the boreens, why should I not make a map of the islands, for which endless summersful of visitors would thank and pay me? The idea appealed to me so deeply that I began work that same day. My conceptions of what could be expressed through a map were at that time sweeping but indefinite; maps of a very generalized and metaphorical sort had been latent in the abstract paintings and environmental constructions I had shown in London, in that previous existence that already seemed so long ago, but I had not engaged myself to such a detailed relationship with an actual place before. The outcome, published in 1975, was a better image of my ignorance than of my knowledge of Aran, but it was generously received by the islanders, prospered moderately with the tourists, and brought me into contact with the specialists in various fields who visited Aran. During the subsequent years of accumulation towards the second version of the map, published in 1980, I have walked the islands in companionship with such visiting experts as well as with the custodians of local lore whom I sought out in every village, and have tried to see Aran through variously informed eyes—and then, alone again, I have gone hunting for those rare places and times, the nodes at which the layers of experience touch and may be fused together. But I find that in a map such points and the energy that accomplishes such fusions (which is that of poetry, not some vague "interdisciplinary" fervour) can, at the most, be invisible guides, benevolent ghosts, through the tangles of the explicit; they cannot themselves be shown or named. So, chastened in my expectations of them, I now regard the Aran maps as preliminary storings and sortings of material for another art, the world-hungry art of words.

However, although the maps underlie this book, the conception of the latter dates from a moment in the preparation for the former. I was on a summer's beach one blinding day watching the waves unmaking each other, when I became aware of a wave, or a recurrent sequence of waves, with a denser identity and more purposeful momentum than the rest. This appearance, which passed by from east to west and then from west to east and so on, resolved itself under my stare into the fins and backs of two dolphins (or were there three?), the follower with its head close by the flank of the leader. I waded out until they were passing and repassing within a few yards of me; it was still difficult to see the smoothly arching succession of dark presences as a definite number of individuals. Yet their unity with their background was no jellyfish-like dalliance with dissolution; their mode of being was an intensification of their medium into alert, reactive self-awareness; they were wave made flesh, with minds solely to ensure the moment-by-moment reintegration of body and world.

This instance of a wholeness beyond happiness made me a little despondent, standing there thigh deep in Panthalassa (for if Pangaea is shattered and will not be mended by our presence on it, the old ocean holds together throughout all its twisting history): a dolphin may be its own poem, but we have to find our rhymes elsewhere, between words in literature, between things in science, and our way back to the world involves us in an endless proliferation of detours. Let the problem be symbolized by that of taking a single step as adequate to the ground it clears as is the dolphin's arc to its wave. Is it possible to think towards a *human* conception of this "good step"? (For the dolphin's ravenous cybernetics and lean hydrodynamics induce in me no nostalgia for imaginary states of past instinctive or future theological grace. Nor is the ecological imperative, that we learn to tread more lightly on the earth, what I have in mind—though that commandment, which is always subject to challenge on pragmatic grounds if presented as a mere facilitation of survival, might indeed acquire some authority from the attitude to the earth I would like to hint at with my step.) But our world has nurtured in us such a multiplicity of modes of awareness that it must be impossible to bring them to a common focus even for the notional duration of a step. The dolphin's world, for all that its inhabitants can sense Gulf Streams of diffuse beneficences, freshening influences of rivers and perhaps a hundred other transparent gradations, is endlessly more continuous and therefore productive of unity than ours, our craggy, boggy, overgrown and overbuilt terrain, on which every step carries us across geologies, biologies, myths, histories, politics, etcetera, and trips us with the trailing *Rosa spinosissima* of personal associations. To forget these dimensions of the step is to forgo our honour as human beings, but an awareness of them equal to the involuted complexities under foot at any given moment would be a crushing backload to have to carry. Can such contradictions be forged into a state of consciousness even fleetingly worthy of its ground? At least one can speculate that the structure of condensation and ordering necessary to pass from such various types of knowledge to such an instant of insight would have the characteristics of a work of art, partaking of the individuality of the mind that bears it, yet with a density of content and richness of connectivity surpassing any state of that mind. So the step lies beyond a certain work of art; it would be like a reading of that work. And the writing of such a work? Impossible, for many reasons, of which the brevity of life is one.

However, it will already be clear that Aran, of the world's countless facets one of the most finely carved by nature, closely structured by labour and minutely commented by tradition, is *the* exemplary terrain upon which to dream of that work, the guidebook to the adequate step. *Stones of Aran* is all made up of steps, which lead in many directions but perpetually return to, loiter near, take short-cuts by, stumble over or impatiently kick aside that ideal. (Otherwise, it explores and takes its form from a single island, Árainn itself; the present work makes a circuit of the coast, whose features present themselves as stations of a *Pilgrimage*, while the sequel will work its way through the interior, tracing out the *Labyrinth*.) And although I am aware that that moment on the beach, like all moments one remembers as creative, owes as much to the cone of futurity opening out from it as to the focusing of the past it accomplished, I will take it as the site of my book, so that when at last it is done I will have told the heedless dolphins how it is, to walk this paradigm of broken, blessed, Pangaea.

I. SOUTH

BEFORE BEGINNING

The circuit that blesses is clockwise, or, since the belief is thousands of years older than the clock, sunwise. It is the way the fire-worshipper's swastika turns, and its Christianized descendant St. Bridget's cross. Visitors to holy wells make their "rounds" so, seven times, with prayers. This book makes just one round of Árainn, though seven could not do justice to the place, and with eyes raised to this world rather than lowered in prayer. On Easter Fridays in past centuries the Aran folk used to walk around the island keeping as close to the coast as possible, and although nothing has been recorded on the question it is inconceivable that they should have made the circuit other than in the right-handed sense. This writing will lead in their footsteps, not at their penitential trudge but at an inquiring, digressive and wondering pace.

I start at the eastern end of the island. The road from Cill Rónáin through Cill Éinne continues past the last village, Iaráirne, and then makes a sharp turn north to a little bay; there is a stile in the wall at that turn from which a faint field-path continues the line of the road eastward, across smooth turf in which hosts of rabbits are digging sandpits, to the exact spot I have in mind. Here one can sit among the wild pansies and Lady's bedstraw with the low rocky shore at one's feet, and get one's bearings. Behind and to the left is level ground of sandy fields, and dunes in the distance. To the right the land rises in stony slopes to the ruins of an ancient watch tower on the skyline. A mile and a half ahead across the sound is Inis Meáin; the third island, Inis Oírr, is hidden behind it, but the hills of the Burren in County Clare appear beyond, a dozen miles away. Since the three islands and that northwestern corner of Clare were once continuous—before the millions of years of weathering, the glaciers of the Ice Ages and the inexhaustible waves cut the sea-ways between them—the land-forms visible out there, a little abstracted as they are by distance, can be seen as images of Árainn itself in the context of its geological past, and it is valuable to read them thus before going on to clamber among the details and complexities of the way ahead, so that an otherwise inchoate mass of impressions may find an ordering and a clarification.

Since this opposing, western face of Inis Meáin is cliffed it is in fact like a cross-section of Árainn. The highest land lies across the centre, and from there to the south the skyline declines evenly to sea level, giving the southern half of the island the appearance of a long dark wedge driven in between sky and sea. The cliffs' ledges and the great platforms of rock along their feet all have the same slant as the skyline, so that the island is visibly made up of a small number of thick parallel layers slightly canted to the south. But if this is an image of Árainn, it is from a time before its southern range of cliffs was formed, for Inis Meáin's coast is low on the south and stands well out beyond the general line of Árainn's Atlantic cliffs. Why the ocean has been able to cut back just one of the three islands into south-facing cliffs is a question to which certain features of the extreme western tip of Árainn may suggest an answer—but that is as yet a dozen miles of walking and a hundred pages of reading ahead.

While the profile of Inis Meáin's southern half is simple to the point of monotony, that of the northern half has a wild vigour recalling one's experience of that strange island; it hops and jumps down from the central heights, and then reaches the north in two long strides with a sharp fall between them. The land is enlivened by these little scarps; the houses are in their shelter, the wells at their feet, the boreens wind up and down them. Árainn is the same except that the aprons of bare rock below the terraces that carry the villages are not so wide; here, as in Inis Meáin and Inis Oírr, the terrain south of the ridge-line is uninhabited, severe, disconcertingly open to non-human immensities, while the northern flank of the island is at least raggedly shawled with the human presence. In fact over parts of the north the fabric of history is so closely woven that it can be as oppressive as the more elemental spaciousness of the south, and for all their beauty neither landscape is a forgiving one.

This side-view of Inis Meáin shows the formation of the terraces with diagrammatic clarity: first the topmost of the great beds of limestone slanting up gently from the south is broken off short by a north-facing scarp; the next layer continues a little farther north before being similarly ended, the next runs still farther north to form another tread of the stair, and so on. There are five such terraces, with three less distinct ones below them, and they can be traced the length of the island chain and indeed matched with similar terraces in the hills of the Burren—at least the geologist can match them, by means of slight variations in the composition of the limestone and in the fossils to be found in each stratum. In some places the scarp-faces separating them are considerable cliffs of up to twenty feet in height, in others they dwindle to broken slopes so that the terraces are not immediately distinguishable and it would be hard to count them, while elsewhere minor subdivisions become more prominent than these major ones—and in the face of these, the usual and generous ways of reality, any diagram having done its work goes on to demonstrate its own inadequacy.

Beyond and above the northern tip of Inis Meáin as viewed from this spot stands the outline of the Burren, which can be seen—through a bewitching gauze of sunshine and cloud-shadow —as a further, more inclusive diagram of Árainn's geology. The northernmost end of the sequence is the promontory on the south of Galway Bay called Black Head, a great rounded hill rising to about a thousand feet. A well-marked terrace, showing from here as a long streak, silvery below and dark above, crosses the face of this hill, strikingly parallel to the general slant of Inis Meáin. Above this level the profile of Black Head rises in indistinct steps, which elsewhere in the Burren are very clear but here have been rounded off by glacial action. These are the strata that correspond to and were once continuous with those of the Aran Islands. The unterraced hillsides below them in the Burren represent the roots of Aran below sea level. To see what once lay above these strata one has only to follow the Burren skyline south to a long dark plateau the southern end of which falls away out of sight behind the heights of Inis Meáin; this is Slieve Elva, a high bog-covered tract of shales that dominates the bright limestone slopes below it. These great thicknesses of shale once covered much more of the area, and above them were further depths of flagstone, still extant a little farther to the south where they form the Cliffs of Moher. All these rocks, laid down as sediments under various conditions and heaved up into a gently sloping plain by slow earth-movements, have been worn away piecemeal by the two hundred-odd million years of exposure to climates varying from the tropical to the arctic. The process may seem so hugely unimaginable as to be irrelevant, but many features of the ground directly underfoot here are only comprehensible in terms of the pressure of the thousands of feet of rock that once bore down on it. And the process of stripping, not just to the bone, to the bare rock, but of the rock itself and its fossil bones, continues today. Rainwater swilling across the surface has washed an inch or two off its thickness even in the comparatively brief span of man's presence here. Unless vaster earth-processes intervene Aran will ultimately dwindle to a little reef and disappear. It seems unlikely that any creatures we would recognize as our descendants will be here to chart that rock in whatever shape of sea succeeds to Galway Bay.

THE ARCHITECTURE OF DESTRUCTION

But where is all the rubble from these gigantic demolitions? Finer than dust, most of it, and dispersed by solution into the sea whence it came. The particles sifted and sorted out by currents into muds, sands and shingles along the sheltered north coast are another remnant of it, while the results of the sea's most recent and crudest hammer-work lie along the coast south of the point this book starts from—the tumbled blocks of stone shouldered above high-water mark by the waves that broke them out of the layers of rock immediately seaward, leaving a shore of steps and ledges, convenient fishing-seats for the lads of Iaráirne. Among them is a slab about twenty feet square and four or five feet thick which always catches my attention as I walk that way, because its upper surface is curiously webbed with what look like lengths of petrified rope. These are traces of burrows made by some invertebrate mud-dweller of the ancient sea-bed. Deposits of sediment have filled in the burrows and then, under the pressure of further accumulations, hardened to preserve their form. But these fossil casts are now outgrowths of the *top* of the limestone block, which itself was formed by a continuation of that sedimentation; therefore the block is lying upside-down. As I pace out its canted deck, and later on at home when I calculate its weight at a hundred and twenty tons or so, I begin to acquire a sense of the forces that shook it free from its bed and overturned it.

This "storm beach" or "boulder beach," as such banks of broken stone above high-water mark are called, fades out a couple of hundred yards to the south in the lee of a rising cliff, the beginning of Árainn's precipitous Atlantic face. The cliff is a continuation of a little scarp, the riser of one of the island's terraces, that comes down to the coast here and turns south along it. One can begin to understand how these terraces were formed by looking at the face of this cliff near the coast. The lowest three feet of it are composed of soft shales and clays, which have been eroded back to leave the more resistant limestone overhanging above them. If this undermining continues, a cliff-fall will follow, and then, if and when the fallen and shattered rock weathers away or is swept aside by waves, undercutting of the cliff will begin again, and stage by stage it will slowly be eaten back into the hillside.

The process can be seen at its most dramatic by following the shore southwards under the cliff. It is possible, if the tide is out and the seas not too high, to reach the easternmost angle of the cliff and look round it at a spot where the swells coming up the channel from the open ocean thrust into a cave they have excavated in this same shale stratum, and columns of foam are blasted out through them by the air trapped and compressed by their inrush. Over on the coast of Inis Meáin the same thing is happening at a point halfway along the cliffs, where if there is any pulse in the ocean at all it is timed by the repeated building-up and falling-down of a tower of white water against a perpetually drenched and blackened rock wall. The two places are both called Poll an tSéideáin, the cave of the blown spray. After a south-westerly gale the Inis Meáin example is a superb sight, a gleaming space rocket launching itself out of solemn turbulences up the one-hundred-foot cliff face, to be mysteriously transformed into a great vague fading bird and swept inland by the wind. Seen from Inis Meáin, and responding to a south-easterly, its Árainn partner is almost equally impressive, and the cliff above and beyond it so smooth, grey and apparently indestructible with its long sheer walls and massive square-cut overhangs that it has the grandiose inhumanity of a space-age fantasy fortress of steel, artillery thundering at its base. In reality, the cliffs are extremely vulnerable. In 1980 a livid scar appeared on Inis Meáin's face just opposite this point, where a piece like the façade of a three-storey house dropped off one night. And here in Árainn the cliff's clean facets show that it is breaking up along a threefold system of weaknesses: the partings between the almost horizontal strata, and the vertical fissures deeply dividing the limestone, one set of which run parallel to the coast at this point, with the other at right-angles to them. So under the blows of the sea the coast is shedding great rectangular blocks and slabs, and owes its style of awesome impregnability to a triple predisposition to failure.

CONNOISSEURS OF WILDERNESS

The ruinous stone tower that tops the hill here was perhaps a lookout post, as it commands such a fine view of the seas to north and south as well as of the channel below, but how old it is nobody knows. It is called Túr Mháirtín, Martin's Tower, as it was when the first Ordnance Survey was made in the 1830s. There is a path leading in this direction from the village of Iaráirne called Bóithrín Mháirtín, Martin's "boreen" or little road, which suggests that at some period this forgotten Martin owned the land around the tower, but again nobody knows. The ruin, which has recently been overzealously reconstructed by the Board of Works men, measures seventeen paces round and stands to a height of about ten feet. At the time of the first Survey it was described as being solid, but it looks to me as if it was always hollow, and the original masonry on the north side includes some long blocks that protrude into the interior like a crude stairway. Otherwise its stones are as uncommunicative as its history.

Legend, however, has more to say about it: this then is the tomb of a saint from Inis Meáin called Gregory of the Golden Mouth, Grióir Béal an Óir. The site of this hermit's sojourn in the wilderness of Inis Meáin can be seen from the tower; beyond the little bay and its bright shinglebank on the opposite coast is an inland cliff that has collapsed into a line of huge stone blocks like the carriages of a derailed train, and St. Gregory's cave is a burrow among these. There the unhappy recluse gnawed off his lower lip in a spasm of anguish over the sins of his early life (according to the chronicler monks) or simply because he was hungry (as I was told by a more down-to-earth Inis Meáin native)—and a golden lip grew in its place. When St. Gregory felt death approaching, regarding himself as unworthy of burial in the holy soil of St. Enda's Árainn, he asked the monks of that island to abandon his body to the sea in a cask, which they did, and found on their return that the cask had reached Árainn before them. The little bay, just north of the starting-point of this book, called Port Daibhche, the harbour of the barrel, was its landfall. So the humble saint was buried in Árainn after all, high on this proud headland overlooking the barren island of his lonely struggle and the Sound named after him, Sunda Ghrióra.

In its drift through time Gregory's story has become entangled with others. Thus, when dying in Rome as Pope Gregory he ordered his body to be launched on the Tiber, a tablet on its breast, and eventually came floating home to burial in his native Aran. As Gregory the Fairheaded, Grióir Ceannfhionnadh, he was beheaded by a tyrant at Cleggan in Connemara, the name of which town derives from *cloigeann*, a head; and then (as if to harmonize this tale with his Aran legend) he rose up, cursed the people of that locality, carried his head to a spring (now a holy well named after him), washed and replaced it, and came home to Inis Meáin.

These legends are all faded now. Fishing boats used to dip their sails to the tomb of St. Gregory of the Golden Mouth, but nowadays the lobsterboats that come throbbing by below regard it only as a useful sea-mark; an Iaráirne man remembers hearing that the old folk used to come here looking for gold teeth; a touch of golden lichen illuminates the tower's lee side, and that is all.

The slopes falling south from the tower to the coast where it turns to face the full power of the Atlantic are scaly with loose stone, and as harsh and desolate as any in Aran. It is a wild spot to which the magnetism of sanctity steered the desert father from Inis Meáin, and it seems that as such it appealed to another connoisseur of wildernesses, the English artist Richard Long, who in 1975 left his mark, a small stone circle, nearby. It still stands in part, a group of limestone splinters jammed upright into crevices of the rocky ground, about three hundred yards south of the tower. Long's work takes him to the remotest parts of the earth, where he makes some construct like this out of what is to hand—stone, of necessity, in this instance—frequently impermanent, often circular or spiral, a passing shadow cast on nature by a restless culture, and then photographs it and exhibits the photographs with accompanying trophies of maps, stones and words in the air-conditioned, neon-lit art galleries of capital cities. I first saw this circle depicted on the poster of an exhibition in Amsterdam, and later made finding it the object of an hour's wintry loitering about this deserted corner of Aran.

THIS VALE OF TEARS

In the last century emigrant ships sailing out of Galway for America used to come through Sunda Ghrióra and sometimes had to wait for days in the lee of the south-east point of the island for a favourable wind. Then if there were Aran people on board their relatives and friends who had already said goodbye to them and may even have held a wake for them, knowing that in most cases the parting was forever, were given another sight of them by this chance that was perhaps more cruel than kind, but at a distance that must have made it an unreal, wordless and ghostly reappearance. The way by which the bereaved came down to the shore to wave and weep is a little valley called Gleann na nDeor. This phrase is the Irish equivalent of the old preachers' platitude for this world as a place of sorrow, "the vale of tears," and even if the traditional account of the origin of the name I have given is perhaps uncertain, a weight of bitter truth about Aran's past hangs about the place now because of it.

There was another cause for mourning here once, on the 16th of August 1852 (a date every Aran man, woman and child seems to know), when fifteen men were drowned, fourteen of them from Cill Éinne and the other from Iaráirne. They were fishing from the great rock terrace under the cliffs around the point, at Aill na nGlasóg, known in English as the Glasson Rock (the *glasóg* or *glasán* is the black pollack, a type of shorefish for which the spot is well known). It seems that a freak wave rose out of a calm sea and swept them away; the misfortune occurred on the Feast of the Blessed Virgin and was seen as a consequence of working on the holy day, for rock-fishing was then a livelihood, as it still is for a few men of the eastern villages. The ballads, one in English and the other in Irish, that commemorate the tragedy mention Gleann na nDeor as the way by which the bereaved came down to the shore, and it is often supposed that the placename refers to the tears shed over the bodies of the drowned there. In fact it anticipates the event, for it was recorded by the Ordnance Surveyors in the 1830s. (Misrecorded, rather, since the map has it as Illaunanaur, anglicizing Oileán na nDeor, island, instead of glen, of tears. The error has imposed itself on one or two islanders who reverence the written and official word more than the spoken folk memory, and on my first attempt at a map of Aran.)

Finally, an islander has suggested to me that the name refers to the dew which early morning fishermen sailing by see sparkling on this grassy plot among the grey stones—the dew, proverbially both fresh and fleeting, which still out-cries all human tears.

OCEAN WALLS AND WINDOWS

In the days when all visitors were assumed by the islanders to be of superior birth, the rock-fishermen at Aill na nGlasóg often had a genteel audience watching them from the clifftop, and the big triangular boulder perched on the very tip of the point that served as a seat for these observers became known as Cloch na nDaoine Móra, which an Aran man would translate as "the big-shots' stone." Some day a wave is going to climb the cliff with enough residual power either to shift the stone a little farther inland or drag it back into the sea. All the more exposed coasts of Aran carry a rock-bank above the levels of the highest tides, and where, as here and elsewhere on the south coast, this "storm beach" actually lies above cliffs thirty to eighty feet high, is composed of vast numbers of blocks it would take many men to move, and furthermore is separated from the cliff's edge by a clear space of ten or twenty feet or more, then the impression given of the sea's power is overwhelming.

It is indeed difficult to find a vocabulary for the combination of the prodigious and the orderly that such natural phenomena display. Most accounts of the Aran Islands, including my own first attempt, give one the idea that these stones have been hurled up over the cliffs from the bottom of the sea, whereas in fact they have been stripped off the rim of the cliff and moved inland by small degrees. Revisiting this spot after the winter of 1981–82, I found startling evidence of this process. A block of freshly broken rock, white with the unweathered calcite of innumerable fossils, caught my eye just a few paces east of the boulder described above. The detached piece was about two feet square and five feet long, and lay askew along the mouth of a trough-like recess of exactly the same dimensions running in from the cliff's edge. There was half a fossil coral in the lower left-hand face of the block, and the other half of it was in the right-hand wall of the recess; clearly a wave had knocked the piece like a splinter out of the rim of the cliff, spun it on its axis and dropped it almost upside down back into its place. No doubt it had been detached from its substrate before this happened, by long ages of shocks and blows, and the unremitting discreet persuasions of daily temperature changes and trickling solvent waters; no doubt too in some future winter storm a wave will mount the sixty or seventy feet of cliff and flip it out of its present awkward rest, and then someday another wave will slide it inland and add it to its accumulated predecessors on the storm beach. By such repeated touches a rampart up to ten or fifteen feet high has been assembled all along this next three miles of south-facing cliff, so that the interior of the island is invisible from the broad promenade of ground swept clear of loose rock along the cliff edge.

On Inis Meáin around the low-lying south-western point there are two or three hundred yards of smooth, cleared rock-terrace between high-water mark and the gigantic storm beach, and as the cliffs rise from there towards the north the storm beach gradually approaches them and fades out on their brink at a height of a hundred and sixty feet above sea level. Inis Oírr too has an impressive storm beach, topped off by the hull of a freighter wrecked off the coast some years ago. These mighty works have been done partly by gale-by-gale, winter-by-winter processes as described above, and partly no doubt by more drastic events like the "Night of the Big Wind" of 1839 which is said to have buried in boulders the prehistoric stone huts on the peninsula of Dúchathair two miles west, or by such combinations of equinoctial tides and millennial storms as may only have occurred a very few times since the Ice Ages left Aran a bare slate, as it were, for the compilation of this reckoning. The only force tending to the destruction of the storm beach once formed, apart from the slow weathering of individual stones, is cliff-fall, which in places has overtaken the retreat of the storm beach; for instance at Dúchathair it is interrupted by deeply carved inlets, and on the western side of the bay next to the Glasson Rock boulders of the storm beach are tumbling off a cliff that has been cut back under their feet.

This little bay of which the Glasson Rock forms the eastern arm is divided into two amphitheatral halves by a narrow peninsula with a rock terrace below it, and in the deeply undercut recesses of either half is a sea-cave leading back to a blow-hole or "puffing-hole." The more spectacular of these chasms, which one comes across with casually horrific suddenness if not forewarned, is the eastern one, a rectangular opening in the ground about thirty-three yards from the clifftop, a dozen yards across and rather more than that from front to back. On its inland side one can scramble down natural steps and ledges to where it opens out sideways into black dripping vaults like some waterlogged upside-down Piranesi dungeon. On calm days a tongue of green and light-filled water mutters below, but when the tide is high and the wind in the right direction waves come breaking up these steps and strew the ground inland with sand and shreds of seaweed. The power with which water has now and again been funnelled up and jetted out of the opening can be judged from the storm beach which here loops back from the cliffs and lies sixty yards inland of the hole, the intervening sheets of rock having been swept bare and the stone skimmed off it or smashed out of the slope of the puffing-hole heaped up in a ten-foot bank. That is not all, for a few yards outside that bank is a second, smaller one, and a third beyond that again. These outer banks must be relics of very ancient commotions of the sea, for no wave could reach them now over the inner bank, which itself was not built in recent days. Immediately to the north-west a little meadow very different from its barren surroundings has come into existence where sand, blown up the puffing-hole and carried across by the south or south-easterly winds that would drive waves directly into the sea-cave below, has accumulated in a slight hollow. It is called Muirbheach na gCoiníní; the first word means a stretch of sandy coastal land, and this is the *"muirbheach* of the rabbits," which are softly housed here by grace of this freak outfall of the storm.

The western puffing-hole is much smaller and lies inland of the storm beach; it is about a hundred yards from the clifftop. Its opening is a ragged grassy funnel above a narrow cleft of rock in which the sea spleenwort fern grows. Occasionally a sigh of spray hangs in the air over it, the sea can always be heard in its depths, and sometimes in spring a nesting chough explodes out of its rocky muzzle as one peers down, and flaps black and screaming overhead until one moves on.

LITTLE SEÁN'S BOULDER AND OTHER STONES

The grey terrain west of the puffing-holes, cut off from the sea by the jagged ramparts of the storm beach, and with the island's low bare ridge-line as its inland horizon, looks like the birthplace of rock itself. The ground here sloughs off scales of stone, which men have set on edge, close-stacked, to make walls for countless fields, and like giant eggs in these comfortless nests are dozens of huge limestone boulders, some of which have split apart and lie in pieces as if already hatched. These rugged boulders are quite different from the smooth slabs of limestone lying everywhere; they were carried here by ice, which ground them into rough ovoids before dropping them as the glaciers melted back at the end of the last Ice Age thousands of years ago. These glaciers had radiated out from an ice-cap on the mountains of the Joyce Country thirty miles to the north, and most of the "erratics" they brought with them are of Galway's granite, but the chunks of limestone that are so profusely scattered across the eastern end of the island must have been torn out of the ground somewhere not so far to the north, either on Aran itself or from the floor of what is now the Sound between it and the granite country. They are all individual and characterful objects, which lead one on into strolling from field to field as through the rooms of some weirdly metamorphosed sculpture gallery. Rain has worked into the tilted flanks of the boulders, carving terraces for miniature rock-gardens of wall-rue ferns and little herbs with starry blossoms in white or purple: scurvy grass, herb Robert, etcetera. Some boulders have been so deeply eaten by rainwater that they have come apart along their parallel fracture-planes and now lie in three or four thick slices stacked aslant. One or two have small lean-to pens for goat-kids built against them out of the curious shards of stone the ground crops in this part of the island. The biggest of them all, ten feet tall, is called Mulán Sheáin Bhig, Little Seán's boulder, after some long-dead toiler in the unpromising plot it overshadows.

The boulder-streak (as the geologists term such an assemblage of glacial erratics, because when plotted on a map it appears as a streak marking the course of the ice that brought the boulders) leads one away from the coast towards the ridge-line, and beyond that down again to near the starting-point of this book. Once engaged in hunting out a way through these tiny, bare, deserted fields, with the curious paths and gaps and stiles that link them into sequences, it is difficult to turn back. Field follows field with the unending incalculable oddity of the prime numbers in their sequence, that ultimate mystery of arithmetic. But the quest for Aran's interior mysteries is reserved for the sequel to this book, and I must return from this incursion, to the cliffs of the south.

PROSPECTIVE

About half a mile west of the Glasson Rock at a little point called simply An Coirnéal, the corner, the coast adopts the general west-north-westerly direction it holds to all the way to the farther end of the island. Headlands appear one beyond another, chapters still to be read of an unfolding tale; the inlets are hidden, but the recesses of the deepest of them lie less than half a mile north of the direct line of sight from here to the most westerly point visible, eight miles away, so the tortuosities of the coastline are constrained within surprisingly narrow limits. The succession of bays and capes, which reaches superb climaxes to the west, begins quietly with a meandering row of little alcoves, each only thirty or fifty yards wide, cut into low cliffs, the massive storm beach set well back from them so that one can walk the clifftops easily, and broad, stepped terraces of rock-pools exposed at their feet when the tide is out. This stretch of coast is so finely detailed, and the Iaráirne man I walked it with when I was collecting its place-names—one of the best of the older generation of Aran folk, keen and hardy in mind and body, a small man bird-like on the roof when mending a thatch, a fisherman who builds his own currachs, a villager who can enter into my sense of the wider significance of his local lore—was in such good form that sunny day that my wind-torn old six-inch map of the area was almost obliterated by my notes and markings. I will only mention a representative few of these placenames here, which introduce themes—what the sea gives, and man's keeping of the land—to be expounded in detail by other shores of Aran.

The third of these little alcoves, going west from An Coirnéal, is Poll an tSail; the basic meaning of the first word, which rhymes with the English "owl," is "hole," but it has to be translated as inlet, bay, cave, valley, hollow, pool or pond, according to circumstances. This, then, is "the bay of the baulk of timber," and around it stand Ailltreacha na Giúise, the cliffs of the pine timber. Many of the older houses of the islands have rafters cut from beams washed ashore and carried off and hidden before the coastguards or the landlords' agent got wind of them, and even today islanders keep an eye out for such prizes, as I do myself. Recently an elderly and, as I had thought, frail couple, neighbours of ours in the west of the island, managed to drag a thick tree trunk eighteen feet long up a steep shinglebank to where they could bring a cart for it. When I made some remark about this feat the old lady replied, *"Ní raibh ann ach pléisiúr!"*—"It was nothing but a pleasure!"

The next bay is named Poillín na gCleití, the little bay of the feathers, but only from some chance observation of scattered seagull feathers, as the seabirds the old cliffmen used to catch and pluck to fill pillows and mattresses nest on the higher cliffs to the west, not here. Next door (for these bays are on a household scale) is a deeper inlet called Poll Neide, after one Ned. Surnames, being few, are little used in Aran and most families have a nickname which is either the Christian name of some forbear or derives from some joke or anecdote about a forbear (and as most of the latter type are offensive to the people concerned and not to be used to their faces it is impossible for me to give any of the dozens of current examples, interesting though they are). However, Muintir Neide (the Ned folk, one might say in English) are a well-known Iaráirne family; their holding is a long strip of land coming down to the coast here, and it would have been in this inlet that they gathered seaweed to put on their land. Seaweed rights used to be grimly defended, and were closely defined in terms of types of seaweed and the times of year at which they could be gathered, and even where they could be dried; for instance the Iaráirne people had the right to spread seaweed to dry on the piece of the Neides' land by the shore here. The next bay to the west, a rather large one, was well known specifically as a place where large amounts of the red *Laminaria* weed drifts ashore and could be easily fetched up the low cliffs to be burnt for kelp; it is called Poll na Feamainne, the bay of the seaweed. Beside it is An Darna Poll, the second bay, so called because coming from the west it is the second one after the boundary wall of the territory of Iaráirne village. And so the final bay of this Iaráirne shore is the next, An Poll Sleamhain, the slippery bay; it is the green *Enteromorpha* seaweed that makes the shore slippery wherever fresh water flows over it from springs, as here.

A CLASS DIVISION

The boundary wall of Iaráirne's territory is immediately recognizable if one climbs the storm beach just west of the last-named bay and looks inland. The horizon is given by a low ridge half a mile away, from which walls come down towards the shore, dividing up a grim and grey landscape into a number of strips of crag and pockets of rough pasture. But, to the west of the wall opposite this point the divisions are large, and to the east of it they are small. The difference used to be even more marked, as the land in the west was redivided or "striped" in the Thirties and distributed among the people of Cill Éinne and Iaráirne. And on the northern slopes of the island where what is being divided is comparatively productive land rather than so much grimness and greyness, the contrast between tiny patches on the one hand and broad acres on the other speaks for itself: the huddled portions of the exploited seem to mutter against the complacent spread of the wealthy. Specifically, what one sees here is the border between two of

Árainn's twenty-four *ceathrúna* or "quarters" which have had quite different histories: to the east lies Ceathrú an tSunda, the quarter of the Sound (being adjacent to Gregory's Sound), consisting of the smallholdings of Iaráirne farmers; to the west is Ceathrú an Chnoic, the quarter of the hill, formerly a single holding known as the Hill Farm, which went with a fine lodge on the hillside near Cill Éinne village, the villagers themselves being landless fishermen or having small plots in the next quarter to the west, an area rather dismissively called An Screigín, the small stony place. The Hill Farm's history, which with the lapse of time has fallen apart into picturesque anecdotes, and the miserable consequences of its monopoly of the best land of Cill Éinne, belong to *Labyrinth*, the account of Árainn's interior. Here we turn back to the coast and note that the shore ahead, that of Ceathrú an Chnoic, is or was serviced by a road, while that of Iaráirne's land is not. The road, a wide, untarred and unwalled track, comes over the ridge of the hill that hides the Lodge to the north-west, crosses broad crags, the more recent "striping" of which has interrupted its course with a couple of walls, then turns eastwards along the coast in the lee of the storm beach, and ends abruptly against the boundary wall. It was famine-relief work of the late nineteenth century, and like most such projects what little utility it had (for the transport of seaweed and wrack from these low-cliffed and accessible shores) was to the benefit of the larger landholders and not to that of the hungry wretches who laboured on it for their daily dish of boiled maize.

SEA-MARKS

One can take this road from the boundary wall as far as the next large bay half a mile to the west, or follow the same arc of the coast on the clifftops, which is preferable since the road is a dreary track of depressing associations and is deprived of a sight of the sea by the storm beach; or if the tide is out one can climb down onto the terraces below the cliffs and meander along among the rock-pools on the sea's own level. This *leac* (as such a sheet of rock is termed here) is over a hundred yards wide in places, and is one of the most spacious wave-cut terraces of Aran. It is called Leac na gCarrachán, and the bay it leads round into is Poll na gCarrachán, both names deriving from that of certain shoals half a mile or so off shore here, called Na Carracháin, which merely means the rocky patches or stone-piles.

Being a landsman I have not visited Na Carracháin, but the old boatmen have told me the spell or Open-Sesame that would get me there: "*Mant Beag ar Ghob an Chinn; Teampall Bheannáin ar na Clocha Móra*" ("The Little Gap on the Point of the Head: St. Benan's church on the Big Stones"). The Mant Beag is a dip in the Cliffs of Moher on the eastern skyline, and it has to be lined up with the southern tip of Inis Meáin, a spot nearly always conspicuously flashing white with breakers. For the other bearing, the little ruin of St. Benan's church, the only building visible from here, high on the hilltop over Cill Éinne village, must be aligned with certain huge boulders precariously balanced on the edge of the cliff on the west side of Poll na gCarrachán. The currach-fishermen had dozens of these runes to guide them to good fishing grounds and keep them clear of danger. They often involve places the fishermen had never visited and to which they gave names their inhabitants would not recognize. Thus Na Simléir, the chimneys, is the Cill Éinne fishermen's name for a place near Gort na gCapall that the farmers of the village cannot quite equate with any of their land; a tiny patch of green grass clinging to the brink of the cliff below Túr Mháirtín is well known to Inis Meáin boatmen as An Réallóg, whereas few Árainn men would know it had a name at all. (The word *réallóg* itself has died out of Árainn's speech although it occurs in a number of placenames there, whereas it is still in use in the smaller islands, for an unfenced plot of good land in a waste of crag.) And men from all three islands, on hearing that I have mapped the area, have asked me about what they call An Garraí Gabhann, the pound, up on the hilltop just east of Ballyvaughan in County Clare; it is a natural formation, not particularly striking on a close approach, that looks like a great enclosure from a distance, and when it appears around Black Head it throws a signal farther and clearer than any lighthouse to men on the sea out to the west of Aran. Thus offshore usage recreates the surrounding landscapes; like a poet I know who finds his lines by glancing along titles on library shelves, so the fisherman low among the waves raises his eyes and picks words off the land with which to write sentences on the sea.

SIGNATURES

The scale of the coast begins to increase westwards from Poll na gCarrachán. The bays are more deeply excavated, out of higher cliffs; the storm beach stands fifty yards or more inland of the cliffs, falling back in wide arcs to yield even more ground around the side of each bay opposite to the prevailing south-westerlies. The grandly sweeping way so formed along the clifftops is as smooth and clear as if it were paved with flagstones.

For a few months in 1975 another art-work by Richard Long stood on this natural exhibition site, a ring of stones which M and I first saw when the plane bringing us from Galway happened to turn and bank over the spot, an instantly recognizable mark that told us who had visited the island in our absence. The following Sunday we made an expedition there as if to authenticate this signature, for things seen from an aeroplane, like dreams, lack a certain validity in recollection. We found it after a long walk, on the small headland immediately west of the giant sea-mark boulders of Na Clocha Móra. It was an elegant work, a circle about twenty paces across of small limestone blocks from the storm beach, that skimmed the brink of the cliff with an aesthetic, almost dandified, poise. It did not withstand the criticism of the autumn storms, however, and on a later visit we found that every bit of it had been tidied back into the storm beach again.

The loitering eclecticism of such Sunday strolls perhaps allows mention of two other signatures of sorts in the rock of this stretch of coast, one geological and the other legendary. The first is a thick sprinkling of tiny white dots, little granules of calcite a couple of millimetres long and pointed at either end. These are the fossils of an alga, or perhaps of the spore of an alga, called *Saccamenopsis*, which lived in the seas from the sediment of which this particular stratum of rock now lying along these clifftops was formed. *Saccamenopsis* was only found to occur in Irish rocks a few years ago when it was discovered in the Burren, though it is well known in the corresponding limestones of Derbyshire in England. The plant must have flourished for a comparatively short period, geologically speaking, and the absence of its traces from other strata makes this one a useful marker-bed for the geologist, recognizable wherever it is exposed.

The other signature left on this shore was made at some date not strung on the same thread as those of *Saccamenopsis* and Richard Long, by a sea-horse that leapt up the cliffs and skidded inland on the rocks. I was led to its hoofmarks by an islander, and as he had some difficulty in finding the exact spot I carefully noted how to do so: a field-wall leads up the hill from a bay called Poll Dick a quarter of a mile north-west of Na Clocha Móra, and the marks are about four paces east of this wall and forty paces from the clifftop. They consist of a series of horseshoe-shaped ripple-marks in the bed of a rivulet worn by rainwater in a sheet of bare rock. Nearer the wall is a smaller, fainter set, attributed to the foal of the sea-horse. I have met nobody, apart from a well-known bar-keeping Münchhausen of Cill Rónáin, who claims to have seen a sea-horse, but several islanders knew folk of the last generation who did, and the stories are not disbelieved. The blacksmith remembers that when he was a child he overheard a man telling his father at the forge about how he went fishing at Aill an Ára, a cliff a mile west of this point, and saw a *capall fharraige* or sea-horse and its foal swimming below, whereupon he wound up his line and never went rock-fishing again. And once, I am told, a man called Dirrane and his crew got a terrible fright when a sea-horse came up beside their boat. Sometimes it used to happen that a mare kept in a field near the shore would produce an unexpected foal, and the *stail fharraige* or sea-stallion would be held responsible. Such are the stories I have heard, and they are much the same as those Lady Gregory collected here in 1898.

NINE FATHOMS

Low tides lay bare a wide terrace under the cliffs from Na Clocha Móra to Poll Dick, and half-way between these two places is a spot called Dabhach an tSnámha, the swimming-pool, a name that points out a striking feature of such rock-floors backed by cliffs: their surfaces are what the geologist calls "mamillated," having smoothly swelling projections, which are in fact sometimes breast-shaped as the etymology demands. These convexities flow into equally rounded concavities, so that the rock has a curiously organic undulating surface, and retains the falling tide in fantastic cups and wayward baths that invite one to loll in sun-warmed shallows. Liam O'Flaherty has written a story in which a young girl makes the discovery of her own body among the pools and mounds of just such a terrace of the shore near his native village farther to the west. Why does this so readily eroticized rock-surface occur below sheer cliffs, as if a concern for privacy entered into its making? The connecting link is the layers of shale and clay that separate the limestone strata at various levels. The cliffs come into existence where they do because the waves excavate a clay band that happens to lie within their range, and so progressively undermine the limestone above, which collapses and is demolished. Therefore the terrace below the cliff is formed from a stra-

tum that immediately underlay such a clay band, and its characteristic surface has been exhumed by the waves from beneath the
clay.

The mamillation, though, is not the result of wave action but
of some process of erosion during the original deposition of the
clay. This took place when the floor of that ancient sea of the
Carboniferous era had been brought up by one of its periodical
oscillations to lie exposed to the air. Weathering then broke up the
topmost rock-layers and reduced them to a soil, of which the present clay bands are the fossil remains. This soil of course bore generations of plants, and the humic acid of their decomposition
seeped down in rainwater to the limestone bedrock, which it cor-
roded. This diffuse chemical action of a mild acid held in the
sponge of soil and vegetable fibre is enough to explain the
smoothness of the rock surface it produced. And if that ground-
water tended to accumulate in any initial depressions of the bedrock, rounding them out into bowls, the result would have been
the topography of coalescent hollows and mounds now revealed.
Similar processes are known to be at work today in areas of limestone covered by soil and vegetation, for instance in the Burren.

Such are the links, as a geologist has explained them to me, between these mamillated surfaces and the cliffs that overhang them,
between the earth-movements of the Carboniferous era and a
story of O'Flaherty's—links not in any simple "chain of being,"
but in the network of being, which consists of tangle within tangle
within tangle, indefinitely, but of which nevertheless we can tease
out a thread or two here and there.

This terrace of beguiling tubs and hummocks ends in a little
bay called Poll na gColm, the bay of the doves, under a westward-
jutting bastion of the cliff; Poll Dick lies just beyond. The first
name refers to the rock-dove one occasionally sees hurtling along
the faces of the precipices it nests on, the wild forbear of the
street-pigeon of town centres—though it is difficult to associate
that jostling, motley, mangy throng scavenging underfoot on

Galway's pavements or in Trafalgar Square with this discreet solitary, briefly glimpsed from the clifftops, a blue-grey arrowhead on a shaft of wind.

The second bay, Poll Dick, is a superb cauldron of roaring whiteness in wild weather when waves rushing round the salient of the cliff beat into the undercuttings of its recesses and send seahorses of foam leaping up its walls. There is something unnerving in the way the waters withdraw from it in the slack of the wave, regroup with apparent deliberation, draw breath and swell up, and then come crashing tumultuously in again, rearing and licking around its rims, and leave its terraces streaming with hazy, rainbowed cataracts. In calm weather this is a favoured fishing spot; its deeps are directly below the cliff, so that one can sit on Ulán Cúl le Gréin, the "ledge shaded from the sun," on the northern face of the little arm of cliff that almost encloses the bay, and drop a line into water even when the tide is out. Dick, it is supposed, was an *habitué* of the place; that is not an island name, however, although a Rickard Fitzpatrick owned Aran in the early eighteenth century, and one could imagine him taking a sunny day off from his turbulent Galway career to doze on the shady ledge of this corner of his domain, his mayoral hat over his eyes.

The next bay to the west is Poll na Naoi bhFeá, the "nine-fathom bay," that being the length of line needed to fish from its cliffs. A fathom is six feet (originally it was the distance from fingertip to fingertip of outstretched arms). I have heard an elderly Aran man complain that the young shop assistants in Galway embarrass him by pretending not to understand when he asks for so many fathoms of rope; the old man and the youngster would have resentfully shared a moment of that insecurity which makes the first vow never to leave Aran again if he can help it, and the second to suppress his memory of country ways and even his Irish language, wanting to be as different from his parents as are the pigeons strutting at the shopdoor from the wild dove inured to the spray of the sea.

Fishing from these cliffs is not just for sport and supper. I

learned the names of these places from old Antoine Ó Briain, one
of a well-known Cill Éinne family of rhymers and *seanchaí* or custodians of lore, when I found him fishing here one day. He was
catching fat golden-red ballan wrasse, called *ballach* or rockfish
here, which he would later fillet, salt and cure in the sun, for sale
to the dealer who comes out from An Cheathrú Rua in Connemara where this Aran product is still relished—I remember buying some myself there once thinking they were kippers, and as I
had not soaked the salt out overnight the more I cooked them the
tougher they got until they were as unpalatable as an oily doormat
and had to be thrown out. Antoine had brought his bait from the
shallow northern shores: little crabs he tore the shells off and winkles he cracked with a stone before filling his hooks with the hor-
rible living mixture. His line had two hooks and was weighted
with a stone which he swung underarm two or three times before
letting the line fly out (the men who fish the taller cliffs to the
west whirl the weight around their heads so as to carry the line
clear of the cliff face). Rockfish lurk close to the crevices of under-
water cliffs; the practised fisherman can drop his line in exactly
the right spot. Antoine did quite well that day; I carried his sack of
sixteen fish home for him over the crags, and it nearly defeated
me. The price he was expecting (this was in 1979) was "two score
pounds a hundred," the hundred being actually a hundred and
twelve, as in hundredweights.

The nine fathoms of line must mean that the cliffs here are
about fifty feet high, and in the next half mile they double in
height, to the peninsula on which stands the ruins of a Celtic
stone fort, Dún Dúchathair. As the cliff rises the storm beach becomes intermittent, being interrupted by deep and comparatively
sheltered inlets. Each peninsula has a wave-cut terrace at its foot;
on the east of the nine-fathom bay it is called Carraig an Bhrutha,
the rock of the surf, and on its west it is Leic Uí Ghoill, Gill's flag-
stone, which is a dangerous reef extending far out from the coast.
Below the peninsula before the fort the terrace is An Creachoileán
Istigh, the inner *creachoileán*, and a great rectangular slab forming

a grim little island off it is An Creachoileán Báite, the submerged or drowned *creachoileán*. The island writer Tom O'Flaherty, Liam's brother, used to translate this word, which occurs in a dozen or more placenames around the islands, as "Island of Woe," as if it derived from *creach*, woe or ruination, which is picturesque and well-suited to such dark and threatening reefs, and perhaps this is the true origin of the word, which is not in the dictionaries.

I notice that on the Ordnance Survey six-inch map the head of the bay between the *creachoileán* and the great fort is marked "Barally." This is the anglicization of *barr aille*, literally "top of the cliff." Aran people refer to the whole southern coastline thus; obviously one of the surveyors asked someone on the spot the name of this place and wrote down the answer without checking its extension. A common phrase here for a fruitless endeavour is "*ag dul go Barr Aille gan tada*," "going to Barr Aille for nothing," for the islanders almost never visit these tall cliffs without good reason, and there are many whom no reason at all could bring to this mortal edge of their holding.

DÚCHATHAIR

From inland the fort of Dúchathair appears a slouching mass dark against the southern sea-spaces; hence, no doubt, its name, from *dubh cathair*, black fort. It consists of a single wall of immense thickness built of rough, unmortared limestone blocks, which defends the outer hundred yards of a peninsula from landward attack, sheer or overhanging cliffs a hundred feet high making approach from the sea impossible. Two fat buttresses of masonry like that of the wall are the work of the nineteenth-century restorers, and knowing this it is easy to subtract them in the mind's eye from the grand unity of the whole and indeed to replace the blocks of which they are composed on the top of the wall whence they had fallen. The skyline of the wall is rather slumped, but at its highest, where it crosses a slight hollow running down the centre of the peninsula, the wall presents a twenty-foot face, very even, and slightly inclined inwards. Before the wall an area of crag is closely set with long stones jammed upright into the crevices; many of them have been taken for fencing or are now fallen, but enough remain to show that they would have been a formidable obstacle to a direct storming of the fort. At either end some length of wall has been lost with collapse of the cliffs; what remains is an arc, convex towards the land, about ninety paces in length. There was a gateway at the east near the cliff which fell away more than a hundred and fifty years ago. Until recently one entered the fort by picking one's way across fallen masonry on the brink of this cliff, but now a gap has been cleared there, for better or for worse, and the wall comes to a neat and stable end a few yards short of the edge.

The inside of the wall has two terraces running around it, as if for viewing the Atlantic horizon that completes its circle. The remains of a number of stone huts clustered like the cells of a wild bees' nest cling to the wall's base in the double shelter of its concavity and the grassy hollow in the middle of the peninsula. Only the bases of their walls remain and these have been tidied up into stout curved arms of stone that embrace half a dozen ideal picnic spots of flowered sward. To seaward the turf is more salt-blasted and intermittent, and the south-western side of the promontory bears a storm beach of jagged flags, among which a few hollows can be read as the sites of a line of stone huts said to have been overwhelmed by the storm beach on "The Night of the Big Wind," the 5th of January 1839.

The outer parapet and the two terraces of the big wall are each the top of an individual thickness of it, for it is composed of three contiguous layers one inside another, totalling sixteen to eighteen feet in thickness at the base, and each raised to a different height. A fourth terrace along the base of the central length compensates for the sag in the ground-level there, and all the terraces and the topmost parapet are linked by little flights of steps running directly up recesses in their inner faces. There is a low aperture under a heavy lintel in the base of the wall, inside the innermost of the huts built against it, from which a tunnel about two feet high runs directly into the wall. This has only recently been opened up; I was shown it first in 1978, and it is not mentioned in any descriptions of the fort, although a tradition that there had been such a tunnel was recorded around the turn of the century. By the light of my match it appears to be about sixteen feet long; its floor is the bare ground and it is roofed across with long slabs, and when I crawled to the end of it I saw a chink of light above me, so it reaches very nearly to the outer surface of the wall. Such passages are well known in many cashels, but this is the only such structure apart from very small recesses to be found in any of the Aran forts. Like the underground chambers or "souterrains" found in many of the Burren's cashels, they probably served as storage places and in some cases as shelters or escape routes. This tunnel looks as if it might have been intended as a secret exit or sally-port that could have been knocked through to the outside of the wall should the gate have been forced by an enemy.

The whole organization of the interior of Dúchathair gives one an immediate impression of resolute, concerted and ingenious application to an imperative purpose. But as one paces and puzzles about it and inquires into its genesis, doubts besiege and overthrow one's initial certainties. Firstly one learns that the interior was a tumbled wreckage when the restorers set to work in 1880, and as earlier records of it are vague it is not known how much of the present arrangement of terraces and steps is a result of their preconceptions of what a prehistoric fort should be. However, it is likely that the general scheme of a layered wall rising in terraces is correct as this recurs in Aran's other cashels and in many elsewhere. But how exactly would such terracing be of advantage in defence? It appears that each thickness of such walls is a complete wall in itself, faced with carefully coursed masonry and infilled with loose stone, so that if the outer thickness were pulled down the next would stand unharmed. But any attackers in a position to pull down part of the wall would have been able to scale it too, and then would have had the advantage of height in fighting their way down the terraces within. It has also been suggested that the stepped construction was an aid in building, but then the islanders of today who are periodically called in by the Office of Public Works to rebuild a collapsed section of one of the dúns quickly rig up a little hoist to raise the stones directly up the outer face of the wall rather than heave them up from terrace to terrace, and this would not have been beyond the original artisans.

Perhaps the terracing was adapted to some feature of life within the cashel—but what sort of life could that have been? Since there is no spring in or near it, and given its exposed situation, it can hardly have been inhabited for more than brief periods of danger, or perhaps of ceremony. Even the monks who came to Aran in search of a landscape to scourge the senses lodged themselves in nooks of its milder northern slopes and wrapped at least a fold of cliff about their shoulders against the blast of the ocean. Are these gloomy parapets and gardens of spikes an architecture of fear or of display? Perhaps the people of Dúchathair with its standing army of stone sought to impose upon folk of lesser forts, and were in turn overawed by the spacious outworks of Dún Aonghasa.

Since none of the dúns has been studied by modern methods (and the same is true for all but a very few of the scores of comparable cashels in Ireland), it is not even known if they were inhabited simultaneously or not. Folk-history ascribes them either to the Fir Bolg, one of the mythical invading races from whom the modern Irishman has come dwindling down, or to "the Danes," the Vikings whose seaborne raids made the mediaeval monks fear calm weather. Who indeed could have built such monstrous nests of stone, and especially on such a wind-racked, spray-blasted extremity of the habitable world as this, but remote ancestral beings, half man and half force of nature, or else mysterious foreign pirates so rapacious that only stormy weather gave respite from their fiercer storms?

Archaeologists are rightly tentative in all they have to say about the origins, dates and purposes of such cashels, which are perhaps only miscalled "forts." In general it is agreed that they were built by a Celtic people, a cattle-raising society with a warrior aristocracy of whose life-style the Irish heroic legends give us a glorified view. Some cashels date from the Iron Age and perhaps most from early historic times, while a few were certainly inhabited in mediaeval times and one or two to within living memory. Aran's two coastal examples, Dúchathair and Dún Aonghasa, both have the *chevaux-de-frise* (as the defensive bands of set stones are called, after the Frisians, who having no horses used a similar device of spikes against cavalry attacks), and this feature may indicate that they are some centuries earlier than the two inland forts and perhaps date from the Early Iron Age, a few centuries BC. But their purpose, for all their purposeful air, remains obscure.

Dún Aonghasa, four miles to the west, will allow me to amplify these suppositions and their evidences, but in leaving Dúchathair, and in the dearth of sounder information, I will pass on a theory I heard from a Cill Rónáin farmer about the *chevaux-de-frise*. This was, he tells me, a defence not against men but against hordes of wild pigs that infested the land in those days—his evidence for these is the vast numbers of stones lying everywhere which can only have been rooted up by pigs, and the name of a certain area of the island, Creig na Muc, the crag of the pigs, where no pigs have been kept in island memory. The stones of the *chevaux-de-frise*, he points out, are set just far enough apart for the inhabitants of the dún to run in amongst them when hard-pressed by the pigs, which themselves would have been too fat to follow. So, mighty residences of stone fall bit by bit into the sea, the myths of huge cloudy lords quit them, and the irrepressible if shrunken folk-mind repopulates them, even before archaeology has done so, with normal-sized mortals devising witty solutions to pig-sized problems, just like their original true inhabitants, whoever they were.

STYLES OF FLIGHT

The sea makes a ferocious attack on the peninsula of Dúchathair, and may after a few more centuries leave a remnant of the fort isolated on a sea-stack, for it is cutting through the neck of the headland from the bay on its west, eating out colossal overhangs from which one can look dizzily down at breakers crawling among giant debris of past cliff-falls. In the last century there were traces of another fort on the headland on the other side of this bay; it was described as having a wall six foot seven inches thick and enclosing a stone hut eighteen foot six across. Nothing can be made out now of either fort or hut among the tumbled slabs of the last of the storm beach, which ceases here as the cliffs beyond the next bay are unscalable by the waves of any storm.

The headland of the vanished fort is Binn an Phrúntaigh, the cliff face of the *prúntach* or young black-backed gull. No doubt that species does nest here, and I often see one go drifting by, alarming the lesser gulls, for it is a huge bird and a nest-robber. But the most familiar gull on this particular cliff is the mild little kittiwake. An aerial survey of sea-birds in 1970 estimated the nesting population of kittiwakes in Árainn at eight hundred and twenty pairs. In spring one can watch them here assembling on the ledges below and greeting each other with childlike cries. They are trim, sea-grey birds with a crisp, newly painted, nautical look due to the unbroken black of their wingtips, which distinguishes them from the other gulls, in which the black of the wingtips is dashed with white. They are marvellous fliers too, circling around the bays with a buoyant, yacht-like glide that makes the herring gulls and common gulls appear to be perpetually stumbling over invisible irregularities of the air. One soon learns to recognize birds by their styles in this three-dimensional rite performed each spring in a dozen great theatres of the cliffs. The fulmar—a rather short-bodied grey bird, not a gull though very like one in appearance—is the most dazzling performer, in a more mechanical mode than that of the dreamy lyrical kittiwake; it rides the updraughts of the deep cliff walls without a sign of effort apart from minute adjustments of the angle of its stiff, blade-like wings to maximize the efficient use of the air's impetus, sometimes looking about it with a turn of its short neck as it whirls by, like a pilot abstractedly glancing out of the cockpit of a little plane as he gives a deft touch to the controls. This bird has only nested on Irish shores during the last decade; formerly its breeding ground was Icelandic, but a century ago it started to expand its range enormously, for no well-understood reason. For nine months of the year the fulmar never rests from flying, far out over the Atlantic. In February, it comes shorewards, though never venturing inland, and nests on cliffs such as these, from which it can drop itself directly into flight by shuffling itself off a ledge, its legs being degenerate and almost functionless. Once when I had ventured a little way down such a cliff-face I disturbed a mating pair of fulmars, and saw the male throw himself into space off the back of his partner. It is strangely disturbing to watch a fulmar approach its nest a dozen times or more before landing, sweeping up to the site and falling away from it into another wide circuit over the water, before it finally commits itself to a stalling flop onto the ledge, as if it were as distrustful of solid ground as we would be of the empty air beyond the brink that separates its world from ours.

Islanders tell me there are puffins at Binn an Phrúntaigh too, but I have never seen them on Aran's cliffs, though they nest on the Cliffs of Moher and I once saw one from a boat not far offshore from Aran. However, the commoner auks, the similarly plump and black razorbills and guillemots, line the ledges here in hundreds during the nesting season. Sometimes, as if they suddenly tired of sitting in rows on the cliff face, a group of them will hop off and go whirring down to the water in a long sagging arc, skim close above the surface with the motion of clockwork mice, and sit in rows on the sea for a change. And the big black cormorants go by, flying very low, with necks outstretched, making that same urgent line across the water as a wild goose against the sky, and carrying their absurd courting gifts of scraps of seaweed, tokens of nests to be.

WRACK

A bay half a mile wide separates the sequence of cliffs so far described from the loftier range to the west, and corresponds to a valley that breaks through the island's escarpment ridge here. The valley is broadest to the north-east where it embraces low land between the villages of Cill Éinne and Cill Rónáin, but as it approaches the southern coast it rises and narrows into a gorge that fades out just short of the cliffs. This gorge must have formed along large joints of the limestone—it shares the general direction of the major set of joints—and these same lines of weakness no doubt have led to the formation of a striking feature called An Aill Bhriste, the broken cliff, at the point of the coast nearest the head of the gorge and in the centre of the bay's arc. Here a great mass has come half adrift from the clifftop, and forms an arch between it and a rock-stack based on the terrace below. When you are close to the spot it all looks so firm and long-lasting that its top of green turf invites you to hop over the ragged chasm onto a perfect picnic site. But then when you look back from farther along the cliffs and see how the stack below leans outwards and that weighty fallen blocks are wedging open the crevasses you jumped, you have a vision of the inevitable crumbling of the whole crazy pile, carrying you with it into the foam.

For the lads of Cill Rónáin the gap opened up by this incipient collapse is an invitation to scramble down to the terraces which run a long way to the west under the cliffs at sea level. I watched two of them recently salvaging a floating spar down there and heaving it up from step to step of the jumble of blocks that hangs like a wrecked staircase between the cliff and the rock-stack. This bay was always well known for the flotsam that accumulated in it, and its name, Poll na Brioscarnach, refers to fragments of wreckage. In the last century there was a winch on the clifftop for hoisting up timbers, and I am told that the O'Malleys, who had the Hill Farm, kept a man stationed here to claim anything of value that came ashore. All that is left of the winch is a rusty iron peg set in the ground at the head of a wide track that comes through the valley and reaches the coast just east of the rock-arch. This road was another nineteenth-century famine-relief project, and is still of use to the men who have fields in An Screigín, the quarter of Cill Éinne it traverses. But its final section, now walled off, served no purpose other than the transport of salvage, and only an isolated and apparently pointless length of it remains, ending mysteriously in mid-air eighty feet above the sea.

ARGUMENTS FROM WEAKNESS

This scrap of history's jetsam, the bit of road abandoned on the clifftop, at least serves to mark a corner of Cill Éinne. The exact boundary is the field-wall between it and the rock-arch, and the next half-mile of land, around the bay and up the hillside to the western skyline, belongs to Cill Rónáin people. This skyline is the beginning of the island's central plateau. The stone fort of Dún Eochla, high on the inland shoulder of the plateau, stands out to the north-west, and from it the skyline runs as evenly as a roof-ridge, with only the slightest southwards dip, to the coast ahead, where it ends in a boldly jutting headland, An Aill Bhán, the white cliff, so called from the cladding of bright calcite on its vertical eastern face. The promontory terrace below the cliff is equally simply named, An Pointe Fiáin, the wild point—"And it is too!" added the retired fisherman who gave me its name, his jaw suddenly setting as if he were once again gripping the tiller to take his lobster boat out of the sheltered bay, around the point's white thunders and into the track of the great rollers coming from the west.

Walking on around the bay from the rock-arch towards the high white promontory, and keeping as one thinks well away from the edge because of the undercutting of the cliffs, one jumps over a field-wall to find an opening at one's feet that gives like a window onto a plunging view of waves breaking on a beach vertically below. This little chasm is called simply Poll Talún, the hole in the ground; it is marked on the Survey maps as a puffing-hole, but the arch of the overhang it opens into is so lofty I doubt if anything more than spindrift is sent up it even by the wildest storms. The young men of the village used to boast about having jumped across it, but erosion, or else degeneration of the race, has made that game too dangerous now. Aran's last fox, according to a local story, evaded its hunters for a long time because no-one could discover where it had its earth, until one day someone saw it slinking down Poll Talún. Then the hunters lay in watch nearby and found out that the fox lived on a ledge in the vault of the cliff below, which it reached by clamping its jaws on a fern that grew in the bottom of the hole and swinging itself down. So they cut the stalk of the fern half through, and the next time the fox swung on it the fern broke and let the beast fall into the breakers.

This shameful anecdote has its setting, if not its excuse, in a lapse of the rock itself; the opening in the roof of the overhang is due to a small fault that shows up as a fissure in the cliff face and a little valley running inland obliquely, north-westwards from it. A fault is a dislocation of the strata (as opposed to a joint, a break that leaves the strata on either side of it in their original relative positions) and here by peering over at the face of the cliff one can see that the layers of rock on the west of the fissure are displaced a foot or so downwards relative to their continuations on the east. Faults are the exception in Aran, and the land-forms, from such major features as the long skyline terminating in the promontory ahead, to the little crevices of the rock underfoot, have been carved out by erosion along the joints, the lines of least resistance. And since these joints occur almost throughout the island in two sets, each astonishingly parallel, the most developed ones trending north-north-east and the others at about ninety degrees to that direction, a great rectangularity underlies all the oddities and complexities of the landscape and even the network of field-walls. Poll Talún, on the other hand, owing its existence to a fault rather than a joint, lies askew in the fields around it, and jars with the pattern.

Some of the joints of the major set are filled with crystals of calcite, a purer form of calcium carbonate than that which makes up the limestone itself. These crystals have been deposited from a flux of hot aqueous solutions that forced its way up through such planes of weakness in the rock during some remote geological period of thermal activity in whatever strata lie deep below the islands. Such veins of calcite show up, especially in the bare rock of the shore, as white lines, of all thicknesses up to a few inches, and sometimes continuing for dozens of yards as straight as rays of light. And where a freak of cliff-fall has entirely removed the rock on one side of a calcite vein, the free face revealed is badged with white, as is An Aill Bhán here and the sides of several other headlands orientated along the major joints.

A steep climb along the coast past the white cliff brings one onto the edge of the plateau; that threshold attained, the eye is suddenly made free of new expanses, broad and lofty by the measures one adopts after a time in Aran, and disquietingly secretive despite their utter openness. A mile to the north the long and level ridge-line, behind which the inhabited slopes of the island fall away, carries three empty monuments like three blind heads gazing over the plain: a roofless signal tower of stone and a half-ruined lighthouse, both unmanned and unlit for more than a century, and the darkly peering bulk of the huge Celtic cashel, deserted since prehistory. In summer it is unusual to see anyone moving along the narrow paths, walled with stone, that angle their way through the plateau's thousandfold replication of small crookedly rectangular fields. In winter cattle graze here and there in these fields, and one may occasionally meet a lad sent up to bring a sack of feed-beet to them, for this level of the island carries a thin soil and a healthy pasture useful as winterage; it corresponds to such plateaus of the Burren as Slieve Carran and Turlough Hill, and in that district too it is the custom to drive the cattle up onto the hilltops in the autumn and bring them down in spring. The limestone that gives rise to this soil, in both Aran and the Burren, differs from that of lower levels with their tracts of bare, smooth, pale-grey pavement; it is rougher in texture and darker in hue, and the geologist would recognize it as dolomite, a sort of limestone in which some of the calcium carbonate is replaced by magnesium carbonate. It seems that this exchange of calcium for magnesium ions takes place in hot and very salty water, so that occurrence of dolomite is an indication that these limestone beds once underlay a shallow and evaporating sea.

Where exposure thins out the grass near the clifftops one can see that the stratum now underfoot has a characteristic pattern of fissures too; joints of the major set rather regularly occur a foot or two apart, so that the rock surface is divided up into long plank-shaped sections separated by gaps of a few inches. And as if to emphasize that one is treading new ground here, a thin layer of a blackish mineral called chert occurs over wide areas of this terrain, either just a few inches below the surface, when it is visible in the sides of every fissure, or on the surface itself, where it fragments into little bricks. Chert is a form of silica that occurs in sheets or nodules in limestone; it is a non-crystalline substance with a coke-like texture, and it gives the ground here a charred look that makes both natives and visitors speculate about a volcanic origin for Aran. In fact chert has its birth in water rather than fire, though how exactly it comes to form such layers is a matter of debate. Sea water contains some dissolved silica, which various marine creatures can extract for use in the building of their own skeletons. For instance the single-celled animals called Radiolarians, which form a large component of the ocean's planktonic life, have an internal skeleton of silica, and in certain circumstances the accumulated remains of their teeming, quickly succeeding generations will collect as an ooze on the sea-floor; trapped under succeeding layers of other sediments the gel of silica will eventually be compressed into a layer of chert. Again, some sorts of sponges also use the sea's silica to rigidify themselves. After their death the tiny "spicules" of which their skeletons were composed lie scattered on the sea-bed and in the course of the ages are incorporated into rock along with all the other sediments. Later, water percolating through the rock—rainwater in Aran, for instance—will redissolve the silica of the spicules, leaving them as empty cavities, and on reaching saturation will precipitate it at another level. Thus it could be that chert bands were formed millions of years after the deposition of the rock in which they are embodied.

So, just as the calcite in An Aill Bhán seems to pick out in white a vertical element of the island's hidden structure, here one of the horizontals of its three-dimensional geometry is, as it were, underlined in black. For the two sets of joints, giving rise to fissures running in two directions at right-angles and dividing the strata vertically, together with the almost horizontal partings between the strata, constitute a skeleton (one made up of weaknesses rather than strengths) very like the system of cleavage-planes in a crystal of the cubic order. In other parts of the island this underlying logic is hard to see among the incidentals of the terrains, but the headlands, bays, terraces and overhangs of the great cliffs the sea has carved out of this upland have been modelled, with sweeping decisiveness and on a grand scale, according to the cubic schema of fissure-planes and strata-partings, and the giant crystallinity of Aran made manifest.

And the setting of this rough gem? Correspondingly vast, almost immeasurable, leaving the walker of the clifftops a microscopical figure assailed by immensities that pry at cracks in the self: the sea's temper, whatever it may be, unchecked to the horizon, where in the south Mount Brandon in Kerry is a mere shadow seen when rain has cleared the air, and there is nothing at all to the west but the sky of the hour; and this sky colossal in all its moods, sometimes raising shield upon shield of tenuous greys against the blinding voids behind it, sometimes opening out into unsoundable rooms opulently furnished with cumulus in white and cream, delicately stratified in various perfections of blue, flawed only by the course of transatlantic flights from Shannon, along which slow silver darts rise one by one far in the south-east, arc silently across the dazzling heights and sink to the western horizon while their murmurous voices are still lagging past the zenith; I have seen their departures follow on so closely that three or four are glinting in the sky at once and their vapour-trails entwine and merge and are scored into the blue as if the sky itself were weakened, fissured and veined, along an invisible line of pre-destined fall.

THE CLIFFMAN'S KINGDOM

A cliff face is ignored by the conventional map, which leaves its extent unrepresented except by a mere line between the spaces devoted to sea and land. Nevertheless it has its geography, and sometimes its history too. In Aran, where it was for generations a hunting-ground for fowlers, the cliff has its named and familiar paths, its exits and entrances, hazards and amenities, haunted spots and favourite nooks. As a part of the island that humanity shared with the destructive and superhuman forces of wave and wind, a region to which access could only be won through rare personal qualities and which was ultimately as uninhabitable as the open sea, the cliff face was a wide province of the islanders' mental landscape, a theatre of anecdote, tradition, boast and dream. Ever since I first heard tales of this extinct part of Aran life I have looked back into it with appalled fascination, like that which drives one to peer over the brink of the cliff itself. Perhaps the odds and ends of lore I have collected, and a few of the earlier accounts, can be knotted together into a rope that will let me down to salvage something of the quotidian weirdness of those times. And, in descending the cliff of the past, a little geology seems a useful peg to start from.

Men visited the cliff face because birds dwelt on it, and the ledges that house the birds exactly correspond to the terraces on which men have their homes along the island's northern slopes. Both owe their existence to the layers of shale that lie between the limestone strata; on the cliff face the shale has been picked out

and worn back by the elements' direct onslaught to leave ledges
between the limestone beds, while more complex processes of erosion have worked on the same shale bands to produce the inland
terraces. These ledges run horizontally around the bays and headlands, dividing the height of the cliff into a number of sections
like the storeys of a façade. In general the cliffs rise from east to
west. Near the eastern end of the range they are of a single
storey—there is a shale band at their base but the cliff face is uninterrupted limestone. At Dúchathair they have two storeys, with
the ledge between them about half-way down the cliff face. Along
the central section of the range there are three storeys, and on the
very highest cliffs, west of Dún Aonghasa, there are four. In places
the lowest storey stands forward of the rest as a broad terrace
edged with a small cliff of its own, and in others it is worn back
into wide-arched caves so that the storeys above appear to rest on
pillars. This geography is hard to make out in the dizzy perspectives from the land's edge that are all one can get where the cliffs
run straight, but certain huge salients and re-entrants of the
higher cliffs allow one less oblique views of it. For instance, walking westwards from An Aill Bhán, it is impossible to see much of
the cliff below, although the first of its recesses, An Poll Gorm, the
blue cave, is big enough for one of the island's small trawlers to
sail into. But after half a mile a turn of the coast reveals the inner
and farther walls of a magnificent bay with deeply incised ledges
running around it, one third and two-thirds of the way down its
sheer cliffs. This is Poll an Iomair, so called no doubt because it is
shaped like three sides of a square *iomar*, a trough or font. In
spring it is the island's most populous breeding ground of sea-
birds; a pair of ravens too usually comes sweeping up over its rim
with defiant cries as one approaches. Multitudinous flotillas of
guillemots and razorbills assemble on the sea at its mouth on
sunny afternoons in April, and fly in clouds up onto its shadowy
precipices with the coming of dusk. Throughout the nesting season birds are packed close all along its ledges, like books on
shelves. Their aboriginal clamour resounding across the two hun-

dred yards of dark water between the echoing walls of stone soon becomes oppressive, and it is sometimes a relief to turn inland, away from such prehuman, unearthly, sights, and sounds. Yet this savage place was like one of the island's fields, cropped every year, and perhaps has been so since the Stone Age. Its ledges, wet with ground-water flowing out of the shale bands, its slimy rock-slabs the waves explode over and the low-roofed caverns they surge into along the foot of its walls, were all ways to a livelihood for the cliffman, who prowled them at night and alone.

This bizarre hunt is of unknown but certainly ancient origin. According to some casuist the old monks must often have blessed, the flesh of certain sea-birds partook of the nature of fish rather than of meat, as is explained in one of the very earliest accounts of the islands, written by Roderic O'Flaherty in 1684:

> Here are birds which never fly save over the sea and therefore are used to be eaten of fasting days, to catch which people go down with ropes tied about them into the caves of cliffs in the night and with a candle light kill abundance of them.

John T. O'Flaherty gives more details of the custom, in the first of the modern accounts of Aran, published in 1824:

> The numerous and lofty cliffs of Aran are well stocked with puffins, which are sought for by the agent, Mr. Thomson, chiefly for the sake of the feathers. He employs cragmen, or clifters, to procure these birds, allowing 6d. for every score they bring. The operations of these cragmen are not less perilous than curious. They provide themselves with a large cable, long enough to reach to the bottom of the cliff; one of them ties an end of this rope about his middle, holding it fast with both hands; the other is held by four or five men, standing one after the other, who are warned by the cragman, when arrived at the haunts of the puffins, to hold fast. Here the cragman gets rid of the rope and falls on the game

with a pole, fastened to which is a snare he easily claps on the bird's neck, all being done at night; such as he kills he ties on a string. His comrades return early the next morning, let down the rope, and haul him up. In this way he kills from fifteen to thirty score per night. Quantities of large eggs are also taken out of these deep cliffs. In the summer of 1816, two unfortunate men, engaged in this frightful occupation of cragman, missed their footing, and were instantly dashed to pieces.

Perhaps puffins were common on the cliffs in those days, and certainly they used to be caught in the way O'Flaherty describes on Tory Island, but it may be that some details of this account are mistaken, as is nearly every mention of plants and animals in his article. In more recent descriptions of the cliffman's trade, and according to the stories I have heard myself, the killing was done with the bare hands. However, the huge numbers of birds that O'Flaherty mentions are certainly correct. In 1929 a former *ailleadóir* or cliffman, Mícheál Ó Maolláin of Baile na Creige, describing his methods, mentioned catching eight score cliff-birds (that is, guillemots) and two rock doves in the cave of An Poll Dubh, handing them out one by one to his companion who wrung their necks, and killing thirty score birds at Gleann an Charnáin (both places are towards the western end of the cliffs). In Aran this Ó Maolláin was called Micilín Sara (Sara's little Michael), from his mother's name. He was so well known on the cliffs that, as I have been told, the raven would fly across and start swooping on him as soon as he started off down the main road from his house with his rope on his shoulder; then Micilín would brandish his otter-spear at the bird and swear to make a widow of it. According to one of the many stories still remembered of him, constables searching for illicit brews of *poitín* once came across the remains of large numbers of cliff-birds around his cottage. It was of course illegal to catch them without the agent's permission, and the fine was five pounds a bird. When all the beaks and legs had been collected up and counted, Micilín Sara was charged with the taking of thirteen score birds. But when the case came to court the judge was persuaded that this was Micilín's first and last offence, and reduced the fine to a penny a bird.

Razorbills, guillemots and black guillemots, puffins and cormorants were the birds usually taken on the cliffs. Both eggs and birds were eaten, the young cormorant and the razorbill being particularly prized—though one could get tired of them, and *blas an seachtú crosáin*, the taste of the seventh razorbill, was a commonplace phrase for a flavour made nauseous by surfeit. The flesh also provided oil for lamps, a horribly smoky oil to which that of the basking shark's liver was preferred when it could be got. The feathers used to be sold in Galway market, and provided the island itself with its filling for pillows and mattresses.

The hunt was conducted as follows. The men would walk across to the cliffs at dusk with the rope, which was often a communal investment. One end of it would be tied around the cliffman's waist and between his legs, and the other made fast to an iron bar driven into a crevice or wedged in a cairn on the clifftop. A team of up to eight would lower the cliffman, guided by signals from a man stationed out on a headland from which he could watch the progress of the descent. The cliffman would carry a stick to keep himself clear of the cliff face while swinging on the rope, and wedges to help him round awkward corners of his climbs. Having reached the chosen ledge the cliffman would remain crouched in it until darkness came. When all the birds had flown in from the sea and settled down to roost he would begin to crawl along, and would silently murder the first bird he came to, putting one arm round it to stop it flapping—for a cormorant with its five-foot wingspan could have knocked him off the cliff—and giving a couple of quick twists to its neck with the other hand before it could raise the alarm. Then he would move on, pushing the dead bird before him until it was up against the next victim, which thus would not feel his hands until it was too late. The dead birds would be strung on a cord by a running loop around the neck. At dawn the cliffman would be hauled up again, bent and rigid with cold and cramp.

Because his was such a dreadful trade—the sea constantly picking at the unsound rock of the ledges, the weather unpredictably changeable in the middle of the night, the village rope a poor thing of frayed and knotted pieces—the cliffman's exploits and narrow escapes provided the community with serial stories which were not the least valuable product of the cliff face. Micilín Sara's little cottage in Baile na Creige was the great talking-shop of the middle of the island, and the young people used to gather there every evening to hear real cliff-hangers, old and new, recollected or reinvented. Some of these stories are still current, and Micilín's words and gestures, which have been fondly reproduced for me time and time again, portray him as a curious, rheumy-eyed, twisted little cat of a man who could make a comedy out of the stuff of nightmares—of getting his head stuck when trying to squeeze under an overhang, so that he could move neither forward nor backwards, or of having to crawl backwards along a ledge too narrow to turn in, pulling a bagful of peregrine falcon fledglings after him. There was a court case over one of these chicks which Micilín Sara had sold to some visitor instead of to the agent who had commissioned him to get them; I have had Micilín's Aran-Irish oaths and witty interjections from the dock rehearsed to me often enough, but they are still as incomprehensible to me as no doubt they were to the judge in the case. Another story records what were nearly his last words, when he was saved from death by a companion called Conneely. Micilín had jumped down on top of a cormorant perched on a ledge that sloped outward and was slippery with droppings, and found himself sliding towards the brink astride the great flapping bird. Thinking he was riding to his death he cried out, "Give my blessing to all the old neighbours who live down on the Creig!"; but Conneely, who was a huge strong fellow, put out a long arm and dragged him back by the hair. His farewell seems oddly formal for such an occasion, but then, as the man who told me the tale explained, "Micilín Sara was like a king among the people of Baile na Creige!"

It seems that early in this century the islanders got permission to catch the seabirds with nets lowered from the clifftops, and the cliffman's skills were no longer needed. The smaller nets were worked from above by three or four men, but to manage the larger ones another team had to be positioned in currachs at the foot of the cliff. An expedition would be made only once or twice in the season, between the arrival of the birds around St. Patrick's Day in March and their departure near the Feast of Our Lady in August. The net would be lowered past each of the ledges in turn, its bottom edge kept well in against the cliff as the tendency of the birds was to fly downwards from the ledges. However, it often happened that the birds merely cowered back into the ledges when they saw the net, and this difficulty was overcome by a local invention, the *dorú drárs,* a pair of white *báinín* drawers on the end of a fishing-line or *dorú,* which would be lowered beside the net and jerked at the right moment so that the drawers flapped against the cliff and flushed the birds from their retreat.

Even the netting was given up perhaps fifty years ago, and the cliff no longer plays much of a part in the islanders' lives. In fact most of them shun that side of the island, and sometimes when a man has to visit his cattle in a field by the cliffs, he will hurry home knowing that his wife will be anxious about him. Over the last eight years I have walked the cliffs hundreds of times, in all weathers and all seasons, and the occasions on which I have met anyone over there are so few that I can remember them all individually—the man fishing with a long line from the cliff west of Dún Aonghasa, another looking out for basking sharks from a sheltered recess above An Pointe Fiáin, a group of Cill Éinne men disconsolately loitering near Dúchathair one holiday weekend when the pubs had run out of beer, and only one or two other such encounters. The last of the *ailleadóirí* were old when the people from whom I learn of them were young, and their way of life, unlike that of the boatmen and farmers of the last century, has no successor today; like the cliff face itself it is turned away from the existent Aran, and seems to look back into a dateless past.

One last anecdote, of Micilín Sara's father from whom he inherited his calling, preserves all the comic, mediaeval eeriness of that life. One dark evening—for it was no good going down the cliff on a bright night—having lowered the cliffman onto his ledge, the lads decided not to go back to the village, because it was near St. John's Eve and the nights were short. So they lit themselves a little fire of cowdung in a field and settled down to wait for the dawn. When they got bored with talk they amused themselves by throwing bits of the flaming dung over the cliff. In the morning they pulled the cliffman up again. "Ah lads," he said, "I had a hard night of it last night, fighting with the Devil! But I drove him off at last, though he was putting out sparks to Kerry!"

A MARINE CATHEDRAL

The western wall of Poll an Iomair is formed by An Bhinn Bhuí, the yellow cliff, a long sheer-sided peninsula of awesome gravity and bulk. The lowest level of the cliff is prolonged below its southern sea-façade into a series of great steps the currach-men call An Altóir, the altar; to me, though, the cormorants that stand there wrapping their black wings about them like shawls seem to be playing the role of beggarwomen around the cathedral's portal rather than of priests before its altar. The field that roofs this rectangular peninsula is fenced on one side by a wall and on three sides by nothing, and it is a fine place from which to marvel at the sublime procession of headlands to the west. However, it is wise to keep clear of the brink, especially in gusty weather; an islander warned me—and I pass on the advice—to beware of "the suckage," for "A sort of hurricane could pick you up and whirl you over, even if you weighed ten tons!" All the same, I remember that on a day when gales made it impossible to see, speak or think near any of the other clifftops, we found a mysteriously becalmed spot on the very tip of this peninsula. It was a day of explosive sunshine, and the waterfalls that usually hang from the shale bands in the cliff faces after wet weather had been reversed by the updraught and were rearing back over the land in dazzling arcs. The gales had lasted for weeks; maddened hills of water were careering around the bays below, and in the distance we could see green surges bursting half-way up the three-hundred-foot cliff under Dún Aonghasa and sending their glittering spray high over the fort itself.

I have visited this place too on a calm summer night by a full moon that laced the sea with mercury all the way across to Clare, and in a wintery dusk when the screaming choughs were blown by like scraps torn out of the night, and a crescent moon and evening star followed the sun down into western cloudbanks. But whatever the play of light and darkness about it the headland itself is always unshakeably majestic; not even Atlantic fog can quite dissolve its materiality. The winter storms are nevertheless battering at its juncture with the land on the western side, where rock-falls have left upside-down staircases in its wall and a deep cove is being rounded out, a process which will someday leave the headland as an isolated stack. A Cill Éinne crew was lost in this cove eighty years ago, through carelessness in a playful sea; they were working too close inshore, and an unexpected swell picked up their currach and smashed it and them against the cliff, a casual sacrifice to the cult of this marine cathedral.

The bay on this western flank of An Bhinn Bhuí used to be very important to the men of Baile na Creige, whose territory this is, in the days when timber was carried as deck cargo and a proportion of it lost overboard in rough weather, and during the World Wars when wrack was plentiful. The semi-circular arc of cliff (called An Cró; the word covers many kinds of round holes and farm enclosures), deeply undercut and floored with shelving rock, is a natural trap for anything drifting in with the prevailing south-westerlies. In the second field west from the headland two short lengths of wall about five feet apart are still to be seen, the supports on which baulks of timber were sawn up, and just beyond the next field-wall there are grooves worn by ropes in the rim of the cliff where men used to be lowered the two hundred feet to sea level. In the sort of weather that brings rich pickings the breakers come thundering up the rock terrace below and the descent had to be carefully timed to land the cliffman between two waves. One old man who used to go down here explained to me that there were two suitable points of descent into An Cró, one of which was more "advantageous" than the other—its advantage was that it landed one on a spot from which it was possible to run quickly up a slope and get out of range of the oncoming wave, whereas from the other landing-point it was a longer run and one was invariably caught and drenched. Going down was pleasanter than coming up, he told me. On the descent one could counteract any tendency to spin as soon as it started, by kicking out with the leg on the side towards which one was turning; however, when being lifted off the shore it was impossible to know which way the rope would twist to begin with, and all one could do was to "close your eyes and clench your teeth to stop the dizziness getting into your head."

SEATS ON THE CLIFFTOP

One field farther to the west the cliff makes a small outward turn, and in the angle is a recess of the clifftop called Uláinín Bhriain, Brian's little ledge, after a man who, it is said, was sitting reading there one day when the breeze lifted a page out of his book and dangled it in mid-air before him, so that he leaned forward to grab it, and fell over the cliff. Perhaps this story has been confused with another concerning Gleann Bhriain, Brian's Glen, close by. Here this doubly doomed fellow one day saw strange horses trespassing on his land. He went up to them, put a halter on a mare and jumped on her back. But these were sea-horses; the halter slipped off and the mare galloped straight to the cliff with Brian clinging to her mane, and plunged beneath the waves. If two conflicting versions of the one fall have been passed down, perhaps it scarcely matters; we all go over the cliff in the end, whether we would ride on horseback or lean towards the literary, and Brian's one death is at least twice remembered.

Binn na nIasc, the cliff of the fish, is the name of the next headland, and on its eastern face is a little recess in the clifftop called An Chathaoir, because it is exactly like an armchair. It is a fine spot in which to sit and watch the wind circulating the fulmars in the bay below, like a juggler with a dozen boomerangs. An accumulation of winkle shells shows that this is also the customary perch of some fisherman, and in fact a number of empty cigarette packets tucked into crevices around tells me that one of the most reclusive of the village lads, whose identity I can guess, regards the seat as his own.

The ground falls sharply from the east to the west flank of this headland, for this is where one of the inland scarps, corresponding to one major division of the limestone, comes to the coast. As usual there are springs associated with the shale band at its foot, and the fresh water that falls over the cliff just west of the headland is said to be responsible for the unusual size of the limpets on the shore below, from which it is called Aill na mBairneach, the cliff of the limpets. To gather them the islanders used to climb down a jumble of blocks, now in a dangerous state of suspended collapse, in the inner angle of the headland, to a ledge called Ulán na Téide, the ledge of the rope, where there were iron pegs fixed on which to tie the seven fathoms of rope needed to reach the bottom. Shore-food such as limpets and the seaweed called *sleabhcán* made the difference between death and survival for the Aran folk and the Connemara refugees who came here during the Famine, and even in the earlier decades of this century some poor families depended on it. Limpets are still occasionally gathered as a delicacy, tough but tasty, though from more accessible shores than this. Even the shells had their uses, for children, as I have been told, used to cook up spoonfuls of sugar in them over the turf fire "when we had no pennies for sweets."

From Binn na nIasc one has a view inland for the first time, as the coast descends from here onwards to the low-lying neck of the island; Dún Aonghasa, on the cliff's edge at the shoulder of the next upland, is seen in profile against the sky, a mile and a half ahead. Three little villages appear, lying apart in this intervening lowland: Gort na gCapall near the southern coast and not far away, Cill Mhuirbhigh far to the north-west near the other coast, and on the horizon directly inland a few of the rooftops of Fearann an Choirce (Oatquarter)—among them that of our own house, which signals to us across grey-green latitudes of crag with the little flag of its darkly vivid cypress, the instant we reach this spot in returning from a walk along the cliffs. We often rest here, on sunny afternoons. At Aill na mBairneach one is about a hundred feet above the sea and on a level with the gannets sailing by just offshore, which seem also to be idling along in enjoyment of the summer skies—bright-skinned beauties in long black gloves, out of a Sargent portrait—until one of them suddenly checks in mid-air, half-folds its elegant slim wings, and plunges vertically, avidly, disappears in a plume of spray, and surfaces a few moments later to lumber into the air with a mackerel in its beak.

Not far along the cliff from Binn na nIasc is an extraordinary detached pillar of rock that appears to be frozen in the act of staggering into the sea bearing a little green field on its head. I have the impression that it has leaned farther out from the cliff during the years we have known it, and the Gort na gCapall people whose bit of land is being alienated in this way tell me that goats used to jump out onto it, and that the village lads used to put a plank across the gap to fetch birds' eggs off it. It is called simply An Aill Bhriste, the broken cliff, and its top is a little square garden of sea-pinks, scurvy grass, samphire and sea beet, beyond the reach now of any goat. It feels odd to see one's own home together with such an impending earth-change in the one landscape. The stack will probably fall in one of those equinoctial storms that shake our house in autumn, but I hope it goes, with a gorgeous wallowing splash, on a day of crazy spring breezes when we happen to be sitting on Binn na nIasc watching the sea attack the keyboard of the cliffs with the rolled chords and flashing cuffs of a Romantic virtuoso.

We visit this shore in other seasons and other moods too. One bitter winter afternoon, the nadir of a Christmas holiday, I was walking along this cliff with my closest friend and our two loves, when something made me stop. I found myself standing in a circle of ragged, blackish mushrooms. The others stopped too and stood looking at me. Not one of them would join me in the sinister circle—perhaps only because at that stage of the walk no two of the four of us were on speaking-terms. I respect ancient forms, even if I do not believe in fairies, so I took care to come out where an outcrop of rock interrupted the circle. That evening I mentioned the incident to an old man from the west of the island. He was impressed: that means that you are an angel, that your prayers will be answered, he told me. This was flattering, but I pricked up my objective folkloristic ear: what was the exact connection between being an angel and having your prayers answered? The old man explained that this was something he had learned in America where he had spent some decades during the Depression. He had been lucky enough to get a job as a boilerman in a convent, and one day a young nun had told him that she was in some trouble and asked him to pray for her. He said that he was not much good at praying but he would have a go—and a few days later the nun came up and thanked him for his prayers, saying that he was an angel, and that her troubles were over. The story did not quite make sense to me, until I pictured this young girl running up to him and crying out "Gee Patrick, you're an angel! Your prayers were answered!" The light-hearted Americanism, deeply pondered for years by a simple soul, brought back across the ocean, was the spore from which the whole magic circle of misinterpretation had grown.

BRACHIOPODS AND BULLETS

Half a mile beyond Binn na nIasc one has to climb down another scarp that runs inland at right-angles to the coast, and the decrease in height evidently brings the clifftops in occasional reach of the waves, as the storm beach starts again at this point. The scarp is a little cliff in itself where it parts from the coast. In its face is exposed a bed of fossil shells, and the material of the storm beach has evidently come from the same stratum as it is full of the same shells. Most of them belonged to sea-creatures called brachiopods, which occurred in such numbers in the Carboniferous era that certain limestones are almost wholly made up of their remains. Brachiopods are superficially rather like such two-shelled molluscs as the mussel and cockle, but in fact they represent an earlier branch of the evolutionary tree and have a more primitive body-structure; for instance molluscs do have heads, although they may not be very apparent in such examples as the mussels, whereas in brachiopods the mouth and principal sense-organs are not so grouped together at one end of the body. Another difference between them and the bivalve molluscs is that the latter have one valve of their shells on either side of the body while brachiopods have one valve below and another above the body. Most of the space inside the shell is taken up by the organ with which they both breath and feed, a pair of feathery spirals covered in minute vibrating hairs, which keeps water flowing in and out of the shell, absorbs oxygen from it, filters out food-particles and passes them to the mouth. Their archaic structure has by no means meant their entire extinction, for although they no longer dominate the seas as they did three hundred million years ago, there are still over two hundred living species, mainly in Pacific coastal regions, and one or two in Irish waters too. However, the type most prevalent in the seas when Aran's rocks were being laid down is long extinct; it was the largest of them all, *Gigantoproductus*, and elsewhere it grew up to fifteen inches across. It looked rather like a scallop except that both its valves were arched, the convexity of the lower one fitting into the concavity of the upper. Its shell was of calcite, and so wherever a cliff face cuts through a bed of them, exposing every conceivable cross-section of shell, its contribution to Aran's substance is an abstract frieze of gleaming white arcs and ovals. In other types of brachiopod the coiled internal organ was supported by a forked ingrowth of shell. One of these, *Davidsonina septosa*, occurred here, and has identified itself for us by a letter Y, the trace of this supporting structure, within the oval outline of its fossils.

Where the sea has smashed down a section of rock face enclosing a shell bed, one can find specimens of all its contents lying among the rubble, as on the storm beach that starts at this point of the coast's decline towards the harbour of Gort na gCapall. Once I picked up what looked like a brooch or pendant of stone, in the form of a flat spiral coil just over an inch across—the fossil shell of a sea snail, *Euomphalos*, identifiable by the cross-section of its tube, which is nearer to a pentagon than to a circle. It was such a covetable object in its compactness and density that I carried it home with a twinge of guilt, as if there were some means of restoring it to its previous owner which I had neglected.

Whenever I pass this place I keep my eyes open for another kind of memento too, for the Gort na gCapall people tell me that they used to pick up spent bullets here. The basic reason why the ground brings forth this ominous crop is clear if one looks at the nature of it. The land below the scarp is barer than any seen so far, and of a hard, smooth limestone that gives rise to wide, unbroken pavements. Gort na gCapall, the rooftops of which are visible a quarter of a mile inland, has nearly all its land on this terrace of the island or on the one below it which is of similarly sterile rock. Thus it has more than its share of the worst land, and what it has of the good was coveted in the last century by a powerful neighbour, O'Flaherty of nearby Cill Mhuirbhigh, the local J.P. and the largest landholder in the islands. So it was that the men of Gort na gCapall were the most militant of Fenians and Land-Leaguers during the "Land War" of the 1880s, and this is where they came to practise firing the guns they had stolen from the barracks in Cill Rónáin. The place was well chosen; the road comes no nearer than the village, and should the police or coastguards have shown themselves on the open crags closer than that, the rebels knew of a way down the cliffs just two fields to the west to a sea-cave called Poll Uí Néadáin, in which they could hide their arms.

The history of this conflict will find its place at the site of its terrible culmination on the great cliffs west of Dún Aonghasa, but at the present point I will turn aside to note a happier reason for the villagers' assembling here. Just inland of the storm beach is a short length of wall against which they used to play handball, on a stretch of ground where absolutely nothing grows, which lacks even the fissures in which at least a goat could find a few mouthfuls of herbage, but is therefore all the more suitable to be the floor of a ball-alley. Passing homeward from the storm beach, absorbed in wondering how to unify my finds more securely than by a belletristic chapter heading, it can happen that I fail to hear the ringing steps and urgent cries of the long-dead players here.

HARBOUR WITHOUT BOATS

Gort na gCapall is the only one of Árainn's fourteen villages, and indeed of the twenty-six villages in the three islands, not to have land reaching to the north coast; Fearann an Choirce, north of it, is the only one not to have an outlet to the south, while all the rest have a strip of territory from sea to sea. Nevertheless, Gort na gCapall is no exception to the rule that the villages stand in the lee of the escarpment out of which the island chain is formed, for here the ridge-line makes a loop to the south that brings it to the Atlantic coast, and although the village is within quarter of a mile of the ocean it is at least partially sheltered by the slight rise of land on its south. Its landing-place, however, in the bay to the south-west of the village, is open to the stormiest quarters, as the immense storm beach that fills the lap of the bay shows. It is a dangerous landfall; no sand or shingle mediates between the ocean swell and the naked angles of the shore. The little concrete slip built in 1956 was never of much use as the engineers, contrary to local advice, sited it by a vertical rock face against which a currach could easily be thrown by a wave.

A century ago, I am told, there used to be about fourteen currachs here. Nowadays the men of Gort na gCapall are either farmers who supplement their income by taking tourists about the island in their pony-traps in summer, or trawlermen working out of Cill Rónáin, and it is over a decade since a currach was launched in this bay. The currachs used to be kept propped upside-down on little piles of stones on the wide expanse of flat rock behind the storm beach called Creig na gCurachaí, the crag of the currachs, and here they were regularly re-coated with tar, which left each currach's resting-place outlined on the smooth rock in black, and this curious after-image of the vanished fleet still persists.

The bay is called Port Bhéal an Dúin, literally the port of the fort's mouth; the fort is Dún Aonghasa, three-quarters of a mile to the west, and the word *béal* is often used for an opening or bay of the sea. The storm beach wrapped around the bay completely hides it from view as one approaches it along the path from the village, and to reach the landing-place one has to clamber over great battlements of wedged and tilted blocks onto the sea-washed terraces without. Every feature of the bay has its name, though many of them are almost forgotten, now that a detailed knowledge of its accesses and obstacles is no longer a matter of survival to the boatmen. It is divided into two halves by a promontory called An Charraigín Gharbh, the little rough rock; the western half, too full of rocks to bring a currach into, is for some reason called Poll an Mhaide Lofa, the bay of the rotten stick, and the slip is in the eastern half, Béal an Phoirt, the mouth of the port. In its approaches is a rock over which rises An Mhaidhm Bheag, the little breaker, which according to a Gort na gCapall man who wrote me an account of bringing in a currach there, dominates the passage "like a Hydra." If the sea was at all rough it took a four-man crew to bring in the currach sufficiently quickly, during the brief lull of three or four smaller waves that would follow immediately after three big breakers had been counted on An Mhaidhm Bheag.

On the east of the bay a wide rock-terrace almost as rectangular as a pier slants gently down into the sea; this is Na Leacracha Sleamhna, the slippery flags, and a sunken rock off it is An Bád Fada, the long boat. The shape of this terrace is due to the parallelism of the joints of the limestone; its western edge has been formed along a major joint, and it is divided from the next terrace to the east by another joint that has been enlarged into a deep channel, An Scailp Mór, the big cleft, which was once well known for the valuable spars and other wrack left in it by the falling tide.

The terrace beyond the cleft continues under the cliffs for a few hundred yards back as far as Poll Uí Néadáin (Ó Néadáin's cave, if my informant's interpretation of the sound of the name is correct). This terrace has a domestic name, Leic an Níocháin, the flagstone of the washing, for it has the "mamillated surface" already seen on corresponding terraces farther east, and its beautifully rounded rock-pools were used by the village women for washing clothes in. A similar shore-name is associated with several other villages in the three islands. Synge, in his book on Aran, notes that this practice of washing clothes in sea water was the cause of much rheumatism as the salt left in the material made the clothes perpetually damp. However, there are no flows of fresh water big enough for such washing and it would have been a heavy labour to collect enough bucketsful from the little springs, especially in dry weather. Nowadays of course the housewives of Gort na gCapall have hot and cold water on tap, and Leic an Níocháin is visited only by a few discerning summer sunbathers, for the pleasure of its polished knolls of warm stone and exquisite green aquaria in which tiny translucent creatures hover and dart. It is a secluded and delectable spot—over which an entire cliff face has recently leaned forward, tearing open a crevasse a yard wide and thirty yards long in the land above, and threatens soon to add its ruins to the scattering of thousand-ton dice previous cliff-falls have flung down upon the inviting resort, as if to say, these severities are of the soul of Aran, and the odds against it tolerating languorous ease for long are heavy.

THE WORM AND THE ROOT

If as an artist I wanted to find a sculptural form for my intuition of the Aran landscape, I would not think in terms of circles. Aran's circles of stone, the great inland cashels and lesser ring-forts, the ancient hunchback huts, Long's evanescent inscriptions, can be read as fearful withdrawals from these bare spaces or as egocentric stances within them, habits of thought born elsewhere and merely sojourning here, not deeply rooted in the specificity of Aran. In other landscapes the rounded might be equated with the natural and the right angle with the human contribution. Here, though, it is as if the ground itself brings forth right angles. Because of the limestone's natural partings along its vertical fissures and horizontal stratifications, the oblong and the cuboid are the first-fruits of the rock. These are the forms that coerce one's footsteps in this terrain, and hence have directed the evolution of the chief human stratum of the landscape, the mosaic of fields and the paths that side-step between them. These too are the forms that come to hand in picking up a loose stone to build a wall—and so the field-patterns rhyme with the patterns of the stones in their walls. On the largest scale the rectilinear skylines and stepped flanks of Aran remember their origins in the nature of the rock.

A block, then, would best embody the essence of Aran's landforms—or, since I am dealing in abstractions and have undergone the metamorphoses of contemporary art, the absence of a block, a rectangular void to stand for all blocks. And since the sea is the most decisive sculptor among the various erosive agents that disengage Aran's form from its substance, let this void be filled by water, reversing the relationship of sea and island. Site it on one of the great stages of rock below the cliffs; do it on a prodigious scale, a spectacle rather than a gallery-piece; let the ocean dance in it, and the cliffs above step back in wide balconies to accommodate the thousands who will come to marvel at this kinetic-conceptualist, megalominimalist, unrepeatable and ever-repeated, sublime and absurd show of the Atlantic's extraction of Aran's square root!

What I have imagined, exists. An exactly rectangular block over a hundred feet long has somehow been excerpted from the floor of a bay in the cliffs, a few hundred yards west of Port Bhéal an Dúin, and the sea fills the void from below. This is Poll na bPéist, the hole of the worms, or The Worm-Hole as it is called for English-speaking visitors; the word *péist*, like the English "worm" in its older acceptances, covers everything from sea-monsters to the grubs that pullulate in rotten seaweed, and nobody knows what sort of creeping thing was originally in question here. It is impossible to see how deep the hole is, and I do not know if the missing block lies in fragments in a sea-cave below or whether it was blasted upwards by the surges and washed off the terrace. On a calm day and at low tide one can reach the spot by following the lowest level of the shore under cliffs that rise westwards from Port Bhéal an Dúin. The rock underfoot here is inhabited by countless purple sea-urchins, each of which has excavated a hole an inch or two deep for itself, and the population is so dense that the rock-surface is reduced to a layer of fantastically fretted, brittle spikes. The gap between the line of surf and the foot of the cliff narrows as one goes westwards; sometimes a seal raises its head from the waves close by to watch as one negotiates the shrinking passage. Then the cliff turns at right angles inland, and on following it one finds oneself on the stage of a natural theatre, with the oblong abyss at one's feet. On such days the water in it is usually still and dark, sunken into itself, leaving the sheer sides too deep to climb. It measures about thirty-six by thirteen slippery paces, and looks like a grim and sinister swimming-pool, the work of some morose civil engineer. However, despite its dank walls and impenetrable depths, the idea of swimming in it is not quite out of the question. Members of a sub-aqua club from Belfast have explored it, and swum out to the open sea through the cave below. And once I met an amiable fantasist here who told me how he had swum in it by moonlight with a beautiful girl forty years ago; it was, he said, one of those holiday affairs: he never even asked her name, and they never met again ....

If, while one has been peering into the dark waters or exchanging amorous reminiscences with strangers, the tide has crept in and cut off retreat at the outer angle of the bay, one's best chance is to scramble up the rock-wall, deeply canopied in places and perfectly sheer in others, that shadows the broad pavements around the pool; a climb of sixteen or twenty feet brings one onto a wide terrace, above which another forty feet of rock completes the height of the cliff. This intermediate level is immediately recognizable from its amœboid rock-pools as the "mamillated surface," and here it is very evident that it once underlay a clay band, for erosion of the softer material has opened up a horizontal slot all along the base of the cliff above it, four to eight feet high and in places up to forty feet in depth; one can walk into this dripping cellarage, with its wavy floor and low, fossil-studded flat ceiling, and see that its rear wall is of clay, all glistening in the dark with seeping ground-water.

At high tide or in stormy weather these terraces are out of the question, and to see Poll na bPéist one has to struggle along the spray-blown clifftops and hold onto stones of the boulder beach up there to avoid being hurled over by the violent gusts. On such days the gladiatorial display in the arena below features primaeval chaos pitted against fundamental geometry. Each breaker floods the lower terrace and pours in torrents of froth down the sides of the shaft to meet the turbulence bursting up into it from below; the water's surface comes roaring up between the polished walls, alive with the snaking trains of bubbles that perhaps suggested the name of the place, swills its excess over the brink into the fleeing wreckage of the wave now retreating from the terrace, then sags and falls back with dizzying speed into the spray-clouded depths of the vault. Throughout the tumult the rock itself conducts a rigorous demonstration of its own theorem, like a deaf mathematics lecturer oblivious of his rowdy students; through the pelting spitballs of foam one can see that, for instance, the eastern wall of the hole lies in exactly the same plane as the east-facing wall of the upper terrace just to seaward of it, both having been determined by the same joint, which is visible as a finely drawn line crossing the rock-floor between them.

One of the most curious features of this, Aran's most striking natural curiosity, is that there is no legend attached to it. The writer Tom O'Flaherty pointed this out fifty years ago, and if there had been any traditional tale about the place he would certainly have known it, as a native of Gort na gCapall. He adds that it is time someone invented a story, but I am not sure that I agree. These encircling, overhanging terraces cruelly intent upon the entrance to the tomb or dungeon below suggest frightful rites; Ariosto has an episode of a maiden sacrificed to a sea-monster on the coast of Ireland, and one could toy with the idea that it happened here. But since it seems that even the most voluble of folk traditions has been left speechless by the place, perhaps it is fitting that this void, this abstract exemplification of Aran's elements, should remain an emptiness without an explanation.

DÚN AONGHASA: THE DIRECT APPROACH

On fine Saturdays and Sundays in summer a line of slow-moving coloured dots slants across the hillside west of Cill Mhuirbhigh—tourists climbing the path from the village to the famous prehistoric fort of Dún Aonghasa. For many of them this is the culmination of their visit to Aran. The intentions of thousands of their predecessors have prepared a way for them that channels their own intentions, in a self-perpetuating process. The jarveys who wait with their pony-traps at the quay in Cill Rónáin for the steamer from Galway assume that every day-tripper will wish to visit the Dún, and indeed tend to override any hesitations on the matter. Amenities well sited on the road from Cill Rónáin to Cill Mhuirbhigh prosper, while those elsewhere fade. Many visitors find the path up to the Dún too steep and rough for enjoyment, but every spring a little more work is done on it, and improved stiles, whitewashed arrows and fingerposts make it ever less likely that anyone will stray from the groove. The ancient and remote fort is a cog of a world-wide machine, hauling up a chain of expectations almost as predictably as a ski-lift.

The "development" of this touristic resource has not been pressed very far as yet, but the convenient and profitable process within the constraints of which most visitors approach the Dún must already be a diminisher of potential experience. Often the steamer's time-table permits only a cursory scramble about the ponderous walls, while the bare space they enclose, as the nominal object of the day's journeying, must be unfulfilling. The hasty frontal assault wins as little from the place, although it now lies open and undefended, as it would have done two thousand years ago when the walls were manned and the gateway closed with a thick wooden door. Like a great personage long inured to the public eye, the old fort guards its privacy by a bland vacancy of expression; it gives one the impression not only that one has seen nothing but that there is nothing to be seen.

Of course there are ways of penetrating time's defences which a daytrip precludes. One can take a hint from the distant glimpse of the fort's lofty profile against the clouds, and recall all the dreams that have been dreamed about it, or one can tread its ground step by step laden with the doubts and disagreements of the archaeologists. This book commits me to both these approaches, and to the attempt to fuse them into some more adequate awareness of what it is like to be in Dún Aonghasa—but still I often look around the place, baffled and a little despondent, and feel that the citadel might after all fall more readily before the casual glance of a tourist.

DÚN AONGHASA: A LEGENDARY PERSPECTIVE

There is one view of the Dún that sometimes, for me, sets it in the most rarely accessible regions of romance, and that is from a point below the cliffs which may be reached by following the terrace that forms a balcony above Poll na bPéist westwards to the corner of the next bay. This is An Sunda Caoch or Blind Sound, which curves so deeply into the low-lying waist of Árainn that from a distance out to sea it appears to be a sound leading between two islands; it is said that a sailing vessel that made this mistake found itself caught on a lee shore and was wrecked in the bay. Here it is that the sea will some day break through and divide the island—the belief recurs in Aran folklore and, I have been told, in Aran people's dreams. In fact in 1640, according to Roderic O'Flaherty, "Upon an extraordinary inundation, the sea, overpowering that bank, went across that island to the north-west," which must mean to the bay of Port Mhuirbhigh only half a mile away on the north coast. But the cliffs around Blind Sound still stand ninety feet high at their lowest, and whether or not there is any truth in that old record, the Aran prophecy of the division of the island will only be justified in a geological timescale that will long have made all our lore and our nightmares irrelevant.

The terrace leading on from Poll na bPéist dwindles into a ledge where it turns with the cliff into Blind Sound, and it is from this corner that one suddenly sees the Dún exalted, on the crest of the headland opposite. For the cliffs treble in height as they encircle the farther arc of the bay, and the dramatic change of scale projects one's gaze into legendary perspectives. If the setting sun is riding into the bay on the backs of the waves, illuminating the vastness of the opposing precipice in golden detail, while the solemn recession of promontories beyond goes back step by step into rose-petal impalpability on the western horizon, then the setting is definitive: Dún Aonghasa, heavy with centuries, dreams upon a pinnacle of another world.

This other world can only be that of Celtic myth, a wide western province of the human mind. Here, at the grandest level of interpretation, the primal elements such as light and darkness, the air, the depths of the earth and sea, establish their dominions and hierarchies through battles and matings, as gods and goddesses. In another reading, some of these warriors and lovers turn out to be our great-grandparents, while others, much diminished, still lurk in the corners of our fields and minds as the fairy host, the *púca*, the leprechaun, the banshee and other reminders of the precarious nature of the equilibrium achieved by those cosmogonic politics. Aonghas, the legendary leader of the Fir Bolg and founder of the Dún, figures in various written mediaeval reconstructions of this much more ancient body of traditions, and principally in *Lebor Gabála Érenn*, "The Book of the Taking (i.e. conquest) of Ireland." This tangled tale of the early invasions of Ireland was put together by degrees from the eighth to the fifteenth century by monastic scribes, who had learned to look at the old Gaelic lore, their birthright, with the eyes of Christendom. In order to make head or tail of even Aonghas's limited role in this pseudo-history one has to realize the potency and complexity of the material its compilers had to work on, and the ideological urges behind their highly creative treatment of it.

The pantheon of prehistoric Celtic religion had included many deities representing natural forces, some of whom would have been worshipped under a variety of names in different parts of Europe; many Celtic tribes were named from deities probably regarded as ancestors, and over a period of centuries the tribes had been stirred by mass migrations under the pressure of Teutonic peoples and the Romans. Thus the traditions of the Celtic inhabitants of Ireland in the early years of this era would have been full of battles and invasions led by beings of unearthly power, and were incorporated in a vast, many-layered mythology in which dim memories of real events merged with symbolic accounts of the origins of the natural and social orders, a rambling, repetitious, contradictory palace of echoes in which every question about the present could be answered by the past. The Irish-speaking and Church-trained scribes brought powerful but alien tools of thought to bear on this oral lore, both unifying and distorting it: the art of writing, a sense of chronological history, a revelation of one God who superseded all others. Exposed to the light of Christianity the nature-deities had dwindled into heroes, witches and ogres, and now dates had to be ascribed to their existences. The resultant scheme of history had to be convincingly rooted in the Bible story, and to branch out into the genealogies by which the dominant families, under whom the scribes worked, justified their status. *Lebor Gabála* is a summation of this giant task of simultaneous elucidation and mystification.

The principal families of the Early Historical period, and especially the Uí Néill dynasty of Tara, claimed to belong to a stock called the Goidel, and the main business of *Lebor Gabála* is to trace the descent of this people from the Creation to their arrival in Ireland, and thence down to the compiler's own era. However, Ireland was not empty when the Goidel came, and so the narrative breaks off at that point and goes back to the time of Noah, in order to follow out the histories of various peoples, including the Fir Bolg, said to have invaded Ireland before its definitive "taking" by the Goidel. Each of these waves of precursors had already been extinguished or expelled, with insignificant exceptions, apart from the last of them, the Tuatha Dé Danann, and these were eliminated by the Goidel. The book can then proceed with its demonstration that everyone who matters in Ireland is a Goidel.

As the Bible tell us, Noah had three sons, Shem, Ham and Japhet. Ham, accursed because he saw his father drunk and naked, sired the Canaanites and other benighted races. Shem's descendants included Abraham, and the Bible follows their story, while *Lebor Gabála* follows the offspring of Japhet, which include not only the Goidel but all the other inhabitants of Ireland since the Flood. Altogether the three sons fathered seventy-two peoples, who shared one language until they tried to build their way up to Heaven by the Tower of Babel and God frustrated their purposes by giving them seventy-two different languages. One of Japhet's great-grandsons extracted a language from the confusion to pass on to his own grandson, Goidil, from whom both language (Goidelic, Gaelic) and race (Goidel, Gael) are named.

The story of the Goidel continues in a form closely modelled on that of the Israelites: both peoples are invited into Egypt but are oppressed there, both are delivered by their respective leaders (who in one version actually meet). The subsequent wanderings of the Goidel are more wide-ranging than those of the Israelites under Moses, however. They are expelled from Scythia after their leader Mil (from whom they are often called the Milesians) kills the king there; they withstand the lure of the Sirens, like Odysseus, by filling their ears with wax; they fight with the Amazons. Eventually they reach "three-cornered Spain" and take it by force, and build a city there with a tower to protect it, and "from that tower was Ireland seen on a winter's evening."

Whereas the story so far is evidently a Christian and classicizing concoction, the next few sections treating of the earlier inhabitants of Ireland come from sources much closer to Celtic myths of the origins of things. The first person ever to land in Ireland was a woman, Cessair, with a band of fifty women and three men; she had been warned by Noah about the Flood and had sailed here to avoid it. On landing the women were divided between the three men, one of whom, Fintan, flees before his responsibilities. This breaks Cessair's heart and she dies, and then all the rest are drowned by the Flood except for Fintan, who hides in a cave and survives to write the poem that tells us of this history. It seems that this legend was a flood-myth in its own right—the name of Cessair's father is Bith which means "life" or "world," and Fintan is the son of Bochna, "ocean." But it has been disrespectfully chopped about to fit in with the Noah story.

The second invasion was that of Partholon, a descendant of Japhet. His people clear some of the plains of Ireland, and certain lakes burst forth in their time. They fight the Fomorians, a race of one-legged, one-armed, one-eyed demons led by Cichol Clapperleg. This was the first battle to be fought in Ireland, it lasted a week and "not a man was slain there because it was a magic battle." However, Partholon was wounded and died not long afterwards of the venom of the wound. Perhaps some ancient ritual underlies this story, representing the daily or annual warfare between pro-human and anti-human forces: the sun or the summer growth of vegetation and plenty, against darkness, winter and want. Eventually all nine thousand of his people die of the plague, again over the space of a week, and this clears the stage for the third invasion, that of Nemed.

Nemed, another descendant of Japhet, came from "the Greeks of Scythia" with his four sons. He fights repeated battles against the Fomorians, and like Partholon he clears various plains in Ireland, further lakes burst forth, and he dies of the plague. His progeny have to pay exorbitant taxes to the Fomorians in wheat and milk, and eventually attack the Fomorian stronghold, a tower in the sea. The tide comes in during the battle and drowns all the remaining Nemedians except for one shipload of thirty warriors. One of these, Britan, fathers the British nation. Another goes to Greece and his progeny returned after two hundred years of servitude there; they are, at last, the Fir Bolg. The descendants of a third Nemedian go to "the northern islands of the world" to learn druidry and heathenism and devilish knowledge, and come back to Ireland two hundred and fifty years later as the Tuatha Dé Danann. They expel the Fir Bolg, but are themselves defeated by the Goidel. Long afterwards the Fir Bolg return, and their adventures bring them to Aran; but in the long run they are of no consequence and the history of the Goidel continues unperturbed by them, to the times in which that history was written down. Nevertheless, these incursions of a people marginal to the historical scheme are the most interesting part of *Lebor Gabála* especially when read, as it were, in the shadow of Dún Aonghasa, and so I will follow the fortunes of the Fir Bolg in more detail.

Lebor Gabála offers various explanations of how that branch of the Nemedians who underwent servitude in Greece came to be called Fir Bolg, which seems at first sight to mean "men of bags." Either they took bags of clay with them from Ireland because the King of Greece gave them a noisesome territory full of noxious reptiles, and the soil of Ireland is lethal to such pests; or the Greeks made them carry up bags of earth to spread on rocky flags and make flowery plains; or they eventually made long currachs out of their bags in which to sail back to Ireland. More recent explanations of the name are perhaps less naïve but even more various, as we shall see.

The return of the Fir Bolg from Greece was the fourth "taking" of Ireland, which they ruled for thirty-seven years under nine successive kings. The last of these was Eochu:

> There was no wetting in his time, save only dew: there was no year without harvest. Falsehoods were expelled from Ireland in his time. By him was executed the law of justice in Ireland for the first time.

This Golden Age was ended by the coming of the Tuatha Dé Danann, the branch of Nemed's progeny that had studied wizardry in the north of the world. *Lebor Gabála* argues with itself as to whether they were men or demons:

> Though some say that the Tuatha Dé Danann were demons, seeing that they came unperceived . . . and for the obscurity of their knowledge and adventures, and for the uncertainty of their genealogy as carried backwards: but that is not true, for their genealogies carried backward are sound. Howbeit they learnt knowledge and poetry: for every obscurity of art and every clearness of reading, and every subtlety of crafts, for that reason, derive their origin from the Tuatha Dé

Danann. And though the faith came, those arts were not put away, for they are good, and no demon ever did good. It is clear therefore from their dignities and their deaths that the Tuatha Dé Danann were not of the demons nor were they *sídh*-folk [i.e. fairy folk].

Nevertheless the anti-pagan scribes cannot quite suppress the wondrousness of this troupe, and their deeds as recounted in *Lebor Gabála* and in many other legends make it certain that they were deities of the Celtic religion. Their name means "the people of the goddess Donu"; their leader on arrival was Nuada, probably to be identified with a god Nodens who was worshipped at the Romano-British temple of Lydney in Gloucestershire; another of their number was Ogma, probably the Gaulish god Ogmios; the most famous of them was Lug, the Welsh Llew, whose nature as a sky-god shines through all his deeds and who has left his name on various towns such as Lyons, Laon and Leiden which grew from centres of his worship. Lug's successor was the Dagda Mór, the Great Good God, and his daughter was Brigid, a fire-goddess from whom the tribe of Brigantes took their name, and whom tradition has converted into a Christian saint of particularly luminous legend.

The comparatively humdrum Fir Bolg were no match for this dazzling throng, who travelled through the air in dark clouds to Ireland, darkened the sun for three days and nights, and demanded "battle or the kingship." In the ensuing battle of Mag Tuired, the plain of towers, a hundred thousand of the Fir Bolg were slain. There was a second battle of Mag Tuired twenty-seven years later in which the Tuatha Dé Danann defeated the Fomorians, and a rather vague passage of *Lebor Gabála* suggests that the Fir Bolg led the Fomorians on this occasion. The battle site was anciently identified as Moytirra in Sligo, but a later tradition transferred the site of the first battle to near Cong in Mayo; there are impressive groups of cairns and stone circles on both sites which have been fancifully explained in terms of these battles.

Whether or not the Fir Bolg were concerned in both battles, the result was that the remnants of them took refuge overseas in islands that have been identified as Rathlin, the Scottish Arran and Islay, and elsewhere among the Picts. By the time of their return from this second exile the situation had changed again, the Tuatha Dé Danann had been defeated by the Goidel, and there was a king, Cairbre, ruling at Tara in Meath. The Fir Bolg, led now by Aonghas son of Umor, petitioned him for territories around Tara that included many important sanctuaries, and in return Cairbre demanded their service in the building of his great fort, each side accepting four sureties or guarantors for the compliance of the other. But Cairbre soon imposed intolerable taxes on the Fir Bolg, who left his territory for that of Queen Medb and her consort Ailill in Connacht:

> They struck westward, along the bright sea,
> To Dún Aonghasa in Ára,

and the verse version of *Lebor Gabála* (a mnemonic doggerel which was perhaps the form in which it had been orally transmitted) goes on to specify where the various leaders of the Fir Bolg established themselves, principally on the south and east of Galway Bay. For instance Irgus took "Cend Boirne," which is Black Head at the mouth of the bay, Bera took a point of land probably to be identified with Finavarra near Ballyvaughan, Taman took Tawin Island at the head of the bay, and Aonghas's son Conall settled in the territory of Aidne on the south of the bay. In the Aran Isles, apart from Aonghas at his Dún, there was Concraide in Inis Meáin, where the fort, Dún Chonchúir, is attributed to him, while Mil (not to be confused with the Goidel of that name) took a place called Murbech or Murbheoch, which is rather tentatively identified with Cill Mhuirbhigh by some commentators. However:

> From the day that Cairbre heard of it,
> his temper mounted high;

> he sent forth a summons, wherever they should be
> to his four sureties...
> Bring to me, said just Cairbre,
> the nomad multitudes of the Sons of Umor:
> or let each man of you bring his head
> as I pledged you for a season.

Now Cairbre's sureties included no less a hero than Cú Chulainn, and Aonghas took council with his friends before deciding to send his three brothers and his own son Conall in single combat against the four champions. Conall fell before Cú Chulainn himself, and is buried (with his father) under Carn Chonaill in his territory of Aidne; the other three were vanquished too, and lie under "The Hillock of the Heads," somewhere in Mayo near Clew Bay. The prose version of *Lebor Gabála* concludes this episode with a brief note on the uncreative nature of the reign of the Fir Bolg, and the unimportant communities they bequeathed to history:

> No forts or entrenchments are reckoned as having been dug, nor lakes to have burst forth, nor plains to have been cleared, in the reign of the Fir Bolg. Of their seed are the three communities who are in Ireland not of Goidelic stock: to wit the Gabraide of the Suc in Connachta, the Uí Thairsig, and the Cailleoin in Laigen. Those are the adventures of the Fir Bolg.

POSTHUMOUS CAREER OF THE FIR BOLG

For centuries this extraordinary group of texts has been read in search of light on questions ranging from the age of Dún Aonghasa and the racial constitution of the Aran Islanders, to the origins of the Irish, the prehistory of the Celts in general, the nature of their religion, and the mythic dimensions of the human psyche. In the last century attention focused on questions nearer the beginnings of this spectrum: the apparently historical content of the *Lebor Gabála* was paramount, the knots and contradictions in its detailed genealogies and chronologies were to be resolved by careful scholarship, while the legendary stuff was patronized as the childish fantasies of mediaeval fabulists. More recently it has been the latter end of the spectrum that caught the eye; the half-suppressed otherworldly content of the book is seen as more important and in a sense truer than the fictitious lists of ancestors, in which it is the repetitions and inconsistencies that may be decoded for evidence of the structures of the underlying myths. When I tried to pursue the old-fashioned question of the age of Dún Aonghasa through the successive readings that have been made of *Lebor Gabála*, I found myself on a wild paper-chase through not only the mythic dimensions of the human mind but some of its lesser dimensions too. Here are some of the landmarks I noticed; any one of them could conceal some subjective tunnel into the Dún, but objectively they lead nowhere.

The earliest description of Dún Aonghasa is that of Roderic O'Flaherty in his *West or H-Iar Connaught*, written in 1682:

On the south side (of the island) stands Dun-Engus, a large fortified place, on the brim of a high clifft, a hundred fathoms deep; being a great wall of bare stones without any mortar, in compass as big as a large castle bawn, with severall long stones on the outside, erected sloapewise about it against assaults. It is named of Engus McHuathmore, of the reliques of the Belgmen in Ireland, there living about the birth-time of Christ.

O'Flaherty assumed the identity of the Fir Bolg with the Belgae, a confederation of Celtic tribes whose continental history is fairly well known as they were Julius Caesar's fiercest opponents and he recorded much about them in his *Gallic Wars*. They inhabited the north-east of Gaul (and gave their name to the country of Belgium), but claimed to have originated farther east, beyond the Rhine. Shortly before Caesar's time they had made settlements in the south-east of Britain; the famous Caractacus was a Belgic chieftain who was dispossessed by the Romans and led resistance to them from the fastnesses of Wales. It seems possible that Belgic tribes contributed to immigration into Ireland under Roman pressure, but nothing is recorded on the question.

O'Flaherty's identification of the Belgae with the legendary Fir Bolg was generally accepted by the great nineteenth-century Irish Celticists, for whom Dún Aonghasa was "the last standingplace of the Firbolg aborigines of Ireland, ready to fight their last battle, or take a fearful and eternal departure from the rocks they had contested foot by foot." The words are those of William Wilde, spoken within the Dún itself to the scholars of Ireland assembled in banquetry, and to the islanders looking on from its terraced ramparts. The occasion is worth reliving here, for on that day in 1857 the ancient fort must have brimmed with the fervours of the age. In that year the British Association held its meeting in Dublin, and Dr. Wilde, as Secretary of Foreign Correspondence to the Royal Irish Academy, had proposed, organized and conducted an excursion of the Association's Ethnological Section to the Aran Islands. A steam yacht chartered in Galway had carried seventy eminent excursionists to Cill Éinne, and from there, by way of various Christian and Pagan sites, the party had tramped the rocks to Dún Aonghasa. In the words of the official reporters of the proceedings, Martin Haverty:

> This was our culminating point of interest—the chief end and object of our pilgrimage....This was the Acropolis of Aran—the Palace-fortress of the days of Queen Maeve,— the venerable ruin which Dr. Petrie...described as "the most magnificent barbaric monument now extant in Europe." We can here only describe its dimensions, its remote antiquity, its site on the beetling brow of the precipice, its walls,

now reduced to little more than crumbling piles of loose stone; but the indescribable feelings of sadness, of awe, and enthusiasm, which the place inspired, cannot be conveyed to the reader by any words of ours.

Haverty goes on to tell of the unpacking of the hampers, the enjoyment of an abundant dinner washed down with some excellent sherry, the warmth of the sun, the gentle murmurs of the Atlantic far below, the ocean breeze that fanned the august assembly. Then the Reverend Dr. MacDonnell, Provost of Trinity College, Dublin, was voted into the chair (a table-like rock near the cliff edge), and the speeches began. Dr. George Petrie proposed the toast to old Mr. O'Flaherty of Cill Mhuirbhigh who had been his host thirty-five years earlier when Petrie was engaged in the first serious study of Aran's monuments, then largely unknown to the outside world. Next Dr. Wilde recapitulated the progress of the present excursion and paid tribute to various members of the party: Dr. Petrie, "the pioneer of philosophic antiquarian research in Ireland"; Dr. O'Donovan, whose letters written in the course of his work for the Ordnance Survey of 1839 were the source of Wilde's own opinions on Dún Aonghasa and remained for half a century to come the best accounts of Ireland's ancient monuments; his colleague in the Ordnance Survey, Eugene O'Curry, "the chief brehon and lexicographer of Ireland—the true, the genuine Irishman, to whom the people, the history and the language of his country are the breath of life"; Samuel Ferguson, "who, to his valuable contributions to the science of the antiquary, has so happily blended the popular fascination of the poet," and Frederick William Burton, "whose pencil has so accurately portrayed the living generation of the island."

Then Wilde, after sounding the Firbolgic trumpet-note with which I introduced him, concluded by appealing to the islanders to refrain from pulling the Dún apart "for the paltry advantage of catching a few rabbits"—for it seems that it had suffered dreadful delapidations in the years since Petrie's first visit (a period which included the Great Hunger, when catching a rabbit was by no means a paltry advantage). Wilde's peroration insists on the ethnic continuity of Aran:

> Remember, above all, that these were the works of your own kindred, long, long dead....You have a right to be proud of them; they are grand monuments of the brave men your forefathers were, and of how they laboured and how they fought to defend the land they left to you and your children. Do you defend them in peace as they defended them in war, and let your children's children see strangers coming to honour them, as we have done today.

After nearly a score of other speeches including one from the French consul, in French, inviting the party to visit his own land, and one from Professor O'Curry in Irish, reiterating the anti-rabbiting plea, a committee was voted into existence to report on the state of Ireland's monuments to the British Association. Finally, reports Haverty, "a musician, with bagpipes, played some merry tunes, and the banquet of Dún Aengus terminated with an Irish jig, in which the French Consul joined *con amore.*"

So, for a few summer hours in 1857, the mind of Ireland assembled and disported itself in this great stone skull lying abandoned on the clifftops of Aran. But the glowing certainties it was celebrating—that the old invasion-myths were basically true, that the Fir Bolg were Celts and the Araners their descendants, that the rest of Ireland was similarly or even more loftily descended from heroes whose names and deeds are preserved to us—were to fade with the waning of the century and the rise of a more sceptical scholarship. In 1902 the Clare archaeologist T. J. Westropp, who had devoted much of his life to an extraordinarily fresh-eyed examination of many hundreds of the ancient forts (or "cahers" as he calls them, from the Irish word *cathair*), and whose outlook was not limited to Ireland, wrote:

The Firbolgic origin of the cahers has been impressed upon Irish archaeology by the great names of Petrie and O'Donovan, supported by Lord Dunraven and Miss Stokes, popularised by many writers and accepted by a large body of antiquaries without any thought of the vast impossibility involved in the legend and its hopelessly weak foundation. Even if the legend of the sons of Huamore be not a sun myth as Professor Rhys suggests, even if it rested on some earlier and better authority than (it should appear) a poem of the tenth century, still, the story in that poem is alone enough to undermine the popular belief; and it is surprising that any of the above antiquaries should have been carried away by so wild a theory. We are called upon to believe that several hundred, if not a couple of thousand of stone forts were built by a handful of fugitives who were able to live in nine raths in Meath, and were exterminated or scattered in a year or two after settling in Galway, Mayo and Clare. The prose version only names Dún Aonghus; the poem in addition tells how Ennach built a fort in Clare in the neighbourhood of Dael; and one manuscript adds "thus they dwelt in fortresses." On this tiny base rests the vast inverted pyramid of theory which attributes the cahers of Kerry and Cork to a tribe never even stated to have settled in those counties, and the innumerable cahers of Clare, Galway, Mayo, Sligo and other districts, to this short-lived little band. After this utter impossibility, the question of the historic value of the legend sinks into unimportance.

Here Westropp himself seems to be taking *Lebor Gabála* needlessly literally, if only to dismiss its testimony. However, the Fir Bolg still held their interest for students of the Irish past, and as the antiquaries of the old regime gave way to the specialized archaeologists and philologists of the new, the old tales were subjected to more ruthless and varied interpretations than ever before. The mutually contradictory views held either successively or even simultaneously by the Celticist John Rhys about the turn of the century, for example, defy summary. As a minor consequence of these far-reaching controversies the presumed date of Dún Aonghasa shot back and forth like a shuttle through the centuries. The tone of the debate was immoderate in proportion to its abstruseness, each protagonist dismissing his opponent's case unargued and with heavy sarcasms, which leave the reader unedified. R. A. S. Macalister, the editor and translator of *Lebor Gabála*, has this to say in his introduction (of 1941) to the section dealing with the long-suffering Fir Bolg:

> We may discard all "Belgic" and similar theories without discussion. We need not waste time over the "bags of earth" about which our historians tell us. Kuno Meyer's explanation is by far the most reasonable, that *Fir Bolg = Fir i mBolgaib = bracati* or breeches-wearers. Thus interpreted it becomes a term of contempt for the "lower orders," applied, by those who wore the dignified flowing costumes which the sculpture of the "High Crosses" depicts for us, to those who found it more convenient, in the life of activity in which their lot was cast, to have each leg separately clothed. This however is only a secondary application of the story. It is really no history, but a member of the same mythological complex as the rest.

Nevertheless Macalister believed the *Lebor Gabála* to derive from folk traditions of genuine events, and in particular that the "takings" of Partholon, Nemed and the Fir Bolg reflected a Pictish (and therefore in his view, non-Celtic and even non-Indo-European) invasion of Ireland in the Early Bronze Age. It was the Picts, then, who built these fortresses, "silent but eloquent witnesses to the terror inspired by the Sword-Men" (i.e. the Goidel), and who "made their last despairing stand" on the Aran Isles. On this theory the date of Dún Aonghasa flew back at least as far as 1000 BC.

"Macalister's appropriation of Meyer's ghostly breeches," along with every other modern theory, was dismissed with cackles of derision by the philologist T. F. O'Rahilly in his book of 1946, *Early Irish History and Mythology*. For him the old identification of the Fir Bolg with the Belgae was correct, and "as there is no reason to question the accuracy of the tradition that attributes their erection to the defeated Fir Bolg, it is permissible to conjecture that these remarkable fortresses were constructed probably in the second century BC." As to the meaning of the name, O'Rahilly presents a fascinating theory, the basis of which is quite beyond lay judgement, but which certainly restores the lustre of cosmic origins to the rather earthy image the "men of bags" had acquired. *Fir Bolg*, it appears, is a mere periphrasis of an earlier name for them, *Builg*, which is not just the plural of the word *bolg*, bag, but like many names of Celtic tribes a pluralized form of the name of a deity.

O'Rahilly produces independent evidence that there was indeed a Celtic god Bolg, and argues that that name would derive from a hypothetical Celtic word *bolgos*, having the same Indo-European root as the Latin *fulgur* and the German *Blitzen*, and like those words meaning "lightning." This also explains the name of Cú Chulainn's ultimate weapon, the *gai bolga*, often mentioned in legends about this Celtic hero; it is the spear of the lightning-god, the thunderbolt. Another hero, Fergus Mac Roich, had a similar weapon, a sword called Caladbolg, which on this interpretation would mean "crushing-lightning"; through Welsh legend and Latinization of its name this lightning-sword ended up in the hands of another Celtic hero, King Arthur, as Excalibur. The name of Aonghas occurs repeatedly in the otherworldly pedigrees of the Fir Bolg, and it is only going half a word beyond O'Rahilly himself to claim that our Aonghas is of the illustrious company of heroes who wield the lightning, sign of their former status as gods of thunder.

However, although it seems to be accepted that there was a god Bolgos or Bolgios, O'Rahilly's wider theses about the nature and origins of the various Celtic immigrations have not found favour, and nowadays the Fir Bolg are not expected to throw light upon such questions. There is no reason to think that the forts of Aran are the work of an embattled people, least of all one making its last stand, and contemporary ideas of how one layer of Celtic culture came to dominate over others are too complex to be represented by a story of an invasion. For the time being the Fir Bolg will have to wait until some new approach to the past gives an unexpected twist to the kaleidoscope and brings their curious name once more into prominence in the pattern of evidence.

Even the Aran man, who himself used to carry earth to make fields out of rocky flags, whose boats were, until the introduction of canvas, leather bags stretched over a framework, whose monumental breeches still amaze the visitor, and who therefore might be expected to show some filial reverence for the Fir Bolg, attributes the forts to "the Danes," that is, the Norse raiders of the ninth and tenth centuries, as do country-folk all over Ireland. This theory seems to have been originated by the fifteenth-century Welsh historian Giraldus Cambrensis and popularized from the eighteenth century on by various writers, before Ireland began to reclaim her own prehistory; a confusion of the Tuatha Dé Danann with the Danes has probably helped its spread. In the only folktale I have heard in Aran about the Dún, from the best of our surviving story-tellers, its inhabitants are nameless cannibals preying on the islanders. The mother of a baby boy they had carried off complained to a blacksmith (who lived near the shore north of Fearann an Choirce), and he persuaded a girl he knew who worked as a servant in the Dún to make an impression of the key of its "hall door" in dough and smuggle it out to him. He made a key from this mould, and with it the islanders got into the Dún one night while its inhabitants were asleep and killed them all with spears or by throwing them over the cliff.

However, in County Clare I did hear a scrap of folklore that is perhaps a faint echo of the Firbolgian epic. A Ballyvaughan man told me that Dún Aonghasa and a certain fort high on the shoulder of Black Head were built by a king and given to his two sons, because they were always fighting and he wanted to settle them with a sea between them. Now the name of this fort is anglicized as Caherdoon-fergus on the Ordnance Survey maps, but according to Westropp "Fergus" is an error for "Irgus," who is stated in *Lebor Gabála* to have settled at Black Head—and indeed the native Irish-speakers of Gleann Eidhneach or Gleninagh nearby do seem to me to call it, very correctly, Cathair Dhúin Irghuis. And of course Aonghas and Irgus were indeed brothers, two of the sons of Umor.

These fragments only confirm that the Fir Bolg, who originated in thunderclouds, are now lost in the ashes of cottage firesides and the dust of libraries. There is no access to the Dún's actual past through its legend. And similarly, since those terraces below the cliffs from which the Dún is seen aloft in mythic splendour cannot be followed around Blind Sound, one has now to retrace one's steps some distance to regain the clifftops, before beginning the steep approach by way of archaeology.

DÚN AONGHASA: A CLOSER LOOK

The three walls of Dún Aonghasa form irregular semicircles, one within another, to which the cliff's edge supplies diameters. The innermost is a massive cashel of unmortared stone blocks, open to the two hundred and seventy foot cliff at the very south-eastern corner of Aran's western plateau. The other two walls, of less imposing dry stonework, are not concentric with the inner cashel but enclose much more of the hillside to the east than of the plateau to the west. Thus the eastern sector of the outermost wall comes to the cliff no less than three hundred yards downhill towards Blind Sound, and as it is very dilapidated there one can easily step across it without realizing its connection with the distant parapets above.

Approaching the Dún from this angle along the rising coast, one notices that the eastern sector of each of its walls stands directly above a slight sharpening of the slope and follows the almost straight line of a little scarp crossing the hillside from the north to the cliff edge. The outer wall encloses about eleven acres of rough grazing no different from the rest of the hillside, profusely set with the harsh blue jewels of the spring gentian in March or April, when the thin turf is still cowed by winter. Over much of its length this wall is about six feet thick and stands nowadays to a height of five feet. In its northern arc is a low entrance, lintelled with several seven-foot long blocks, which is loosely filled with stones, for this first line of defence (if that is what it was) nowadays functions as a field-wall. It appears that in any case it was an afterthought or was never intended to do more than protect cattle at night from the casual thief or wolf, for within it, before the next wall, is a band of stones set like spikes in the ground, which obviously begins the cashel's more formidable defences. This abattis or *chevaux-de-frise* is from thirty to eighty feet deep, and on the east it occupies the steeper slope immediately before the foot of the middle wall. The stones are three or four feet long, upright or slanting outwards, close-packed, and must have been much more of an obstacle than the thinner array before Dúchathair. The wall behind them is eight feet thick and eleven feet high, and for most of the way round it is terraced on the inside. At its northernmost point the terrace is interrupted by a gap within which is a blind entrance on the inside of the wall, measuring about four feet in height and width. There is also a break in the wall where the path from Cill Mhuirbhigh comes up, following a walled avenue where it passes through the abattis. The area enclosed measures about four hundred feet from east to west along the clifftop, and about three hundred feet from the cliff to the north. It is more level, but again the eastern sector of the high innermost wall rises from a steep little scarp which becomes in fact a vertical six-foot podium of rock where it approaches the cliff.

This final wall is impressively bulky; it bulges outwards in places and in spite of the weighty buttresses the restorers piled against it in the last century, bits of it occasionally avalanche down, whereupon local men "build it up rough again, like the rest of it" according to instructions from the Board of Works. Many of its stones are scabbed with dark lumps of chert, a layer of which outcrops on the plateau here at a level corresponding exactly to the stratum noted farther east. The wall is nearly thirteen feet thick and eighteen feet high, and is pierced on the east by a gateway only about three and a half feet wide and just over five feet high under the outer lintel. The ground rises through the thickness of the wall here, and to compensate for this the ceiling of the entrance, of long stones set across it from side to side, rises in steps from outside to inside. The jambs of the door, which incline inwards slightly, are of the same coursed masonry as the rest of the wall. On either side of the doorway a continuous vertical joint runs up through the masonry, and other such joints occur at intervals around the wall, suggesting that each sector, and the gateway itself, was built by a separate work-force.

The space within the cashel is roughly a semicircle, open to the cliff edge and about one hundred and fifty feet across. The inside of the wall has two terraces each about four feet wide; these are linked by flights of steps, one on the north of the gateway going directly up the wall like a ladder, and another on the western arc that slants across the wall. At the foot of this stairway is a low lintelled recess about five feet deep forming a rectangular cell in the wall. The details of these terraces and steps may be misleading because by the time restoration was undertaken, in 1881, the interior had become very ruinous, and no attempt was made to mark where original work ends and speculative reconstruction starts. However, it is certain that the wall did consist of three thicknesses each separately faced, for Westropp saw the ramparts before their "destructive re-edification," and noted where the fall of part of the outer layer had exposed the well-built face of an inner layer. Similar two- or three-layered walls occur in several major cashels in the Burren; it is a more stable method of construction than the normal one of a single thick wall with well-built inner and outer faces and an interior packed with a mass of smaller stones, which tend to settle and cause the faces to bulge and even burst. Usually the inner layers are not carried up as high as the outer and form terraces such as one now sees in Dún Aonghasa, but according to Westropp the reconstruction in this case is incorrect, for the inner and outer layers were originally carried up higher than the middle one, which thus formed a sort of sunken walkway around at least part of the top of the wall.

The garth inside the cashel is of quite smooth and level ground except for one rectangular area by the cliff edge that stands a foot or two above the rest, the remains of a stratum that elsewhere has been removed and perhaps furnished blocks for the wall. The Aran people call this platform An Bord, the table. It is inconceivable that the garth was always as undefended against the assaults of the wind as it is now; at the very least there must have been a parapet along the edge of the cliff. O'Donovan was quite sure that the cashel was originally a complete oval and had been halved by recession of the cliff. However, I think cliff-fall of this magnitude over the comparatively short time of two thousand or so years since the building of the Dún would have left the sea below full of great blocks as it is elsewhere below the cliffs, but in fact it is fairly clear at this point. Others have held that not only the inner wall but all the defences were once closed perimeters, and indeed that the fort defended a land that stretched miles to the south; but while it is true that the cliffs have been cut back from a coastline farther south, that took place over a time-scale at least a thousand times longer than the history of Dún Aonghasa. And there are other cashels on cliffs, in situations where cliff-recession can be ruled out. In the Burren Lios Mac Síoda and Cathair Chomáin both stand on inland cliffs that form part of their defences. The latter is not unlike Dún Aonghasa, though it is rather smaller and very much more symmetrical; its outer two walls abut on the cliff as do those of Dún Aonghasa, but the ends of its inner wall turn inwards at the cliff edge and are continued along it as a slighter parapet, so that the area enclosed is almost a full circle. On Árainn itself there are the remains of a substantial though little-known cashel just north of the village of Eochaill, which is a full circle although it comes within feet of a twenty-foot inland cliff. However, these various cases of forts on cliffs do not throw direct light on Dún Aonghasa. It is only commonsense that suggests that the garth cannot have gaped at the void as it does now; but then the vast scale and extreme situation of Dún Aonghasa should perhaps warn us that commonsense had little to do with its construction.

On the level land to the west the three walls of the Dún are much closer together, and around the north-west there is an extra detached sector, a fifty-yard length of single-terraced wall, between the middle and the outermost walls. This anomaly is rather puzzling. In Westropp's diagram it is shown as a loop attached to the middle wall at either end. However, it is not so attached, except by a modern field-wall, and as Westropp points out it was originally part of the middle wall itself. It looks as if there were at one time four walls around the Dún, and that for some obscure reason the two intermediate ones were partly demolished and the remaining lengths cobbled together to make one rather buckled and kinked perimeter. If we number the walls one to four counting outwards from the central garth, this is what the work entailed: the removal of the eastern sector of wall two, the removal of the western and northern sector of wall three, and the building of a new, slightly oblique northern sector to link up the loose ends, leaving the western sector of wall three unattached. As soon as it is pointed out, it is obvious that this is what has been done (though it is much more easily read off an aerial photograph than recognized while walking the site), for the inner limit of the abattis, that hugs the foot of the middle wall around its eastern sector, diverges slightly from it across the north and follows its old track to link up with the isolated remnants on the west. But why such a vast labour was undertaken, to produce such a botched job, remains incomprehensible.

Although it is one of the biggest and the most dramatically sited of the cashels of Ireland, most of the features of Dún Aonghasa—its multiple walls, their height and thickness, its abattis and lintelled gateway, its terraces and steps, even its situation on a high sea-cliff—can be paralleled elsewhere, and it is foolish to speculate on its origins and purpose except in the context of the many hundreds of large stone or earth forts throughout Ireland, or indeed throughout all the former Celtic realms of Europe. That it is so huge is evidence of the self-confidence and stability of the community that built it, not of their fear of imminent overthrow. The siting of its walls seems to show some not very consistent care for tactical advantage; the abattis looks as if it were meant to be taken seriously; but there is no spring within the walls and so the Dún could not have held out against a long siege. This exclusion of wells, which is almost the rule with Irish cashels and those of other regions, was perhaps to avoid pollution of the water-supply. The other Aran cashels, and many of those elsewhere, have foundations of stone huts within the garth, but there is no trace of such here, and as the enclosure is of rock bearing only an inch or two of turf, it is unlikely that excavation would produce much evidence of living quarters, or of much else. The few finds that have been picked up here—flint arrowheads, a bronze fibula or brooch about two thousand years old—have no obvious relationship to the age or the purpose of these walls. It seems unlikely that anyone would choose such an exposed situation to live in except perhaps for brief periods when attack threatened, or for ceremonial purposes. But this is not Tara or Cruachain or Cashel, a natural centre for a wide province, famous in legend and history as a seat of kings and a meeting-place of a people; nothing is recorded of it save for its nominal connection with the perhaps fictitious adventures of the Fir Bolg.

In general the raths and cashels of Ireland are thought to date from the Early Historical period, with a few going back as far as the Iron Age, and others dating perhaps from mediaeval times. Cathair Chomáin, for example, one of the few to have been excavated, is thought to have been occupied for two comparatively short periods in the ninth century AD, though a much earlier date, in the Early Iron Age, has recently been suggested. The smaller ringforts (as they are conventionally termed) were simply walls to protect stock, around a farmer's hut. Strong farmers perhaps expressed their status in that pastoral society by adding an outer wall or two; in fact ancient Irish law-tracts lay it down, at least as an ideal, that a man of such and such a rank should have so many walls to his cashel. But the scale of Dún Aonghasa together with its extraordinary cliff-top perch seems to exempt it from such comparisons. I do not know what degree of conceit and indifference to personal comfort would have made a man a laughing-stock in the Heroic Ages, and I would rather believe the place was built for the worship of storms, to which it is well adapted, than to impress the neighbours. It is generally thought to date from a few centuries BC, in the Early Iron Age, but on rather vague grounds—the occurrence of the abattis in similar cashels of that age in Iberia, which is a likely source of influence on prehistoric Ireland, and so on. Ultimately nothing definite can be said as yet about the purpose of Dún Aonghasa; perhaps a more detailed modern investigation would provide an answer, but the stony terrain is unpromising.

I usually glance around Dún Aonghasa with a slight sense of exasperation on leaving it, not just because archaeologically speaking it is a puzzle, for archaeology in itself is not my concern, nor because as a romantic materialist I would have preferred it in its unrestored state, described as "a weird chaos of ruined heaps," nor yet because it has been drained of poetry by over-frequentation, by me among the thousands, but because once again I have failed adequately to *be* in this strange place, this knot of stone from which the sky has broken out. So I promise to come back and try again, to approach it from a different angle, take it by storm or moonlight, bring a measuring tape or a bottle of wine. But in this mood of frustration I leave it for the moment with this tart comment, that could be read as a feminist one, on its military pretensions, from the two women writers Somerville and Ross, who walked to it over the rocks from Killeany Lodge where they spent a long hot fortnight in 1895:

Of its kind, it is reputed to be as perfect as anything in Europe, but it is an unlovely kind. Three invertebrate walls of loose stones...sprawl in a triple horseshoe to the edge of a cliff which, with its sheer drop of three hundred feet to the sea, completes the line of defence. The innermost of the three ramparts encloses a windy plateau where, in times of siege, the Firbolg Prince Aengus, son of Huamore, probably enjoyed the society of all the cattle in the island, and of an indefinite number of wives.

No, such flippancy will not do at all! I shall have to return to Dún Aonghasa.

PERDITION'S EDGE

From the western walls of Dún Aonghasa one can survey the tableland beyond, a grey-green puzzle of fields and walls that slants evenly and almost imperceptibly across to the south and stops in mid-air three hundred feet above the sea. All the features of the central plateau recur here, for this surface is carved out of the same strata: the thin layers of chert exposed here and there that break up into fragments like children's building-blocks; the monotonous network of fields (about fifteen hundred of them, I estimate) of various sizes but nearly all of a rectangular shape that seems to usher one towards the cliff; and underlying this pattern the regular jointing dissecting the surface by shallow fissures into strips a foot or two wide that also direct one towards the edge, where some of them jut out beyond the cliff top like fingerposts to the horizon. Because of the height of these cliffs the strange landscape continues almost unchanged right up to its abrupt cessation, which, approached from inland, can scarcely be called a coast, the region of interplay between land and sea being hidden and apparently reduced to a line of mathematical intangibility and finality.

Only the most exceptional seas can fling spray over these cliffs and so the flora of the stony pastures persists right up to the edge, but crouching ever lower against the blast. The lank-stemmed harebell of the inland fields is reduced to a height of four inches at thirty paces from the cliffs, and at a yard from the brink its stem is only an inch and a half long and its bell lolls on the ground. Similarly in the hayfields of the sheltered northern slopes centaury grows eighteen inches tall, on the open crags it is half that height, and here on the clifftop it is a compact knob of pink blossom an inch high. The yellow cat's-ear is prominent here in late summer, its stem prostrate and its flowerheads hardly lifted off the ground, among hunched sprigs of Lady's bedstraw and elegantly abbreviated fairy flax. These dwarfs stand up out of a sward that clings to the rock like a skin, mainly composed of thyme and the little Gothic rosettes of buckthorn plantain, but comprising dozens of other plants reduced by exposure to a botanical shorthand only the expert can read. Thus the scale of what is underfoot shrinks as the edge is approached, where all commentary on this world of fascinating minutiae is brought up short by the overwhelming generalization of the void.

A line of portrait busts of Roman senators could not display a nobler sequence of profiles than do the headlands west of the Dún. Here the cliffs have three and in places four massive storeys of limestone separated by deeply scored ledges where the sea has licked out the crumbly layers of shale. Often the upper storey projects beyond the one below, and in places the lowest level forms a wide terrace onto which the waves break at high tide. The cliffs of Achill are seven times higher than these and yet are not so imposing because they slant into the sea, whereas these cliffs are sheer or overhanging. A fall from the Achill cliffs would be an ignominious slithering panic, but here it would be an unimpeded parabolic plunge. However, the idea of falling is not so insistent here as it is on the lower ranges to the east, where the movement of the waves below is not so dwarfed and hushed by distance and one feels oneself in a more immediate comparison with the forces of the sea. Here, though, the space outside the brink is so far beyond the human scale that it fills one with the breath of oceanic well-being and a lofty self-confidence.

Nevertheless people have vanished over this edge. Carraig an Smáil, which Tom O'Flaherty renders as the Rock of Perdition in his stories of the old cliffmen, is an ill-famed angle a hundred yards west of the Dún, from which a Gort na gCapall fisherman went down. Nobody knows how he came to fall, but although this was nearly a century ago what ensued is still remembered with some bitterness in the village, for boatmen of another family found his body in their nets many days later, and let it go with the tide rather than bring it ashore as it was so loathsome, and this caused a rift between the two families that lasted for decades.

Only once or twice in the course of many walks have I met anyone fishing from these western cliffs, and the unnerving spectacle, made world-famous by Robert Flaherty's film *Man of Aran*, is now almost extinct. Having baited his hook with periwinkles brought from the low northern shores, and searched around for a suitable weight—a stone a few inches long, preferably with a waist to tie the line round—the fisherman stands on the brink and either swings the stone to and fro underhand or whirls it around his head in a few great slow circles before letting it fly far out into the air. However energetic the cast the height of the cliff is such that the stone always seems to fall close to its base. The fisherman sits down with his heels stuck out into space and leans forward with the line delicately held over one finger; in the barefoot days he would have run it between two toes. By experience and inheritance he knows exactly where the wrasse are waiting, just off the edge of the terrace below. The tug of a bite brings him convulsively to his feet. It is easier to haul the catch up if the cliff actually leans out over the water, and to the onlooker standing a little aside out of range of the whirling stone and who can see the extent of the overhang, this spasm of activity on the cracked lip of rock looks suicidal. Sometimes a fisherman will leave his line in a cleft of the clifftop when he goes home, knowing that no one will touch it. Recently an Oatquarter lad went back to his habitual perch, to find that not only his line but the place itself had disappeared overnight.

The cliff face itself is unvisited territory nowadays. The main routes of this portion of it were two ledges, continuous for a couple of miles westwards from the Dún and linked in certain angles of the cliff by vertical, stair-like climbs. The *ailleadóir* or cliffman would enter his chosen ledge at dusk east of the Dún where the rising ground brings the clifftop up past the level of each ledge in turn, or he would be lowered onto it from above by a team. Both the *aragaint* or ledges and the *strapaí* or stairs are much altered since the days of the cliffmen of the last century, being blocked by rock-falls in places that were clear, and cleared by erosion in places that were blocked. One man who had discovered his own route down to sea level when he was a boy and offered to show me it, was unable to recognize the entrance to his *strapa* when we reached the spot, and I was glad that I had prudently declined his invitation and that we had not carried the necessary so many fathoms of rope all the way along the cliffs.

The names of these old ways are being washed away too, and the memory of those who traversed this dark obverse of the path-system above is similarly lapsing into the fabulous. The anecdotes I have picked up of their exploits are as evocative as scraps of a lost cycle of legends. Hearing about the man on whom the ravens dropped pebbles while he was raiding their nest, or of the man who was battered by the wings of a cormorant in the darkness of a narrow crumbling shelf, or of the brothers who saved themselves by climbing the cliff-face at night when the weather changed and the waves started to reach up into the ledge they were crouched in, I envisage the cliff as the field of a strange hands-and-knees chivalry, across which an order of knights pledged to the vertiginous crawled forth to do battle with black-winged monsters. Simultaneously I see these heroes as bent, wheezy little old men with a comic turn of phrase, for this is how the islanders I talk to recall them; it seems that those vigils on the windy ledges were conducive to wit as well as to catarrh.

For the *ailleadóir* the cliff was primarily a geography of variously productive places and the handiest routes to them. The terrace below the cliff a couple of hundred yards west of the Dún, on which the tides leave little pools of water, for instance, was Leac an tSalainn, the flag of the salt, and it was worth going there in hot weather to collect the salt from around the rims of the evaporated pools. Aragaint an tSraoilleáin, the ledge one third of the way up the cliff in the first big bay west of the Dún, was a famous place for cormorants and guillemots, and many a feather pillow came from that ledge. If the cliff was haunted in places it was no more so than the villages; if there was a Scailp an Phúca, the goblin's cleft, in the east of that same bay, it was still as useful a shortcut as Róidín an Phúca, a lane in Cill Rónáin. Nevertheless, and whatever the importance of its product in the way of bird-flesh, eggs, feathers and oil, fish, limpets and driftwood, this was an alien territory, a world turned on its edge and subjected to a draconian law of gravity, and those who ventured into it must have brought back something of its savagery to their wives and hearths, as a Gort na gCapall man I have heard of brought back peregrine falcon and raven chicks, to rear them up and to pit them against each other in cock-fights. And when the cliffmen led their sons out along these ledges for the first time and were agreeably surprised by the lads' steadiness of nerve, they probably suspected from their own experience that the children had been secretly testing themselves on the cliffs for years, as both boys and girls still occasionally do.

TIDES OF THE OTHER WORLD

Half a mile west of the Dún the façade of the cliffs is recessed as if around the forecourt of a sombre and majestic public building. A falling tide leaves the smooth pavement of this great rectangular courtyard bare and black, and the bay is named An Sraoilleán from this sprawling, slippery rock, which is what the word means. The cliff that looks down into the bay from the east is Binn an Ghlais; the sense of this name is not quite clear, but it seems to refer to an appearance of greenness, perhaps of the turf along its rim. Half-way along this cliff one can step down onto a little ledge, a balcony trimmed with thrift and sea-campion in spring, or scentless mayweed and sea-aster later in the year. Long ago this was the favourite fishing perch of the three sons of a woman called Nora, and it is known from them as Ulán Chlainn Nora, the ledge of Nora's family. These young men were pilots, and they lived in a cottage by the "Seven Churches" on the north coast, from which they could keep a look out for sailing vessels coming into Galway Bay from the west. One day, when there was "a stir on the sea" as the Aran men say, they saw a ship sailing up the North Sound, and hurried down to the shore to launch their currach, intending to intercept the ship and offer to guide it through the rocks and shoals of the bay. But the ship vanished as they rowed out, and the great breaker of An Gleannachán overturned their currach and drowned them.

The history of Nora's sons is not the only tale of Aran men lured to their deaths by fairy ships. The seas of Aran are or were as haunted as its hillsides, lanes and precipices, and drifting scraps of sheer malice—flotsam from that great shipwreck of evil, the Fall of the Angels (for that is one supposed origin of the fairies)—could entangle themselves in the fishermen's lives at any moment. Some tracts of sea are more ghost-run than others; the shadowed tides of An Sraoilleán in particular bring in the supernatural as other bays collect wrack of the human world. With the flood the breakers roll farther and farther up its slanting floor until they enter caverns that look like dark slits along the base of the cliff; seen from so far above their movement is slow and deliberate, and on a day when Aran is windless and the breakers have their origins in a storm long past or far out to sea, their silent disappearance one after the other under the low arches has the solemnity of a great funeral procession entering a cathedral. Such a place is a natural breeding-ground of stories. Here is a translation of what an islander wrote for me about this bay:

It always was a ghostly, weird place. The evening that Colm Mór, Labhràs Phatch Sheáin and Patch Tom Sheáin were drowned off the north coast of the island, there were several men in currachs at anchor in the mouth of An Sraoilleán fishing for bream. They hadn't heard a hint or a rumour of the misfortune. At twilight they felt something strange and ghostly about them that they could not understand. They drew together. They knew that the sounds they heard were coming from the other world—talk and tumult and old warcries of "abú, ullallú!" And then they suddenly saw an apparition of boats and currachs in the bay and lights peering out at them from the cliffs. There was a noise of battle and slaughter, of boats coming ashore and launching out again. They heard disputes, threats and blows. They took fright, and, winding in their lines and pulling up their anchor stones, they rowed off as fast as they could.

And on reaching home they would have heard of the overturning of a currach in calm waters close to the shore near Mainistir, and the drowning of three men—a tragedy which is ascribed by the island's oral history to drink, whatever unearthly conflicts it may have occasioned in the catacombs of the sea.

LIFE ON THE BRINK

"I'll do it if I can, as the billygoat of Binn an Ghlais said!"— "*Deanfad mar fhéadaim, mar a deir pocaide Bhinn an Ghlais!*"—is an old Aran saying used in tricky undertakings. What the billygoat was up to on this, Aran's highest cliff, has unfortunately been forgotten, but the saying still captures something of the essence of this place, the contrast between the gloom of the abyss and the airy ardour of life on its brink. Even rabbits seem to live dangerously up here, burrowing in gullies of crumbling shale that give onto the direst drops; in fact it is the dog that chases them that is likely to go over the edge, as in one of the short stories in which Liam O'Flaherty celebrates life's dance towards death.

Spring exhibits its delectable blend of spontaneity and ritual on the clifftops as elsewhere; each time it comes round the same wayward impulses inhabit new bodies exactly like those of last year, or perhaps the same bodies rejuvenated, at exactly the same times and places. There is always a pair of wheatears flitting about and calling to one another in a little glen just outside the Dún's western defences. The Aran belief is that they winter in caves on the cliff face, but in fact they fly to equatorial Africa each autumn and arrive back in March; as an islander rather oddly put it to me, "If you don't see them on St. Patrick's Day, you'll see them a day or two before that." At that season, too, a pair of inky-black choughs are often to be seen hopping heavily from stone to stone of the Dún's western *chevaux-de-frise*, stropping their curved red beaks. Choughs are rare nowadays; as jackdaws, their rougher, rowdier cousins in the crow family, have spread, so the similar-sized (but slimmer, more fastidiously black and elegantly beaked) choughs have become restricted to a few such western outposts as this, where nesting pairs are not uncommon on the great cliffs. Often there is a bachelor party of a dozen or so unpaired, yearling birds, high and buoyant above the Dún, flinging themselves about in aerial riot, soaring with wing-feathers spread like long fingers against the brightness, then folding themselves up into black fists and abandoning themselves to a few seconds of free fall, scattering their fierce shrill, down-curving cries like ragged scrapings of zinc. Couples of ravens perform a similar dance, but on a spectacular scale befitting their much greater size. The ravens' courtship flights take them up into skies so spacious they become black dots to us and to each other, but each pair of these circuits springs like vast invisible wings from a fixed origin on the clifftop, one of which is above An Sraoilleán; I have the impression that just four couples spaced out as far as possible each year hold and divide the entire range of cliffs between them. Aran people delight in telling one that the raven can fly upside-down, and indeed it does so for certain instants of the spring. The raven, flying high in the sight of its mate, half-folds its wings, lets itself plunge and turns over on its back for a moment as it swings through the sky like the clapper of a bell, and its call at that supreme moment is a single deep chime as evocative of marriage as is its normal croak of funeral.

The irrepressible every-day, every-field plants that flower on the clifftops have already been mentioned, but this particular range, the mile or so west of the Dún, is the last refuge of a little rarity that, having lingered on almost since the end of the last Ice Age, is now reduced to this marginal existence, if it is not, in Ireland, on the verge of extinction. This is *Astragalus danicus*, the purple milk-vetch; its loose clover-like heads of violet flowers catch the eye here in May, and throughout the summer its small neat leaves, pinnate like those of the common vetch but ending with a leaflet rather than a tendril, are easily recognized in the short turf. It is common only on these particular clifftops, occurs sporadically in one or two places on the north coast and in Inis Meáin (notably in the new graveyard), and nowhere else in Ireland. In Europe it is a plant of the tundra and high mountain pastures, and presumably it was widespread in Ireland when this country was recovering its vegetation after the retreat of the glaciers. Now, on this uttermost edge of its former range, it finds conditions similar enough to those of its old habitats to blossom and seed, because of rather than despite the adjacent gulf.

DIVISIONS OF THE LAND

The western wall of An Sraoilleán is noticeably different from the other cliff faces; it is smooth and vertically streaked, as if it has been half-melted. In fact it has been subjected to extreme stresses, for this is the effect of a fault, where the rock has fractured and the land on one side of the fracture has moved relatively to that on the other. The plane of this fracture is almost vertical and at right angles to the general line of the coast. As the cliffs have been eaten back by the sea, rock on the east of the fracture has fallen away and exposed some of the opposing rock face; the fault, then, is older than the cliffs. Although the fault extends through the entire thickness of limestone from clifftop to sea level or below, the relative movement of the two sides has been very small, as one can see at the point where the fault plane reaches the cliff. A thread of water finds its way over the brink just here and in fact has cut a little cleft into this weakened zone, in which the various thicknesses of rock on the west of the streamlet visibly match up with those about six inches higher on its east. The little valley resulting from erosion along the line of the fault runs inland for about a third of a mile in a direction a few degrees more easterly than that of the major set of joints, and even on an Ordnance Survey map showing only the field boundaries it can be recognized as a slight distortion of the field pattern, which otherwise is largely controlled by the jointings. Faults are infrequent in Aran, as they are in the western parts of the Burren, but both faults and folding of strata become more noticeable towards the western tip of the island, and, as will become apparent, a fault may have initiated the development of the whole line of cliffs.

The name of this headland that closes off An Sraoilleán on the west, Barr an Leath-chartúir, means "the head of the half-cartron" —which lands one on the middle of the multiplication table of a system of land-divisions that dates from mediaeval times. It is based on factors of four. The four townlands of Árainn are each divided into carrows or quarters, each of which is divided into four cartrons, each of which contains four croggeries or fourths. These terms are anglicizations of Irish words: *ceathrú* (quarter), *cartúr* (cartron) and *cnagaire* (croggery). A *cnagaire* is sixteen acres, the nominal size of a holding that "could feed a cow with her calf, a horse, some sheep for their wool and give sufficient potatoes to support one family." This nineteenth-century formula gives the whole scheme a basis in rustic idyll, it would seem, but there are complications in adjusting it to reality. First, each of the four townlands of Árainn has *six* quarters. (Inis Meáin's two townlands and Inis Oírr's single townland, though, have just four quarters each.) The three western townlands, Eoghanacht, Cill Mhuirbhigh and Eochaill, each measure very close to 1800 acres; Cill Éinne townland has 2296 acres but if its unproductive sandy tracts are disregarded it is not far off the same size as the rest. However, if a *cnagaire* is sixteen acres, a townland (even if it has six quarters) should only be 1536 acres. Thus there is a certain latitude of allowance for bare rock, even if not as much as one would think reasonable. Perhaps, though, this calculation should start from the old "Irish acre," which was about one and two-thirds the size of a statute acre. In that case a townland of six quarters would contain no less than 2594 statute acres. This seems to indicate that those basic croggeries (the very word speaks of stony ground!) on which the tenants subsisted were of niggardly measure.

It follows from the above, as the mathematicians say, that a *leath-chartúr* is thirty-two acres, give or take a few acres hardly worth giving or taking.

I have not been able to identify the particular tract of land referred to in the name of Barr an Leath-chartúir, and in several other cases I have only just been in time to catch the dying whispers of the island's oral record of such minor subdivisions. Only the townland boundaries are shown on the Ordnance Survey maps. In 1980 it was only with difficulty that I found one or two people in each village of the island who could show me at least parts of the boundary walls of the nearby *ceathrúna* or quarters, but I was able to complete a record, with only a few doubts and gaps, of this incredibly complex apportioning of land between the villages, which having long lost its function is now being obliterated by the swapping of parcels of land to rationalize scattered holdings. The names of most of the individual *ceathrúna* survive though the sense of some has become obscure, and here and there I was shown a wall that formed part of the otherwise forgotten boundary of a *leath-cheathrú* or half-quarter, for many of the quarters, themselves narrow strips running across the island, were divided longitudinally into still narrower pieces, each with its name, of which a few are dimly remembered.

However, with one quarter I had no difficulty as it is a single holding and its borders are therefore marked in red on its owner's Land Commission map, which he kindly lent me. The way in which it came to be a single holding, over a century ago, is also scored in red, on the island's communal memory. As I gathered its history piece-meal from various people, I heard more bitterness expressed over this particular case of "land-grabbing" than over any other in the catalogue of Aran's wrongs—not against its present owner, who is everyone's obliging neighbour, but against his distant predecessors the O'Flahertys of Cill Mhuirbhigh.

The quarter in question is called Ceathrú an Turlaigh, and its eastern boundary wall comes zigzagging across from the north coast to the western side of the bay of An Sraoilleán. Over most of its course this wall like all the others obeys the promptings of the joint-system, so that each length of it either runs south-south-west or at right angles to that direction; near its southern end it is slightly deflected by the distortions caused in the field-pattern by the fault described above, as if it were briefly tempted by an analogy between the geological and social stresses that have riven Aran, and it finally reaches the cliff on the east side of Barr an Leath-chartúir. A little gully running out onto the cliff face immediately west of that same headland, was the site of the most horrific incident of Aran's "Land War," the "cliffing" of the O'Flahertys' cattle just over a century ago. But to explain this event and relate it to the tensions such boundaries as those of Ceathrú an Turlaigh have inscribed on the face of the island, I need first to set a wider scene.

AN "AGRARIAN OUTRAGE"

The name Ceathrú an Turlaigh refers to a *turlach*, a hollow in which a lake appears from time to time as the level of rainwater held in the fissures of the surrounding rock fluctuates with the weather and the season of the year. There is such a hollow called An Turlach Mór about three hundred yards inland from the cliffs just west of Barr an Leath-chartúir; it is a closed valley comprising a few large pastures often waterlogged in winter and almost always damp and lush through the rest of the year, in startling contrast to the dry stoniness of the land in neighbouring quarters. Ceathrú an Turlaigh also includes fine sandy grazing on the north coast, and on the whole it is more productive than any other quarter west of Cill Mhuirbhigh.

However, during the Famine and the decades of chronic want that followed, the small tenants of this quarter were no more able to make ends meet than the rest, and when rents could not be paid evictions followed; those who were not evicted or forced by hunger to leave a home that could not provide for them were disposed of by the offer of tickets for the emigrant boats. As an islander explained to me: "The big-shots didn't care where they went, to Cill Rónáin or Inis Oírr or America, just so long as they got the hell out of Ceathrú an Turlaigh!" And as the long-settled population evaporated in this way, the landlord's agent was able to lease the entire quarter to the O'Flahertys, already the island's largest landholders. No doubt the agent considered this a progressive step, a reform of a hopelessly archaic fragmentation of productive capacity. Perhaps he even believed that the surviving population of Aran would someday join him in regarding their distress, bereavement and loneliness as necessary to and justified by the inauguration of a more rational order. The economic theology of the time would have strengthened this man, Thomas Thompson, at whose name I have seen old Aran men shake their sticks, in the repression of his humanity, as the latest versions of such doctrines armour the hearts of his like today. The only beneficiaries in fact, apart from the agent himself and the landlords (who were far away and cared nothing so long as they received a couple of thousand pounds out of Thompson's takings each year), were the O'Flahertys. By the end of the 1870s James O'Flaherty was master not only of the fertile lowlands around Port Mhuirbhigh but of the Hill Farm in the east and Ceathrú an Turlaigh in the west. He was, simply, The O'Flaherty. His house had expanded from a thatched cottage into a plain two-storey, slate-roofed, mansion which by Aran standards was palatial. The constabulary barracks stood before it, and like his father before him he was the island's Justice of the Peace.

But for his version of justice the islanders did not return him peace. They too were strengthened by voices from the outside world, for Aran's case was that of much of Ireland, and opposition to rack-renting and evictions was being organized both overtly and covertly throughout the country and articulated in Westminster itself. Although the Fenian uprising of 1867 had been a dismal failure, Ireland was still threaded through with the remains of a secret, nationalist, revolutionary organization. Gladstone on taking office in the following year had announced his mission to pacify Ireland, but while his Land Act of 1870 had given the tenant who could pay his rent a degree of protection against eviction, towards the end of the decade bad seasons and competition of cheap grain from America had made paying the rent impossible for the men of few acres, and the Act was no longer a hindrance to the landlord who wished to clear surplus tenantry off his estates.

The number of evictions soared after the long wet summer of 1877 had brought the country to the verge of famine again, and the local and immediate resentments of the peasantry which had always found their outlet in sporadic acts of violence against landlords, agents, bailiffs and "land-grabbers," as those who occupied land from which others had been evicted were called, became forces which both the Fenians in hiding and Parnell in parliament wanted to control and direct in pursuance of their various hopes for Ireland's future. At a mass meeting organized by Michael Davitt at Westport in June 1879, Parnell lent the voice of his urbanity and reason to the oppressed, and in return pocketed their spontaneous rebelliousness as a card to be played or held in reserve in his own unfathomable parliamentary game:

> A fair rent is a rent the tenant can reasonably afford to pay according to the times, but in bad times a tenant cannot be expected to pay as much as he did in good times....Now, what must be done in order to induce the landlords to see the position? You must show them that you intend to keep a firm grip of your homesteads and lands. You must not allow yourselves to be dispossessed as your fathers were dispossessed in 1847....I hope...that on those properties where the rents are out of all proportion to the times a reduction may be made and that immediately. If not, you must help yourselves, and the public opinion of the world will stand by you in your struggle to defend your homesteads.

The National Land League was founded by Michael Davitt a few months later with Parnell as its president, and the "Land War" was declared. Throughout Ireland there were mass-demonstrations that obliged many landlords to reduce rents on the spot. The Land League concerted action physically to prevent many evictions, and could dispose of the funds necessary to house and feed at least some of the dispossessed. It won the support of the local clergy and the Hierarchy, instituted an alternative system of courts, and by 1880 could be described by *The Times* as "a very distinct and potent government which is rapidly succeeding the Imperial government." Gladstone responded in the following year with, on the one hand, a Coercion Act which allowed him to arrest various

Land League leaders, and on the other with a second Land Act which guaranteed "the three F's"—fixity of tenure, free sale of the tenant's interest and improvement on vacation of the holding, and fair rents, to be set by a Land Court. By 1882 the crisis was over at least for the time being; Parnell had been arrested and released on an understanding that he would call off the agitation and co-operate with the Land Act, under which tenants were already winning rent decreases, and that the Coercion Act would be repealed. The attention of both Parnell and the country as a whole soon turned to more directly nationalistic matters.

The climactic event of Aran's Land War exactly coincided with the peak of Ireland's fever. I am told that at this time James O'Flaherty had his eyes on an area of good fields called An Caiseal (no doubt from the cashel of Dún Aonghasa on the hill above it), which bordered his own holding in Cill Mhuirbhigh and was leased in small lots to the people of Gort na gCapall. Opposition to his depredations was led by the Fenians, now Land Leaguers, of that village, among whom Mícheál Ó Flaithearta (Michael O'Flaherty) who later fathered the novelist Liam O'Flaherty, was prominent.

The plans for the destruction of James O'Flaherty's stock, which took place on the 7th of January 1881, must have been carefully coordinated. James O'Flaherty had twenty-one cattle including a bull grazing near An Turlach Mór at the time, according to oral history, which has preserved many curious details of the event. (Newspaper accounts though mention thirty heifers of O'Flaherty's and three belonging to his retainers.) The Land Leaguers rounded them up, blindfolded them and herded them down the gully nearby to the edge of the cliff, from which they fell more than two hundred and fifty feet into the sea. By pre-arrangement, children were banging empty buckets and playing jew's harps on the roads at that hour, to prevent the distant lowing of the terrified beasts reaching the ears of authority, and the conspirators came home unhindered.

Arrests were made after the discovery of the crime, but evidence against particular persons was lacking. In May of that year Michael O'Flaherty and his brother-in-law Thomas Ganly, the local secretary of the Land League, were added to the other suspects in Galway Gaol; after three months in prison they were offered release on condition of signing an undertaking about their future behaviour, which they refused to do, and by the end of September they had been released unconditionally. A "cess" covering compensation to James O'Flaherty was to be levied on the household rates, and opposition to this communal fine, including the violent repulse of the police, bailiffs and hired roughs from Galway who came out to enforce it, rumbled on for decades. In the end it was paid off by degrees, but James O'Flaherty hardly saw the three hundred pounds he was awarded, as he died in November of the same year, aged sixty-four. According to the newspapers he "received the Last Rites," but Aran lore has it that his last living dealings with the clergy were rather of the opposite nature. It is said that as he was stepping into the boat at Cill Rónáin to go to the court hearings in Galway a curate on the quayside said to him "May you never come back!," to which a bystander added "Amen!" The curate turned on the other man and said, "That's a terrible thing you've done, saying Amen to a curse!" And indeed O'Flaherty did not come back, but was found dead one morning in his hotel bedroom.

That dramatic year of 1881 does seem to represent the beginning of a process of redress, a slow and painful progress towards amelioration in which national and parochial history oddly conspired. Nationally the "agrarian outrages" of those years around '81, the cattle-maimings, house-burnings, attacks upon landlords and bailiffs, boycotts of land-grabbers, and above all their political orchestration by the Land League, won significant concessions, and these were felt in Aran when the Land Court sitting in Cill Rónáin in 1885 reduced the rents on the average by a third. The Gort na gCapall men had followed Parnell's urgings and had "kept a firm grip" on their holdings in An Caiseal. The expansionism of the Cill Mhuirbhigh O'Flahertys had been halted, and their estate was soon to decline, for it happened that James had left no male heir and his eldest daughter married into gentry, the Johnstons of Doolin in County Clare, who had no Aran roots, and were expensively addicted to drink and fox-hunting. As financial ruin approached, the outlying portions of the estate had to be sold off. The Hill Farm in Cill Éinne (after tragi-comedies to be detailed in a sequel to this book) was eventually "striped" and distributed among smallholders, while Ceathrú an Turlaigh went to an Aran man returned from America rich enough to buy it as a single lot. Even the Cill Mhuirbhigh farm itself, with the passing of the last of the Johnstons, has become in some respects an Aran holding like the rest.

And so it appears that this little kink in the edge of Ceathrú an Turlaigh, the brief cattle track that led the puzzled beasts from peaceful grazing to those four seconds of black panic before their deaths, is a site (one of hundreds) of a certain historical crisis, as well as of a shameful deed, which is how most Aran people see it. When I peer down here, sickly, to the breakers crawling on the rocks below, I know why this story is one that sticks in the throat of oral history. I fear that some islanders will be displeased that I have told it, though it has been at least mentioned in print before. One or two have said to me that it would have been fair enough to throw the landlords over the cliff, but that it was a shame to treat the innocent beasts so. In the long exchange of insults that has always accompanied the Connemara men's dealings with Aran, for instance, the "cliffing" of the O'Flahertys' cattle has been the substance of a jibe and a reproach, as I have been told. Our eldest, best and most prolix story-teller could not bring himself to say much to me about the event but this: "*Ba mhór an náire é. Ba mhór an peaca é!*"—"A great shame it was. A great sin it was!"

FEAR OF FALLING, FEAR OF FAILING

Cataclysms are in preparation beyond the bay in which O'Flaherty's cattle fell to their deaths. The western boundary wall of Ceathrú an Turlaigh, which runs to the point of a headland called Binn an Turlaigh on the west of the bay, crosses a fissure a foot or so wide, thirty yards inland and extending almost all the way across the headland for a distance of a hundred yards or so; it seems that an enormous area of at least an upper stratum several yards thick is detached and has begun to slide outwards. A third of a mile farther west, just beyond the next headland, is another fissure, nearer the edge but much wider and deeper, called Scailp na bPlátaí, the cleft of the plates, because a stone thrown down it disappears with an echoing clatter that is supposed to sound like the breaking of plates. Scailp na bPlátaí is wide enough for a rock-climber to wedge himself down between its sheer faces, and it is the beginning of a traditional route to the terraces at the foot of the cliff three hundred feet below. The details of the climb, as recollected for me by an Aran man who some forty years ago was one of the last to do it, make me feel the chill breath of vertigo. While I can play with the idea of getting down the fifty or sixty feet of Scailp na bPlátaí with the aid of the various fallen blocks and granite boulders wedged here and there in its jaws, and working westwards along its gullet to a window-like opening in the cliff face, my imagination quails at the next stage of the descent, Ulán na mBos, the ledge of the palms of the hands, so called because it is apparently necessary to sit on it and use one's palms to ease oneself sideways along it, first southwards and then eastwards around a corner of the cliff. This leads one to Ulán na Téide, the ledge of the rope, where one attaches seven fathoms of rope and lets oneself down onto the top of An Clochar, a tower of debris from an ancient rock-fall stacked against the cliff to a height of a hundred and fifty feet or more. Scrambling down this stone-bank or *clochar* presents no difficulties, it seems.

The sagging megatons of rock that have pulled open the *scailp* overhang and will eventually collapse into a cavern called An Poll Dubh, the black hole. The sea-cave in its depths is said, in all geological improbability, to connect with An Loch Dearg, the red lake, on the north coast; a piper once entered it and was never seen again, though his music is sometimes heard under the village of Creig an Chéirín. Tom O'Flaherty mentions this legend in one of his autobiographical pieces. According to him the piper was a fugitive outlaw from Connemara, and "anyone who hears his mournful music will before long be called to the Piper's Castle, from which none return." A similar tale is told of a cave in Inis Oírr said to connect with one in Inis Meáin, and in this case the music is heard from under Carraig an Phíobaire or Piper's Rock in the channel between the two islands. The almost identical legend of Poll an Phíobaire, the piper's cave in Camas, Connemara, suggested one of Patrick Pearse's Irish stories for children, and both the name and the tale occur elsewhere in Ireland. I am told by a spelaeologist that similar legends are widespread in other countries too, connecting certain caves with the traditional musical instruments of the locality. Orpheus himself was probably not the first musician to visit the Underworld.

The central interpretations of this universal theme are in the hands of Freudians and others, but perhaps the Aran instance could be spared for adoption into a personal mythology. Thus: the artist finds deep-lying passages, unsuspected correspondences, unrevealed concordances, leading from element to element of reality, and celebrates them in the darkness of the solipsism necessary to his undertaking, but at best it is a weak and intermittent music, confused by its own echoes and muffled by the chattering waters of the earth, that reaches the surface-dweller above; nor does the artist emerge; his ways lead on and on, or about and about.

The ruinous pagoda of An Clochar has its base on a broad terrace that runs back around the headland and as far east as Binn an Turlaigh. A hundred-yard-long arm of this terrace extends southwards into the sea from below the point of the headland like the deck of a foundering aircraft carrier. In wild weather the waves clamber onto Leic an Chlochair, as this sheet of rock is called, but on calm days it stands serenely out of the water, an ideal platform for any fisherman able to face the climb down the cliff. Only cormorants fish there now, but it used to be a famous place for catching mackerel, wrasse, pollock and especially bream, as these last could only be caught in plenty from a shore that faced into the wind, and such a position could nearly always be found on this long peninsula.

A Gort na gCapall man has written me a lyrical account of a boy's first expedition with his father and other men of the village to Leic an Chlochair. They walk along the cliffs to Scailp na bPlátaí before sunrise, carrying ropes and fishing gear in baskets on their backs. The boy follows his father down the cliff to the Leic without difficulty, and spends magical hours there as the red-gold dawn blazes along the cliff face and the rockfish come in in shoals. He sees the life of the cliff foot: a silky-furred seal spends the morning in diving and putting its head up to watch them with curious eyes from Cloch na gCollach, the stone of the males, a flat rock on which seals mate just east of the Leic; otters hunt for their breakfast even more nimbly than the seal, a skua harries the gulls to and fro until they disgorge their last meal which it catches in mid-air, and the basking shark dozes in the sparkling water within a few yards of the fishermen. But when it comes to time to go home the lad looks up at the seagulls as small as swallows around the top of the cliff, and remembers the story of the clumsy fellow who slipped and swung on his rope over An Poll Dubh out of reach of the cliff face, and of the man who fell screaming from Ulán na Téide. He masters his panic enough to scale An Clochar, but when he is half-way up the rope-climb the raven of An Poll Dubh swoops out at him and he is paralyzed by fear, so that his father has to climb up after him to encourage him with a clip on the ear and tell him that it is no harder than the little cliff under the village so long as he keeps his eyes on the rope. His pride reawakened, he completes the climb, and is never again afraid of Leic an Chlochair.

No doubt this climb was an initiation for many lads. Younger children used to play up and down another climb in the eastern angle of the headland, where there is a way down to a grassy ledge called Ulán na mBuachaillí, the ledge of the boys—although I have heard of at least one woman who visited it in her girlhood. The man who showed me it kept well away from the edge, crouching down to clutch the ground and saying "I used to go down there when I was young, but look at me now!" In those days the usual Sunday afternoon pastime of children from the western villages, strictly forbidden by their parents, was to go down the cliffs after birds and eggs, which having brought to the top they had to throw down again, not daring to risk a beating by bringing them home. Although many children thus became immune to vertigo and are still at ease when sitting on the clifftop and leaning out with a fishing line, others had terrifying experiences they never told anyone about and never got over. There are men who have not visited the cliffs for half a lifetime and still occasionally wake up shuddering in the night as the ledge crumbles or the rope parts in their dreams.

This psychopathology of the clifftops finds its ultimate expression in a plank of rock that projects from the brink a quarter of a mile west of Scailp na bPlátaí. It is about two feet across and eight or ten inches thick; it looks about fifteen feet long and was once rather longer until someone paced it out and the end broke off under his weight. That at least is one version of the origin of its name, An Troigh Mhairbh, the dead step. Island tradition specifies that it was an English army officer who walked out to the end of his life here, and according to one cryptophallic telling of the tale he was driven to his death by the mockery in the eyes of his newly wedded wife: "Go on! Even the village lads go as far as that!" she cried when he hesitated half-way along its length. This fearful rock-spur is well-known in Connemara folklore as An Troigh Mharfach, the deadly step or foot. In the Connemara tale when the man has paced out every step of the spur the woman urges him to pace out "the step that isn't there," and he steps over the end of it. It is certainly true that Aran lads used to dare each other to go some way out onto it, and Tom O'Flaherty mentions an old cliffman no longer able to tackle the cliff face who could not resist the temptation every now and then of walking out and standing on the very tip of the projection.

These reveries over the void reveal their deathly and obsessional side in such stories, a concern that lies deeper than a perverse harping on the theme of challenge to a narrowly conceived virility. It is because of the inadequacy of our step to the earth that bears it that we are fascinated by "the step that isn't there." Implicit in this book is the conviction that to refuse "the leap" of faith is the honourable alternative and, if fully accepted, the more demanding one; these demands are what I hope to clarify for myself through the writing of it. At this stage in the construction of my metaphysical Aran, however, I can already clearly identify An Troigh Mhairbh as the antithesis of that good step which would be, if one could take it, the human equivalent of the dolphin's wavelike plunge among the waves.

LOOKING BACK

Because I know little about it, the final mile of this sequence of the highest cliffs has, now I come to write about it, a certain grand simplicity in my memory. I have walked it often enough alone, and in conversations with people from the western villages I have heard many of its placenames mentioned, but since it is so remote I have not been able to persuade any of the elderly men who could give me its lore in detail to accompany me there, and so the pairings between names and places remain indeterminate and therefore barren. This fortunately permits me to compress the decrescendo into a few generalities and bring my book swiftly down from dizzy elevations to a moment of relaxed retrospection.

The last of the tall promontories is Binn an tSléibhe Mhóir, which answers to and derives its name from An Sliabh Mór, the big hill, a low ridge crossing the uplands, beyond which the island declines step by step to its western tip. At each stage as one follows this descent along the cliffs a wider view opens up to the north-west. The little uninhabited Brannock Islands appear off the end of Árainn, low, flat and curiously shaped like two bits from a giant jigsaw puzzle, with the vertical white-black-white-black-white of the lighthouse on the farther of them. As one advances, a vast panorama pivoting on the lighthouse is slowly revealed. Far away on the Atlantic horizon are the glittering teeth of the Skerd Rocks and their leaping breakers; then comes Slyne Head and the first low hills of the mainland, and then by degrees the deep heart of Connemara unfolds such an arcanum of colours that it appears a painted fantasy realm quite unattainable from the grey shores of Aran; I remember that, having looked across at it for years, I could still hardly believe in it when at last I went and climbed among those mountains and learnt with my hands their strange sphagnum-greens, heather-wines and scree-silvers.

Once past An Sliabh Mór the coast steps down sharply over a scarp leading inland to the village of Bun Gabhla hidden in a hollow to the north. Then the gravity-demons that rule the heights make a last stand on An Carnán, a curious turret of rock, half a conical hillock left hanging over the sea by recession of the cliffs. A cliffman who had spent some years in America and forgotten his native skills fell to his death here once. He was being lowered down on a rope, and clumsily let himself turn away from the cliff so that the rope caught in a crevice. The team tried to jerk it free, and it broke.

Half a mile on, the coast drops again by one main division of the limestone, where the upper storey of the cliff turns inland and runs northwards. A ledge marking the shale band between that storey and the one beneath it leads back along the sea-cliff from that same place, and although it narrows rather alarmingly at one point and there is still a considerable drop of perhaps forty or fifty feet below, one should master one's nerves and go along it and look up at the face of Binn an Iarainn, the cliff of the iron, which is marvellously streaked from top to bottom with every colour of a rusty spectrum.

The opening of this ledge (Ulán na gCrosán, the ledge of the razorbills) is a natural resting-point from which to study the final quarter-mile of coast that lies ahead, a study that throws a light on all that has gone before, the entire succession of the bays and promontories of Barr Aille. A storm beach has formed along the lower tract of shore between this point and an isolated flat-topped hillock that terminates the southern coast. This hillock stands a little south of the general line of the coast, and the glen that cuts it off from the rest of Árainn is, with one exception, unique in the island in that it runs parallel to that line. The heaped boulders of the storm beach obscure the nearer end of the glen, but one can see that it is continued in an east-south-easterly direction by a little gorge running down into the sea, where breakers seem to extrapolate its trend back along the line of the cliffs. The southern side of this gorge is a peculiarly smooth rock face like that of the fault-plane revealed at An Sraoilleán, for the relative movement here has left the strata on the landward side of the glen about twelve feet lower than their continuations on the seaward side. Apart from the two very small faults encountered previously, this is the first sign of such disruption of the rock-layers we have come across, every other valley in Aran being explicable in terms of erosion opening up joints of the limestone, without relative movement of the ground on either side.

If on a map one rules a line through this glen and produces it back along the entire length of the south coast, one finds that the line passes just offshore of all the major headlands, and that nearly every point of the cliffs is within a quarter of a mile of it. Now this overall straightness of Árainn's cliff coast calls for geological explanation, and perhaps this fault provides it. Could this be the initial weakness that formed as it were the starting-line from which the cliffs have been slowly eaten back by the sea? Or is there another fault farther out and parallel to this one that explains the linearity

of the coast? At one time, presumably, the strata that dip so regularly across the breadth of the island to the cliffs continued in the
same gentle slope to sea level, as they still do in Inis Meáin and
Inis Oírr. Some such break in their structure may have initiated
the development of the cliffs—a development that is still proceeding, for the sea's steady excavations are in fact increasing the height
of the cliffs as they are cut farther and farther back into the sloping strata. We are talking here, most soberly, of processes continuous over tens of millions of years; the fallacy of the wilder theories
that have been spun about formerly existent land to the south of
Aran, inhabited by Celts and guarded by the dúns, is that they fail
to distinguish between such geological aeons and the brief thousands of years of the human presence. In fact this little glen is like
a window in the whole human experience; to look back through it
along the headlands that stand as if fixed for all eternity, one behind another to the limits of vision, is to look into the jaws of
time.

This valley of such theoretical potency is called Gleainnín an
Ghrióra, the little plateau south of it is Maoilín an Ghrióra, a
maoilín being a flat-topped hillock, and the wide terrace sloping
gently into the sea south of that is An Gríóir itself, the Gregory; thus
the saint is celebrated at either end of the island. The eighteenth-
century natural philosopher, Richard Kirwan of Galway, had a
theory that Galway Bay was originally a granite mountain that
was "shattered and swallowed," and he notes that there was a vast
mass of granite called the Gregory on one of the Isles of Aran,
which was shattered by lightning in 1774. However, it seems that
the local tradition was merely that it disappeared one night. No
doubt it was an especially big glacial erratic like the other granite
boulders of Aran, and if it stood on the terrace now known as the
Gregory it is quite possible that a storm swept it off, for gigantic
blocks of limestone have come and gone here in the time I have
known the place.

An Maoilín itself is cliffed on the south and west, and a few
paces beyond its western face the terrace of An Gríóir is separated

by another small vertical drop from the final, most westerly, expanse of the shelving rocky shore, Na Leacracha Móra, the big flags. This little cliff again marks a fault and it is faced with calcite (the rust-tinged white crystals like little skew-sided bricks) and quartz (the tiny glittering crystals with six-faceted pyramids on their ends), which were deposited geological ages ago from hot solutions forcing their way up the fault-plane from deep in the earth. Faults tend to occur in lattice patterns; this one is roughly at right angles to the larger one aligned with the cliffs, and there are one or two more of either orientation to the west and north. As well as such breaks in the continuity of the rocks, vague undulations of the limestone thicknesses and the shale bands are visible all around this end of the island. For instance if one looks back at An Maoilín from Na Leacracha Móra one sees that its strata are slightly arched. Nothing similar is to be seen elsewhere in the islands or in the corresponding strata of north-west Clare as far as the south-eastern limit of the Burren, where a much more intense folding has produced the strange swooping terraces of the Mullach Mór.

An Grióir itself, the great field of rock standing out into the sea south of An Maoilín, is the most sociable spot on the whole southern coast. On a fine Sunday afternoon in August when the mackerel are coming in on a rising tide a row of men and boys from the western villages stands along its edge, casting out their lines as far as they can to where the gulls and gannets are diving. After walking the cliffs we often stop there to sit on the uncomfortable wave-nibbled rock and watch a friend reel in the silver flashes that will be our dinner, and look back along the way we have taken. From this viewing-platform uniquely set out beyond the line of the cliffs and mysteriously exempted from the engulfment of all the rest of the land that formerly stood south of the fault-line, one can see and try to identify all the headlands, one beyond another, fading back from vivid reality into gold or grey oblivion, bearing with them their seabirds, flowers, brachiopods and ghosts of the old cliffmen. However beguiling the sun and breeze, however fascinating the life and lore of the clifftops, I can never walk those heights without bringing home like burs on my clothes the seeds of nightmare. This retrospective spot itself belongs in spirit to the northern reaches of the coast, which are more frequented, more touched by the life of roads, fields, and villages, more humanized. The long cliff sequence of this circuit of Árainn, a walk along the brink of one's own unbeing, is now completed.

II. EXCURSION

Seán and Beartla, fishermen of Bun Gabhla, like to catch the BBC coastal weather reports at 8:05 a.m. before deciding whether or not to launch their currach for the day. They had promised to give me a lift out to the Brannock Islands on the first suitable morning, so I had set my alarm clock to wake me in time to cycle the four miles westwards to Bun Gabhla for the moment of decision. From my bedroom window the North Sound looked smooth enough to me, so I dressed and ate, and leapt onto my bike. It was a grey morning, in the April of a belated spring. The ease with which I sailed up to Seán's bungalow high on Aran's westernmost hill should have told me there was more wind at my back than I thought. Seán, opening his door, looked surprised to see me. "You're not going anywhere today!" he said, and led me through to the kitchen. The four children were waiting around the table with silent sleepy smiles while Bríd buttered scones for them. Behind them the picture window held a dark panorama of the Connemara coast eight miles away, and Seán pointed out the sparks of white flickering all along its base, tiny images of the breakers one could expect on Aran's southern shores that day. The radio was impassively reciting a familiar litany of winds veering south and south-west, increasing gale force 8 and severe gale force 9, etcetera, in a string of sea areas including Shannon. But Shannon is a vast tract of ocean and many a gale out there never troubles Aran; and Beartla's coming in for the conference at that moment (silently materializing in what was evidently his habitual way, without knocking) also gave me hope that the day was not quite out of the question. But then again my few previous encounters

with Beartla had led me to associate him with weather unsuitable
for whatever is in hand. Once I had found him pulling rye for
thatch on a sweaty July afternoon, savagely yanking the handfuls
out of the ground and beating the soil off the roots with vicious
blows against his boot; once gloomily looming up on his bike out
of a wet white mist, going to milk a distant cow; once slamming
nails into splintery boards to make a shed for his donkey at the
bitterly windy gable of his cottage. Bríd handed round mugs of
tea, and while I chatted with the children I kept an eye on the two
tall Aran men standing in the window against the sky they were
weighing up. Seán's wide-shouldered stance and gingery aureole of
whisker and hair spelt robust commonsense, Beartla's lank darkness a pessimism verging on despair. Beartla's body is a long line of
what would be poetry if one could only get the hang of its metre:
a loose linkage of lean and rigid lengths, a Swiss knife of bladed
and pointed implements (scythe, pitchfork, spade) capable of unexpected leverages (crowbar, pickaxe) and fierce twists (wrench,
vice), which works with dogged grimness or folds up completely
(crouched under a wall from the rain) or sprawls abandoned (leaning back in his chair till nearly horizontal, heels at the hearth and
hand raised at the gaping door of his cottage to every passer-by);
his brows, nose and lips are blades at work too, sickles and bill-
hooks, impatiently and dangerously hacking away in the long
hummocky field of his face, around two deep eye-wells brimming
with darkness, tenderness and melancholy.

Beartla's eloquence is not verbal; Seán on the other hand has a
word for every moment. Now he interrupted Bríd's marshalling of
the children for school to make them show me the baby wild rabbits they had in a cardboard box; and then, as Bríd recaptured the
children, stuffed their arms into sleeves, hung satchels about them
and herded them out to the car, he told me what a plague rabbits
have become on the islands in recent years. They are destroying
pastures, and it seems cattle refuse grass fouled by them. Many
Aran people will not eat rabbits as they believe they interbreed
with the half-wild cats that live on the crags; a neighbour of Seán's

had actually seen a rabbit and a cat in a field doing something which Seán wouldn't quite specify but which proved the point. I said that that was completely impossible, and that the cats one sees waiting by rabbit holes are hunting, not courting. But Seán was doubtful. "You wouldn't know," he said. "The cats and the rabbits down on the football-field are getting that friendly they're practically walking about hand in hand!"

It seemed to have been decided in the meantime that it was worth going down to the shore at any rate, so we finished our mugs of tea and left the warmth of the kitchen range. Seán took Beartla on the pillion of his scooter and I followed on my bike, whirring down the twisted mile of road and track that finally jolts to a stop among the stones of Cladach Bhun Gabhla, the shore pertaining to Bun Gabhla village. We climbed the shinglebank and considered the outlook. This is Aran's most westerly shore, and the nearer of the two uninhabited Brannock Islands faces it across half a mile of rock-strewn water. Waves were rolling into the channel from either end; not very menacing ones, I thought, but my companions looked dubious. And then the waves were suddenly much larger; grey humps were bulging and jostling in the middle of the channel and blasts of foam were jumping over the southern point of the island. This was decisive. We turned away, and without a word Beartla wandered off along the tide-mark, stopping here and there to pick up a few thick stems of sea-weed, flinging them up the shore to be added to a small collection of them he had drying on a wall nearby. (An alginates factory in Connemara buys these "searods" at a price that makes collecting them worth while when nothing better offers.) Meanwhile I per-suaded Seán to walk a sector of the coast to the north with me and tell me the names of all its ins and outs. But after half a mile or so the rain came on heavily. Seán took a short cut directly up the crags to his house on the skyline; I turned back for my bike and cycled home drenched.

The gales gave up the game after a few days and a suitable morning showed itself in my bedroom window. It was still and grey as I cycled westwards; a few small cloudbanks were sitting on the water in the North Sound. The children and Bríd were about to go eastwards to school and Seán and Beartla westwards to the shore when I arrived. By the time I had caught up with them again they were inspecting the currach which was lying upside-down supported by its thwarts on little piles of stones, with one or two others by a field-wall near the end of the road.

Currachs, being made of tarred canvas stretched over a framework of laths, are easily holed on rocks and easily repaired by tarring on a canvas patch. Some people still make their own currachs, but this one had come from the boatyard in Inis Oírr where an aged craftsman pursues his hereditary trade. Seán told me that it had cost him £30 in 1968. (One like it would cost six or seven hundred pounds today.) The Aran currach is a narrow keel-less boat, sharp-prowed and square-sterned, with two to four thwarts; Seán's had three thwarts and was twenty-one feet long, which made it a heavy load for two to carry down to the water—but to have a third man sharing the catch would have been uneconomical. Seán's currach, thick with old patches and lumpy black from repeated tarrings, was worn but water-tight. He heaved up its prow, Beartla crept in under it and straightened up with the forward thwart on his shoulders, Seán went in behind him and shouldered up the rear thwart, and then they walked slowly and unsteadily under the eclipsing load, holding it by the thole-pins, up the shinglebank and down over the slippery rocks to the margin of the sea. (Books on the West of Ireland invariably liken a currach carried thus by two or three men to a giant black beetle, very accurately; but the sight always makes me see, nonsensically, a short procession wearing a huge communal hat.) At the water's edge Seán and Beartla lurched sideways and let the currach roll off them into the foam swilling over a sheet of rock that has been slightly improved into a slip. Then they got into their bright yellow oilskins and put their gear into the currach—buoys, nets, bait, two oars, the outboard motor, a flask of tea and a bag of buttered scones. A few stones for ballast and a little plastic bottle of holy water jammed behind a rib of the bows completed the outfitting. I asked them to put in another pair of oars so that I could try my hand at rowing. They intended to visit lobsterpots set here and there around the Brannock Islands, and it was decided they would land me on the farther island, where the lighthouse is, transfer me to the nearer island after a few hours, and collect me from there at the end of the day.

The first pots were not far away, so the morning silence was spared the motor for a while and Beartla and I took the oars. I was to take the stroke from him, behind me in the bows. The currach oar is a hefty pole with one face of its outer third flattened to give a blade no wider than its stock. A thick triangular tab with a round hole in it on the side of the stock fits over the thole-pin, a stout wooden peg set in the gunwale. The handle is long, to give more leverage, and so the two oars overlap and are pulled cross-handed. I soon found out that the beginner tends to bump the knuckles of one hand against the opposite handle; the trick, as Seán pointed out, is to keep the handle on the windward side higher than the other, the difference in angles of the oars then compensating for the tilt of the boat away from the wind. The stroke is fast and rather short. In fact we shot off as if in a race— probably Beartla was trying to test my stamina—until one of his thole-pins snapped and he did a complicated jack-knife into the bows. As he moodily groped around under himself for a replacement for the pin and battered it into place with a stone from the ballast, Seán made a few sententious observations such as: "That would be bad, now, if we were under the cliffs!"

The first two pots hauled up were empty, so Seán mounted the outboard and we sped away round the southern point of the first island, outlying slabs of which reared up over us black and dripping, with the sea fighting itself in clefts and caverns below. Seán shouted out little volleys of placenames and pointed wildly as we drove past the promontories and I wrestled with my flapping map and notebook in the spray. I got An Bodach Crom, the hunch-backed lout, in the right place at any rate, on the outside of the south-westernmost point; the cliff profile with its tiny punched-in nose and great barnacled chin was unmistakable. Then we were approaching the south-east corner of the farther island, where a long jetty about a yard wide comes angling out, with a flight of slippery little steps down its outer face. A heavy swell coming round the corner made the currach buck, and Seán inched us in with extreme caution, while Beartla held me back from trying a leap until the three or four small waves that always follow four or five big ones came; then at a moment when we were almost motionless: "Out with you, quick!"—and I was slithering up the steps on all fours while the boat wallowed away below me. The jetty deposited me, rather shaken and chilled, on a wide wet flag of rock, where I paused to wave to the fishermen as the currach pranced off into the uneasy ocean.

A faint worn mark led across the rock-sheets to a neatly consolidated gap in the mighty storm beach that hid the interior of the island. The Irish name of An tOileán Iarthach, the western island, as it is called, is anglicized as Earragh Island, but in English it is more often called Rock Island. It is in fact all rock, as I saw when I passed through the gap in the storm beach, except for one or two little hollows in which there is enough soil to have prompted someone, probably a bored lighthouse keeper, to project a vegetable patch, which had not prospered. From the gap a track leads north to the high-walled enclosure about the lighthouse and its living-quarters. I diverged from the track and roamed to and fro across the interior as far as the rock-bank that sprawls over much of its western half, feeling rather self-conscious ferreting about in the silent emptiness under the cold observation of the crystal-headed tower. The only human touches to the intimidatingly barren terrain were a few roofless outhouses, a ruined limekiln and occasional wedge-marks in the rock where blocks had been levered out for the building of the lighthouse over a century ago.

By degrees I worked round to the gateway of the great barracks-square and went in to look at the tower (cylindrical, white with two broad horizontal bands of black, and a little green door) and the living-quarters (a long, single-storied building of grey cut limestone, with more green doors), and after some knocking found one of the keepers in a room full of comfortable smells and warmth. A radio was giving out brief yelps and long crackling silences. The man keeping an ear on it couldn't leave his post but said that if I wanted to go up and see the light I was welcome to do so; the tower was "on the latch." I crossed the yard again and opened the green door of the lighthouse. A spiral staircase led me up, green banister-rail of iron on the left and a curved grey wall of impeccably cut stone full of fossil shells on the right. A lacy black floor of cast iron surrounded the light, a gigantic prismatic pineapple of glass and brass, a model universe inhabited by rainbows and sunbursts. I tried to summon up a practical understanding of it and thought about Fresnel lenses and acetylene lamps for a bit; I dutifully copied from a plaque on the wall:

Earragh Lighthouse
Light first established 1st Dec. 1857
Present apparatus 1904
375,000 candelas
115 ft above High Water

—and then I gave up and turned to survey the dismal geography below. The island is a battered oval plain a third of a mile long from north to south, with a hillock added onto the north-west where a long point of rock runs out into the waves, which today were fretful. The storm beach encircles all the low-lying ground except to the east of the tower, and it has spilled inwards over much of the western sector. Outside it in that direction is a hundred yards of wet rock shelving smoothly into a rim of surge and spume, and beyond that nothing but the wan curve of the world that hides America. I soon descended to the frowsty room with the radio, where several men were now gathered.

It transpired that I had chosen a bad time to call, for the helicopter bringing a relieving crew was even now on its way from its base at Cork, while the departing men were busy packing, their minds on the coming "month off" rather than the expiring "month on." A polygonal radio argument was in progress between the helicopter pilot, a controller at Shannon airport, and the various lighthouses to be called at in some order which was to be optimized. I soon saw that the Lighthouse Service's toughest logistical problem is the productivity of those empty hours of the "month on," the ships-in-Dimple-Haig-bottles, lighthouses made of matchsticks, balsawood Connemara cottages, raffia-work stools and red-sails-in-the-sunset done in luminous string pegged out on black velvet, all fragile and voluminously wrapped, which their originators felt should have precedence in the helicopter's hold over empty gas-cylinders and the like. At last the pilot, rapidly approaching the point where he had to decide whether to head first for South Aran (i.e. Inis Oírr's lighthouse), "Slyne" (Slyne Head light, off Connemara) or "North Aran" (the Earragh light), ordered everyone to go and measure and weigh their luggage and count the gas-cylinders. The room emptied except for an Aran man I knew slightly.

The lighthouse keeper (I generalize) is of a phlegmatic and inward temperament, engendered perhaps by the tinned diet of baked beans and Irish stew or the restriction of exercise to left-handed ascents and right-handed descents of the corkscrew stairs. But along with a formidable capacity for long silences, he has deeply buried resources of sardonic humour. We were talking about a school of dolphins we had both seen playing in and out of the bay at Cill Mhuirbhigh over a period of a few days not long before. I described how they had danced on an evening of silken calm, leaping clear of the water in graceful arcs that crossed in pairs; as I had sat in a little field above the bay to watch, their plunges had been the only sound in the world. He listened to me expressionlessly, then turned his eyes to the dingy window and the dingy sky beyond. "That's right," he said, "and on Sunday morning they were all kneeling on the beach!"

Then the buzz of the helicopter was heard and I went out to see it come, ladybird-red, hunched and leaning forward urgently. (Every second Friday we see it go by, a bright noisy little punctuation mark in Aran-time.) It clattered down and posed on tiptoe within the circle whitewashed on the bare ground of the yard. The rotor spun impatiently while the doors slid back, three men leapt to the ground, wrestled their bags and boxes out of the holds below, ran crouching under the blast to the living-quarters and disappeared through the little green doors as if eager to begin their month's vigil; the departing crew ran out equally eagerly, stuffed their goods in, slammed the curved gleaming scales of the hatches and scrambled aboard; the helicopter hopped into the air at a tilt and blew away over the high wall, thistledown in a hurry, and was gone. As the silence recollected itself I found myself alone in the yard.

At a loss, I loitered out of the gate and climbed onto a rock to see if Seán and Beartla were coming for me yet. The currach was far away off the north of the other island, and stationary. Land, sea and sky agreed on dullness. Fighting the abject determination of mood by weather, I set off on a slow scientific tour of unpromising terrain to the north-west. I saw some grey-green leaves of rose-root, and the more usual Aran maritimers such as sea-pink, sea-campion, pellitory and wild angelica. In the deep crevices was a mysterious splendour of buttercup-gold: rank-stemmed and profusely flowering lesser celandine glowing in the dimness three or four feet below ground. And a more unusual find, a dwarf version of scurvy grass (a form of *Cochlearia danica*, I thought, but the botanical establishment later identified my specimen, rather hesitantly, as *C. officinalis*) in which the leaves were plump kidney-shaped pastilles only two millimetres across and the flowers were equally minute white stars.

I also saw one or two rats scuttling from crevice to crevice; they are there because of the lighthouse and despite the fact that a keeper once brought in some of the highly reputed magic soil of Tory Island to discourage them. Because of the rats, no birds nest on the island. But I did notice a collared dove sitting on the very farthest rock of the north-west headland and staring out to sea as if to make the point that the whole of Aran has now been colonized by these recent arrivals (for this species has expanded across Europe from Turkey since the Thirties; it first nested in England in 1955, in Ireland in 1959, and has been part of the street-life of Cill Rónáin since about 1973 so far as I can discover). The perch of this specimen suggested some thoughts about the oddness of the dusky Levantine coming within sight of the glacial fulmar, for that species only started to spread south and east from Iceland in the 1870s, and now nests nearly all round the coasts of Ireland and Britain. But communities of different birds are not only mutually infertile but mutually invisible, it seems; nor did my thoughts come together fruitfully, so I moved on. Desolation threatened; I wished I were at home. I was bored and cold by the time I came round to the landing-place again. The currach was lurching in to the quay, and I had to steel myself for the slimy steps and the awkward jump aboard.

Landing on the other island is much easier as there is a bay on its south coast where a currach can be nosed onto a little beach of sand. Two islets, each a single four- or five-acre slab of rock, stand protectively south and south-east of the bay and are joined to its western arm by a natural mole of jumbled boulders called An Clochar Bán, the white stone-heap, from the brightness of its outer face perpetually shuffled and scuffed by the sea. The bay is simply An Caladh, the harbour, and it is so sheltered that the Bun Gabhla men have their *potaí stóir*, the big wooden cases in which the catch of lobsters is accumulated and kept alive until it is worth taking across to Ros a' Mhíl, floating at anchor here.

But the protection offered by An Clochar Bán can be delusive. As we edged in through the shallows Seán told me about a drowning here long ago. Two Connemara smugglers were sailing by on their way to Kerry with a cargo of *poitín*, the illicit barley spirits, when rising seas forced them to run for this bay. (Their boat was a *gleoiteóg*, a small version of the "hooker," Connemara's famous single-masted wooden work-boat.) They moored the boat and came ashore to sit out the night and the storm in the lee of a boulder. But with the storm at its height on the top of the tide, waves began to break over An Clochar Bán and burst into the bay from the rear. One of the men went down to see if the moorings were holding, slipped between boat and shore, and was swept away in the darkness.

Seán went on to tell of an incident early in this century when several Bun Gabhla men were weather-bound here for a few days. Their friends and families could see them across the raging channel but had no way of getting food to them. The local agent of the British steam trawlers that used to call in at Cill Rónáin in those days, a retired English army officer called Smith, persuaded one of the trawler captains to sail round, and the men were got off successfully. But Smith suffered a fall on deck during the rescue which re-awoke an old war wound, and he died not long afterwards. (The Aran lifeboat service was instituted, in 1927, as a result of the publicity this event attracted, I have been told.)

Fortified by these precedents, I made ready to be marooned once more. By this time the sun had bored through the greyness and was sprinkling the little bay with welcome. The Aran men jumped ashore with me to stretch their cramped limbs for a few minutes, and we discussed the island's name. Since not even Seán had an opinion as to its significance, I gave them some of the various suppositions I had come across (thus thoroughly muddying the wells for future researchers).

According to the Placenames Department of the Ordnance Survey, this island is Oileán Dá Bhranóg (and hence by anglicization Brannock Island, whence the two islands are collectively The

Brannock Islands). So far as I know the only warrant for adopting this version of the Irish name is a mention in O'Flaherty's *West Connaught*: "There is a waste island on the south-west side, called Oilenda-branoge, where they go to slaughter seals yearly, and where there is abundance of samphire." O'Flaherty here is using English phonetic values to convey the sound of the Irish name; the official Placenames Department version gives it a grammatically respectable spelling, but the sense remains obscure.

Bran is an old literary word for "raven," so some writers have suggested that the name means "island of the two little ravens," the *-óg* being a diminutive. But *bran* also means "bream," a fish that used to be a feature of this coast (and *brannóg* means "gudgeon" according to the dictionaries and perhaps could refer to sundry small fish locally), so other derivations are possible. Again, a stone carrying the inscription in Old Irish, "Pray for Bran the Pilgrim," was found in the last century at "The Seven Churches" in Eoghanacht, and started some fusty speculation among scholars that a hermit saint called Bran lived here; *Dá Bhranóg* could then mean "your little Bran," for such affectionate and respectful possessives occur in other placenames of saintly origins.

All this, however, presupposes that the sound of the name is as represented by the official spelling, whereas both Aran and Connemara fishermen call it Oileán Dá Bhruithneog, and several of them have told me that a *bruithneog* is a batch of potatoes roasted in ashes such as outdoor workers might make for themselves in a hearth of a few stones put together. One Araner from whom I heard this derivation drove home his point by acting out for me the part of a boatman clambering ashore on the island, looking down in surprise and saying (in Irish) "Aha! Two batches of roast potatoes!" Can one imagine that this mythical boatman would go on to say "Therefore let this be the Island of the Two Batches of Roast Potatoes!"? An expert in the field of placenames to whom I mentioned this supposed derivation replied that "Some joker must have invented it." Perhaps so, but for all its absurdity it is the only current understanding of the name among the frequenters of the place.

Now, if the original sense of a placename cannot be retrieved, how does one prevent a placenames-study degenerating into the sterile exercise of preferring old mistakes to new ones? And even if a degree of probability is attainable, is a name's origin always its most vital factor? A placename (of the questionable sort I am discussing) is perpetually gathering and shedding meanings; it comes down to us a loose bundle which may or may not still contain that kernel, the intitial grain of sense that set it rolling through time. Taken as a cluster of more or less untutored guesses at its origin, the placename (in this wider interpretation) may appear ridiculous—witness the present agglomeration of raven, bream, pilgrim and roast potato. But if read as a mnemonic for a history of the mind's responses to a mysterious marriage of sound and place, the placename can be a word of power—a password, perhaps, to that "step" foreshadowed in the introduction to this book.

Some of above I imparted to Seán and Beartla as we ramped on the shinglebank and expanded in the sunshine. They assented guardedly, and withdrew to their narrow boat and wide sea. I turned and strode inland. A dozen donkeys grazing a thin sandy pasturage raised their heads to see me pass. There are perhaps twenty acres of not very nutritious grass here, of which the penultimate village of Aran, Creig an Chéirín, has the grazing rights, rather than Bun Gabhla as one would expect. Sometimes sheep are brought out here by currach in summer, and donkeys not wanted for work are towed out swimming and left to breed. There is a price to be got for donkeys from the tinkers who periodically call round Aran looking for them; so some of these castaways will ascend to the comparative heaven of being children's pets or seaside diversions, if they survive the purgatory of spray-soaked winters and parched summers here for long enough. Some do not survive, and there are skeletons on the closely nibbled turf to remind one of it. I skirted two or three of these revolting tents of bone and tattered hide, and went on eastwards, wondering what Bran the Pilgrim, if indeed he did penance here, felt that he deserved of the Hereafter. A natural train of thought brought me to the chocolate and the apple in my shoulder-bag; I found a soft and sheltered bank of the eastern shore looking out towards Árainn, where smoke was rising from the chimneys of Bun Gabhla up on the hill, and sat down to eat.

Blue was winning over grey, above and below. I began to savour the aimless life of the beachcomber, and stretched myself out, feeling a not-unpleasant vacuum in my mind. After a while of dozing, a sound like mice rehearsing a crowd-scene opened my eyes. A fleet of small birds, portly as bath-ducks, black with neat white flashes on either wing, was bobbing in the ripples beyond my boots: ten black guillemots. My mental note-taking reminded me that my project was to see all that was to be seen on this island in the time it would take Seán and Beartla to visit a dozen lobsterpots. I jumped to my feet, and a hundred herring gulls flapped up from a ridge close by to the north. There I found a swathe of boulders whitewashed with droppings, and nests everywhere among them, little pads of grey grassy stuff, but no eggs as yet. I looked for terns as I had heard that they nest here, but it was still too early in the season for them. Beyond the ridge I climbed a rise to the west, and found myself looking down a most unexpected cliff onto a sea-washed terrace fifty feet below. The cliff was deeply undercut. Two rectangular caverns ran far back into it under my feet, and huge blocks had dropped out of the overhangs to leave two long lintels above their entrances; the larger of these lintels was a single forty-foot span, accurately cut to a section about four feet wide and six deep. I followed the clifftop south and then west again to look back at this Egyptian fantasy of Nature. The caverns were massively pillared, and shafts of sunlight slanted down into their shadow from the openings above. I wished I had time to clamber down to the terrace and explore those operatic portals, strike a pose perhaps (to the applause of herring gulls?) as High Priest of some netherworldly cult. I was amazed that I had never even heard report of this, the most magnificent piece of Aran's cliff-architecture. Later I learned from the currach-men that it had no name; they supposed that it must have come into existence since the time of the *seandream*, the old folk, that dateless but definitively extinct generation to which the naming of every feature of the islands, if not of the world, is attributed.

The cliffs steadily declined from that magnificence towards the south-west, and the storm beach I was following along their tops grew and finally merged into the great bank of boulders, An Clochar Bán, that shields the little anchorage from westerlies. Seán and Beartla had not yet reappeared, so I set out along the *clochar*, slipping among mounds of seaweed and gurgling rock-pools, towards the islet a quarter of a mile to the south-west.

This appendage to Oileán Dá Bhranóg turned out to be a scale model of Árainn itself, as it rises in terraces from a low northern coast and then slants very slightly southwards and ends in cliffs. The other islet just east of it has the same form; so does An Creachoileán Mór, another islet attached to the south end of the Bun Gabhla shore, and so does Maoilín an Ghrióra, the curious flat-topped hillock separated from the rest of Árainn by the fault-line running back along the general trend of the whole cliff coast. If that fault, which could be connected with the origin of the cliffs, also extends westwards, it should pass under An Clochar Bán (and then just south of An tOileán Iarthach), and these four strikingly similar little end-stops to Árainn would lie along its southern side, like a row of points of suspension....And indeed I found a slanting cleft running in the right direction; it was obscured by boulders and seaweed and the first limbs of the incoming tide (and I haven't yet inveigled a geologist out there to check that it is a fault); but when I looked along its course to the east-south-east, there was the little valley of the fault-line, Gleann an Ghrióra, making a notch in the skyline of Árainn through which all the headlands of the Atlantic coast appeared one behind another in diminishing perspective to the horizon, as simple in their old age as ABC.

The islet I had now reached, a two-hundred yard slab of rock (An Gob Thiar, the western tip; the other is An Gob Thoir, the eastern tip), must have been much frequented by previous generations as it has a number of named features. Along its western face is a shelf called Leic na Creathnaí, from its dense red carpet of *creathnach*, a sort of dulse, a small edible seaweed which used to be gathered here. I tried a bit: deliciously sweet and salty, and then chewy, with a savour fading to rubbery zero. Dulse is still sought after in the West of Ireland. Country women take an apron-pocketful of it to nibble while standing behind their vegetable stalls or baskets of eggs in Galway's street market, as I have observed. Beyond this "flag-stone of the *creathnach*" is the cliff-profile of the hunchback bully, An Bodach Crom, which Seán had pointed out earlier in the day. Beyond that again, the last few feet of the islet are almost divided from the rest by a fissure full of surging sounds, Scailp na mBallach Mór, the cleft of the big rockfish. And finally Carraig na bPiseog, the rock of the bream (the Aran for "bream" being *piseog* rather than *bran* as in the dictionaries). Standing on this ultimate fisherman's perch from which one can cast an eye over an uninterrupted hemisphere of ocean—I saw the currach coming to fetch me home, and turned to hurry back across rocks and seaweed and the little gasping inrushes of the tide.

Seán and Beartla had finished putting the day's catch into the crate moored in the bay by the time I reached the sand, and I splashed out through the shallows to meet them. There were fat little starfish washing about in the bottom of the currach, and a few rockfish giving occasional twitches in a bag under a thwart. I was pleased with all I had seen; they were moderately content with their takings of sixteen lobsters, though they had been doing better before the storms. And now they were eager to be home, and sent the currach skipping through the waves to Bun Gabhla shore. We threw all the gear ashore and leapt out. Beartla, looking off towards the horizon, silently filled the plastic bag I had brought for plant specimens with crab claws for me (the disarmed crabs having gone into the *pota stóir* to feed the lobsters). Then they rolled the boat upside-down, raised it on their shoulders and staggered up to its parking-place. They ran back for the engine, the oars, the rockfish for their supper. "That's our day's work done!" cried Seán delightedly. They stepped out of their oilskins and left them exactly where they fell on the shinglebank, and I suddenly understood what a familiar and private place this wilderness is to the Bun Gabhla men, who expect to see neither tourists (except during a few weekends of high summer) nor their own womenfolk here, and scatter their clothes and nets about it without a thought, the utmost of their care being to put a stone on top to stop them blowing away if it might turn windy. The two fishermen roared off on the scooter and I toiled up the hill after them on my bike, tired, but feeling the day's moods settle down and jigsaw together into contentment. Seán was at the door of his house as I came by, and I turned in to thank him and to drink my tea. I asked him to check all the placenames I had scribbled on my map and make sure I had them all in the right positions, which he did most scrupulously. The children were just coming in from school as I left.

III. NORTH

PREMONITIONS

The score of miles that will close the circuit of Árainn, leading back from the Bun Gabhla shore by way of the north coast to the eastern tip of the island, begins with a brief reprise of the cliff-theme of the southern coast, and thereafter unfolds its own individualities. Individualities in the plural, because the experiences it offers oscillate between two extremes. The grim rock-banks of the more exposed stretches of coast, in grey weather almost intolerably desolate, alternate with bays in which a degree of shelter has allowed the accumulation not only of bright sands and shingles but of history, of a residual human warmth that the fogs and winter storms do not quite dispel. A walk that takes one in and out of these bays dips into various eras of the past—the Age of the Saints, the centuries of Aran's military significance, the birthpangs of the modern fishing fleet, the brief and dazzling reign of Flaherty the film-maker—each of which has brought lasting life to its elected sites. On the other hand the intervening monotonies were dedicated only to a laborious task, perennial throughout the darkest times but now abandoned, the cropping and burning of seaweed; and that whole long Kelp Age has no monument other than a few stones scattered and scarcely identifiable among millions of others on the storm beach.

In general the severity of the coast moderates from west to east, from the cliffs that face the north-western gales, by way of low rocky shores and shinglebanks, to the sand dunes in the shelter of Cill Éinne bay. The smaller bays that punctuate this modulation (one can distinguish about a dozen of them), and in particular Port Mhuirbhigh which almost makes a separate island out of the western third of Árainn, produce the sort of focusing of the landscape that is one of the ways in which mere location is intensified into *place*. By these hearths even the wandering sea pauses. On the coasts between them, however, even the most soundly situated human can wander into uncentred and uncentering moods.

LEVIATHAN

The north-western coast of Árainn, from the wind-shadow of the Brannock Islands to the point where it turns east and faces Connemara, is open to the Atlantic, and rises in cliffs to stand against the gales and look out onto the ocean beyond Slyne Head. A fault parallel to the one at An Grióir breaks this mile of cliffs into two ranges, the western one lower than the eastern. One can walk around the coast from Port an Choma under the lower cliffs on a wide terrace of green-fringed rock-pools. If the weather is blowy one may have to time a dash between a rock-pool and the foam leaping up over the edge of the terrace at one point, but unless the tide is very high one can usually pick one's way around a jutting angle of the cliff called An Coirnéal, the corner, to the loveliest seclusion of this rarely visited facet of the island. There is an odd rakishness, a mettlesome spirit, running through the cubism of the rocks of this natural esplanade, which must be the combined effect of its undulant surface, the general twist the nearby fault has given to the vicinity, and the carefree poise of a square-faced block—I am sure it must measure forty feet each way—that has detached itself from the cliff against which it leans one elbow, and stands on two fat little legs looking as if it were about to skip into the sea with the ponderous charm of one of Picasso's surreal beach-girls. Just beyond it a boulder-filled creek marks the fault, and by comparing thicknesses of rock one can see that the terrace one is standing on here matches up with a level thirty feet higher in the cliffs on its east. This is quite insignificant compared to the faults geologists can trace in other parts of the world, with vertical "throws" of thousands of feet or horizontal displacements of many miles, but this disruption is on an exhilarating, only-just-superhuman scale, like the Picasso bather; the gloss of its slanting fault-face on the other side of the creek makes its energy palpable, and yet by scrambling up the wave-worn cleft of the fault-line to the clifftop beyond it one can surmount the little cataclysm in a couple of minutes.

From these higher cliffs, one fine Easter Sunday, I watched a basking shark rolling lazily in the sun-filled water below. I remember the date because the visitor with me had just discovered a few dusty shards of chocolate-egg in the bottom of his knapsack, and I associate the unexpected taste unfolding as we rested there with the materialization of the strange shape in our idle view. Its black dorsal fin arose first and its long snout with a little bow-wave, and then we saw its submerged bulk vaguely embodied in a slowly gliding net of ripple-shadow and sun-spangles. As its mouth gaped, its gills opened like five huge ruffs. I could not say how big it was—basking sharks of over forty feet in length and weighing more than three tons have been recorded, but I think our specimen was not quite in that class. By an irresistible paradox this, the world's biggest fish, eats only the smallest specks of life, and when it comes to the surface to yawn and loll about like this it is straining plankton out of the copious floods of water (up to twenty tons a minute) pouring in at its mouth and out by its fringed gills. In Irish it is called *An Liamhán Mór* or *An Liamhán Gréine*, the great *liamhán* (is this word derived from the biblical Leviathan, I wonder?) or the *liamhán* of the sun, and in English it used to be known in these regions as the sunfish too, because of its appearing inshore in the spring, to browse off the billions of copepods and other small fry multiplying in the sun-warmed surface waters. Not much is known of the rest of its life, except that after a winter of fasting and torpor out in the deeps it seems to make its way slowly northwards up the Atlantic coasts of Europe, and disappears again.

The commercial value of the basking shark, which lies in the oil from its gigantic liver, used to be so high that in the eighteenth and nineteenth centuries the shark fishery was second only to the herring in importance for the Galway Bay fleet. The men of Aran, Connemara and the Claddagh, Galway's fishing quarter, used to hunt the monsters from small open boats with hand-held harpoons. There is an account in Tom O'Flaherty's *Aranmen All,* given in suitably gargantuan terms, of how his grandfather organized the man of Gort na gCapall to the hunt when after many years of absence the sharks were once more spotted from the clifftops. All available tackle—"spears, gaffs, bocáns, pocáns, buoys, bireógs, straimpíns, long knives and poles and chains taken from a ship wrecked at the Big Cleft"—was assembled and carried down to Port Bhéal an Dúin; a spear was attached by a rope and a cable to a chain wound around a big boulder in a deep pot-hole of the shore; five three-man currachs were launched, a shark was eventually speared, and when it had run itself to exhaustion another team of fifteen men hauled it ashore. The livers used to be boiled in iron cauldrons to extract the oil, which was sent to the mainland in barrels. Some of it was used in Aran for burning in the little lights called *muiríní,* consisting of a piece of rush as a wick lying in a scallop-shell of oil; shark oil was preferred to dogfish oil when it could be got, as it was less smelly and smoky. But when paraffin become available the oil lost its value, and the fishery was abandoned.

It seems the shark was absent again for years around the turn of the century, but it had reappeared a few seasons before Robert Flaherty arrived to make *Man of Aran,* and the shark-hunt was revived to give him a climactic episode for the film. Flaherty even had ideas of interesting buyers in the oil from the sharks caught on that occasion, and so restoring the industry to the islands, but the price at that time was too low for profit. Since then nobody in Aran had troubled about the fish, until the day described above on which we watched one from the cliffs and at the same time an idea was occurring to an Aran man on the hilltop behind us. We met him on our way home—a Cill Rónáin trawlerman who, when on land, spends as much time as possible looking at the sea, and on Sundays likes to put the family in the car and drive to some vantage point from which he can use his binoculars while they drowse and squabble and read the newspapers. This time he was watching a small trawler out in the North Sound which he told us was a Norwegian poacher making a big killing in a shoal of basking shark. Every few minutes we could see splashing as a shark was hauled on board and its carcass flung off again as soon as the liver had been cut out. At that time such plunderers had little to fear from the sparse patrols and mild penalties that guarded Irish fisheries, and in any case this massacre was not one to which the local fishermen objected, as they preferred the risk of catching one of the drifting corpses in their salmon-nets to that of a live shark entangling itself and destroying the net entirely. The Norwegians' example interested our Aran friend considerably and it prompted him to make enquiries of a firm in Achill Island, where the shark is still caught in fixed nets off the headlands. He found that there is a market for the oil, which has engineering applications as a fine lubricant—we were even told that a few drops of it went to the moon with the Apollo missions—and for the fins, which end up in Chinese shark's fin soup. So two or three owners of half-deckers entered into agreements with the Achill concern, and hired and mounted harpoon guns, and in the following year, 1980, the ancient fishery was briefly resurrected. Ever since *Man of Aran* the basking-shark hunt has been part of the romantic myth of Aran, and such was the interest in its revival that more boatloads of journalists than trawlers set forth, and many more photographs than sharks were taken. In fact sharks were few that year, and a vast amount of costly diesel fuel was burned in criss-crossing the seas from the Cliffs of Moher to far out beyond the Earragh lighthouse looking for them, and then in creeping up on them close enough for an inexpert harpooner to take a shot. The fishermen eventually tired of hearing from ambivalent shore-loafers like myself that a shark had been spotted, off the other end of the island the day before yesterday; then the salmon season took precedence and the harpoon guns were dismantled. The experiment was tried again with similar results in 1982, so one hopes that from now on the sun-loving basking shark will be able to take its vast and mysterious stroll, at least through Aran waters, in peace and safety.

A DIFFICULT MILE

The transition from one type of coast to another, from sheer cliff to low-lying rock-sheets bearing huge storm beaches, is accomplished in three dramatic steps around the most northerly arc of the island's perimeter. First the lower two-thirds of the cliff face steps out beyond the upper third, which continues eastwards as an inland scarp; a quarter of a mile farther on the bottom storey of the remaining sea-cliff moves outwards again while the upper storey runs on eastwards, and finally this last sea-wall divides, dwindles and straggles inland as benches of a stony slope above a shore of shallow rock-shelves. The upper of the two wide terraces between these three lines of cliff successively discarded by the coast is called Scrios na gCapall, the *scrios* of the horses, and the lower one is An Scrios Mór, the big *scrios*. This word means (in Árainn at least, for I have not come across its use in placenames elsewhere) a tract of land not much divided up by field-walls, and it occurs in half-a-dozen names of such areas around the island. In other contexts it means destruction or ruination, a scraping, or a thin covering (of soil, for instance). It may be that none of these connotations is relevant to the Aran usage. Scrios na gCapall in fact has comparatively deep soil from the weathering-out of the thick clay band under the cliffs behind it, together with one of the few aboriginal patches of soil, a reddish laterite formed by rotting of the limestone in a subtropical climate, that has not been scraped away by the Ice Ages. So it is a grassy area, and not only were horses grazed on it but before rabbits become the plague they now are throughout the island people used to come here to hunt them.

An Scrios Mór, which lies lower and is within reach of the spray, is craggier, and although local people tell me that waves cannot climb up onto it, there is a storm beach along its edge, dating perhaps from five thousand years ago when the sea level was rather higher than it is today. Waves driven by modern storms can in any case very nearly scale the forty-foot cliff below this terrace, for after a long period of high but not unheard-of seas I noticed bright unweathered scars where a great weight of stone had been chipped out of its rim only just below the storm beach.

Grimness and desolation intensify from here on, as the coast falls more and more into the power of the sea. This storm beach fades out as the cliff carries it inland, but another starts on the lowest level where the tides come flooding in over wide flats and shallow steps of bare rock. At first it is merely a string of big isolated blocks swept along from under the last of the cliffs, but as one follows it eastwards it becomes a great reef up to twenty feet high that snakes along the coast, dividing the flat shore from the little fields in its lee, into which it occasionally spills stone-falls when a wild winter has heaped up its crest beyond stability. The going is harder now. If the tide is full one has to choose between stumbling from boulder to boulder along the knobbly spine of the storm beach, or sacrifice the sight of the sea and climb wall after wall of the fields inside it; but if the tide has withdrawn one can pick one's way along the slippery flags uncovered, the interior of the island hidden by the looming rampart on one's right but with the left open to the lovely distances of Connemara.

Sometimes this difficult mile, from the last of the cliffs to the bay of An Gleannachán below the village of Eoghanacht, can close on the mind like a trap, especially if one has spent one's spirits on the exhilarating heights and is beginning to count the plodding steps homeward. Then if a sea mist annuls the beatific vision of

Connemara and the waves turn leaden and the sky hangs low, the generalizing monotony of the rock-bank is suddenly replaced by a dreadful multiplicity of individual boulders, each an ugly confusion of angles and edges. With every pace one's mood darkens. These endless ankle-twisting contradictions underfoot, amorphous, resistant, cutting, dull, become the uncountable futilities heaped upon one's own shores by the surrounding ocean of indifference. If then one could elevate gloom into metaphysical despair, see the human race as no taller than that most depressing of life-forms, the lichen that stains so many of these bare stones black, one might, paradoxically, march on with a weightier stride that would soon outwalk the linear desert. Instead, the interminable dump of broken bits and pieces one is toiling along stubbornly remains the merely personal accumulation of petty worries, selfish anxieties, broken promises, discarded aspirations and other chips off a life-worn ego, that constitutes the path to one's own particular version of nowhere. And then, is it not a conceit, that further convicts one of conceit, to read one's own misfortune into even these random sheddings of processes so many magnitudes vaster than the human span of space and time? But at such moments it seems the only alternative is to let these supernal processes grind all one's concerns down into utter insignificance. Whereupon, rebelliously struggling through this clogged precipitate of scourings worn off its housing by the gyrating sea, this lumpish outwash of the wasting-away of the Earth, this dandruff of a seedy cosmos, one begins to feel that even if the whole did have a meaning narrow enough to be discovered by or revealed to such infinitesimals as Man, it would be one which we, honouring ourselves as dust, should decline to read or make our own. Better to keep our eyes on the ground, our ground, wary of the next stumbling-block and the crevice crouching behind it ready to snap at the ankle like a bad-tempered dog.

Here and there, though, even on this surly shore, is a nascent significance. Once I found a hatched egg-shell of black rubber, a broken fishing-float that had drifted over the ocean from Cuba and made me think of revolution and renewal. And a doll's arm waving from between two stones, an infant gesture, a birth-cry impossible not to heed. Many foam-born amoeba-goddesses of wave-worn polystyrene bring archetypal touches in art colours to the grey of the storm beach. From all over our plastic Babel come greetings in bottles labelled Drink-Me/Drink-Me-Not in effaced print and unknown languages. These and innumerable other fragmentary and ambiguous emblems, washed up here to be pounded to bits or imbricated whole among the stones, fatten the rock-bank, and shorten the way.

In fact the way itself is not without interest, once one's perceptions are reborn. Two shifts of waves a day work over the rock-bank, cracking its stones together and sorting the fragments. While its inland slant is greyish-black except for an occasional red-tinged chunk of dolomite or glinting ovoid erratic of granite, its weather-flank is scuffed silver bright. And, as a pilgrim's progress, its rigours ameliorate eastwards. Its beginning in the west is of cabin-trunk-sized blocks, then they are tea-chest-sized, then parcel-sized, for whatever the local weather, billows entering the North Sound with the accumulated energies of an Atlantic wind-pattern strike at this shore obliquely, rolling stones eastwards as well as upwards before lapsing into the arms of gravity and abandoning them on the bank, and the smaller pieces are each time carried a little farther than the larger. When a stone finally cracks up its remains migrate even faster; as corners and edges are blunted the chippings are swirled onwards. By the time the storm beach rounds the point into the bay of An Gleannachán it is a smoothly curved and flat-topped dam of heavy shingle, which retains an oval of brackish water called Loch Dearg, the red lake.

The appearance one after the other of a few species of plants accompanies this process by which the terrain becomes less inimical to life. First one sees a thin straggle of herb Robert on top of the bank, a small reddish thing with neat little pinkish-purple flowers, almost indefeasible in Aran; then the dull nettle-like pellitory, and a few long strands of bittersweet with its blue-and-yellow poison-warning flowers and tempting glossy red berries. On the shingle-dam by the lake grows the rarest of Irish shore-plants, seakale, which used to be such a striking feature here that the place is marked Sea Cabbage Point on the old Admiralty charts. It has declined to only about twenty plants now, and until recently it was thought to be extinct elsewhere in Ireland. In 1981 I found two unrecorded colonies of it on the Connemara coast, at least one of which has in fact always been there. However, it does seem that the species has had a narrow escape from extinction, at least in the wild, for it has of course been adopted into cultivation. A few plants recently appeared in Inis Meáin, but this is its only station in Árainn. Here every spring its gnarled and contorted rootstocks thrust aside the massive shingle with new growth; the leathery, prehistoric-looking blue-green leaves unfurl, and suffer the caterpillar like any common cabbage; its massed flowers are white and sweet in June, and fall to reveal many-branched seedheads, bearing round capsules, like fantastically complicated molecular models, which are smashed down and deeply drowned in stone again by the winter storms.

The grading of ever-finer beach material continues around the curve to the bay's most sheltered recesses, where there are even deposits of sand, and where for that reason one will perhaps exchange the first spoken words of this dour trek, with a man filling his cartrailer or the baskets on his donkey with sand to spread on his potato-patch or to make concrete for a septic tank. A road comes down to the shore here from Eoghanacht village, just quarter of a mile inland, and so while pausing to chat one can consider whether to follow it and hope for a lift along the main road, or to let the lovely curve and nearly tints of the outswinging shingle-bank beyond lead one on, to the further trials and visions of a coast which is proving to be more subtly challenging than the tall cliffs.

THE SEAWEED GATHERERS

The pale shinglebanks of An Gleannachán frame a dark half-oval of shallow and seaweed when the tide is low. Sometimes one sees a man moving slowly to and fro out there, stalking and stooping just like the shore-birds that come in clouds to pick over the sea's leavings. Perhaps he is collecting periwinkles for bait before going to some taller shore to fish, but if the season is late spring or summer he may be gathering the edible seaweed called *carraigín* or "Irish Moss," which he will spread to dry on the short grass of some field by the shore, and sell to a mainland wholesaler through an agent in Cill Rónáin. Some of it goes abroad; in London, for instance, little cellophane packets of it can be bought in the more expensive stores, in health-food shops and in corner groceries catering to nostalgic Irish exiles. A few packets even come back to the Aran shops and are sold at amazing prices (65p. for two-and-a-half ounces in 1982, when the pickers were getting £4 a stone for it), and not only to tourists. Next to whiskey it is the Aran people's most trusted cure for coughs and colds; they simmer a few sprigs of it in milk or water and after straining out the insoluble bits drink the resulting bland and soothing essence of rock-pool. We have occasionally used a thicker brew of it as the basis of a sort of blancmange, which is nutritious and soothing but soon palls, and no doubt it has other unexplored potentials, but so far the picking and drying of it has afforded us more health and pleasure than the eating.

On some still day between May and August we go down to a shore like An Gleannachán and spend an hour or so paddling in the sun-warmed pools and groping under the leathery fronds of the larger seaweeds draped over the rocks for the small round clumps of *carraigín*, that come away softly in the hand. Searching these limpid recesses, perturbing the surface of their waters as little as possible, is like trying to recall the images of strange but soothing dreams. Some of the living things waiting there evade the eye by stillness, some by swiftness and others by transparency, while every now and then one goes wavering by wrapped in incredibility rather than invisibility; I remember in particular a sea hare, a few inches of deep red, slowly rippling worm-stuff shaped like a hare, or rather the reflection of one in uneasy water.

The *carraigín* itself is beautiful in its life and in its dying. There are two sorts, that grow intermingled; the slightly taller tufts with inrolled, dark brownish-red fronds, are what the biologists call *Gigartina stellata*, and the more common, smaller species is *Chondrus crispus*, which has flat, dark red fronds with mobile touches of phosphorescence on their tips like liquefying sapphires. These delusive jewels vanish as soon as the weed is lifted out of the water, but when it is spread out on the ground for the rain and dew to wash the salt out and the sun and wind to bleach and dry, it goes through a sequence of colour changes that is enough to compensate for the withering of the satisfactory load one had lugged home wet and living into an almost weightless few handfuls of crumpled tatters. As its initial, glossy midnight-chestnut pales by coalescence of spreading lunar patches, each last spot of darkness dissolves into an auroral flush of greens, pinks and oranges, and then after a few days, if one has luck with the weather, flaccid ivory is replaced by suntan crispness.

Of course for those few men who want to or have to augment their income by gathering *carraigín*, it involves more labour and less aesthetics, and this final stage can be anxious. Once I fell into conversation with an old man considering his small heaps of *carraigín* in a field by An Gleannachán. He eyed the darkening clouds and fingered his chin doubtfully, saying "If I thought it wouldn't rain, now, I'd leave it out for another night. But, the way it is, you wouldn't know...." If it got soaked at this stage it might rot before it dried again, and then the task of picking out the bad bits would be added to that of picking out the dead winkles in it, and at the price he could expect it was scarcely worth the trouble. As much at a loss as he in this ancient dilemma, I could not advise. Eventually we propped the sticky masses against the wall of the field where the wind could blow through them, and left it to fate.

The only other seaweed product exported from Aran nowadays is the *slata mara* or searods, the thick stems, three or four feet long, of the seaweed *Laminaria digitata*, which grows at or below the level of low tide, and comes ashore among the great masses of brown tangleweeds thrown up on the beach by winter storms. Gathering searods is a much more considerable business both in scale—the shore of An Gleannachán produces six or eight tons of searods yearly—and the rigours of the work. It even has its effect on the landscape, for many of the island's shinglebanks have a ribbing of low walls built out of the shingle on their inland slopes, over which the rods are hung to dry; in fact some of the storm beaches of Inis Oírr, where searods are gathered much more intensively, have been largely remodelled by the building of drying-stands for them. Nevertheless, when one first comes across the scene, perhaps on some quickly fading afternoon when land, sea and sky are thick with winter, the solitary man knee-deep in the sodden weed-bank, dragging out the club-like stems with their gnarled hold-fasts and flinging them heavily up the shore one by one, seems to be engaged in a task so wild, forlorn and picturesquely aboriginal that one is not quite pleased to learn that this is no mere local, archaic and obsolete mode of survival, but the first stage in an industrial process of international ramifications.

The rows of searods arranged side by side across the tops of the neighbouring field-walls represent a sum of money—not the fortune they suggest when still juicy red, but more than one would expect from their shrivelled grey thong-like look after a few weeks' exposure. When thoroughly dry they are laid and tied in rectangular stacks, and in May trailer-loads of them are hauled to Cill Rónáin pier to await the coming of a personage known in the islands as *Fear na Slata Mara*, the searod man, who weighs and pays and oversees their shipment by trawler to Cill Chiaráin on the Connemara coast. There by the harbour are the slovenly sheds of a factory, surrounded by reeking mountains of other sorts of seaweed delivered by lorry from various parts of the mainland coast. Aran's contribution like the rest is fed into one of the two furnaces—

huge cylinders turning on an axis of roaring flame—and reduced to a powder, which a little freighter, the *Saint Ronan*, takes in lots of four or five hundred tons directly to the works of Alginate Industries Ltd in Scotland. There, together with the similar product of many other regions of the North Atlantic coast, it is made into a thickening agent used in various manufacturing processes. In icecreams, paints and cosmetics, a little of it eventually finds its way back to Aran.

Gathering searods is an intermittent occupation for a few Aran farmers in the winter when little can be done on the land. "It puts the time by," one or two of them have told me, and indeed a superfluity of time is one of the rigours of the season. A man might expect to gather one or two tons of searods, or even more, in the course of a winter. The lump of cash comes in handy, and buys a calf when the grass is greening to feed it. In the Seventies the island was producing about thirty tons a year; Inis Oírr was producing twice that, alternative employment being scarcer there, while Inis Meáin contributed much less as comparatively few searods come ashore there. The price offered is announced by Arramara, the Cill Chiaráin concern, each year, and as one would expect with such a broadly useful constituent, it follows general economic trends. It rose rapidly in the mid-Seventies in line with that of other raw materials, and then reflected the subsequent depression, and is now responding to demand again. In 1973 it was £15 a ton and in 1984, £70.

In general, the number of searods washed ashore is thought to be declining, and Arramara's technical experts attribute this to the expansion of the lobster-fisheries, though it is not known if it is the lobsterpots themselves that injure the growing weed or whether the removal of lobsters encourages the proliferation of their prey, the sea-urchins, which themselves feed on seaweed. However, a lot of searods rot uncollected on the shores of Aran these days, as the deeply scored habit of labour, a value stubbornly outlasting the necessity that decreed it, wears away with the older generation. A ton of dried searods represents a weary number of

cold, wet, stooping hours, and few of the younger men are constrained economically or psychologically to follow the old ways.
In the past, although the traditional allotment of the shores always
meant that if through age or illness a man was no longer able to
gather the searods on his portion, they would remain ungathered
there for some years, eventually a younger relative would take
over. Nowadays there is little competition to keep bright the honour of the shore's divisions, and if the number of searods lying disregarded on a certain beach reminds us that old Tom or old Seán
has taken to his bed, we suspect that it is not tradition but indifference that leaves them scattered there.

ON THE SHORES OF THE PAST

The two long man-forsaken miles of shore from An Gleannachán
to Port Mhuirbhigh are alleviated by the pleasant little bays of
Port Chonnla and Port Sheánla, where one may at least sometimes
hear the ring of a spade on stone from a nearby potato-plot, even
if tall field-walls hide the digger; the intervening lobes of land,
however, carry one out into deep solitudes although they lie in
view of the houses ranged along the hillside half a mile inland. The
fields of the coastal plain either have no soil at all—An Chreig
Dhubh, the black crag, is the name of a typical one of these unre-
generate tracts—or only a shallow layer built up by many annual
applications of sand and seaweed hauled from the shore. The
storm beach—a confusion of jagged slabs where it emerges from
the shelter of each bay, a smooth shinglebank where it turns into
the next—divides this bare lowland from an unemphatic shore
which is merely its final descent, by way of slight steps and broad
shelves of rock, into the fields of seaweed that stretch out towards
the vague limits of low tide. Such an expanse of intertidal rock extending from a headland is called a *cora*, and to the "black crag"
on the land correspond An Chora Dhubh Thiar and An Chora

Dhubh Thoir, the black *cora* of the west and of the east, which continue the shores enclosing An Gleannachán far out into the sea like two dark horns. The former *cora* blows an almost perpetual visual fanfare, the trumpetings of white foam from the rollers that break across the shoal in rounding the headland to shape themselves into the curve of the bay. Indeed there is always more colour and spectacle out there, where the terns hunting for fish flicker against the sky and shriek like wet glass before shooting themselves like darts into the sea, and the occasional lobsterboat in sea-worn blues and whites chugs by clinging to the bucking waves. But the shore itself is dark as with sad memories, a deep depression that both rebuffs and pleads for interpretation of the few remaining signs of the vigorous, rancorous, laborious and sometimes joyous comradeship it hosted before it was forsaken.

The waning and extinction of the old shore-life was sufficiently prolonged into this century to be briefly illuminated—old moon in the arms of the new—by the first brilliant generation of island writers. Máirtín Ó Direáin has jotted down a note of one of its good moments in a poem called *An tEarrach Thiar*. ("The Western Spring" will have to do as English for this title, but it could also be the late spring, or even, stretching a grammatical point, a spring of the old days, of the Dublin literary figure's Aran origins, for the word *thiar* and its derivatives have two sets of meanings as intimately related as warp and woof: one is connected with "west" and the other with "back," as relative position in space or time. Further, the frictions of Irish history and geography have given the concept of "the West" such a charge that *thiar* is almost as potent a word as *sean*, old, is in Irish. Indeed this whole book, like all possible books on Aran, could be read as a footnote to the full explication of these two simple Irish words. But the following line-by-line translation of Ó Direáin's poem does not presume to look into such mysteries.)

Fear ag glanadh cré	A man cleaning earth
De ghimseán spáide	Off the tread of a spade

Sa gciúnas séimh
I mbrothall lae:
  Binn an fhuaim
  San Earrach thiar.

In the mild quietness
Of the heat of the day:
  Sweet the sound
  In the western Spring.

Fear ag caitheamh
Cliabh da dhroim,
Is an fheamainn dhearg
Ag lonrú
I dtaitneamh gréine
Ar dhuirling bhán:
  Niamhrach an radharc
  San Earrach thiar.

A man throwing
A basket off his back,
And the redweed
Glistening
In sunshine
On a white shinglebank:
  A lustrous sight
  In the western Spring.

Mná i locháin
In íochtar díthrá,
A gcótaí craptha,
Scáilí thíos fúthu:
  Támhradharc sítheach
  San Earrach thiar.

Women in pools
At the lowest ebb
Their petticoats tucked up,
Reflections beneath them:
  Peaceful trance-vision
  In the western Spring.

Tollbhuillí fanna
Ag maidí rámha
Currach lán éisc
Ag teach chun cladaigh
Ar órmhuir mháll
I ndeireadh lae;
  San Earrach thiar.

Languid hollow strokes
Of oars
A currach full of fish
Coming to shore
On a slow golden sea
At the end of the day;
  In the western Spring.

Ó Direáin was born (in 1910) in the village of Sruthán just a few hundred yards from An Gleannachán, and many of his writings commemorate the shore-work of his childhood; conversely, various placenames of the Sruthán coastline refer one back to his work. The title of his collection of prose pieces, *Feamainn Bhealtaine*, "Mayweed," could indeed be taken as symbolic of literature's gathering-in of the old shore-life, for it is the Aran term for the banks of redweed cast up by the gales of spring. Ó Direáin's reminiscential work often returns to this sea-harvest in the fresh of the year, and it is the moments of relaxation from toil, of stillness and contemplation, that shine most brightly in the memory of that child whom Sruthán thought of as a lazy dreamer—while in fact he was already at work, picking up the whole village, its cottages, fields, shore and folk, to carry them across into our world:

> The taste and smell of bread and butter come back [*aniar*, from the West] to me through the mist of years. The sheet spread on a convenient mossy hummock in a corner under a high wall. . . .The midges would come with the sultry heat of midday. . . . A long sunbeam over the weedbank making a lustrous frame of the midges.
>
> A man taking his rest for a moment. Looking out at the bay, the islands of Connemara little blue fragments in the haze, like blobs of blue spittle left by a sea-dragon on its way to the western world. The Connemara boats nearer in view, their sails furled. The crew catching fish for dinner perhaps. The man pulls his bobbled cap off with one hand, takes a piece of tobacco out of it with the other. He pushes the tobacco into his mouth. He tightens his woven belt around his waist and starts to fill baskets again.

Against Ó Direáin's nostalgic watercolours one can set Liam O'Flaherty's lurid oil-painting (from the story "Poor People') of a man from a sick and hungry household labouring "in the poisonous cold of a February morning":

> The edge of the sea was full of seaweed, a great load spilling from the deep, red, slime-covered, dribbling in with every wave that broke murmuring in the darkness of the dawn.
>
> Patrick Derrane came running down the road with a pitchfork on his shoulder, his rawhide shoes squelching with

the wetness of the road, a white frieze smock tucked into his waist-belt, his slim body shivering with the cold. He reached the sandbank and saw the seaweed in the tide through the darkness, being sucked in and out by the mighty slow movement of the sea. He uttered a low joyous cry and ran down, running ankle-deep in the soft sand....

The seaweed must be gathered and the potatoes must be planted because another winter was coming after the warmth of summer, another winter with cold and sickness and hardship. The great whip of poverty lashing his back, driving him down the beach through the soft sand.

He had no thought of his wife or of his son or of his hunger, walking rapidly back and forth from the sandbank to the tide, lifting the seaweed on his pitchfork and spilling it in a slipping heap. He worked wildly, gritting his teeth against the cold. He only remembered the crop he had to sow and that great lash of hunger, the dread spirit that ever taunts the poor, reminding them of the hardship that is to come, deadening the pain that is present....

The sun rose, daylight sparkled on the land, on the beach and over the sea. The birds awakened and sent their sweet music dancing through the depths of the sky. The cloak of red seaweed on the beach shimmered like freshly spilt blood on which the sun is shining, against the dark blue background of the freezing sea.

Derrane had gathered a great heap of seaweed, ten loads for a horse. He went home. Weak after his sickness he was hardly able to walk the road. His thighs were scalded by the brine. And now that he was going home, he remembered the sadness that awaited him there, lamentation and a grave being opened.

The shore's own indications of its past—a few scarcely noticeable stones, the significances of which have been given me by sons and grandsons of the old seaweed-gatherers, and a handful of obscure placenames—are meagre. It is a faded picture, but these writers and one or two others have preserved at least some of the authentic pigments for its restoration. This is a task to which I am prompted by my own limited experience of shore-work (groping in pools left by the ebb of generations), as well as by many conversations with former labourers remembering their tidal fields, in words which remind me that not all the genes of poetry in that first literary generation were foreign to their Aran stock.

Certain small boulders visible when the tide is low in the bay of An Gleannachán mark a convenient start in this work of restoration, and from there I work eastwards.

SHORE DIVISIONS

Two boreens come down to An Gleannachán, the one from Eoghanacht already mentioned, and another from the next village to the east, Sruthán. The boundary between the two villages is the west wall of the latter boreen, and the boulders lying in the shallows of the bay are the continuation of this boundary towards low tide mark. Thus the Sruthán people could gather seaweed off the eastern half of the bay and the coast around the headland to the middle of the next bay, Port Chonnla. Within this division by villages subdivision by households was equally clearly established. These finer details are largely forgotten now, but when I spent a day cutting "blackweed," as the dark seaweeds of the upper shore are called here, my instructor, task-master and host was careful to show me the boulder and the rock-pool that delimited his ancestral patch.

These long-standing regulations of the shore have not always prevented disputes. On the north coast of Inis Meáin, for instance, the name Cladach an tSiúite, the shore of the quarrelling, is said to derive from the fact that weed always seemed to drift ashore there exactly on the boundary between the two townlands.

I have even heard an old history of Gort na gCapall men being killed in a brawl over the divisions of weed on Cill Mhuirbhigh strand. And sometimes when wind and tide combined to bring weed ashore in great quantities it was "a case of every family for itself," as the Aran writer Pat Mullen tells:

> At such times my father was like a tiger. He yelled at us and cursed us up and down the shore as we gathered the seaweed in the tide and filled our baskets, which he would carry up the beach and then come running back again for more. On a pitch-dark night he would hurry just as much as in broad daylight and would never let us rest until we had gathered more seaweed than anyone else. I tried to carry my first basket of seaweed when I was fourteen. I wasn't strong enough and it brought me down, but I was growing strong quickly and a few months later I managed to carry my first basket, and I was very proud.

On certain gently sloping shores weed could be cut in partnership and left where it lay because the rising tide could be trusted to wash it in rather that sweep it away along the coast, and then after the tide had turned it could be divided up at leisure. But this measure of co-operation gave no quarter to the feeble or lazy. Pat Mullen again:

> In such a shore a man to be fully qualified must be able to change his knife into either hand and with each be able to cut equally well. I remember once I got a chance to go cutting on such a shore. I was to get my first man's share as a cutter. I felt very nervous as a full score of men walked down the path towards the shore, each man having made, long before, his choice of a sharpening stone—and on these they were carefully whetting their special knives to razor edge. It was my father's job as every man there well knew. He was a first-class knife man, but he was now looking for some better

work somewhere else and threw me in his place....On my first day I kept close to my Uncle Jim, thinking it would be safest to be under the arm of a relation; but I was mistaken because he soon began to give me hell, shouting out so that everyone could hear, that it was a shame that I should be looking for a man's share.

Weed gathered in common like this would then be divided into as many heaps as there were workers, and the heaps allotted by the following procedure, which was also used in sharing out a catch of fish amongst a boatcrew, and which a Sruthán man described for me. Little objects picked up on the strandline served as tokens for the casting of lots—a seashell, a fragment of driftwood or searod, a wisp of seaweed and so on, to the requisite number. While the rest looked away, one man would arrange these objects in a row across his two palms from thumb to thumb, close his fists over them, and take his place behind the row of seaweed stacks. Then he would call on each of the others to name his choice of token. When he opened his hands and revealed the order of the tokens, the stacks would be assigned to their owners in the corresponding order, from one end of the row to the other. A very similar way of casting lots was used in Clear Island off the southwest tip of Ireland, according to an account taken down from an old fisherman there in the Thirties. In his words it was done so that "nobody would have a straight mouth or a crooked one on him" when he got his portion. The Stone-Age folk who gathered shellfish round Ireland's coasts probably did the same. In comparable circumstances today we would appeal for justice to coins or to pieces of paper marked with our names, that is, to the basic apparatus of our daily lives. The old shore-folk picked their talismans off the naked strand, and threw them away again without a thought.

BLACKWEED AND REDWEED

The Araners distinguish about thirty types of seaweed, each with its own advantages and disadvantages as fertilizer for various crops or as the raw material of kelp. The main division is between *feamainn dhubh*, blackweed and *feamainn dhearg*, redweed. The former comprises the dark-toned *Fucus* species that grow on the upper and middle shore, and of which acres are exposed by the ebb on such shallow stony bays as An Gleannachán. The redweeds are the huge tangleweeds, mainly *Laminaria*, growing around low water mark and only accessible to cutting when the tide is far out, on such rocky promontories as An Chora Dhubh on the east of the bay.

There are various types of blackweed, as I learned on that day I spent cutting it. The most favoured is *feamainn bhoilgíneach*, or "belly-weed" as it is called in English here, the familiar bladder-wrack; all these names refer to the air-sacs like big blisters that float its leathery thongs. Blackweed should always be cut rather than pulled, so that its holdfasts remain on the rock and soon sprout new growth (and one should not lose the penknife and at the end of a tiring day have to spend an extra half-hour groping for it in the swilling tide, as I did). After stooping to cut for an hour or so it is a relief to stop and pile the weed into the big square basket of woven osiers—and after stumbling under that dripping load through the rock-pools and up the shinglebank it is a relief to return to cutting. The first attempt at straightening up under a full basket convinced me of the superiority of another method of bringing cut weed to land, no longer used in Aran, which is to assemble it into a *cleimín*, a flat bundle about ten feet across, tie a rope around it, and tow it ashore when the rising tide floats it. Vast amounts of *feamainn bhuí*, yellow-weed (the knotted wrack, *Ascophyllum*), a seaweed of sheltered waters uncommon in Aran, are still harvested in the landlocked bays of Connemara by this method for sale to the factory at Cill Chiaráin; there are usually several *cleimíní* moored by each little jetty of that coast, and one may see men making amazing leaps from raft to raft of seaweed as they pole them out of the shallows around the off-shore islands where it is cut and assemble them into little flotillas that a small boat will tug to the mainland. This is still a very slow business even with an outboard motor, and the progress of a rowing-boat towing a *cleimín* is almost imperceptible however the men strain at the oars; and so, short of further mechanization, it seems there is no way of bringing weed ashore without back-breaking effort.

My friend's shore-marks were irrelevant that day as there was no one else cutting blackweed then or indeed on any other day of that spring. Has anyone cut weed anywhere around the island since, I wonder, or was my mentor the last to do so? A hundred years ago vast tonnages of it were cut each spring, mainly to fertilize the fields before potato-setting in March and April; it was not the best weed for kelp-making. The island's hooker-owners used to make a bit of money at that time of year running blackweed to Galway and Kinvara, whence it would be distributed by cart around the countryside and sold to farmers as fertilizer, but this trade died when guano from South America began to be shipped to Galway early in this century.

If nobody troubles with blackweed nowadays, a certain amount of the redweed is still used, though even this more easily obtained natural fertilizer is being replaced by the usual industrial products. These weeds are exposed as prostrate forests whenever the tide withdraws sufficiently, which it does in the spring tides, that is, those tides on two or three days just after each full or new moon. This twice-monthly showing of the island's blood-red margin imposes itself on the attention of anyone who stays here long enough, although it no longer dictates the cycle of shore-work, for enough redweed is brought ashore by the gales of winter and spring to save its few users the trouble of wading out to cut it. Every now and then in the beginning of the year I and my philosopher of the shoreline go down to the bay nearest our village and consider the state of the *bainc*, the heavy deposit of macerated redweed that accumulates on the outer slopes of the shinglebanks throughout the winter. When it is judged to be sufficiently *preasáilte*, that is, pressed, compacted and rotted into a black maggoty dung, we "straddle" the grey mare and take her down to the shore for one of her rather infrequent days' work. The straddle or *srathair* is a wooden bridge that sits across the horse's back like a large saddle, with pegs from which a sally-rod basket hangs on either side. A thick layer of straw under the straddle protects the hide from the brine of the seaweed. With pitchforks we fill the baskets, piling yet more *bainc* onto the straddle until the *bord* or load is a tall cone. When we lead the mare up the shinglebank she watches carefully where she places her forehooves among the turning stones, but the hindlegs it seems have to look out for themselves and tend to trip and slip. At the roadside we push the nodding superstructure of weed off the straddle and then, one on either side, we unhitch the ropes that hold up the hinged bottoms of the baskets, so that they fall open simultaneously and deposit the rest of the load on the ground. Then we rest for a moment, praising the mare for her steadiness and rubbing her nose—her master always cups her eyeballs in the palms of his horny hands in a way that looks uncomforting but which she seems to like—and take her down to the weedbank again. After a dozen or more such turns, having exchanged the whole short winter afternoon for a hillock of weed, we go home to tea, bringing an acrid whiff of horse-sweat and sea-rot into the house. The next morning we put the mare into the shafts of the "common cart." How long all these adjustments of the ropes and chains and hooks of the harness seem to take! How anxious I become in trying to follow instructions about them in Irish, while the mare, to me a compendium of unknown forces, stirs and twitches and rolls her eyeballs, making me think of a saying her master has given me to the effect that while a horse only thinks of killing you once in its life, a mare does so seven times! At length we are ready and go rattling down the hill to the shore, the pitchforks bouncing beside us on the cart. Yesterday's mound seems to have shrunk a bit, but it still makes three cartloads since the way is steep and the mare young as yet. If squalls break across the island one after another as they often do at that time of year, forcing us to spend time crouched under a wall by the roadside looking at the mare hanging her dripping head, the three journeys take all day, and I learn not only the Irish terms for countless details of horsecraft and seaweed lore, but also a slower mental pulse, which dreams away the distinction between minutes and hours and threatens to stretch my city-cut days into the baggy lunar months and earth-heavy seasons of Aran's old fields and shores.

WOMEN'S WORK

If the structure of the year is a very loosely fitting harness around the Aran farm nowadays, and chafes for that reason, in the past it cut, blinkered and bitted a life ruthlessly driven by want. Each household planted as many ridges of potatoes as a whole village does now, and as soon as the weed this demanded was gathered in spring, stacking of more weed for the summer's kelp-burning began. Less weed ended up as *bainc*, ready heaped for easy loading, because so much was snatched from the waves before it reached shore, such was the islanders' need. Redweed used to be cut too, and as this could only be done at the ebb of the especially big spring tides around the equinoxes, the calendar whipped everyone to the shore on such occasions. A story by Máirtín Ó Cadhain, *An Taoille Tuile*, "The Flood Tide," gives us the urgency of the work, its consequent erosion of gentle feelings, and perhaps a moment of fierce joy in the elemental struggle. In this case it is co-operation that adds to the stress, as two households sharing the weed of a particular *cora* each feel bound by a competitive sense of honour to make the larger contribution. One household is represented by Pádraig and Máiréad, a newly-married couple, and the other by an older man, An Loideanach, and his two daughters. They meet by arrangement on the shore at dawn—the setting is Ó Cadhain's native Cois Fharraige west of Galway, but I picture it as An Chora Dhubh Thoir by An Gleannachán. Pádraig and Máiréad find the others waiting for them, the two girls sitting on their upturned baskets and An Loideanach striding up and down the shinglebank gnawing on his pipe:

> "On my conscience," he said, between jest and earnest, "I thought devil a wisp of seaweed would be cut on the Cora today! I never saw newlyweds killing themselves with hurry to get up!"
>
> "The tide has gone out a bit," said Pádraig, crestfallen.
>
> "Gone out a bit! and it as good as low water! This is the second day of the Spring Tides and if we don't hurry today and tomorrow there won't be another ebb this year good enough for cutting the deep reefs of the Cora!"
>
> "It's a big Spring Tide," said Máiréad simply. Because she had gone to America so early in her youth she now had no more than a smattering of some home concerns, the names of which were woven into her memory.
>
> "Big Spring Tide!" said An Loideanach with the look of a bishop hearing some terrible blasphemy uttered in his presence. "The great Spring Tide of the Feast of St. Brigid! You're not experienced in Spring Tides yet, my treasure, and they're not what's on your mind!"

Pádraig starts the day full of consideration for his tender bride and carries her basket down the shore for her. But once he bends to the task of proving himself the equal of all three of the Loideanaigh together, Máiréad is left to her own tentative and feeble efforts among the blackweed of the upper shore, and is told off by the older man first for wasting time gathering limpets and then for cutting the wrong sort of weed, the juiceless serrated wrack that, he tells her, would still be lying unrotted in the stony earth by autumn. The men have waded out waist-deep onto the farther reaches of the Cora to cut the large redweed called *coirleach* (strapwrack), and the women are ordered to follow as soon as the water-level has fallen a bit further. Once the tide turns the women start to carry the weed up the shore to the place where it will be spread to dry. Máiréad feels the sweat warming the brine running down her back and the salt burning her fingers, raw from the ropes of the basket. As the sea gains on the Cora the men also have to turn from cutting to carrying for fear that the weed already cut might be lost to the tide again, and the conflict sharpens. On each journey up the shore Pádraig is already emptying his basket at the drying-place while the Loideanaigh are just passing high water mark and Máireád is still at the foot of the beach. In the culmination of the race against the rising tide Máiréad goes after a bit of yellow-weed, and Pádraig's tolerance is exhausted:

> "Get out of my way!" said Pádraig, going in thigh-deep to wrest the last of the prey from the greedy sea. Máiréad straightened up, her mind instantly alerted by that voice. A rough, unfamiliar voice. A voice from some realm other than that of plaintive letters, of beguiling companionship, the realm of the pillow. With the spasm that ran through her the seaweed bladder burst between her fingers and spurted a dull reddish slime up to her cheek.
>
> The darkness she saw on Pádraig's forehead at that moment was as inhospitable and sullen as the black furrows the rising wind was making in the angry face of the flood tide.

Contemporary Aran attitudes to the part women played in the old shore-life are complicated. I have been told with a certain pitying pride by their offspring, now themselves elderly, that Aran women sometimes had to work at the seaweed until late in their pregnancies. (Whether any Araners were actually born on the shore I do not know, but from County Clare I have heard of a woman giving birth on a shore below cliffs, and the baby being hauled up the cliff face with one of the seaweed baskets while the mother continued cutting weed below so as not to loose the ebb.) In a dis-

cussion of the scene in the film *Man of Aran* in which that supporting role, the Woman of Aran, is allowed her moment in heroic silhouette, bearing a monumental basket of weed, against a backdrop
of raging elements, I have heard an Aran man flatly deny that
women ever did such work. This retrospective chivalry is not the
rule, however. Whereas Flaherty's film caused offence to islanders
in the past, when the way of life it recreated was still too salt in the
memory for nostalgia and the simplicities it heroized were seen as
brands of poverty, today its stilted naturalism can be smiled at and
its colossal energies relished. And in celebrating strength and endurance Flaherty was true to a persistent Aran value. Many feats
of the *seandream*, the old people of the shore, are still remembered.
For instance I have several times been told of a woman who could
carry her backload of seaweed from the shore near Port Chonnla
up a mile of rough boreen to her field on the skyline, without
pausing for rest. In looking for a wife the Aran farmer of those
days, whatever his other ideals of beauty, modesty and gentleness,
had it in mind that she who could not carry a burden would be
one. As a bitter old Aran saying puts it, "*Is é moladh na mná óige,
a droim bheith fliuch,*" "Praise of the young woman, that her back
be wet"—wet, that is, with the brine from a basket of weed.

POETS ON THE SHORE

Port Chonnla, a steep-sided little cup of a bay with a teaspoonful
of sand in it, marks the end of Sruthán's shore; the boundary wall
comes down the middle of the tiny beach, and the coast beyond is
the portion of the Cill Mhuirbhigh villagers.

Before cockcrow, some sixty years ago, two little boys came
down the boreen from Sruthán, determined to be the first at work
on this shore. But they had got up so early they suspected it was
still Sunday night rather than Monday morning, and this was
making them anxious:

In the two villages only one man would defy the Sabbath, and he used to gather his seaweed on this shore; he would have a big stone laid on each heap and be back in his bed before anyone else had thought of stirring. He used to make as much kelp on his own as the head of any family with twelve to help him. It was said that "people" gave him a helping hand, and one would gather from the way in which it was said that these people were not from the angelic realm. But not even he was down on this particular morning.

Before us was a bank of weed that could not be exhausted in a week however much was taken out of it. The green madman who had been foaming at the mouth a couple of days earlier was now a slack fool, the red belch of the weed bank cast up before him. As soon as we put a hand to the weed we noticed as it were hundreds of little red sprites clowning about like drops of rain in a shower. There was fear as well as fun in the little startled cries that came from us on seeing those tiny spark-like beings. Nowhere could we stick our hands into the bank without being up to our elbows in these malicious little fellows.

"The Day of Rest, definitely!" I said. "Hadn't we better go home?"

The children were Máirtín Ó Direáin and his younger brother Tomás (who has also published poetry, though his work has not been collected as yet). The poet in exile mulls over the same questions as do those who have never left the old shores, but tends to bring books to bear on them. Máirtín Ó Direáin writes:

Where did that name [An Gleannachán] come from? Where did Port Chúnla come from? Should it be Port Chuanla? Or Port Chonnla? Was it from there that "Gentle Connla of the flowing golden hair" was taken to Tír na hÓige, the Land of Youth? God be with the *Old Celtic Romances* of schooldays.... Can the placenames experts solve the question?

I have put Ó Direáin's question to the experts, and they could not solve it, so the name rests in indeterminacy, the seedbed of at least one variety of poetry. As to An Gleannachán, another local writer, Colm P. Ó hIarnáin, who lives close by that shore, would derive the name from *gleann an chuain*, glen of the bay, and has taken that phrase as the title of his collection of short stories in Irish. I would prefer a less strenuous interpretation if one were forthcoming.

Other names of this shore are equally elusive. Buaile Ghaeil, the name of an area around an inlet just over half a mile south-east of Port Chonnla, appears to mean the Irishman's pasture, which would be odd in an island largely composed of Irishmen's pastures; another exile from Aran has written to me deriving it from the mythical hero Gael named in the pseudo-histories of the Invasions of Ireland (and other places such as Scailp Eireamháin, a little cave in Oatquarter, Trácht Míl, a beach in Inis Oírr, and Inis Oírr itself, are named from other "Milesian" ancestors of the race, Eireamhán, Mil himself and Ír, according to my correspondent). The placenames specialist must distrust the poet's affinity for the far-fetched, but anyone walking this blank stony foreshore might be glad that such august shadows have been cast upon it, even if only in error. And then—to turn the tide of this reverie—the name of the headland between Port Chonnla and Port Sheánla sounds like Cora Scaití Ciúin, the sometimes-calm *cora*, and that is how some of the islanders who bother their head with such questions would interpret it, a lovely and appropriate name for this arm of Aran—I have just glanced at it from my window as I write—that almost always sports a lacy cuff of breakers. However, Colm Ó hIarnáin of Sruthán thinks it should be Cora Scair Tí Choinn, the *cora* of the Quinn family's portion; there were people of that name living nearby who might have had seaweed rights there. So shadows of the old shore-workers are interleaved with those of giants and demigods.

FORTUNE AND MISFORTUNE

Rummaging one day among the lumber and dust-filled sunbeams of a neighbour's barn, I came across a huge and ancient implement that clearly dated from some heroic age of toil, although I could not guess its purpose. It had a twenty-foot shaft of wood, with a little wooden blade fixed across it near one end and an iron fork of three curved tines over eighteen inches long at the other. Its owner told me that it was a combination of two seaweed-gathering tools: the shaft plus the crosspiece constituted a *croisín*, and the shaft plus the fork a *crúca*. Later, down on the shore, he showed me the situations in which each would have been used. Just south of Cora Scaití Ciúin, for instance, where the shoreline is an *ulán* or shelf about ten or fifteen feet high, the sea has enlarged a joint of the limestone into a narrow sheer-sided creek called An Uaimh Mhór. (The dictionary-meaning of *uaimh* is cave, but in Aran it refers to such an open cleft in the seashore as this, like its equivalent *fuaigh* in Connemara.) Here the great fork or *crúca* was used for lifting out the masses of redweed packed into the creek by northerly gales. And just off the point of the *cora* itself is a reef, one of the many called An Creachoileán, on which *coirleach* was harvested from a currach with the aid of the *croisín*. The pole was thrust down into the submarine forest of weed, and turned until the *coirleach*, whose fronds are several feet long, was tangled into a huge ball around the crosspiece. It was important, my friend told me, to give the *croisín* a jerk after every turn to break the stems, or else one would end up with such a mass of weed still attached to the rocks that "Fionn Mac Cumhall himself couldn't pull it up!" When the currach was heaped up with eight or ten hundredweight of weed it would be rowed cautiously to shore, the water lapping at its brim.

This business of *croisínteacht* was both strenuous and risky. Once, when walking a Connemara shore, I was startled to see a man apparently sitting in the sea between two weed-covered rocks, reading a newspaper; he had looked up, nodded guardedly and returned to his paper before I had made out that he was in a rowingboat so heavily loaded that only a mere splinter of the gunwale showed above the waterline between the mounds of weed that hid the bows and stern in their draperies. Having brought his cargo across from the islet where he had cut it, he was now waiting for another inch of tide to float him alongside a jetty. Such an operation is delicate enough in the unruffled inlets of Rosmuc, and I could appreciate why this man's greeting of me had been so restrained, but days on which it would be practicable off a "sometimes calm *cora*" of Aran must be very few indeed.

Paradoxically, the difficulties of cropping An Creachoileán were once at the origins of a commercial fortune. There are conflicting versions of this piece of folk-history, but according to the tale my neighbour told me as we leaned over a wall and looked out at the foaming reef, the MacDonncha family of Leitir Mealláin on the opposite coast once owned three *cartúir* of land in Eoghanacht, and therefore had seaweed rights here. One day when some ancestral MacDonncha was wrestling with the *coirleach* of An Creachoileán his *croisín* broke, and he stood up in his currach and swore "I'll never gather *coirleach* again, if I have to beg!" Whereupon he went off to Galway to try another mode of life and opened a little shop, which over the course of generations has become that pillar of the business community, MacDonogh's huge store on Merchants' Road.

But in Aran, over those same generations, the *coirleach* was still wrenched off An Creachoileán, and renewed itself every year; the *crúca* was wielded in An Uaimh Mhór, the *cleimíní* were dragged into Port Chonnla, the blackweed and the red were cut on An Chora Dhubh; *bainc* was pitch-forked into baskets at An Gleannachán, and the baskets carried up to the hungry fields. Aran's back was bent to the rule of the moon, for lifetime after lifetime. A little rhyme I heard from an old lady of Inis Oírr expresses the griefs of that immemorial labour. The places it names are seaweed shores of the south coast of Inis Oírr, but they could stand for any of a hundred such shores of Aran:

Dún an Ní
Bhris mo chroí
Béal a' Chalaidh
Mharaigh mé,
Leic Mhór
A chuir faoi thalamh mé.

Dún an Ní broke my heart, Béal a' Chalaidh killed me, Leic Mhór
put me under the earth.

THE KELP AGE

Dare one wonder what the product of this heart-break was, in
terms of tons per year, of basketloads carried up the shore? Most
of the weed gathered through the winter was for fertilizing the potato crop and for "making land" by covering barren rock with layers of seaweed and sand, but after the potatoes had been set in
March and April yet more weed was stacked and dried, and then
burnt in little kilns on the shore, for seaweed ash or "kelp" was the
island's principal cash product for over two hundred years. In the
1860s and '70s, for instance, between 450 and 750 tons of kelp
were exported annually. Estimates of how many tons of weed
went into the making of a ton of kelp vary and I have read figures
as high as twenty tons, but islanders I have consulted would put it
at about five tons of dry weed or ten of wet weed. That gives a total of around six thousand tons burnt for kelp; then if a basketload
of weed is about a hundredweight, as I have been told, a hundred
and twenty thousand basketsful were carried up the shore every
year during the heyday of the kelp industry, plus I have no idea
how many more to feed the land.

Kelp-burning probably became important in Aran around the
year 1700 as the industry seems to have originated in the west of
Ireland at about that time, spread to the Highlands and Islands of

Scotland within a few decades and rapidly came to dominate the economy of the coastal areas. Its occasion was the demand for various constituents of vegetable ash, especially the soda used in glass and soap-making and (in Ireland particularly) in the bleaching of linen, and to a lesser extent the potash used in the manufacture of alum (for dyeing) and saltpetre (for gunpowder). Wood-ash had been the main source of these alkalies, but with the forests depleted and the import of alkalies of various continental origins interrupted by wars, British manufacturers called for alternative supplies, and the peasants of the Atlantic coast bent their backs to the seaweed.

Hardiman's *History of Galway* (1820) records that kelp sold there initially at 14 to 21 shillings a ton, but that by 1808 it had reached a peak of £13 a ton and the town was exporting 4000 tons a year, most of it made in Connemara. It was Galway's man of science Dr. Richard Kirwan who first devised a chemical estimation of the alkali content of kelp, superseding the old rules of thumb based on appearance and taste. Much of Galway's kelp went to the north of Ireland for use in the linen industry and, according to Hardiman,

> it was found that several gross frauds were practised in making this article by mixing it with sand, stones and other grit matter, to the manifest injury, it was complained, of the linen trade of the kingdom.... Inspectors were accordingly appointed, but even this precaution was found insufficient to prevent its adulteration, in consequence of which the Connemara kelp has of late years fallen into disrepute.

By the time Hardiman was writing the price had fallen to £4 and Galway's exports to 2500 tons a year because, he supposed, of its inferiority to Scottish kelp. In fact the Scottish boom had collapsed too, partly because the Treaty of Paris had opened the way to Spanish imports of alkali made by burning the saltwort plant, and (a more important factor, though not recognized as such at the time) the discovery of a process of synthesizing alkali directly from sea-salt and sulphur.

The smoke of the kelp-kilns might have died away then in Aran as all around the coasts of Ireland and Scotland, but for a fortuitous discovery that had been made in 1812 by a manufacturer of saltpetre near Paris. In the course of experiments to establish why the kelp solution he used was corroding his copper vessels, he isolated a previously unknown element, iodine. The unfolding of the industrial and medicinal virtues of the new substance gave kelp another century or more of usefulness, and it is only within present memory that the exploitation of other sources of iodine, and its replacement in surgery by modern antibiotics, have brought an end to kelp-burning.

It is impossible to identify any material traces of the earlier, eighteenth-century, phase of the industry in Aran. The kilns were slight affairs quickly put together out of the stones of the shore and pulled apart after use. But the history of the second phase can be written around a cluster of derelict structures by the sea, five or six hundred yards south of An Uaimh Mhór. Their importance is in inverse proportion to their prominence, but the roofless gables of the largest form the only landmark along this morose stretch of coast and serve to guide one to the others, which could be overlooked—for the kilns were still the same, ephemeral in form and in substance undistinguished from the shore itself. The iodine-rich redweed and searods of the lower shore were now preferred to the more easily harvested blackweed, but otherwise the practice was unchanged, except that during a brief period of boom around 1870 an element of mechanization was introduced. This ruined factory, called by the islanders Teach an Smáil, the house of the ash, was one of three; another just inland of Port Chonnla, is now scarcely traceable, but the walls of the major establishment, An Teach Mór, the big house, still grimly overlook the great seaweed-shore of Port Chorrúch two miles farther east. Aran's annual production of kelp had climbed from between 120 and 200 tons in the 1820s to over 700 tons at the industry's high point in the early

'70s, and agents were competing to buy it. The rapacious Mr. Thompson, agent to Aran's landlords, had established the "Marine Salts Company" in Galway, with a standing order from London for as much iodine as he could supply. By threat of eviction he was forcing the Aran men to sell him their kelp at his price of £5 a ton (and on his generous definition of a ton, which could be anything from 22 ¹/₂ to 40 hundredweight), when they could have got from £7 to £8 a ton from other dealers in Clare and Connemara. The Aran factories were outposts of his short-lived Galway enterprise, and their tale of extortion, fraud and collapse, as it appears in newspapers, judicial enquiries and even Parliamentary debates of the time, will be read into the record apropos of An Teach Mór, by the waves of Port Chorrúch.

By 1877 Marine Salts was out of business and in the ensuing decade prices were so low that little or no kelp was made. There was a revival in the 1890s and 1900s; the price fluctuated around £4, two-thirds of the population were engaged in kelp-making, the average family producing at least two tons and some families as much as twelve tons. It was estimated that kelp money formed over a third of the total income of a family "in poor circumstances" and nearly a quarter of that of a family "in ordinary circumstances." But after 1908 competition from Japanese kelp and from South American guano as fertilizer caused another fall to the point where it was no longer worth while harvesting the weed. Kelp profited from the carnage of the First World War which cried out for iodine; also in 1917 the interruptions of other supplies prompted MacDonoghs of Galway to set up a factory making fertilizer using kelp made from blackweed, to which Aran contributed. Thereafter, with the discovery of penicillin and the opening-up of other sources for what little iodine was still required, the industry flickered to its final extinction in about 1948. That spring when the kelpers went to Cill Rónáin as usual to get the sacks from the agent they were told that there would be no further buying of kelp. So the stacks of weed gathered and dried through the previous winter went onto the land as fertilizer.

It was during this long autumn of the Age of Kelp that certain innovations were made, quite ineffective in practice, but which at least provided the industry with a few monuments more eye-catching than the shallow traces of the old kilns. For in the Thirties the Free State government, in an attempt to develop the technology of kelp, had specimen kilns of a more substantial and permanent design built on various seaweed-shores, together with enclosures for the storage of the weed. Of the new kilns only two have survived the fifty stormy winters since then in these islands, one almost complete at Mainistir (which will be described when that shore is reached) and another rather ruinous one in Inis Oírr. The enclosures or *teáltaí* (the islanders call them *teaichíní*, little houses) were of two sorts, and one of each can be seen close by the empty walls of the old seaweed factory, Teach an Smáil. The larger is a rectangle defined by low, solidly built walls, about 14 feet by 44 feet inside and with a wide opening in the seaward end, occu-pying the corner of a field by the shore. There is another, inland of An Gleannachán, that fits snugly into the field-pattern, one on the Bun Gabhla shore, and two on each of the smaller Aran Islands. They are floored with small limestone blocks neatly set on edge, between which the brine was no doubt supposed to seep away. The other type was a circle of stout wall measuring about a dozen feet across within, and floored with big ovoid stones from the shinglebank. Apart from the one on the foreshore here which is in good shape, these circles have almost completely vanished. These then are the scanty markers of the failing history—and elsewhere they are probably even fewer, for when I was mapping the whole South Connemara coast from Indreabhán westwards to Cashel I came across only one such kiln and one circular enclosure still standing, on the south of Garomna Island.

Although the Aran labourers appreciated the bit of relief-work money spent on building these things I am told that "not a sop of seaweed ever went into them." According to my guide to the Sruthán shore, the theory was that wet weed heaped into these shelters would dry "by spontaneous combustion," but this was never put to the test as local opinion was and is that "It's hard enough to dry weed hung over a wall, never mind put down in one of them things!" In fact a contemporary publication in which the kelpers were urged to adopt new ways makes it clear that the shelters were only for holding the weedstack, roofed with straw, secure from rain (which would tend to wash the iodine out of wet weed) until the weather should be suitable for spreading, drying and making cocks of it in the usual way. Similarly the kiln at Mainistir was never used though it would have been less laborious to operate than the old type. These innovations came too late to overcome the conservatism of a way of life falling into senility.

Thus the true memorials of the two-and-a-half centuries of kelp-burning are the temporary kilns of the old type, the remains of which are not easy to find among the other stones of the shore. And so at last the never-used circular enclosure near Teach an Smáil has acquired a certain modest function, for it guides one to the site of such a kiln, just twenty-five paces to its south-east. Having seen this specimen—hardly more than a grassy clearance among the pebbles in the shape of a narrow oblong about twenty feet long, with the interrupted remains of an edging of rough blocks of stone along one side—it is possible to recognize others as one comes across them, like fossil footprints of some extinct monster, at intervals along the shore. Here at last we are on the track of the business to which so much of Aran's thought and energy was sacrificed.

SMOKE AND ASH

The firing of the kilns was the crux of the year's shore-work, a midsummer dedication of sweat. It was a time of high excitement and anxiety that called upon all the stamina of the young and craft of the old. For weeks on end the shores would be wreathed in heavy creamy smoke. Over on the mainland the weather-prophets of Casla used to foretell rain if they caught the whiff of Aran's burning seaweed carried across the twelve miles of sea by a south-westerly breeze and held low by a temperature inversion, while at such times the Aran folk would be praying that the breeze would hold steady and the clouds pass unbroken over the island. Luck with the weather, a relentless physical effort sustained over the twenty-four or thirty-six hours of a kiln's burning, and the inherited expertise of generations went into ensuring a successful outcome; a little magic and a degree of roguery were among the ingredients too. From various islanders, the last to practise it, I have pieced together a detailed account of the building and tending of the altars of this rite.

The burning was usually done in June, by which time the great stacks of weed gathered in the spring would be thoroughly dry. The kilns were simply made by clearing a level patch of stony shore (it was important to avoid contamination by sand), arranging a rim of blocks about a foot high around a rectangle three or four feet across and from fifteen to thirty feet long, depending on the amount of weed to be burned, and then carefully pointing and flooring it with *dóib*, the clay dug out from under the inland cliffs of the islands. Before dawn on the appointed day the men would have drunk their mugs of tea and be walking down to the shore with a bucketful of smouldering turfs from the hearth. The kiln would be heaped high with dry briars, pressed down and lit from a couple of turfs thrust in at either end and in the middle. The driest of the weed would be thrown in, and it would soon be burning fiercely if the wind was suitable. It was essential for the wind to be blowing across the kiln if it were not to smother itself, and helpful if it blew from the same side all the time so that the men feeding the fire were not themselves smothered. I have been told, by an elderly man who in his youth saw it done by "the old folk," that a *muileann gaoithe*, a windmill, which was merely a napkin-sized cloth hung between a few sticks, was sometimes erected by the kiln to "draw the wind" to the right quarter. The two long walls of the kiln were termed *balla na gaoithe*, the wall of the wind, and *balla an deataigh*, the wall of the smoke. A strong wind could cool the exposed wall of the kiln to such a degree that the weed on that side would not burn properly, and a little gap would appear between the interior of the wind-wall and the rising column of smoke; at this sign a currach would be brought up to shelter the wall and weed heaped over it to make a wind-break.

Towards mid-afternoon the kiln would be thoroughly raked by six or eight men facing each other in pairs across the kiln and working their *rácaí* to and fro in opposite directions. (One or two rusty specimens of these *rácaí* still lie around the almost defunct island smithy in which they were made; they were iron rods just over a yard long, sometimes fitted with a wooden handle and bent round at the top into a small loop.) When the whole kilnful had been stirred thoroughly until it all ran together into a molten glow, feeding of the fire would be continued. In the middle of the next night the raking would be repeated, and the fire allowed to die down. Flat stones would be placed on the hot mass (round ones would have sunk into it) to cover and compress it. Finally, it would be protected from the rain with a layer of bracken or dry weed, and left to cool. It would be mid-morning by the time the exhausted men went home.

Sometimes it took a night, a day and a night to burn a large kiln. Tom O'Flaherty recalls witnessing the two nights of toil as a child:

About two o'clock the horizon on the north-east lightened and soon crimsoned. The sun was coming up and I was getting sleepy and felt like lying down. Michael advised me to go home and to bed. I told him I would after I saw them rake the kiln. Michael nodded. "Go light on her now!" he ordered. "It's time we gave her the first raking." Then the men got hold of long iron rods and stripping to the waist they raked the burnt seaweed in the kiln from end to end and side to side. They shouted to each other to work harder as the sweat poured from their bodies. When the kelp began to run in a molten mass they stopped and threw more sea-weed on the kiln.

And the following evening:

The seaweed was now nearly all burned. The men were tired, worn, dirty and bleary-eyed after the night and the long hot day. It was midnight when they threw the last wisp on the kiln. Then they got out their long iron rakes and re-peated the process of the previous night. When they had finished, the kelp ran like molten lead. The men put on their white waistcoats and rested while the kelp was harden-ing. Then they put flat rocks over it and dry ferns. Soon it would be ready for the buyer. If it did not test well they would only get a poor price for it. Oftentimes they did not get enough to pay the cost of carrying it to the mainland.

Tragically, much of this titanic effort was later found to be unnec-essary. The Congested Districts Board around 1912 was experi-menting with a less demanding regime of burning which produced a loose ash rather than a clinker. For a long time the buyers resis-ted the idea on the grounds that ash would be more vulnerable to the weather in transport, and would have to be emptied out of its bags to test for adulteration. The kelp-burners too were reluctant to accept that the muscle and wisdom of generations had been mis-directed. However, in time both sides were persuaded that there was no point in fusing the kelp into solidity. Twenty-eight years after witnessing the scenes described above, Tom O'Flaherty re-turned to the same shore and spoke with the new generation of kelpers:

"Will you have her burned tonight?" I asked.
"Faith we will not," he answered. "In half an hour's time we'll be going home and into our beds for ourselves...."

There's many a change on things since you left. You remember how we used to stay up as long as two nights and a day with a large kiln. Every once in a while we got our long iron rods and raked her. We thought she wouldn't be any good unless she was running like boiled tar. Now, faith, we just start throwing in the seaweed, nice and easy, and devil damn the rake at all we put in her. And here's the best of it. When night comes we leave her there and go home and to bed, and around we come in the morning and start up again. We keep on taking our time until we have the kiln burned."

"And doesn't the kelp run at all now and don't you have to break it up with a sledge?"

"Damn the run, O son. They say it's better to have her in small stones or powder. We put her all in bags now. In your time there was no respect at all for the kelp that was in the bags. Everything is different now. We don't work as hard as we used to and though there is no money we live better than we ever did. We are eating meat now my boy!"

Such, then, was the riot and licence of the Kelp Age's decadence; one can hear the note of disapproval. But in the old, classical times to which my informants' memories return, solidity was still accounted a virtue. The kiln would be left to cool for three or four days, and then the stones of one side of it would be pulled away and the block of kelp broken up into handleable bits two or three feet across. One way of doing this was to lever up the slab with crowbars, place a round stone under it where it was desired to crack it, put a handful of straw on top of the slab and give it a sharp blow with another stone on the straw, so that it fractured neatly. The pieces would be piled up and covered from the rain with bracken until they could be carried to Cill Rónáin by cart or to Connemara by boat. The steep-sided creek of An Uaimh Mhór, just north of Teach an Smáil, was one of the dozens of natural harbours from which hookers took kelp across to a firm in Cill Chiaráin, the predecessor of today's alginate works.

But before he would buy, the agent would test the kelp for iodine content. He would crumble together two or three little pieces taken from different parts of the lot, put a pinch of the powder into a test-tube and do something mysterious with a drop of sulphuric acid; the islanders would take it as a hopeful sign if when the treated sample was flung out on the ground they saw a smoke of iodine vapour arising from it. Then after a calculation the agent would announce his verdict, acceptance or rejection, good price or bad. By all accounts this could scarcely be called the moment of truth. As Synge wrote in his compassionate account of Connemara, of 1905:

> In the Galway neighbourhood, at least, no steps appear to have been taken to ensure the people a fair market for the kelp they produce, or to revise the unsatisfactory system by which it is tested and paid for. In some places the whole buying trade falls into the hands of one man, who can then control the prices at his pleasure, while one hears on all sides of arbitrary decisions by which good kelp is rejected, and what the people consider an inferior article is paid for at a high figure. When the buying is thus carried on, no appeal can be made from the decision of one individual, and I have sometimes seen a party of old men sitting nearly in tears on a ton of rejected kelp that had cost them weeks of work, while, for all one knew, it had very possibly been refused on account of some grudge or caprice of the buyer.

Similar memories are still bitter in the islands. As one old man told me, "If you weren't great with the buyer you wouldn't get the price—and then the best thing you could do was leave your kelp on the quay and the next day ask someone else to pretend it was his and get a fair price for you."

On the other hand adulteration of the kelp was a practice almost as old as the industry, and one on which the kelpers were repeatedly lectured. The Annual Report of the Congested Districts Board for 1914, for instance, states:

> The buyers of the kelp complain, and often justly, we fear, that when the seaweed is in a molten state, sand and stones are sometimes mixed with it in order to increase the weight.... All real friends of the kelp-burners urge them to abandon this adulteration.... Buyers make a careful chemical analysis and fix a lower price all round so as to protect themselves.

Sometimes, I have been told, a special batch of kelp would be made from *coirleach*, which is rich in iodine but laborious to harvest, in the hope that the agent would take his sample out of this portion of the load. And on the other hand I was once surprised to learn from my oracle of the shore that *ruánach*, the fleshless thongweed, was favoured for kelp: "There's great weight in *ruánach*!" he said, and when I reminded him that he had previously told me there was little iodine in it he replied, "That's true—but then you'd try to have the *ruánach* in a part of the kelp that wouldn't be tested!"

AFTERIMAGES, AFTERTHOUGHTS

Having thought so intensely about the old shore-days in the writing of these seaweed-sequences of my book, I went back to that coast and walked it once again, from An Gleannachán to Port Sheánla, to see if the images I had drawn from the past and tried to impose on that refractory background had any permanency. But the vivid sea-fowl distracted me from the hunt for enhanced imaginings; I wished I had brought binoculars and bird-book; I saw nothing but the passing show of the present. Later I read an anecdote recorded by Elizabeth Rivers, an English artist who lived here for a time in the Thirties, which suggested a particular interpretation of my fruitless search. An old shore-worker is talking:

"I was passing down by the shore before day and I thought I heard the swish of seaweed being thrown," he said. "I stooped, by stooping I could get the shape of anyone who might be there against the water, and I saw him outlined against the water as he bent down and gathered great armfuls of weed and I heard the swish of the weed as it fell into heaps. He was in the best part of the shore, the part I was aiming for myself, so leaving him I passed on further round the point; I worked there for some hours and then sat down under a cock of weed expecting him, Mike Mór I thought it was, to pass that way. No one came and I went round to see was he still working. The rods were all there undisturbed, no human hand had touched them." He paused as if seeing the scene again in his mind.

"Did you leave them?" I asked.

"No," he looked at me with a quizzical expression and smiled. "I went to work, whoever was there before me I reckoned there was work to be done. We used to believe that great seaweed men came back to the shore, some thought to do penance because of having wanted more than their just share in life; some believed that for a man who loved the shore it would be natural for his spirit to come there after his death."

Now of course those just or unjust shares of the shore are all forgotten and for mile after mile it is the ungrudged portion of such solitaries as love it disinterestedly; nevertheless to search there for its past by the broad daylight of the present, hoping for more than something vaguely seen and heard against the glimmer and plash of the night sea, is perhaps to want more than one's just, or even possible, share in life. But, not granting the objective existence of ghosts, I require all the more precision in their identification. The verbal material I have used in my attempt to recall the old shore-life is unspecific, for instance, about the dress of the labourers; perhaps I should turn to old photographs to impress visual details on my memory before returning to the shore.

The Araner, his gear and garb, have been catching the camera's eye for a century. This eye sometimes has had a rude scientific stare, sometimes a look of love. There are photographs by the ethnographers Haddon and Browne who came here to measure skulls in the 1890s, showing three islanders ranged by height, in profile and full-face views; the symmetry and order of the framing exacerbates every oddity and lopsidedness of the framed. Whereas another islander of that same generation, in one of the photographs Synge made, no doubt as a step in his mysterious transmutation of the Aran Islands into *The Aran Islands*, looks at his strange friend behind the camera with exactly the expression of puzzled affection the poet's face must often have worn—a fine instance of the total reversal the hands of a serious photographer unknowingly induce in the optics of the camera. Then there are untruthful moments concocted for the blink of the truthful eye: in T. H. Mason's *The Islands of Ireland*, of 1936, we are offered photographic evidence of a patriarchally bearded Araner seated at a spinning-wheel before his cottage door. The son of the sitter, now himself elderly, has told me how angry he was, a child, on seeing a stranger photographing "something that doesn't be, a man at a spinning-wheel." Finally (to complete this cursory quartering of the photographic archives), there are the little showers of anonymous and amateur snaps that turn up lodged here and there like autumn leaves in unexpected crannies, such as the packet marked only "1934" which "came into the hands of" *The Irish Times* recently, containing images (the upturned faces of Inis Meáin boatmen holding their currachs against the waves while waiting for goods to be thrown down to them from the steamer, the empty seaward gaze of loiterers on the wall above Cill Rónáin harbour) of ragged, haggard endurance and resignation, from a harsh season.

From such sources, by ignoring so much of what they have to say and by interpreting the rest with the aid of contemporary writings, one could compile a manual of identification of old-Aran-out-of-door, as follows:

Male: Soft black round-crowned hat with a broad brim that together with the beard shades the face completely, or a knitted tam-o-shanter with a bobble on top. Small straight-stemmed clay pipe. Flannel shirt, high-necked small-collared jacket of homespun tweed, and over that a sleeveless tweed *veist* or waistcoat with broad lapels buttoned back. Trousers also of homespun tweed with capacious bottoms (for ease in rowing) and wide legs, usually stiff with patches, having short slits at the outside ankle (so that they can be rolled up); these trousers supported by the *crios*, a four-yard strip of woven material in bright patterns, the only touch of colour in the sombre ensemble, wound around the waist and tucked into itself, not knotted, and requiring frequent tightening in a work-pause as habitual as spitting on the hands. On hot days or at the kiln these outer layers would be stripped off, down to the long under-trousers of natural-coloured wool. Long knitted stockings and moccasin-like *bróga úrleathair* or rawhide shoes, hairy side out—the "pampooties" famed in touristic writings and to which Synge attributed Aran's elastic nobility of stride.

Female: Flannel blouse, black or tartan shawl pulled up over the head during rain (or substituted for by a spare petticoat). When carrying up the big square osier-rod baskets full of wet weed, a sheepskin or goatskin is worn on the back to keep off the brine. Ample petticoat to mid-calf, grey-black or sepia in the old photographs of course, indelibly red in every page of Ireland's romantic history, and more often indigo blue in Aran's reality. Thick stockings and *bróga úrleathair*, or bare feet.

Primed with these distinguishing marks, then, I could set out once again (for instance from the trace of the old kiln described above, and thence south-east to Port Sheánla, so as to finish with this stretch of coast and conclude these conjurations of the shore's past, before turning to other matters), in the hope of identifying the ghost of Kelp Age Man and Kelp Age Woman.

But even as I picture myself doing so, some of those "other matters" (as if the phrase referred to mental solids, liquids and gases), denser than any spirits distilled from old photographs, claim my vision: memories deriving from my most recent, my first, my every visit to this place. Offshore, opposite the fragments of kiln, is a square, flat-topped rock called Table Rock on the Admiralty charts, and in Irish An Corradán (a diminutive, probably, from *corr*, point or angle, and merely expressing the fact that it is a little projection of the coast). On it ten or twenty big dark long-necked birds stand motionless except for an occasional stabbing quarrel or a yawning stretch of the wings, for hour after hour, every day. They are green cormorants, or shags, a little smaller than the cormorants themselves. The field-guides to birds list the distinguishing features of the two species:

Cormorant: Length 36 inches. Bronze-black plumage, with white chin and cheeks. White patch on thigh in breeding season. Immature birds brownish above and whitish below.

Shag: Length 30 inches. Green-black plumage, no white on face. Short crest in breeding season. Immature birds dark brown with little or no white below.

I wonder if the Irish name for the cormorant, *broigheall*, derives from *bráidgheall*, white-throated. I wonder why Aran at least sees the shag as female, for here it is known as the *cailleach dhubh*, the black hag. Running my mind rapidly along the whole northern coast I see that there are just three such parliaments of shags, one here on An Corradán, one three miles to the east below a cliff called An Caipín, the little cap, and one on a rock named from the species, Carraig na gCailleach, another three miles beyond the last. Their sessions have no doubt seen the kelp industry come and go, indifferently. How intensely their angular outlines are imprinted on the loose grey distances seawards! My afterimages of the human generations of the shore, fading into the dimness of old photographs, have no comparable claim on the retina. Can the act of writing hold such disparate materials in coexistence?

Making my way (in thought) along the awkward rock-banks towards Port Sheánla, I can at least work out the answer to the question sometimes put to me by myself and others as to whether or no there will be photographs in my book—old photographs, as if it were a field-guide to revenants, new ones, my own perhaps, as exemptions from the task of description? Photographs and text stand in such different dimensions of the attention, demand attention of such different dimensions, that, for instance a photograph resists quotation, adoption into a verbal context by cutting and commentary, more resolutely than does another text. In particular it is only through description and not by physical inclusion that those troubling likenesses of bygone kelpers can people this described shore of mine. The persistency, recurrency and interpenetration of images in a composed book (and with the word "composed" goes the implication that these considerations need not trouble a guide-book, for example) are to be as modulable as those of themes in music. The page of photographs standing out among pages of print would preserve certain images from the time-flow of writing, of reading—and nothing, living or dead, can be allowed that exemption within the covers of this book. A photograph, then, would disrupt the book as much as an actual sample of Aran stone enclosed between its pages.

To explain to myself what this means for the life-expectancy of ghosts, for example, I stop in passing to look at Port Sheánla. This theatre for potential apparitions, a slight concavity of the coast-line, a little stage of sand and at low tide some flat seaweed-shiny rocks, can be oppressively set in drizzling walls of fog, or lit with transformation-scenes of crystalline dazzle. The first time I visited the spot with M, in early spring sunshine, I overwhelmed her by saying with an all-inclusive and impulsive gesture, "This is Para-dise!"—for the dancing shallows and freshly rinsed sandflats were alive with little waders, and I (Adam with a newly acquired field-guide to shorebirds) was looking forward to naming them: streaky brown dunlins, plump pearly sanderlings, turnstones with harle-quin backs and wings, ringed plovers in black white and choco-late, so many nimble fistfuls of distinctive features. And then an old man, tall and wiry, with a fierce bony jaw, hailed us from the nearby field where he was digging long parallel ridges to plant his potatoes in. "No Englishman can match me with the spade!" he cried, brandishing it about his head, whereupon I hopped over the wall, seized the spade and threw together a yard or two of ridge, not as precisely level-topped and bevel-edged as his own work but creditable enough to surprise him, not knowing that a neighbour had been coaching me in this island art.

These memories of our first wide-eyed appropriation of this lit-tle world, and the counter-claims each new find here still makes on me after a decade of careful looking, interrupt my ghost-hunt, reveal its artificiality. Ghosts are to be created, not found. In so far as my writing can catch them against the same light as it does the stones and stories of my own experience, the old people of the shore revisit it. And when on rounding a headland of this mental march other sights of powerful associations come into view, these ghosts are laid, with the laying aside of this attempt at a resurrec-tion that never for a moment troubled the nothingness of the dead.

MAN OF ARAN

A single-storied, many-windowed house that nowadays gives the impression of being a trifle tired of sunshine and sea breezes enjoys a spacious setting on the western shoulder of the bay at Cill Mhuirbhigh, near an old stone pier. It was built in the Twenties for a Mrs. Sharman of London, a frequent visitor to the island who became friendly with the Johnstons, the successors of the O'Flahertys at Kilmurvey House, and was eventually given this lovely site—a choice that indicates the arrival in Aran of the concept of a view. At that period the glassy display cases in which prosperous Aran trawlermen are now housing themselves would have been inconceivable, and the relaxed, open look of this self-confessed holiday home must have been strikingly alien to an Aran that knew only the shy, sly, little cottage windows that wink and peep, and the cold lofty stare of Kilmurvey House. In 1932 and '33 it was the fitting seat of the great-hearted court of Robert Flaherty, who leased it for himself and his family during the making of *Man of Aran*, the film that Aran people call simply "the Film." Flaherty's definitive remake of timeless Aran was at the same time a definite intervention in Aran history, and one which is rapidly acquiring the moss of myth in its own right. His fame and lavish hospitality brought many visitors to watch him building what appeared to be yet another storey of that sublime and ill-founded tower, the Aran legend; his giant presence redirected dozens of island lives, and his creation, ambiguously situated between documentary and mythology, yearly allures hundreds of romantic pilgrims and journalistic hacks to an island it would please them to see as situated in a changeless and heroic era. But the lasting elements of Flaherty's magnificent construction are certain huge, deep and simple intuitions of the physical universe, for which he hunted here with his camera as he had in the Canadian snows and the tropical Pacific. To suggest that the exotic incidentals of his film measure the subtle, complex and changing surface of Aran is to falsify Flaherty's work and even make it ridiculous

—but in the zeal of promotion that is exactly what Flaherty himself did.

Aran used to suspect that Flaherty's prestigious surname was a mask adopted to help make his way in the islands, but it is mere coincidence that the name appears yet again in local history. Robert J. Flaherty's father was a second-generation Irish-American of Protestant stock who owned and managed an iron mine (the profession may not be irrelevant) in Ironmountain, Michigan, where Flaherty was born in 1884. When the slump of '93 closed that concern young Flaherty accompanied his father to his new post of manager of an iron mine in Ontario, Canada. Flaherty himself later returned to train (briefly, until expelled) at the Michigan School of Mining, and his early years were spent in mapping, prospecting and mining in Northern Ontario and Vancouver Island. In 1910 he was commissioned to explore the iron-ore potential of islands in the east of Hudson Bay, and it was there, in the previously almost unknown Belcher Islands, that he first filmed the Eskimos who were his guides, hosts and friends. He later burned this film (accidentally, he claimed), but from its ashes arose *Nanook of the North*, which was screened in '23 and established him as a celebrant of the primaeval duel of Man and Nature.

His next film, *Moanna*, was set in Samoa, and his backers, Paramount, expected him to find the exotic, as before. But for Flaherty the languor of the lagoon was no equivalent of the wind-blasted icefloes. Even the man-eating shark he had hoped to cast in the adversary role of Nature failed to turn up, and to give his hero something to endure he had to revive a happily extinct ceremony of initiation by all-over tattooing. For his pains, Flaherty too ended up with a superficial film of beauty.

It was on his way to Britain to work on documentaries that Flaherty first heard of Aran, as a place where men pit themselves against mountainous seas in frail coracles, from a stranger met on board ship. (This unknown voice prompting the re-invention of Aran—a person from Porlock perhaps, expiating his interruption of an earlier visionary landscape in creation?) Flaherty later enquired further, and the documentary film-maker John Grierson gave him Synge's *The Aran Islands* and *Riders to the Sea*. After a period of unsatisfactory work in Britain, and a spell of what he termed "mental hookworm," Flaherty came to look at Aran in the autumn of '31, and evidently saw it as the rock from which he too could launch his frail craft against the mounting waves of doubt. He returned to install himself, his wife Francis and their three daughters in the house by Port Mhuirbhigh in the following January.

On his first visit Flaherty had been shown around the island by a Cill Rónáin man, Pat Mullen, who made his living largely by his pony and side-car. As a young man Pat Mullen had been in America—had indeed left a wife running an illicit drinking-house there—and his years of rambling, labouring and moonshining, and then the friendship of educated visitors to Aran, had given him a breadth of outlook that many of his neighbours identified as Socialism and Atheism. He rather naturally now became Flaherty's courier and contact-man, which probably added to the islanders' suspicions about Flaherty's proceedings. Both Mullen and Flaherty have left accounts, or at least streams of anecdotes, of that period (Pat Mullen's were published under the rather opportunistic title of *Man of Aran* in 1935, and Flaherty's are retailed in Arthur Calder Marshall's study of him, *The Innocent Eye*, of 1963). As both men were *raconteurs* it would be in two senses an ungrateful task to search among their entertaining inconsistencies for the truth of various incidents in the cycle of legends that accumulated around the making of the film.

Casting was made difficult by the islanders' fear of alien corruption and by their shyness which wrapped itself in a fierce pride. But, whether by Pat Mullen's ready tongue or Flaherty's geniality, the wages he offered and a discreet donation to the Church, all obstacles were overcome and a cast was assembled that served the half-comprehended enterprise with courage and loyalty.

The three eventually called to stand as the film's nuclear family were a boy from Cill Éinne called Micilín Dillane, a careworn beauty, Maggie Dirrane, whom Flaherty had noticed cradling her baby at her cottage door in Sruthán, and the Man of Aran himself, Colman (nicknamed "Tiger") King, a magnificent young giant whom one of the Flaherty daughters spotted sitting on the quay at Cill Mhuirbhigh. The Kings, hereditary blacksmiths in Fearann an Choirce and an intensely self-respecting family, suspected Flaherty of Socialism. Flaherty had for some time been pursuing Tiger's brother Pádraig for the part, but Pádraig stoutly resisted his destiny (and went on instead to the Heavyweight Boxing Championship of Connacht, and a career in the *gardaí*). The Tiger, however, was at last cajoled into a film-test, and so it was that the eagle profile of the Kings came to be stamped on an Aran that is still current coin.

Memories connected with three buildings scattered around the Sharman house by Port Mhuirbhigh are satellite to those of Flaherty's bright and massive presence. The traditional thatched cottage, with what looks like half another cottage built against it at the rear, was created to be the home of Flaherty's archetypal island family, and its odd design was to enable the taking of cottage-door shots by either morning or evening light. Pat Mullen oversaw its building (its kernel was the arch of an old fireplace he had had carted across from a ruined house in Gort na gCapall), and according to his account the rumour went around that it was to be a "Birds' Nest," as those hated institutions of the Famine times had been called, in which destitute Catholic children were brought up as Protestants. Micilín Dillane's family were particularly anxious about the danger of proselytism, and only the reassurance of the parish priest himself won their permission for Micilín to come to Cill Mhuirbhigh. In 1976 when the American cinematologist George Stoney was making a film or metafilm on Flaherty's film, he came across a fascinating hoard of huge wooden film reels and other antiquated equipment in the loft of the cottage, and arranged for their transfer to an archive set up for the purpose by Raidió Telefís Éireann. Until a few years ago the cottage was owned by Flaherty's daughters who occasionally spent a summer there. It has changed hands a couple of times since and become very dishevelled; now it is being adapted to some other future, but whatever this may be it will always be known as the Man of Aran cottages.

The second building of Flaherty connections lies near the shore to the north of the last; it is a tiny cottage, now roofless, of which only the chimneytop can be seen from the road. Some of Flaherty's many guests were lodged here, and it must have been a charming retreat, in a lush (by Aran standards) water-meadow by the sea, tucked under a flowery scarp. (The place is called Fearann na Bacaí, which probably used to mean "the Field of the Bend," for the scarp echoes the curve of the low-cliffed coastline into the bay, and the meadow follows between. But this sense has been lost to speech, and an islander suggests that the name is really Fearann na bPacaí, "the Field of the Packs," the big canvas bags in which *carraigín* was carried—in which case the gaunt figure of the old shore-life makes its momentary reappearance....)

Among the residents in this cottage was a Newton Rowe, former District Inspector of the Samoan island of Savaii, to whom Flaherty owed a debt of more than hospitality from the time of the making of *Moanna*. Flaherty had been taken mysteriously ill while filming on Savaii, and Rowe had had him carried to his house and nursed him there until he could be transferred to the capital. (The illness was later found to be due to contamination of the pool from which Flaherty drank, by silver nitrate from the film-processing.) Rowe had since left the New Zealand Government Service and had published a denunciation of its iniquities in his book, *Samoa under the Sailing Gods*, of 1930. Now he was a freelance journalist with a novel in mind, and Flaherty invited him to come and write it in this island, in every way the antipodes of Samoa—but of the outcome, if any, I have learned nothing.

Another visitor to Fearann na Bacaí was the English Celticist Robin Flower, most widely known in connection with the Blasket Islands and their literature. He had come to Aran to collaborate with Flaherty on a project for the Free State government, a film called *Oidhche Sheanchais*, an evening of traditional lore, or *The Story Teller*. This, the first film ever made in the Irish language, featured an Aran man, Seáinín Tom Ó Direáin, entertaining a fireside audience with a long tale. I have never seen this film, but when it was shown privately in Dublin in 1934 it won praise from a critic in *The Irish Times*, although as he admits he did not understand a word of it.

The third building, also co-opted into Flaherty's solar system, was an old stone fish-curing shed by the quay. It was taken over by Flaherty's young technical assistant John Taylor as a film-processing laboratory; a darkroom was improvised in one corner, and a generator, the first in Aran, was imported. The shed is hardly used now except for the gear of the one lobster-boat that works out of the bay, and the remains of the darkroom can be seen through its gaping door. A rusty chunk of the generator lying nearby must still be able to power bright memories in a few old islanders, for every now and then Flaherty would decree an evening of *céilí* dancing on the waterfront and send for the island musicians; then a cable would be run out from the generator for lamps to prolong the summer twilight while Francis Flaherty would oversee the local girl she had hired as cook (to whom I owe this vignette) in making trays of butterscotch for the dancers.

Island lore still shakes its head over the dangers to which Flaherty exposed his actors in the scenes of shark-hunting and homecomings from stormy seas that make up most of the film. He has indulged in something between confession and showmanship on the question:

> I should have been shot for what I asked those superb people to do for the film, for the enormous risks I exposed them to, and all for the sake of a keg of porter and five pounds apiece. But they were so intensely proud of the fact that they had been chosen to act in a film that might be shown all over the world that there was nothing they wouldn't do to make it a success.

However, as one old man who had played a bare-foot urchin in it told me, "That was the exaggeratingest film ever made!" And just as Flaherty's telephoto lens had the effect of piling up distant waves into awesome overhangs about to swamp his foreground figures, so every detail of the film's history has been wrought up into the terrific by the combined garrulities of the Aran hearthside and the film-world's dinner tables. Flaherty himself is no mean exaggerator:

> The Aran Islander in order to survive has to fight the sea. The sea around Aran is one of the most dangerous in the world. The craft he uses is a curragh—one of the oldest and most primitive craft that man anywhere has devised.... There was one instance of a crew in a curragh trying to get in to land. The following waves were so overwhelming that when a wave larger than the rest towered behind them, they had to swing round and face it, and then sidle over it, and then turn and run until the next wave came on and then the performance had to be gone through once again. That day the seas were so high that they couldn't make a landing on the island at all but had to keep on and on and finally landed at the head of Galway Bay some 30 miles away. I have never anywhere in the world seen men so brave who would undertake such risks with the sea.

Winter gave Flaherty those scenes of desperate landfalls—the half-drowned crew floundering ashore leaving their currach to be gnashed between wave and rock—that make the beginning and end of the film. And then summer, as if not to be outdone, gave him the central theme he was still waiting for, the giant shark the South Seas had denied him. And in some profusion, if his own account is to be believed:

> One Sunday we sailed through one of these schools [of basking sharks] in Galway Bay. The sharks averaged a length

of about twenty-seven feet, the tail being about six feet across. The school was four miles long. Looking down into the water, we could see that they were in layers—in tiers, tier after tier of them until we could see no deeper. There were thousands and thousands of them.

Pat Mullen managed to find two rusty harpoons tied to a rafter above the fireplace in his grandfather's old house, and took them to Galway for a smith to copy. But a generation had passed away since the basking shark had last been hunted in Aran waters, and Mullen had to seek out a deathbed-ridden centenarian in the Claddagh district of Galway and ask him how to harpoon the Levawn Mor, as he calls it (from the Irish, *an Liamhán Mór*):

"Ha, the Levawn Mor," said Martin, "'tis well I know them and 'tis them that's hard to kill," and his faded blue eyes shone brightly and took on a faraway look. Then he spoke again:

"You must have two hundred fathoms of line, with ten fathoms of it sarved near the harpoon end, so that when the Levawn rolls around on the bottom of the sea trying to get the harpoon out, the cable won't be cut on its skin. It is very rough and full of little sharp points and many a good boatman lost a Levawn that way long ago, for the want of the cable being sarved properly."

"Where will I harpoon it?" I asked.

"On the grey streak under the big fin, but you are never sure of your Levawn until you drive home your second harpoon."

Then old Martin turned over on his other side with his face away from us, and as he pulled the bedclothes up around his head he again murmured: "The Levawn Mor."

With just so much knowledge of the art, Flaherty's shark-hunters set off in a small open boat, a wooden Connemara *púcán*, and rowed up to the tranquil monsters to try out their unfamiliar harpoons, while Flaherty followed with his camera mounted on a larger boat with an engine. But, until Tiger King mastered the skill of striking into "the grey streak under the big fin," the harpoons bent on the impenetrable hide or were easily torn out when the shark dived; and then, because the rope always snapped or the light failed at the crucial moment, not much film had been made by the time the sharks moved on from Aran waters, and Flaherty had to prolong his shooting schedule into the next season. This time he called in a friend from the Hudson Bay years, a retired whaler captain, to show the crew how to mount a snubbing post near the stern of the *púcán* and use it to check or slacken away the rope as the shark ran. The captain brought a harpoon gun with him, and he would use it to put a heavy whale-harpoon into the shark from the larger boat to begin with; then the line would be passed to the *púcán* and the Aran men would use their hand-harpoons when they had hauled themselves close enough to the dying fish. And so at last the record of the noble pursuit was concocted. A few briefer sequences of Aran's more photogenic land-based activities—fishing from the tall cliffs, seaweed-gathering in storms, "making land" by spreading seaweed on bare rock—made up the rest of the film.

The anachronism of the shark-hunt was one factor in the controversy that arose after the film's first screening (in April 1934 at the New Gallery, London), for it was presented as a documentary of contemporary reality—and Maggie, Micilín and the Tiger were brought across to the premier in their homespuns to enforce the point, while a stuffed shark, shortened by removal of a middle cut, was displayed in the Gaumont-British Film Company's Wardour Street window. In the context of those depression years Flaherty's *Aran* appeared to be mere escapism. C. A. Lejeune's opinion was that the real story of Aran was the fight to hold the land against eviction, which Flaherty had not told, while Graham Greene condemned the wearisome affectation of his figures against the sky-line and the meaninglessness of his magnificent photography of storm after storm. In America criticism was more responsive to the theme of "a unit of life—man, woman and child—the continuing link in the human race winning survival in an unending war with the grim impersonality of the elements." Commercially the film did moderately well, and by degrees, as the question of its relationship to Aran of the Thirties has fallen away into the past, its almost abstract splendours have been revealed.

Island gossip about the film often reverts to the idea that there is another *Man of Aran* film somewhere, made up of all the scenes people remember being shot but which they do not find in the film as we know it (and as the islanders in particular and in detail know it, for it is shown repeatedly throughout the summer in the Hall in Cill Rónáin). One of these "missing" sequences haunts my imagination too. John Goldman, who was sent out to Aran by Gaumont-British to cut some sense, or what they would have regarded as sense, into Flaherty's profuse streams of unpre-edited footage, mentions it in the course of justifying his own work on the film:

> Much the worst of Flaherty's profligacy was his addiction to panning the camera. Perhaps the smoothness of the gyro-headed tripod had something to do with this, and touched a tactile nerve in him. One shot—quite pointless in itself—consisted of a complete magazine [200 feet] of an unbroken pan-shot ranging over the perpendicular walls of a cliff from the top—though never showing the skyline—down to the sea and back again until it lost itself. I think he was trying to establish by feeling it the height of the cliff. It was typical of him to try to do this by the camera rather than by cutting. This wanting to do it all *in and through* the camera was one of the main causes of his great expenditure of film—so often he was trying to do what could *not* in fact be done.

Or, perhaps, what the cinema of the time did not *want* done. This visual scaling of the cliff sends me back to the early, Canadian, pages (to me, unversed in film history, much the most exciting) of

Calder Marshall's biography of Flaherty, *The Innocent Eye*. Was this eye in fact always that of a *prospector*, looking into the heart of matter through measurement of its surface? I see Flaherty wandering in a giant landscape trying to subject it to the rule and compass of geology—and then through the Eskimos finding he could apply a more compelling measure to the immensities of snow and ice, that of human endurance. (In a more recent climate he might have been able to unfold about that landscape a more subtle, web-like extension of his measure, human adaptation.) But what was prime, what mattered, was to him not endurance as such (and certainly not the endurers) but the rhythms and structures of a non-human reality. That in exploring the substantiality of place he repeatedly used (as his mine-workers) societies nearing the end of their timelessness, and further blurred their historicity by his unsignaled recursions to their past, identifies him as a poet of the material, rather than the temporal, imagination. And it is because he went so deep in search of its materiality that his Aran stands like a rock after all the buzzing froth of Celtic and filmic exaggeration has fallen from it.

HISTORY OF A STRANGER

To suppress Time, so as to throw the grand material dimensions into relief against that blank, is a masterly way with reality. But even if it does justice to the artist's own splendid simplicities such a work should not pretend to *adequacy* (in a sense that I would like to explain to myself through this book) to even that scrap of the world it takes as its pretext; a million of the little nerves and veins in which Time, as life and sense, works through the material, broken by the great interruption, would cry out against it. Being more concerned with justice to Aran than to Flaherty, I will take up two of these threads (which entangle with the Flaherty story), as example, as reparation, as steps on my way.

The cottage that Flaherty had built to house his Man, Woman and Child of Aran had a modest afterlife once those eternal verities had quitted it, serving the growing tourist trade encouraged by the film. It was rented by Elizabeth Rivers, an English artist born in 1908, who came here in 1935. Miss Rivers, as she was known here, stayed in Aran for most of seven years until she went to London to do her bit in the Fire Service during the Blitz. She returned for a short time after the war, and then settled in Dublin, working with Evie Hone on stained glass, and involving herself with the Independent Artists' Group. She died in 1964.

During her Aran years Miss Rivers supported herself by putting up visitors (poorly off Bohemians, many of them, attracted by the power of Flaherty's romantic vision), whom Pat Mullen would bring over to her from Cill Rónáin pier in his side-car. One of these visitors, Lady Clara Vyvyan, became a friend, and has left a tender portrait of her, and of the cottage's brimming social life, in her book of dreamily bedazzled travels in Ireland, *On Timeless Shores*. Betty Rivers, she tells us, "with her sloe-black eyes and upstanding crest of dark hair and quiet voice, was a very gentle-seeming person of forceful character." And as will appear shortly, she was to have need of that quiet fortitude, for her life in Aran was not always the continuous festival of friendship Lady Vyvyan describes. Unfortunately the "timeless" mode of writing (that of the consciousness on holiday, especially in the West of Ireland) tends to be too diffuse for quotation, but it does nevertheless catch certain subjectively genuine moments, and I like to read her descriptions of those spontaneous kitchen *céilí* dances of long ago in the Man of Aran cottage when wide-eyed visitors found themselves whirling in constellation with mysterious beings who seem to have just lifted the latch and stepped in from the Celtic otherworld.

Elizabeth River's woodcuts of island life, in a style slightly cubicized by her earlier studies at the Academie L'hôte in Paris, hang in a number of Aran homes. She also provided covers for various books (those of Pat Mullen and Tom O'Flaherty, that came in the wake of the Film, and Risteard de Paor's work of young love of Aran, *Úll i mBarr an Ghéagáin*)—likeable and competent work, if unsound on the question of which end of a currach is the sharp one. She was a writer too; I have already quoted from her autobio- graphical *Stranger in Aran*, apropos of the ghosts of the old shore- workers. The book, published in 1946, is one of those slim hand-printed volumes from the Cuala Press with the feel and look of a delicately flavoured and wholesome biscuit. She was evidently a keen and sympathetic listener, and I find her record of Aran's talk (at work and at dances, matchmakings and weddings) more vivid and convincing than the cursory Dufyesque notes with which she illustrates herself. Aran's silences too are well rendered: her ac- count of a wild sea-crossing after which the currach crew lie on the shore for a while and then walk inland without having referred in any way to the dangers they had been through, is in its quietism more telling than all the blustering breakers of other Aran books.

One of the rather vague sketches in *Stranger in Aran* shows young men carrying seaweed up the shore, and in the reminis- cences of those men, now grown old, I find Miss Rivers as an equally vaguely observed figure with a sketchbook looking down at them from the shinglebank. It seems that she was liked and re- spected by the islanders, but her life here was shadowed by the hostility of a cleric of the old school, Father Thomas Killeen, who was parish priest of Aran from 1935 to 1948. This man was agitated by the question of *mná treabhsair*, as the islanders called women who wore trousers, and in a sermon on the topic he recalled the Old Testament (rather than the New) on the stoning of immoral women. Stone-throwing was a pastime for which the young were more usually reproved in Aran, and no doubt the children took the hint joyously when Father Killeen suggested it would be right to let such women know they were not welcome in the commu- nity. Some respectable ladies of Aran still remember with rueful smiles ambushing trousered women visitors to Dún Aonghasa. According to one version of the tale, the first to have to run from the attack were the wife and daughter of a superintendent of police, who complained to the local *gardaí* and were not mollified on hearing that a sermon had been "misunderstood"; shortly afterwards the priest was called to the Archbishop at Tuam and his zeal reproved. Another version has it that he had to abandon his crusade when his own niece returned from America wearing trousers. In any case he restricted himself thereafter to the repression of courting, dancing and dirty books, especially those of Liam O'Flaherty.

Many people, including herself, suspected that Miss Rivers was the real object of the priest's campaign, that he wanted to drive her out, as being an artist and therefore a potential corruptor of the community. Father Killeen is remembered today as much for the wearisome length of the feast-day processions he inaugurated, and to which he was devoted, as for his intolerance of laxity. But once when the headmaster of the Cill Rónáin school asked Miss Rivers to paint a banner to be hung across the road for one of these processions, she agreed only after he had sworn himself to secrecy as to her part in it, for it seems that the priest would have ordered it to be taken down if he had known it was her work. This atmosphere of insult made her unhappy here, but she did not leave, and the absence of bitterness in *Stranger in Aran* is a Christian eloquence. However, the word *stráinséar*, the usual Aran-Irish term for a non-islander, has no undertone of hostility and it is not quite exactly translated by the English "stranger"; so perhaps Miss Rivers did allow the slightest tinge of bitterness to shade the title she gave herself.

FISHERMEN OF CILL MHUIRBHIGH

Fishing (at least for gigantic fish, or if for the humble rock-fish then from gigantic heights) is clearly proper to the Man of Aran, but one cannot imagine him as concerned with *selling* fish, any more than as being priest-ridden or throwing stones at tourists or keeping paying guests. Aran fishermen on the other hand had to make a living not only in fickle seas but in treacherous market conditions. The old wharf-house by Cill Mhuirbhigh pier, the centre of a thriving business fifteen years before Flaherty installed his darkroom in it, resists his mythifications with its own prosaic story of boom and crash.

The pier itself was built in 1893, when the Aran fisheries, which had dwindled almost to extinction in the post-Famine period, were being refounded by the Congested Districts Board. It has never given much satisfaction, as there is insufficient depth off it at low water for any but very small boats. As one shore-critic put it, "You don't build a pier on dry land: that's *my* policy anyhow!"—and indeed the structure does seem to hang back like a timid bather and go sidling along the shore unnecessarily before turning and marching into the chilly water, firmly, but not far.

Twenty years later, the Aran fishery was still based on currachs and small wooden sailing boats such as hookers and nobbies, and the big foreign steam drifters operating in local waters were able to snatch most of the catch from it. Also the Aran crews felt that they were not getting fair treatment from the buyers for what fish they could bring ashore. It was the Cill Mhuirbhigh men who first decided to form themselves into a co-operative society to market the catch. The parish priest of the day, the Reverend Murtagh Farragher, a keen modernizer, drew up the proposals for the co-operative, and the C.D. Board approved. Although the Board warily refrained from giving direct financial aid, it helped in other ways, and so far as I can discover provided the pier building which Flaherty later found so useful.

An Stór Dearg, the red store, as it is called for some reason not now apparent, has a concrete floor with a central drainage channel, and behind it is a small concrete area, now broken up and obscured by plant life, with scupper-holes in its low concrete surround; both were for the wet and messy job of filleting and pickling fish in salt. Here the Aran Fisheries Co-operative Society began business in 1915, curing and dispatching the autumn catch of mackerel, mainly to the American market. The crews still owned their boats and gear as before, while the Society under the management of the parish priest took care of the processing and marketing, and distributed the profits among the crews in proportion to the catches they had contributed. Canon Farragher was a vigorous and enthusiastic organizer but (at least in the hindsight of the C.D. Board's first secretary, writing after the event), not a businessman:

> The Canon was a man of apostolic fervour in fishery matters, no better hand at the tiller in wild weather, and he thoroughly understood the requirements of his people as regards kinds of boats, gear and methods. It was a neglect of the business principles of co-operation that led to the failure of the Society.

During the First World War the foreign fishing boats were absent from Irish waters, catches were better, the American demand for pickled mackerel insatiable, and the fresh fish was fetching abnormally high prices in England. The Society spread to Cill Rónáin and nearly all the Aran crews joined it, though some took advantage of the high prices to make private deals with outside buyers. A cooper was permanently employed making barrels, and it is remembered that at the height of the boom the lines of barrels awaiting shipment from Cill Mhuirbhigh stretched all along the roadside around the west of the bay from the quay. The Board was gratified, but added a cautionary note to its report of 1917:

> The results have justified both the original arrangements made, and the subsequent management of the transactions of the Society, as regards which Fr Farragher was mainly responsible.... It is hoped that when the present high war-prices fall off a reserve shall have been accumulated.

Instead, the Society was overreaching itself. To publicize the high prices it could obtain, it had got into the way of paying or promising to pay the crews for their catches as they were brought in, upon estimates of the future proceeds. Then a large consignment to England had been delayed in transit and was condemned as unfit, so that the Society's finances were already strained when, with the Armistice of November 1918, prices fell sharply. Thousands of barrels already consigned to America had to be sold for less than had already been promised to the crews, and it was found that the compensation claimable for this loss was quite inadequate. The fishermen would have settled for less, but barrels, salt, labour and freight had already been paid for. The Board was full of sympathy for what it termed the Society's "gallant struggle" against the flood of debts, but could not avert the collapse which ensued after a few more loss-making seasons, among recriminations that are not quite stilled to this day—I have seen old men go pale with anger over the seventy-year-old question. Hundreds of barrels of fish were dumped in the bay (which I am told brought bad luck on it, so that mackerel never came there again), and the Society was finally liquidated in 1922.

After the war the British and Scottish drifters returned to these coasts, catches declined and the disturbed state of the country made marketing and transport precarious. Nearly all the motorized boats gave up entirely and the Aran fishery was once again left to the oar and the sail. Among the gloomy reports of successive years from the C.D. Board, the only positive note is in its last, before Independence brought its dissolution in 1923, and it once again concerns Cill Mhuirbhigh. Some boat-owners there had been issued with large-mesh nets and were being paid at a fixed price higher than the normal for the larger mackerel of their catch, which were carefully graded and packed "in accordance with the taste of the American buyers" and exported under the Board's own "Shamrock" brandmark. The net profit on sales of £458 was £78—and that probably represents the last profitable activity in the old shed (apart from that of Flaherty's dream factory ten years later), for the fisheries continued to decline after Independence and by the time of the recovery in the Thirties the industry was largely confined to Cill Rónáin and Cill Éinne.

Ever more decrepit, An Stór Dearg has since served out a post-script to its history as depository for a clutter of buoys, ropes, nets and lobster-pots from a few currachs and small half-deckers. In recent years the last of these lobster-boats, the *Lively Lady*, was part of the furniture of the bay, bobbing at her moorings just off the pier—and now (1982) she is gone, foundered in a heavy sea off Ros a' Mhíl, and with her two of the "lads," Mikey from Cill Mhuirbhigh and Brian from Gort na gCapall, their bodies never found. Coming across odd references to this little boat, identified or unidentified, as I leaf through parts of this book written over the last few years, is to feel time like the rush of salt water in the throat. Time, postscript to postscript to postscript. Time, salt postscript.

WRITING ON THE BEACH

Because the bay of Port Mhuirbhigh curves so deeply into the flank of the island its waters are undisturbed by the currents that sweep along the coast, and so have deposited a beach of fine sand. Onshore winds have carried the sand inland to build dunes, now grassed over. The whole area around the bay is a *muirbheach*, a sea-plain of sandy pasturage; hence the name Port Mhuirbhigh, the bay of the *muirbheach*. There was once a little burial ground or *cill*, perhaps an ancient church site, close to the head of the bay, which in turn has been buried by the dunes so that its only memorial is the name of the nearby village and the surrounding townland, Cill Mhuirbhigh, anglicized as Kilmurvey. The Kilmurvey House farm, which almost monopolizes this *muirbheach*, is the best holding in the three islands.

Sand, then, sets the tone here. A beach the colour of the moon waxes from a poor crescent to a good half and wanes again twice a day. Behind it is another crescent, a pale and ragged area of marramgrass hillocks between a foreshore path and the road going by to the village. Sometimes young visitors set up their tents in the snug hollows of this field, which for some reason is called The Vinegar, and the currachs of the Cill Mhuirbhigh men are kept on their stone stocks in the shelter of its walls. All around are the vivid green and unbroken acres grazed by the cattle of the "Big House"; in contrast, the background of hill-slopes to the south-east and south-west is grey and lined with walls.

All the roads and tracks of this area run to or loiter by the beach. The stony coastline itself seems to holiday here and unwind from its severities. Sunbathers and sandcastle-builders dispel the old equation of the shore with labour and its new one with loneliness, at least for those short and radiant times in which the angle of a gull's white wing against the unstable Atlantic blue defines high summer in Aran. At such hours even the pulse of the breaking waves, the universal constant of all shores, never quite stilled, becomes a whisper, a merely subliminal reminiscence of storm, of winter.

Winter is defined by a bird here too, a solitary great northern diver that comes with falling temperatures from the far north to haunt the bay, and lives for months out there on the heaving waters, rising and falling in time to the crash of waves on the beach, a dark, secretive thing that keeps its distances and refuses one a view, slipping silently under the surface if one approaches the water's edge and reappearing after a long interval farther off, half lost in the poor light. One gives up peering, identifying, and wanders along the heavy ever-repeated landfall of the sea. At this season the resistant depths of colour on land, sea and sky slow down the pace of perception to that of contemplation. If a gleam from the low sun comes across to catch the countless overlapping marks on the sand, then idleness and the absence of humankind can tempt one into the error of thinking: "Signatures of all things I am here to read." Each fallen wave, for instance, rushes up the strand with a million urgently typing fingers, and then at the moment between writing and erasing subscribes itself in a negligent cursive across the whole breadth of the page. Signatures and counter-signatures accumulate, confuse, obliterate. Seabirds put down their names in cuneiform, lugworms excrete their humble marks. And then come my boots to add the stamp of authenticity, not of the endless process of the beach which needs no authentification from anybody, but of my witnessing of it.

Is this an image of the work I have dreamed of, that book—with which the present book has a certain flirtatious but respectful relationship—preliminary to the taking of an all-encompassing stride? A muddled draft of it perhaps, or more usefully a demonstration of its impossibility; for the multitudinous, encyclopaedic inscription of all passing reality upon a yard of ground is ultimately self-effacing. But no; for if the book like the beach lies open to all that befalls it, welcomes whatever heterogeneous material is washed up or blown in, then must begin the magic transubstantiation of all this intractable stuff into the person fit to make the step. A work of many generations, I wonder? Let a few almost frivolous examples of the countless marks that have been impressed temporarily on this particular beach and more lastingly upon myself demonstrate how nearly overwhelming is even my limited and ill-defined project.

In the spring of 1975 almost the entire area of sand between high water mark and the foot of the dunes rather suddenly filled up with low clumps of a silvery-leaved plant never recorded in Árainn before, the frosted orache. This is in general rare on Ireland's western coasts, though commoner on the east, but I heard later that it had turned up at Roundstone in Connemara the previous year, and perhaps a drift of its seeds had come across the channel from there. This insemination has probably not added permanently to the Aran flora, for year by year since then its summer growth has been thinner and thinner, and now it is difficult to find a single specimen. In my capacity as self-appointed resident scientific busybody I kept the botanical authorities informed, and now I read in D. A. Webb's almost-but-of-course-not-quite definitive "Flora of the Aran Islands," published in 1980:

> *Atriplex laciniata*...observed in 1975 on Kilmurvey beach,
> where (*fide* Robinson) it has since much decreased.

The Latinism was new to me; I am tempted to adopt it as a motto.

Similarly, on the 27th August 1977, I witnessed the presence of a small bird running to and fro and pecking at the margins of retreating waves, a slim, stilt-legged, long-beaked wader very like a common sandpiper but with a reddish underside. Unlike the other shorebirds that feed in mixed flocks here from the autumn onwards, and which take flight as one approaches, circle round over the sea and re-alight behind one, this elegant little oddity stayed there, busy and preoccupied, until it was almost under my feet. Later the reference books told me it was a buff-breasted sandpiper, a vagrant from America recorded less than a dozen times in Ireland, and well known as an unusually tame bird—though "tame" is hardly the word for a creature to whom human beings are of no more concern than any other solid obstacle in its way. I referred this observation to higher authorities too, and was informed that a body called the Rare Birds Committee was "sitting on it" and might well accept it as an authentic record, but I never heard the outcome of their incubations. In fact I would say to them "*Diffide* Robinson!," for my certainty about the identification is of the sort oddly called a "moral certainty," which seems to be inferior to a factual one. (For instance, Professor Webb once found on Inis Oírr a certain plant, a little stonecrop called *Sedum dasyphyllum*; at least, that is what the specimen he brought away with him turned out to be. The discovery was unusual enough to demand confirmation, but although he, his acolytes and rivals have like myself diligently searched the place, that particular stonecrop has not been refound. And although he is still "morally certain" about it, he has excluded it from his Aran *Flora*.)

What else? The dolphins, forty or fifty of them, did indeed dance in the bay one year, just as I described to the lightkeeper who saw them praying on the beach. I am told that their splashy leapings are more practical than expressive, and that they were probably rounding up a shoal of fish; also that they were of the species known prosaically as the bottle-nosed dolphin, from their elongated snouts. Aran does not distinguish between the various dolphins and the smaller porpoises, lumping them all together as *muca mara*, sea-pigs, a libellous name for such lithe hydrobats. The expanding ring-waves made by that circus troupe can hardly have shifted a grain of sand on the shore, and I can include dolphins in this catalogue of beach-marks only on the strength of those fanciful, prayerful, kneeprints.

A last impression: a stumpy-legged dog, white with brown blotches, mainly gundog but "with a bit of a seal in him" according to his owner; our adopted pet, Oscar, dearly loved and sadly missed as the death-notices put it. I used to throw a ball for him on the strand, a game that almost killed the neglected creature with delight. If I stood forgetful with the ball in my hand, lost in my musings over the riddles propounded by the sea to the sand, he would wait patiently at my feet, looking up, and very delicately place a paw on my toe to recall me. Then I would glance down and catch him saying, "There are just two ways, or perhaps three, in which you can hope to give supreme pleasure to another living being. You can go home and make love to her who loves you, or you can throw that ball for your dog. This is the time for the second alternative, for the third is to go on trying to perfect your book, which I do not believe you have it in you to do."

No, dogs do not speak. The sea does not riddle, dolphins do not pray, the vagrant bird neither trusts nor distrusts Robinson, waves never sign anything; what I myself witness is my own forgery. One should forego these overluxuriant metaphors that covertly impute a desire of communication to non-human reality. We ourselves are the only source of meaning, at least on this little beach of the Universe. These inscriptions that we insist on finding on every stone, every sand-grain, are in our own hand. People who write letters to themselves are generally regarded as pathetic, but such is the human condition. We are writing a work so vast, so

multivocal, so driven asunder by its project of becoming coexten-
sive with reality, that when we come across scattered phrases of it
we fail to recognize them as our own.

THE LUCK OF THE SHORE

It begins again, complaint of wave against rock, rock against wave,
as soon as one leaves the arms of the bay. The next two miles of
coast are the same as other miles of coast; its generalities—the low
rock-terraces with chipped edges, the blocks flung askew on them,
the clefts licked smooth in them—may be taken as read. But this
is one of our habitual walks, home being just half a mile away up
there on the skyline, and so its asperities have acquired the ease of
familiarity. Here, in this angle between two tons of stone, Oscar
killed his first rabbit, more by luck than skill, and to his own
amazement, while we two convertite vegetarians hesitated between outrage and applause. (I commemorated the deed with a
microscopic portrait of the dog at this point on my first map of
Aran, which intrigued those visitors who noticed it.) Here, where
the terrace stands just high enough above the breakers to carry a
patchy veneer of soil and scattered clumps of the more spray-proof
vegetation, we come in spring to pick sea-beet, the aboriginal
from which the tame garden spinach has been cultivated; its thick
juicy leaves add a primitive savour to our peaceable diet. This is a
good place to look out for driftwood too, for the general eastward
set of the currents brings floating goods inshore from the main
here. Once we lugged home a four-foot baulk to be cut up for fire-
wood, which instead became a peculiarly grim, salty, spider-
haunted, fungus-prone ornament-stand in a corner of the living
room.

This shore is known as Poll na Loinge, inlet of the ship, and the
name applies in particular to a deep and narrow creek cutting into
the terrace, where bodies and cargo from a wrecked sailing vessel

came ashore long ago. The drowned men are buried under flag-stones almost indistinguishable from the rest of the limestone pavement a hundred and fifty yards up and on the west side of the boreen that comes down to the coast road nearby, and the cargo, which was tobacco, was carried secretly across the island and hidden from coastguards in a cave called Poll an Tobac, a third of the way down the dizzy cliff just east of Dún Aonghasa. The inlet of Poll na Loinge marks the end of Cill Mhuirbhigh shore and the beginning of Fearann an Choirce (or Oatquarter) shore. The terrace that constitutes the coastline rises slowly as one goes on, and after another quarter of a mile the little cliff turns and runs inland, eastward, while the shore continues north-eastwards on a lower level. The cliff face at the turn is called Balla na Sáibhéarachta, the wall of the sawing. The blacksmith of Oatquarter still has the great two-man saw, a five-foot blade set in a rectangular frame of wood with a crossbar handle at either end, with which his ancestors used to saw up driftwood spars for rafters. The old men of Oatquarter, he tells me, used to sit in the shelter of the field wall at Balla na Sáibhéarachta, peering out round the corner now and again to see if the tide was bringing in anything interesting, smoking their pipes the while and telling stories, "as happy as the King of England." Once when his grandfather and others were sawing up timbers near Bun Gabhla the coastguards came looking for them, for wrack was Crown property. The men hid the big saw and managed to get away, but King, the blacksmith, left his dividers behind, which the guards found and traced back to him. However, since he was such a respectable character, he was given a sort of unofficial licence to gather and cut up timbers thereafter. Perhaps that was one of the factors in the peace of mind of those Oatquarter elders enjoying their pipes while waiting for what the sea might send; chronology is vague here.

Chronology fades away like tobacco smoke from the next tale, although it is one which is told in the most matter-of-fact way. A man walking by Poll na Loinge one day found a coin in a *bullán* or rock-pool. The next morning he found another one in the same *bullán*, and the following morning a third. Then he told someone about it, and after that there were no more coins. So much I heard from a lady of Eochaill. An Oatquarter man whom I questioned about it was able to give me further details: the first coin was a half-crown, the second five shillings, and the third ten shillings ("Triple!" he added in an explanatory tone, throwing me back into puzzlement just as I was congratulating myself on having got the figures on this otherworldly transaction). He also said that the person who was told about it was probably the priest. Priests of course have always protected their retail monopoly of supernatural benefits by maligning even the pettiest rival outlets; the coins probably found their way into the Church's pocket and the poor peasant was told to have no further dealings with the Devil; and in the face of such distrust and greed the charitable Earth ceased from alms-giving. No, of course I must not impose my own anticlerical and pagan interpretations on the incident. Nor will I join folklorists by filing it under an International Folktale Type number. Listened to in the way it is told by Araners (demanding neither belief nor disbelief) it sounds like any other instance of the happy-go-lucky beneficence of this particular shore. A man found a coin in a *bullán*. The next day he found another. And the next day, a third. Then he told someone else, and after that he found no more. What could be more natural than that?

Concerning more toilsome ways of gaining an income, these Oatquarter shores had certain advantages and disadvantages. Beyond the point where the cliffs retreat inland, the shore is of broad stony shallows backed by a shinglebank. The shallows provide plenty of blackweed, good for manuring the potato-fields but not so good for making kelp. The redweed of deeper waters is not cast conveniently ashore here, for the coastline is so straight that the currents sweep it past to be caught by a great hook of land a mile farther east, on the territory of the next village, Corrúch. Since Oatquarter had no redweed shore of its own it had the right of gathering redweed on Corrúch shore throughout the winter and spring up to the 1st of May. The weed was brought back to the shinglebank, which was the ideal place for stacking it to dry and for making kelp, being high and airy, firm underfoot and free from sand. This is An Duirling Bhán, the white rock-bank. (The word *duirling* applies to the storm beaches of all kinds around Aran's shores, from fine pebble-banks to the rough boulder-stacks along the Atlantic clifftops, and here as elsewhere the whiteness is the work of the sea, rolling the pebbles up and down the outer face of the bank and keeping them well polished.) As "The White Shore" this shinglebank is the setting of Tom O'Flaherty's child-hood reminiscence *The Kelp Burners*, which tells of the night he was allowed to stay up and help tend the fire of an Oatquarter kelper:

> I was not long working when Michael's two daughters came with bread and tea. It was pitch dark now a short distance from the kiln. Like ghosts the two men who were feeding the flames would appear out of the gloom with armfuls of seaweed and vanish again. The two girls who brought the meal sat on boulders in the glare of the light and looked in-tently at the fire. The men paid no attention to them, though they were good-looking girls. Perhaps they were afraid of irascible old Michael. I looked at them and wondered what they were thinking about. Perhaps they were thinking that part of the price of the kelp would pay their way to America. That was the constant thought in those days.

The shiny pebbles of the White Shore occupy only two or three hundred yards of the coastline, and the rest of Oatquarter's allot-ted portion is made up of long bare steps upon which the waves prostrate themselves before the usual ranks of boulders. The few features of this shore are revealed only at low tide, including the one from which it is named Scailp Fhada, a "long cleft," running parallel to the shoreline a quarter of a mile beyond the end of the shinglebank. At the eastern end of this cleft is a big rock-basin called Poll na Mná Móire, the pool of the big woman; who she was is unknown. A third of a mile farther on is a small rock that stands out like a jetty into the deeper water below low tide, Carraig Ghiolla. The man whose habit of fishing from it was so persistent as to leave his name on it, Giolla Ó Direáin, was called Gilbert in English and has been commemorated under that name too, for the island's most luxurious guesthouse, Gilbert Cottage (*recte* Gilbert's Cottage—the error was mine, in painting its sign), which stands in ungainly prominence among the houses half a mile off up the hillside, has grown as if by cellular fission, piling extension upon extension, from the two little rooms of his home of eighty years ago.

Another quarter of a mile along the coast two deep coves side by side, Poll Shíle Mór and Poll Shíle Beag (*Síle* being the Irish original of the name Sheila, and *mór* and *beag* meaning respectively "big" and "little"), mark the end of Oatquarter's shore. The larger of these (very small) inlets was a usefully secluded harbour for the smuggling ashore of barrels of *poitín* from Connemara. Redweed collects in it too, and the giant pitchfork, the *crúca*, was used to lift it out; one can still just make out where steps have been hacked in the wave-washed rock around its rim to ease the way for, perhaps, the otherwise unrecorded Síle, among the anonymous generations of basket-carriers. This is the last of Oatquarter's inadequate little catchments for redweed, and the fact that so much of it goes drifting by to Corrúch's more fortunate shore has always rankled. One oldtimer grumbles to me about the uselessness of the Congested Districts Board (defunct over sixty years ago) who he thinks should have dynamited the shore here into a more retentive configuration. As it is, Oatquarter's has been a shore of scanty and hard-earned profits for individual workers, whereas, as we shall see, Corrúch's lent itself, if only briefly, to large-scale enterprise and the factory system.

THE IRISH IODINE & MARINE SALTS MFG. CO. LTD.

The ruins that loom up as one approaches Port Chorrúch, rather tremendous among the humbly criss-crossing field-walls on the mild slopes coming down the road by the sea, represent an outpost of Victorian industrialism, established here with great ruthlessness only to fail within five years. The roof and rear wall have long vanished, together with the tops of the three tall window-spaces, so that its façade alternates blank oblongs of stone and sky. The sort of architectural gaze, at once exploitative and paternal, that subdued the milling valleys of the north of England, here, in the 1860s, oversaw the labours of peasants in wide seaweed-fields.

It is no accident that one of the earliest attempts to mechanize the kelp industry was sited just here, for its topography makes this Aran's most favoured weed-shore. Immediately over the road from the factory ruins is the beginnings of an immense shinglebank that swings out in a westward-facing concave, as high, level and evenly curved as an esplanade, along the flank of a headland. Every scrap of redweed brought along by tide and current is caught by this bay, and after a storm the shingle slope is plastered three feet deep with it. The deposit piles up, settles and rots throughout autumn and winter, and even today cartloads of this rich, dense *bainc* are fetched away in spring for manuring the potato-fields. The sheltered back-slope of the shingle is ribbed with the low walls across which searods are still hung to dry, though in amounts that decrease year by year. The top of the shinglebank makes a track out to the far side of the bay where the blackweed-shallows run back westwards for hundreds of yards; one some-times sees boys far out on this *cora* leading donkeys, stumbling and splashing, laden with baskets of *carraigín*.

Seaweed-gathering of any sort is not a priority nowadays, and one rarely sees anyone at work out in Port Chorrúch except on the sort of day when the still expanses of the bay give a dreamy slow-ness to the movements of the few isolated figures. At the time of the iodine-boom, however, there must have been lines of shore-workers trudging up the shingle with weed to feed the machinery of the factory, whatever the weather. The price they got, it is remembered, was a penny a basket, or a shilling a *bord*, the load carried on the straddle and side-baskets of a horse. Their paymaster was the land-agent Thomas H. Thompson, who plays his part of villain in Aran history with such gusto. He and two other gentlemen, Sir James Drombraine of Monkstown and Richard Young of Dublin, had founded the Irish Iodine and Marine Salts Manufacturing Company Limited in 1863. By '65 they had a factory in operation in Galway and were building here at Corrúch. An article in the *Galway Vindicator*, dated the 6th of May, 1866, summarizes the nature of the business:

> *Iodine Manufactury* The Marine Salts Co. of Ireland (Ltd.) want to increase their operation. They have a factory at Long Walk, Galway, and buildings in Arran for drying and burning kelp to be taken as ash to Galway. The Company has originated a process of converting seaweed to ash which is patented. There are twenty-six men employed under Mr. Glassford in Galway. The following substances are produced in abundance: Muriate of potash [i.e. potassium chloride] (used in the manufacture of powder, for which there is a brisk demand in Liverpool), Sulphate of potash (used in the manufacture of fine glass), Glauber salts [i.e. sodium sulphate], Soda salts (for the manufacture of coarse glass). The grand result produced in the factory is Iodine, with a standing order from London for as much as possible. The refuse makes manure.

By the following year Sir James Drombraine could claim that Marine Salts was the third largest iodine manufactury in the United Kingdom. The prime necessity was for copious supplies of seaweed for the Corrúch works, and of kelp burnt by the islanders in their individual kilns. Aran was producing around 500 tons of kelp a year and there was keen competition to buy it. Previous to the foundation of Marine Salts, Aran kelp had been bought by agents operating in Connemara on behalf of a Glasgow firm. The Scotsmen were offering £7 to £8 a ton, but this, according to Thompson, was an artificial price, an attempt to crush his company. As agent to the landlords, he had the answer: henceforth the tenantry would sell their kelp only to him, and at his price of £4 to £5 depending on quality, or face eviction. The landlords' rights in seaweed, he claimed, were absolute—though later on he had to admit that the landlords (the fastidiously remote Miss Digby of Landenstown, and the Countess of Howth) knew nothing of his Marine Salts company. This monopoly attracted a lot of criticism in the *Galway Vindicator*, which denounced it and others of Thompson's abuses as "serfdom." In reply Thompson defended the monopoly as a protection for Galway industry and claimed that the Aran men were now getting a better price than the Connemara men. Nevertheless in 1869 the *Vindicator* reported that a man called Milane from The Seven Churches (i.e. Eoghanacht) had been served with notice to quit, for bringing his kelp across to Connemara to get a better price.

There were also complaints of unfair weighing methods. Thompson was not only the sole judge of the quality, by which the price per ton was fixed, but also of what constituted a ton. A defensive letter to the paper from the company states that the standard was 22 ½ cwt (rather than the usual 20 cwt), but a rejoinder from the island's curate, the Reverend Corbett, puts the Thompsonian ton at from thirty to forty cwt; further, the bailiff had announced after Mass one Sunday that "All will make kelp, or..." The curate goes on to threaten to bring this monopoly to the attention of the Government. Next we read of a public meeting (in September of 1869) at which 273 kelp-burners signed an address to Mr. James O'Flaherty of Kilmurvey House, refuting the curate's letter. The Reverend Corbett returns to the attack: no such meeting took place, and the address is a forgery; he challenges Thompson and O'Flaherty to produce twenty of the signatories, or to take him to court. We learn that two of the bailiffs had taken down the names of a crowd of people attending a funeral in Inis Meáin, and that the rest of the signatures had been obtained by O'Flaherty from people who did not know what they were signing; also, that O'Flaherty's interest in the business was that the kelp was carried to Galway in his boats alone.

By 1870 the Corrúch factory had already ceased operations; perhaps the patent process was not a success, or perhaps, as an Oatquarter man tells me (for the tittle-tattle of village against village outlasts industries), "Them Corrúch people put stones in the seaweed to give it weight, and the coggles of the machinery got broken." However, Marine Salts continued to buy kelp, and the monopoly was enforced until 1872 when Thompson permitted the islanders to sell to whom they liked, provided they paid him "royalties" out of their gain. At this time he was offering a price of £5 a ton, but the islanders insisted on selling to the Scottish firm's agent, Mr. Hazell (whose kelp-store is still to be seen at Cashel in Connemara), who was offering £7 plus freight plus 10s. "expenses." Thompson's royalty was levied on the raw weed itself at a rate of 5 to 10s. a ton (or £1 19s on two tons according to another account), and since it took five tons or more of weed to make a ton of kelp this effectively reimposed the monopoly. Thompson was adamant that "On behalf of the owners I have a right to every bit of seaweed that comes ashore and can do what I like with it and charge what I like on it." However, kelp prices were soon to fall disastrously and Marine Salts went out of business in 1877.

Those were dreadful times, in which not only the kelp but all other means of livelihood failed—the fisheries, the oats, the pigs, the potatoes—and Thompson's royalties became a minor item in the litany of his abuses (all of which will be gone into in their place), as events spiralled down towards the Land War and the vicious settling of accounts of '81. The question was exhumed in subsequent court hearings before the Land Court in '84, and even raised in the House of Commons, after which Thomson had the effrontery to claim in a letter he wrote to *The Freeman's Journal* "to put the record straight," that the tenants had paid royalties for many years and had never complained "until now, when all the rights of the landlord are being invaded." In fact, he explains, Marine Salts had been set up partly to offer competition and so keep prices up, for the good of all concerned.

And that is the last word I have found, on the company and its philanthropic activities. Should one require a monument to this out-of-the-way episode of the Industrial Revolution, there remains only a grassy plot sheltered by a tall façade from the winds off the sea, in which the men of Corrúch keep their currachs. For the rest of its stones one might look about the walls of the old cottages on the hillside above.

And now we will let the sea wash the taste of those foul times out of the bay's mouth.

THE FINGERPRINT

At high tide, and especially in calm weather, Port Chorrúch is a place of grand simplicity. The sea follows close below the coastal road that comes from the west to pass before the factory ruins, where the massive shinglebank begins to swing out to the north, the sea curving with it as evenly as wine in a glass, to the farther arm of the bay, a submerged *cora* pointing back to the west, marked even on the stillest days by a ceaseless white pleating of the waters. But as the tide falls the bay becomes more complicated; amorphous areas of sprawling seaweed, sand and rock appear, and only a more prolonged attention can give it back a topography. Here, though, one can be directed by countless previous acts of attention enshrined in placenames. "If you write down the names of all the places here," said the Corrúch man whom I was questioning about them, "your map will be all black!" Certainly the dozen or so that I have recorded represent only a fraction of that antique apparatus, functional in its day but now rusting in disuse, which permitted such a fine discrimination of place on this intensively worked shore.

To begin with, there are two bays, not one: Port Chorrúch Beag, the small one, by the roadside and facing north, a quarter of a mile west of the old factory, and Port Chorrúch Mór, the large one, facing west and backed by the shinglebank. They are separated at low tide by a muddle of stone and water. To sort out the muddle, one can follow in the steps of the shore-workers who cropped it every year. They would have approached it from the road by means of a boreen no more than a dozen yards long leading down between two little fields, which is called Bóithrín na Gairleóige from the tall *gairleóg* or wild leek plants growing in it. It is also called Bóithrín na Scailpe because at the end of it one has to scramble down a little rock-face from which this fraction of the shore gets its name, An Scailp—the word *scailp* covers a variety of rocky clefts and slants. A shallow terrace of the shore that makes a little promontory here at half-tide is An tUlán Buí, the yellow ledge, and as in many other similar situations the yellowness is that of the slimy *Enteromorpha* seaweed marking an outflow of fresh water from a seepage at the foot of a *scailp*. Off the end of this ledge is a patch of sand, Trá na Lugaí, the beach of the lugworms, which provides bait for the Corrúch lads' fishing lines. To the left of this rise two wide steps of rock cut by the waves out of strata of different qualities; the lower has been pocked and fretted by the sea, while the higher (by only a foot or two) has been smoothly polished; they are An tUlán Garbh, the rough ledge, and An tUlán Mín, the smooth ledge. None of these features is more than a few paces across; their names attend closely to the feel of those paces.

To the east of this no-longer amorphous little headland is Port Chorrúch Beag and to its west the inner reaches of Port Chorrúch Mór, interrupted by a scattered reef called Carraig an Choileáin, the rock of the puppy-dog (what small tragedy or comedy has been forgotten here?). A roundish boulder lying on the lower slopes of the shinglebank nearby is An Chloch Mhór, the big stone, and its significance to the shore-workers was that at half-tide the water just laps around its base, announcing that there is just over three hours to go before full tide or low tide. "Isn't it a strange thing, now," said my guide, "that on every shore of Aran there's a boulder marking half-tide!" It seems strange to me that a result of our human ingenuity in using Nature as clockwork when other clocks are lacking should be interpreted as a beneficent ordinance of Nature itself; but the Aran man has an easy acceptance of the strangeness of things that I cannot share. Next, halfway round the curve of the bay, one might or might not notice a little spur of rocks far down on the shore: An Chéibh, the quay; the name points it out as the natural (or is it in part artificial?) landing-place for boats coming into the bay at low water. Just beyond it is another sandy patch, An Trá Bhig, the small beach, and then a large, strange, dark boulder the name of which I will return to in a moment, and which is the perfect back-rest for anyone tired from cutting weed on the great *cora* that stretches for nearly a third of a mile out to sea west and north-west of this spot. I can rest here too, and point out a last few features of the coast nearby. As the tide rises it cuts off the outer reaches of the *cora* by creating a shallow channel, Bealach na Carraige, the way of the rock, through which a currach coming from the north or east can with caution enter the bay, thus saving a long row around Barr na Cora, the tip of the *cora*. And finally, if the tide is indeed coming in, it is already too late to go on another two hundred yards to see the lovely little inlet in the lower shore below the point at which the coast turns east again, for its floor will be flooded and its distinctive feature, a marble-white line running exactly down its centre and out to sea, will be hidden. This is one of those very characteristic inlets of this northern coast which all run inland on the same bearing, about south-south-east, and have been produced by the sea's working its way into a joint of the major set, and abrading it out with rolling pebbles and churning water until it is all sleek, grey, seal-like curves. In this particular instance the joint has a vein of calcite a few inches thick in it, which can be traced across the upper shore to the head of the inlet, into which it plunges to pursue its ruler-straight way along the swellings and hollows of its floor, like the white line in the centre of a road subjected to some dream-transformation. We named this place Scailp Álainn, the beautiful *scailp*, thinking of a friend of ours, Allen, who had died shortly before we discovered it. Later I learned both that I was mistaken in thinking that "Allen" derives from *álainn*, and that the place already had a name, though a rather pedestrian one: An Poll Mór, the big hole.

Individually, none of the names I have mentioned is of much intrinsic interest. But if we think of all the placenames that humanity has applied to the surface of this planet as constituting a single vast fingerprint, can we neglect even its most minute particularities in trying to identify ourselves?

SAILING ON A STONE

The ungainly bulk of rock against which I, like so many before me, rested from my shore-labours, obviously did not originate in Aran. Its blackish complexion, its twisted veins of dull red and its unsplittable hardness would tell a locally knowledgeable geologist that it came from Leitir Mealláin or the south of Garomna, the nearest points of Connemara to Aran. It is in fact, an expert tells me, "a basaltic tuff of the South Connemara group, which has been hornfelsed to pyroxene hornfels facies, from very near the margin of the Connemara granite, probably from the far eastern end of the contact on Garomna Island." Instead of providing a shaky translation for the layman, on the basis of my own very recent acquaintance with its terminology, I will allow the general purport of this dictum to emerge indirectly and by degrees.

An Aran man too would be able to guess the provenance of this boulder, for the difference between Aran's hospitable lime stone and the bitter waterlogged land arising from Connemara's granites and metamorphic rocks has many consequences and is well known to those dwelling on either side of the Sound between them. Most of Connemara south of the Twelve Bens is of granite, which came welling up from the depths of the earth about four hundred million years ago. The rocks into which the granite was intruded were already fifty or more million years old, as they probably date from the Ordovician, a period of volcanic activity in this region, when large-scale earth-movements were beginning to build the mountains of northern Ireland and Scotland. These pre-existent strata consisted of lavas and sedimentary rocks laid down on the bed of an ocean which later vanished in the course of these mountain-building upheavals. The stresses to which these rocks were subjected had already thoroughly kneaded, hardened and "metamorphosed" them even before the intensely hot, viscid masses of granite were thrust up among them from below, whereupon they were reworked, baked and recrystallized to various degrees depending on their distance from the margins of the granite. Nowadays the resultant "metamorphic aureole" (the geologists' term) can be clearly traced in the rocks surrounding the granite outcrops.

All this happened at some depth in the earth, but erosion since then has removed nearly all the original rock under which the granite was emplaced, except for a strip a few miles wide comprising the southern parts of Garomna and Leitir Meallái islands, and the Skerd Rocks out in the Atlantic to the west. The strata exposed in this area represent a three- to five-mile thickness of rock that has been almost completely overturned in the course of its troubled existence, and probably formed part of a pendant projection, within the granite mass itself, from the "roof" of rock above it.

These twisted remains of long-destroyed landforms are known as the South Connemara group, and their component rocks have been studied in some detail, as their physical and chemical make-up contains clues to the making and unmaking of geographies long before Europe and America parted company and the Atlantic came into existence. The papers dealing with them exhibit one of the most lapidary prose styles I have come across. For example:

In the field both pillow and massive metabasites are horn-felsed and now comprise an equigranular mosaic of plagio-clase and horneblende with the latter sometimes defining a L/S fabric (mimetic after S2 and L2) that parallels the axial surface of small-scale folds in the metasediments. In thin section there are ragged poikiloblasts of hornblende and occasionally plagioclase set in a very fine-grained polygonal mosaic of plagioclase, idioblastic horne-blende, needles of ilmanite and irregular granular aggregates of pyrite.... The whole area of exposure displays sillimanite in hornefelsed pelites with biotite as a common porphyroblastic mineral.

Even without looking up all these words (and then looking up all the equally alarming ones used in their definitions, and so on), one acquires a vague sense of the degree to which these rocks have been confounded and refounded in detail and in bulk by processes much fiercer than any that have affected the limestone areas to the south of them. This sample of South Connemara now lying on Aran's foreshore is composed of ash ejected by a volcano, petrified under miles of overlying deposits, crumpled by forces that fold mountains, crystallized by the high-temperature chemistry of molten granite. This hectic period of its history was of course long before even the sea came into existence in which Aran's limestone was to be deposited three hundred and twenty million years ago; on the other hand, it was brought across to Aran by ice-movement (perhaps embedded in an iceberg) in comparatively recent times, probably less than fifteen thousand years ago.

But to explain the full significance, which is double, of this alien stone, I must introduce another aspect of its native land. For the south of Connemara has been metamorphosed by fervours other than the geological—its rock has been irradiated with leg-end by the aureole of Aran's mediaeval sanctity. I can just make out an example of this process on the opposite coast as I lean back against the black boulder and look out across the Sound to Golam Head, an appendage of Leitir Mealláin and the outermost of the chain known simply as Na hOileáin, the islands. Its dark profile is easily identified from here by the ruins of an old signal tower on its highest point, and just to the right of that little upright marker is a tiny oblique whitish fleck pointing down towards its shore. A lad from Leitir Mealláin once rowed me out to Golam Head, which is uninhabited, and among the wonders he showed me there was this broad band of white rock running through the black and pursuing a straight course in the direction of Aran among all the convulsions of the terrain, like a glimmering wake across a stormy sea. A geologist tells me it is a dyke of quartz which was intruded into the older volcanic rock at about the time the neighbouring granite mass was solidifying. To my boatman it was Bóthar na Naomh, the road of the saints, and marked the way the saints took on their pilgrimage to Aran. "*Áit dheas í, Árainn; áit bheannaithe!*" ("A nice place, Aran; a blessed place!"), he re-marked as we stood looking out at it along the direction of this weird white way; and other people in Connemara have said the same thing to me, with a casual sincerity that brushed aside the centuries since the time of the saint. (Connemara! A just quittance for the years I have spent poring over the stones of Aran would be another decade in which to consider the stones of that as-yet hardly described land of marvels. But here it is fitting only for me to touch upon this single aspect of its southern shores, their leg-endary function as threshold to the Aran legend.)

Each of the promontories and archipelagos that reach out from Connemara has its tales of the holy traffic to and from Aran. Even the port of Kilkieran, which is Cill Chiaráin, the church of Ciarán, in Irish, is where it is because that saint went astray on his way to study under St. Enda in Aran. In Na hOileáin there is the saints' road in Golam Head and another in Leitir Mealláin; Inis Bearcháin claims to derive its name from a saint who sailed there from Aran, and Garomna has two ancient churches the stones of which are said to have come from Aran (with an element of prob-able truth, the surrounds of the windows in one of them being carved from limestone). And in the next peninsula, that of An

Cheathrú Rua, I heard a legend linking four or five of its holy sites into the itinerary of another march of the saints to Aran, one incident of which illustrates the great number of these pilgrims with the diagrammatic realism of a mediaeval woodcut: their last overnight stop was at Loch na Naomh, the lake of the saints, on the hilltop near the present town of Carraroe, and the following day when the head of the procession reached the coast (at a point in An Rinn marked by a holy well on the shore, two miles to the south) their leader found that he had left his breviary behind. He told the monk behind him, the message was passed back, and the last of them was able to pick up the book before leaving the lake.

The people from whom I heard these marvels were unsure as to how these migrations went on to Aran, whether they marched over or under the waves. But certain well-known individuals among the anonymous hordes of saints sailed across, or sailed back, on boats of stone. Once they had fulfilled their miraculous function these boats were abandoned on the shore, where they are still to be seen, having reverted to their former status as ordinary boulders, immovably heavy, their reality if anything enhanced by the accretion of legend. As a poetic image of the paradox of faith (which ceases to be faith if it rests on any grounds of reason, and so is essentially committed to the seas of doubt), the concept of the stone boat seems to me even richer than that of walking on water. In its precarious solidity the stone boat is a foundation stone, itself founded on nothing but the possibility of foundering "like a stone."

The most famous of these stone boats is on the Connemara coast south of Ros a' Mhíl. Bád Cholm Cille, Saint Colm Cille's boat, is a great prow of granite, on which the eye of faith can find the marks left by its anchor-chain, the grooves worn by the working of the oars, and the saint's huge handprint in the middle of its slanting deck. Nearby are two "holy wells"—beautifully smooth pot-holes uncovered only at low water, and regarded as having been made by the saint as fonts for the baptism of the pagans; they are visited by hundreds of people on the Feast of St. Colm

Cille, the 9th of June, when Mass is celebrated on the shore. I am told that the boat used to be larger, but such is the demand for relics and souvenirs that it suffers a pious erosion, which I suppose could do away with it entirely if the cult persists for a few more centuries.

In Aran there are two stone boats, of which the best-known lies on the shore near Cill Éinne, the site of St. Enda's monastery. It is called the Currach Stone (and it does look remarkably like a beached currach) or Bád na Naomh, the boat of the saints. Sometimes it is associated with St. Enda but more often with St. Colm Cille, to whom a nearby altar is dedicated. Both in legend and history Colm Cille is the most notable Irish saint after St. Patrick himself, and his cult is particularly strong on the South Connemara coast, where I have been shown thirty or more of those mysterious intertidal fonts attributed to him. In Aran too he is even more highly regarded than the founder of the island's reputation for sanctity, and perhaps in the case of this boat his fame has eclipsed an earlier cult of St. Enda, for in the mediaeval biographies of the saints it is Enda, not Colm Cille, who sails to Aran on a stone. Similarly Aran's other stone boat is called Mulán Cholm Cille, Colm Cille's boulder. This is the stone that initiated my digression to Connemara and back, from the shores of Port Chorrúch. It is hardly known now except to a few of the more traditionally minded folk of the nearer villages.

My personal belief concerning the Port Chorrúch stone is a conditional one: if St. Enda sailed to Aran on a stone, it was on this one rather than the one at Cill Éinne. This is not an article of faith, for I can uphold it with reasons, if only shadowy ones from the age of faith itself. Firstly, in Magradin's *Vita S. Endei*, written in 1390, we read:

The saint then went to a harbour from which he could most conveniently cross over to the island, and having no boat or ship sailed across in a large stone which lay on the shore, and which eight of his brethren shoved into the sea for him.

Therefore, with a prosperous voyage, he arrived at the island, and in a place which is called Leamhchoill.

Actually Leamhchoill was in the south of Garomna, the point of Connemara nearest to the island; the name seems to be forgotten now but it is on Petty's map of 1655. Roderic O'Flaherty, commenting on the above passage, puts the record straight:

> But Leamhchoill, where he is said to have first arrived in the north side of the island, should be Ochoill, for Leamhchoill is in the west continent [i.e. in what O'Flaherty calls West or Iar Connaught], whence is a ferry-port into the island, and Ochoill hath a port for boats to arrive, named from Ochoill, and another called Port Caradoc.

Ochoill, or Eochaill as it is now spelled, is the townland of Aran that includes Port Chorrúch, which is O'Flaherty's Port Caradoc. (I shall puzzle out the meaning of these placenames when I come to deal with the villages of Eochaill and Corrúch.) So the upshot of all this crabbed antiquarianism is that St. Enda landed in Port Chorrúch, therefore that the stone I am writing about is the genuine one rather than the Cill Éinne claimant; further, that St. Enda sailed from south Garomna, and so the hagiographical origin of his stone exactly corresponds to its geological origin.

The last shred of doubt as to the claims of our stone (I say "our," being a patriotic resident of western rather than eastern Árainn) must be dispersed by the fact that St. Enda's next adventure concerns the lake now called Loch Phort Chorrúch, which is behind the great shinglebank of Port Chorrúch. Magradin tells it finely:

> At that time God sent a wonderful cow, which was red in the body and white in the head, to the relief of his poor people [i.e. to the saint and his followers]. This cow sent by God was milked three times a day, the milk of which af-

forded abundance to all the disciples of St. Endeus. And when one day she heard the lowing of another cow in the island, which cow was given by a certain man to the faithful and holy Endeus; then winding herself in a circuitous motion as if giving honour to the Divine Trinity, immediately immersing herself in a pool of sweet water, which is in the island, she nowhere after appeared. Whence it is called from the name of that cow, stagnum na Ceannainne.

O'Donovan (writing in 1839) says that neither this name (Loch na Ceannainne, the lake of the white-headed cow) nor its origin are remembered on the island. However, I have heard both, from a man who certainly did not get them from O'Donovan or his sources. This current version of the legend is less ornate but somehow more appealing to the mind's eye than the emblematic mediaeval one. It seems that in those days Corrúch belonged to a pagan who lived in a castle up on the hillside (its remains, an ivy-covered stone-rick, will be pointed out in due course). The saint and his monks were living on his land on the shore of the lake, and they asked him for a cow, which he kindly gave them. The cow swam across the lake to its new owners, and its white face appearing above the waters gave the lake its name. (I also hear that the pagan's two daughters were converted to "Catholicism" by the saint.)

So much for the material and spiritual nature of the boulder evidently miscalled Mulán Cholm Cille. The rest of St. Enda's legend will crop up here and there, miracle by miracle (his division of the island with St. Breacán, the harbour an angel cut out for him at Cill Éinne, his wrestling match with Colm Cille, etcetera), as we pass the visible traces each of these incidents has left on the impressionable stones of Aran. A more connected account of what passes for his history and of the significance of his foundation will be given when I discuss the monastic remains at Cill Éinne in Labyrinth. But perhaps a defence of my haphazard treatment of the legendary material is in place here, in the form of a remark on the nature of miracles as I would have it. The idea of the miracle is

required as the blazingly distinct emblem of all the possibilities lying muffled in any given place and time. As such, the miracle
must stand apart from all rational orderings; the moment of its
happening must be free from the threads of causality linking all
moments; and its retelling should reflect this if it is to accomplish
the refocusing of our blurred perceptions of the here and now.

Ultimately the only true believer in miracles is one who be-
lieves they do not happen, and all this talk of voyages on stones is
here only as part of something that might appear more feasible,
the taking of a step or two around a certain stone, a blackish lump
of "hornfelsed basaltic tuff," on a deserted seaweed-shore of Aran.
It is not very like a boat, but it has often carried me faithfully to
Connemara. The heat of the earth cooked it, ice delivered it, centuries of aching backs have been sustained by it. What is required
to float it into the miraculous is not an act of faith, but an act of
recollection.

LOOKING INTO OTHER LIVES

The next bay to the west of Port Chorrúch is Port Eochla, so
called as pertaining to the village of Eochaill. But between Corrúch and Eochaill is Baile na Creige, the village of the crag. (All
three are in fact rather arbitrary segments of a scattering of houses
along the mainroad, half a mile inland, and no stranger could tell
where each begins or ends.) Baile na Creige is the smallest village
of the island, and its territory is an irregular strip just three or four
hundred yards wide, running right across the island from the
north coast to the south. Its northern shore is an unemphatic
stretch of the low headland between the two bays named above, a
few minutes of rough walking and enervating nullity that has
never revealed itself to me in any memorable way, about which I
have collected no lore, upon which I have met neither native nor
stranger—and which by the logic of Aran's land-divisions corre-

sponds to one of the most dramatic parts of the southern coast, the cathedral-like peninsula called An Bhinn Bhuí, and the vast cauldron of An Cró on its west. So the man who owns that amazing field on the peninsula, with one wall of stone and three of wind and vertigo and the cry of gulls, also owns a couple of fields, hardly better than damp bramble-patches, down by this shore, while the rest of his holding is in a dozen or so little parcels strung out like beads along the two miles between these extremes.

This northern coastline of Baile na Creige represents a failure in the terms of this book, as I can report scarcely a word from my several walkings of it (except—now it comes back to me—that of a heron I disturbed here one dreary day; a deathly, hoarse *khaaa*, exhaled as it lumbered on grey wings into a grey sky). Therefore I prefer now to retrace my steps from the stone boat, and linger around the "lake of the white-headed cow" for a while before cutting across the headland by the coast road to Port Eochla—all the more so as Loch Phort Chorrúch and its surrounds compose one of Aran's frankest and most engaging landscapes.

On the west of the lake is the great rampart of shingle separating it from Port Chorrúch itself (allowing some seepage of the tide through fissures below, it seems, for the lake has a taste of salt and is not now, if it ever was, a "pool of sweet water" as in the legend, and yellow-green *Enteromorpha* weed grows in it and is gathered to keep the rain off stacks of more useful seaweeds drying on the back of the shinglebank). There are reedbeds along the foot of this shingle shoreline of the lake and around its northern perimeter. The eastern shore is of little fields, that make green capes and promontories, kept trim by grazing cattle; sometimes after rainy weeks the lake reaches across a boreen that runs back to the shore through these fields, and borrows a few more of them for a while. The road goes by close to the southern bank, and there are secretive little steps down from it to a freshwater spring that feeds the lake, opposite an islet upon which the waterfowl pursue their private lives oblivious to the woman filling a pail for her cow there.

One March morning I noticed that this islet appeared to have been paved with large pebbles, and it was only when one of them showed twinges of restless life that I identified them as knots, a species of wader, moderately sized, moderately long-beaked and long-legged, of a nondescript grey, and to my amateur eye at least, chiefly distinguished from the dozens of other waders by its lack of distinguishing features. This whole area, bay and lake, is especially vivified by birds in the winter. All the dark members of the crow family including the raven and the chough, and a few rooks that fly in from the mainland at that season, come to forage on the great bank of rotting weed amassed by the gales on the outer face of the shingle. Countless waders work the rock-pools, following the tide down the shore; one needs binoculars to resolve all these fidgety brown-grey scraps into so many highly distinctive species, and I have never learned to discriminate the half of their individual parts in the web of vibrant calls stretched like taut nerves over the shore. The dunlins, ringed plovers and turnstones all run mingled together, a few redshanks and the occasional greenshank hold aloof, half-a-dozen bar-tailed godwits keep to themselves. The sanderlings, diminutive clowns of this winter circus, amuse us by forming a wavering line across any patch of sand and running down it after each receding wave, picking morsels out of its rim, and then all turning together and running up again before the next wave catches them, matchstick legs whirring under their fat little bellies, keeping just ahead of the spreading foam as if afraid to get their feet wet.

In winter too there are often thirty or forty whooper swans on the lake, together with half-a-dozen mute swans. Occasionally the whoopers all take off with long splashing runs over the water, huge wings labouring, and come sailing low over the shinglebank, necks outstretched, emitting that strange breathy hoot in time to the hiss of their wingstrokes, and land on the waters of the bay, where they rest for an hour or two with heads under their wings before returning to the lake. Sometimes in the depths of winter there comes an isolated day of summer (a pet day, *peata lae*, as they say here) that holds a lens of stillness and clarity over all this life of the shore; each feather, each rustle of a feather, is as incisive as diamond in the memory—at least one feels it so at the moment, but then the day passes and one's impressions of it merge into a dazzled nostalgia.

With spring the gatherings disperse. The whooper swans fly north to their nesting grounds in Iceland and beyond, while the mute swans fight balletic wars until just one pair holds the lake for its territory. I know where some of the shore-birds go, for we find the ringed plovers nesting in the dunes at Cill Éinne, and I remember from my childhood on the Yorkshire moors how the curlews would arrive there in time for my birthday (as I put it, with a child's egotism) in late March (and having so long ago learned their horizon-circling, sky-probing call as the annunciation of spring, to hear it now on their return to the shore in August as the thin premonitory trumpet of autumn gives me a sense in the marrow of my bones of the Earth's curvature and my ageing).

After the curlews have gone in the early spring, the very similar but smaller whimbrel breaks its northward migration here, so picking up (and leaving behind) its local name of *crotach Bhealtaine*, May curlew. And then throughout the summer there are more birds on the lake than on the seashore. Dabchicks and waterhens nest in the reeds, so does a pair of herons, and invariably the mute swans convoy a flotilla of six or eight grey cygnets in and out of their harbour in the recesses of the reedbeds farthest from the road.

The lake is curiously open and indifferent to observation; a few islanders come wildfowling here but not so often as to dispel its trust. The human routes around it—the high walkway of shingle used only by a few men preoccupied with seaweed, the open road that carries sometimes a couple of tourists on bicycles and sometimes a man driving cattle into Cill Rónáin, the boreen sidling through the fields that give covert views of the water through gaps in the reedbeds—at once present the lake to the eye and half avert themselves from it; and the lake-dwellers know and care as little of them as do the figures in a painting of the title on its frame.

I remember that for some reason one spring (it was in 1978) a single whooper swan stayed behind when all the rest had flown, and spent the entire summer pottering about the banks, because whenever it tried to put a foot into the water one of the resident pair of mute swans would come sailing towards it with wings half-raised and head poised on its elegant stalk above a chaos of white plumes—a ruffled rococo beau with a duellist's eye—and the whooper, gauche and gooselike with its stiff straight neck and bland face, would turn away resignedly. Witnessing a little defeat like this almost every time I passed the lake used to make me un-comfortable. Un-swanlike in practical life, having to assume a finely feathered style before trusting myself even to the eyes of the future, I would prefer for my own ego the unflappable self-possession of a heron I watched here once. It had caught a large eel and had just swallowed its head when I saw it, with the rest hanging from its beak. A passing crow had seen it too and alighted nearby hoping to profit in some way. The heron ignored the crow and concen-trated on gulping down a little more of the eel. The crow rose into the air and called up its mate, and the pair of them set up an in-timidating racket, one on either side of the heron, which merely threw back another few inches of eel. The crows tried making lit-tle hopping, flopping flights from one side of the heron to the other, only just clearing its head; but the heron calmly raised both broad wings into a canopy for itself, and after a pause for breath downed the rest of the eel in one violent convulsion. Then it cleaned its beak, eyed the ground narrowly as if to ensure that not a single scale was left for the crows, and took itself off with leisurely flaps.

Enviable bird, gorging on the moment, contemptuous of dark forethought and afterthought! Whereas even as I stand here not-ing every detail of the scene I can imagine some islander pausing from spadework on the hillside above and shaking his head over my wandering and staring about his island; and as I write up the incident I wonder if those haunting eyes, the reader's, which the writer must exorcize if he is to inhabit his work, will read me as I intend myself, or unimaginably otherwise. Perhaps what will last will be nothing of my writing, my thought self, but some chance observation of me, marginal to an anecdote about a bird, or a fiction prompted by my alien name in an old census return, resurrecting me in a body and mind I would not recognize. At this very spot I have done the same to a fellow alien, as I will tell:

The little field to the south-east of the lake, where the boreen around it meets the road, is called Garraí Wilson; a *garraí* is a "garden," which in Aran means a potato- or a vegetable-plot (I remember being puzzled when we were new here by an islander telling me he had a little garden down by the shore; the idea seemed charming, impractical, and absolutely un-Aranish). As for Wilson, nobody remembers who he was, but in the census of 1821 I found:

> Robert Wilson, half-pay Lieutenant; Royal
> Marines, age 36, Head Lightkeeper
> Ann, his wife, age 30
> Robert, his son, age 5
> Ann, his daughter, age 3
> Eliza, his daughter, age 1

In those days the only lighthouse was above Eochaill on the highest point of the island, whence its ruins still look down towards the lake. Wilson must have leased this garden to grow vegetables for himself and that young family living up there on the windy skyline in the disused signal tower by the lighthouse. Why was he retired on halfpay? Perhaps he had a stiff knee which he allowed it to be understood had a Napoleonic bullet lodged in it, but which in fact he broke by tripping over a bollard in Plymouth docks while turning round to look after a passing shop-girl, Ann. I picture him in this field, paunchy, grunting, puzzling ineffectually with his spade of unfamiliar design at the shallow stony soil of Aran. He straightens up, putting his knuckles to his spine, and sees through the reeds a heron swallowing an eel. He stands there open-mouthed, long-dead Lieutenant Wilson, keeper of the long-extinguished light, never suspecting that we are watching him through words, those chinks in Time.

DIFFERENCES BETWEEN LIMESTONE AND GRANITE

On almost every shore of Aran is a spot called Carraig na Móna, Aill na Móna or Poll na Móna, the rock or cliff or inlet of the turf. These placenames are equally common on the southern coast of Connemara. There they mark places where the turf-boats were loaded, and in Aran the places where they were unloaded. Until recently Aran was almost totally dependent on Connemara for its fuel, for whatever timber it may once have had was reduced to scattered patches of hazel scrub centuries ago, and its well-drained ground of many-fissured limestone had never given rise to more than a few shallow patches of peat. Southern Connemara on the other hand, being mainly of impervious granite and having a rainfall much higher than that of Aran, carries hundreds of square miles of bog-land in which, under the living surface of sphagnum moss and heather, a six- or ten-foot depth of plant-remains compressed into peat has accumulated over at least the last three thousand years.

This dense blackness underfoot has been Connemara's major resource, for it could be cut as turf and sold to the grey limestone lands of Aran, the Burren, the Gort plain south-east of Galway Bay, and to Galway city itself. The sea and its complex inlets ramifying deep into the bog-lands provided the means of carriage. Every year throughout spring and summer turf was cut, spread to dry, turned, stacked, brought out of the bogs in basketfuls, carried by donkey-carts down to hundreds of little quays and rocky ledges from which boats could be loaded, and shipped on the famous black-hulled, brown-sailed hookers of Connemara to the bays and inlets serving as ports for each village of Aran, to Ballyvaughan and Kinvara and Galway city. Such was the pressure of poverty on Connemara to sell off the turf that even the *scraith* itself, the top-most layer of living roots, was dried for burning at home instead of being replaced at the bottom of the cutting. The result after centuries of this trade has been the denudation of the outer islands and peninsulas such as Na hOileáin and An Cheathrú Rua, and to a large extent of Rosmuc and Camas at the heads of the inlets, leaving a bizarre terrain in which soggy dells alternate with hum-mocks of bare rock and scratchy bushes—the soft rainlands of the North Atlantic seaboard stirred together with a harsh Mediter-ranean *maquis*. Leitir Mealláin, the outermost of Na hOileáin, was bare more than a century ago and its people had to carry their own fuel four miles from the north of Garomna, the next island in the chain; in fact turf was so precious in Leitir Mealláin that in-stead of the traditional midsummer bonfire on St. John's Eve they would set up an oar to dance round. Garomna is bare now except for a few shallow deposits being cut at present, and so is Leitir Móir to the north of it. Emigrants returning to Leitir Móir from America early in this century used to be amazed to find that the smooth green hill they had played football on as lads had become a gaunt crag of straggling furze and ling, and now the people there have been allocated strips of bog on the mainland east of Camas, eight or ten miles away. The removal of the peat has revealed the heavily glaciated landforms of these archipelagoes and peninsulas. The raw-looking outcrops of pinkish granite are strewn with gla-cial erratics, some of them so huge as to have become well-known landmarks, and often when I have been enquiring about the name of one of these monumental boulders my informant has told me, almost with incredulity, that his or her grandmother remembered hearing the old folk say they had once cut turf off the top.

For Aran the only alternative to Connemara's turf was *buail-treach*, dried cowdung, which was in short supply and trouble-some to collect, and although inoffensive and indeed pleasantly fragrant (it is still in use here and there, especially in Inis Meáin), it gives out little heat, so that if the Aran man complained that the turf he had been sold was damp or crumbly, the standard retort of the Connemara man was "It's better than *cac bó* anyway!"—and *Cac Bó*, cowshit, became Connemara's cruel nickname for the poor Araner.

In fact Connemara was as poverty-stricken as Aran during the last century and the first few decades of this. These two teeming populations, both half-starved most of the time and completely starved very frequently, maintained themselves in life and occasional high spirits by exchanging the products of their meagre soils. The possibility of exchange, of life, lay in the difference between limestone and granite. Aran's rock where it is not bare carries a good grassland, dry underfoot even in winter, but with a tendency to burn up in summer, especially in droughty periods when the shallow soil quickly dries out. At least the horses, which were principally used in winter and spring for carrying seaweed, could be returned to their native hillsides (for most of them were Connemara ponies) for a few months from June. Connemara on the other hand was short of winter pasturage. The cattle there, according to a report of the 1890s, suffered from two diseases, the "cripple" and the "pine"; the first was in fact rheumatism acquired on the rainswept hillsides in spring, and the second mere starvation suffered in those miserable winter pastures of the coastal region, waterlogged and acidic, full of rushes and wild iris. Therefore the Connemara man would bring his cow across to Aran for the winter, paying in turf for its grazing. The Aran man, proud of the nutritious grass that puts such "bone" on Aran cattle, would be contemptuous of the starveling beasts from over the Sound; his nickname for them and for the Connemara folk themselves was *Slóchtaí*, hoarse ones, perhaps because the Connemara dialect sounds low and throaty to the Aran ear, perhaps because the beasts coughed. When the Connemara man came to fetch his cow in the spring he would pretend to be dissatisfied with its condition, and the time-honoured joke was to accuse the Aran man of having used it to carry sand and seaweed up from the shore for "making land." This need to make fields out of bare rock was one of the oddest features of the life of their much commented-on neighbours across the Sound for the Connemara folk, who were rapidly reducing their own hillsides by turf-cutting to as barren a state as Aran's.

Among the goods that came into Aran the most important after the turf was *poitín*, the barley brew made in secret stills in out-of-the-way corners of Connemara and smuggled across either in small quantities buried among the turf or in larger consignments run ashore at night into the little coves of the north coast. Connemara, as a large-scale map shows, is all composed of out-of-the-way corners—islands lost in labyrinthine sea-ways, jigsaw-puzzles of countless lakes hidden among the undulations of vast tracts of bog, glens multiplying and dwindling up into the fastnesses of mountains ever on the watch for the constabulary or the coastguards. Aran had a few stills, too, especially in Inis Meáin, but lacking these natural advantages over the Law preferred to leave most of the business to Connemara.

The other goods I have heard of as being traded across the Sound are an odd assortment. Aran's potatoes are better than Connemara's and often the turf would be paid for half in money and half in potatoes. Osiers or "sally-rods" as they are called here are grown for basket-making in little sally-gardens in damp corners of both Aran and Connemara, but the Connemara ones do not grow long enough to make the circumference of a big turf-creel, and Aran sally-rods used to be brought across for that purpose. Long strips of turf cut from seashore grasslands in Connemara were taken into Aran, rolled up, for laying on roofs under the straw thatch. Aran's salted breams were a delicacy for Connemara. Gravestones levered out of Aran's limestone pavements and decorated and lettered by Aran stone-cutters went out in the turf-boats and now pave the ground in the little seaside churchyards of Connemara. Vast amounts of limestone in its natural state found its way to Connemara too, for a boat that had brought over sixteen tons of turf and was returning empty required up to six tons of ballast. Some of this would be burnt for lime in little kilns by the shore and used in cement and whitewash or spread on the land; so the basic stuff of Aran itself went to sweeten the acid soil of Connemara.

All these minor exchanges were carried on the back of the turf trade and died out with it as other fuels became available here. Perhaps it was a relief to Aran to be delivered from this dependence on Connemara. A vengeful story by Colm Ó hIarnáin of Eoghanacht, "*An Bádóir Santach*," "The Greedy Boatman," describes the Connemara man bringing his cargo of inferior turf into port here, gleefully anticipating the price he is going to extort for it from the islanders who even in the height of summer are desperately anxious about the long wet winter to come. But to his amazement instead of the usual crowd on the quay all eager to leap aboard and help throw the turf ashore in the hope of securing the load for themselves, there is nobody in sight, until a man with a donkey carrying a little barrel of some sort comes by and greets him with such merriment and mockery that the boatman becomes alarmed, cuts his mooring and pushes out from the quay. The Aran man cries after him, "You're not going, boatman, without being introduced to your enemy, the lad that will be there before you whichever harbour or port you go into, that will be on the doorstep before you whichever house you enter? Look, you rascal, look!"—and shows him the barrel, on which is written "Calor Gas."

The end did not really come so emblematically as that, of course. First coal and then briquettes and gas became more and more competitive with turf as the lorry, the train and the steamer won out against the Connemara hooker. There used to be a hundred and fifty hookers working out of Greatman's Bay alone in the last century, and in my explorations of the Connemara coastline I am always coming across their skeletal remains sunk in mud or bleaching behind a field-wall by that shore which is now so silent. The last few survivors of that fleet today are being sought out, lovingly restored, and raced in the summer festivals of little ports all around Galway Bay, and in this year of 1983 one hooker has been ferrying pleasure-trippers to Cill Rónáin from Ros a" Mhíl. So those tannin-brown sails and tar-black, full-breasted hulls, the lines of which are so unexpectedly fine in work-boats of provincial provenance that one marine historian would derive them from such remote and lordly influences as the pleasure-yachts of seventeenth-century Holland, are becoming a familiar sight again after an absence of some years, and the craftsman-families who make them, to designs inherited by the mind's eye only, are busier than they have been for decades.

But the last time I saw a heap of turf on an Aran quay was in Port Mhuirbhigh ten years ago, and I will never see the sight Aran folk recall so fondly, a score of deeply laden hookers lying off the coast with sails furled and the blue turf smoke arising from their cabins where tea was being made and fish fried while they waited for sufficient tide to bring them into the little ports of the villages. Those boatmen of the husky voices and intricate curses have sailed away for ever; the turf has been piled into the donkey-baskets and carried home, the few sods left as if by accident on the quay have been gathered by the paupers, and even the turf-dust has been swept up and scattered on the potato-gardens, Connemara's mite contributed to Aran soil, all for the last time.

Port Eochla, the shore corresponding to Eochaill village, like so many of the shores I have described, is seldom visited. It has no remarkable features, just seaweed-covered boulders exposed at low tide, a curve of shingle, and on its east side a shelf of rock where a boat could come alongside at the flood. One would scarcely notice this rock in passing nor think that it merited a name—but this is Aill na Móna, the cliff of the turf, and what I have written here are the associations waiting off-shore for the tide of recollection rising around that name.

YET TWO MORE BAYS

The shinglebank of Port Eochla gives place eastwards to a scattering of big slabs lying on a rock-bench knobbed with rough nodules of chert. As the bench rises to form low cliffs the storm beach dwindles, and the final stretch of it around the next headland has been cleared and piled aside to increase the grazing along the clifftops. This comparatively high point of a low-lying coast is called Carnán na bhFiach, the hillock of the ravens. A few hundred yards farther on one may be surprised by a deep roaring under foot; the sea has found various clefts in the limestone of the terraced shore and excavated a labyrinthine cellarage in which it sighs and grumbles even on calm days. If there is any swell on the sea, foam comes leaping up through three gaping holes in the roofs of these vaults. Both sand and seaweed accumulate down there, and used to be fetched up by means of ladders. As these puffing-holes were assets to the various people who had rights on this shore they bore possessive names, and the largest of them is still called Scailp Mhikey.

The terrace punctuated by these holes is the western arm of Port na Mainistreach, the bay of the monastery, and on the hillside that rises rather closely behind it are the grey walls of an ancient church and the remains of an almost deserted village, Mainistir, which means "monastery." This is a richly haunted landscape, part of the labyrinth to be explored in the sequel to this book, but here I stick doggedly to the hard going of the shoreline and note some lesser monuments, dating from the kelp-burning era. The first is close by Scailp Mhikey: a kelp kiln of the sort introduced by the Free State government in about 1932, almost complete, and only a little wave-battered, and in fact the only surviving example in the island. It is like an open-topped rectangular box, about fifteen feet long by six wide and three-and-a-half deep, neatly built of the sort of limestone blocks that can be picked out of any rocky spot here. It has an opening like a hearth at either end and two smaller openings on either side, at ground level. Traces of a fan-shaped flagged area before one of the end-openings can be made out. This type of kiln, in which the weed was burnt only for eight or ten hours and raked out as an ash rather than being made to fuse into a solid block, would have been much easier to use than the conventional type, but as I have recounted earlier the industry was failing and set in its ways by the time of these innovations. This particular kiln was never used, I am told. The pile of stones just north of it is the remains of one of the circular enclosures for collecting weed that were built at the same time and equally failed to win favour.

For various reasons Mainistir men did not think themselves lucky in their shore. Along its inner curve, where the coastal road comes close by, it is a very abrupt shingle slope, on which any searods cast ashore tend to be smashed up before they can be collected. The sheltering heights all around made it difficult to dry weed thoroughly, and the steep banks did not provide suitably level and airy sites for burning the weed either. At the east of the bay, for instance, one can see the remains of a kiln of the traditional type, which has had to be perched most awkwardly on the slope of a grassy knoll (the name of which, by the way, is Tóin-le-gaoth, backside-to-the-wind!).

The eastern limb of the bay rises into a cliff thirty or forty feet high called An Caipín, the cap, whose dark and frowning profile is unmistakably that of an Aran man in a peaked cap—a Mainistir man considering the shortcomings of his shore, perhaps, for this point marks the beginnings of Cill Rónáin's much more favourable portion. Off the point between Port na Mainistreach and the next bay are extensive rocky shallows (Carraig an Lugáin, the rock of the hollow) on which the ribbonweed or *coirleach* grows; the Cill Rónáin people used to be able to lead their horses and donkeys out onto it to fill their straddle-baskets. From the far side of this next bay another great reef, An Charraig Fhada, the long rock, stretches half across its mouth, and because of these sheltering arms the bay has still waters and a fine sandy beach. (This is "The Mooltia" on the Ordnance Survey maps, a name that used to be the subject of argument among the wise men of the village; their best opinion seems to have been that it derives from Trá na mBuailte, the beach of the *buailte*, the little pastures of the good sandy grazing-land around it.) The soft sand of the bay made it easy to collect searods here as they drift ashore unbroken, but on the other hand it was hard to avoid the contamination of kelp by the sand.

Of all this sequence of small bays from Port Chorrúch onwards to this, the last one, Port Eochla used to get the best prices for its kelp, as it was free from sand and yet was low-shored and open to the winds. But these workday aspects of the shores, which so intensely individualized them to their slaves and masters, are in eclipse now that the toilsome centuries are past, and only a few old men could tell you about them. Holiday values emerge in their stead: Port Chorrúch for bird-watching; Port na Mainistreach for picking up decorative pebbles polka-dotted in white calcite, fragments from some offshore stratum full of fossilized corals; Trá na mBuailte for sea-bathing, or at least for sun-bathing, or watching dolphins trying backwards somersaults as they were doing, rather gracelessly, last time I was down that way.

THE DROWNED WOMAN

At Trá na mBuailte one feels almost within call of our island capital, Cill Rónáin, for although the village is hidden by a rise to the south two boreens lead back that way and in high summer a few tourists escape down here from the crowded bars and ice-cream shops. Usually, though, this shore is as unpeopled as the rest, and the temptation after so much desert is now to cut inland in search of human-kind, whether neighbours or strangers—but here the coast to which I am committed makes a wide loop to the north-east, and it is only after another mile of walking that a view opens up of the great bay embracing Cill Rónáin harbour.

This curved mile lies around a flat, expansive peninsula scarcely rising above sea level. Turning the headland, with the endlessly odd, angular, secretive field-walls on the right and the shore alternating heaped shingle and strewn boulders on the left, one traverses small sandy, salty, rocky wastelands given over to the rabbits and the stoats that hunt them. A stoat busy at the neck of a bloody carcass twice as big as itself may look up and eye you so boldly as you pass that the old idea, still current in Aran, of its spitting poison comes to mind, and one is relieved when it withdraws itself, thin as a thread of wind, through a chink in a wall.

This vague terrain around the headland is known as An Bhean Bháite, the drowned woman. She from whom it is so anonymously named lies buried just within the sea-wall of the last field before a track begins, that leads one on more rapidly towards the harbour and the town. I suppose it was a seaweed-gatherer who found her left by the tide on the shore here. Her clothing indicated that she came from Connemara, I have been told, and her baby would have been born soon. In those days (but I do not know what days they were; perhaps of a century ago) it was not the custom to bury such human jetsam in consecrated ground, for fear of mixing non-believers with Christian dead, of suicides (such as this unknown mother-not-to-be perhaps was) with good folk legitimately dead not of their own volition. Instead, some peasant more welcoming than the Churches made her part of this, his field, setting a small stone at her head and another at her feet— two more of the untold stones of Aran.

THE FEAST OF SAINTS PETER AND PAUL

And now, after such meditative miles upon stone, one needs company, amusement, excitement—and by one of those coincidences it is the privilege of authorship to command, today is the island's *pátrún* or Pattern Day, the celebration of its patron saints Peter and Paul, and the joyous noise of the crowds assembled outside Cill Rónáin for the sports reaches back even to the graveside of the drowned woman. The track hurries us southwards (for we are turning into the great bay that embraces the harbours of Cill Rónáin and Cill Éinne now); roofs old and new jumbled together appear on the right half a mile off and ahead are the masts of fishing boats and visiting yachts, and the slow-moving black-and-white bulk of the steamer gliding into harbour with its freight of summer visitors. There are three or four bungalows near at hand, a suburb enormously diluted with broad fields and a long brackish lake stretching inland—but we can come back later on to examine the geography, for now the track becomes a seaside road, and the road is packed with people and traffic: families in parked cars, tourists with huge rucksacks, little boys on bewildered donkeys, young heroes carrying oars for the currach races, clusters of girls giggling at the kilts of a visiting pipe band, and reserved elderly Aran men in dark tweed and peaked caps.

At this moment the voice of the technical school's headmaster, amplified into a thrilling and incomprehensible roar, is marshalling the small boys to the Donkey Race in a big hollow field by the road. The modern, multicoloured throng presses through the gaps in the tumbledown field-wall and flings itself on the grassy slopes within while the sombre Aran elders watch from the roadside, kneeling on one knee in their immemorially patient way, leaning a forearm along the top of the wall, sucking their gurgling pipes, spitting carefully in the grass verge. A few of their old acquaintances from the other islands and Connemara are among them, exchanging almost invisible nods of recognition. In the old days the three summer festivals of the region were, according to a scrap of doggerel:

> Lá 'l Caomhaín in Inis Oírr
> Lá San Seáin in Inis Meáin
> Lá Peadar is Pól in Árainn Mhór
> Lá Mhic Dara i gConamara.

(St. Cavan's Day in Inis Oírr, St. John's Day in Inis Meáin, SS Peter and Paul's Day in Árainn, and St. Macdara's Day in Connemara.) On the 29th of June, the day of Pátrún Árann, the Connemara turf-boats would bring in hundreds of people to visit the holy wells and pray in the ruined churches of Aran of the Saints, to sing and dance and drink, to have contests in smoking clay pipes, and to crack skulls with their stout blackthorn sticks. Towards the end of the last century the scandal of faction-fighting led the Church to put down many of the Pattern Days all over the country, but some, like Aran's, lingered on until about forty years ago. In recent times many of them have been revived in more sober forms. In Árainn the Pátrún now is a weekend programme including a lecture or two in the Hall, competitions for *sean-nós* or traditional singing, a celebration of the Mass, two days of sports and currach races, and a presentation of prizes at the Sunday night *céilí* dance.

The Currach Races are taken most seriously, but the Donkey Race we are all waiting for now is the height of the year's absurdities. The whistle blows, dust is raised from the shabby hides but none of the animals will leave the starting-line; in fact two of the riders have been spilt in opposite directions as a pair of donkeys makes a bid for sexual congress, to cheers and whistles from a section of the populace. They are hauled apart and the starter gets the race going by kicking each rump in the line-up, causing a chaos of barging and bucking from which the remaining boys-on-donkeys radiate crabwise in various directions; spectators rush forward and herd them around some approximation to a circuit. One lad can only progress by jumping off, running round behind, kicking his donkey and flinging himself onto it again, and the starter encourages them all with impartial kicks as they come by at the end of the lap. Nobody knows where the race ends, least of all the rebellious, unambitious beasts, but somehow a victor emerges, ringed around with cheers and laughter.

The Bicycle Race is next. A mighty-thighed Bun Gabhla girl has borrowed my bike for the event, my precious rusty-trusty

Raleigh that has fought the gales and grikes and muds of Connemara and the Burren with me, and my heart goes out to it as she assaults a bucketing slope, someone in the crowd shouting "She'll break the chain for sure!" But she collapses in a heap at the bend and other slimmer and more modern models swerve around her to the finish. Now, Throwing the Weight—a fifty-six-pound shop-weight with a loop of rope on its handle, swung backwards and forwards between the legs and then launched into an unimpressive arc. Colm Mór of Inis Meáin, a man of extraordinary lankiness, seventy per cent of it in the legs, used to manage a throw of twenty-one feet in his prime, or so he tells me, but nobody matches that in these degenerate times.

And next come the giants of Aran shambling to the Tug-of-War, trawler-men in whom some studied regime of hauling nets and drinking Guinness has united the Immovable Mass and the Irresistible Force of the old conundrum. But this year they face a visiting team from a city, trim young men all wearing neat little green shorts and matching singlets embroidered with the logo of their club. Under the command of a briskly barking coach the visitors warm up by running on the spot; meanwhile some of the Aran earthshakers seem to be warming each other up with thumps in the ribs from fists that could sink a basking shark. The teams take up the rope, and with one highly co-ordinated tug the visitors have the Araners slithering and sprawling; but then the officious coach tries to push aside an intrusive Aran supporter, who turns on him with a roar and a swing of a bottle, whereupon the visitors become disjointed, and Aran digs in its heels and hauls them to defeat like so many mackerel.

The wonderful series of events continues all afternoon, interspersed with infinite longueurs of disorganization during which we lie on the grass and watch the swallows flitting overhead, or chat with Mrs. Conneely from the west of the island and reckon up with her how many grandchildren she has been blessed with since this time last year. Sometimes there are exotic birds of passage to comment upon; one year a hippy couple and their baby, all wearing many beads and tassels. "Isn't she dirty!" sniffed a Galway matron. "Are they Red Indians?" whispered a child. "I don't know," I replied, "Why don't you go and ask them?" The child went over to them shyly, and came back saying, "Yes, they are Red Indians, and her name's Heather." Then the Ladies' Half Mile was announced, and we all sat up as Heather shed some of her wampum and stood forth, very long-legged in her brief chamois-leather tunic. From the crack of the starting-pistol she left the rest toiling behind her, drifting away from them with an expression of calm goodwill to the world at large on her face, and we became clamorously appreciative. But as the last lap began another girl steadily started to overhaul her, a solid frowning girl in a bouncing white blouse, with inexorable piston-like legs. We shrieked "Heather! Heather!" (or was it Feather?), thinking of the steam locomotive displacing the streaming buffalo herds of the Prairies; and Heather with a backward glance through her flowing hair lengthened that lovely stride, and floated to a serene victory. We were all in love with Heather that summer afternoon, even the Galway matron.

And finally, the Currach Races. We all leave the field and line the sea-wall along the other side of the road. The children scramble down onto the shingle and set tin cans floating to throw pebbles at, while we wait for the four three-man teams to assemble and to be ferried out to the long black currachs pawing at the wavelets on the starting-line. A bang, at long last, and they row past us, the Joyce brothers of Inis Bearcháin in Connemara taking the lead immediately, then Máirtín and his mates from Cill Mhuirbhigh, then an Inis Meáin team, and another we can't identify. They turn around a buoy and head off towards the lighthouse on Straw Island in the mouth of the bay; a squadron of half-deckers and motor boats follows to monitor and encourage. They dwindle with infinite slowness, and turn about another buoy we cannot see. The currachs are ants crawling the length of a pale golden arm, the sand-dunes of the Cill Éinne side of the bay. We do not need to be told by those with binoculars that the Joyce brothers are increasing their lead, for that is inevitable; it seems the Joyces have nothing better to do all summer long than go from festival to festival winning currach races. It is more intriguing to speculate about a little sailing dinghy that appears from the direction of the harbour and shapes for the open sea. The man at the tiller does not look back. The blue wedge of his sail exactly splits the difference between the blue of the water and the blue of the sky. Who is this insouciant loner? How is it that he seems to be drawing away in his wake something of the brightness of the hour? Or is it just that it is getting late and the breeze has suddenly become chilly? Currach races are boring, really. After this heat there will be semi-finals and finals for the Joyce brothers to win; it will all take hours. We begin to think of dinner, and the hilly road home. A vast owl-note from the direction of the quay warns the day-trippers to hurry, for the captain of the steamer wants to have her safe in Galway harbour before darkness falls.

THE MINISTER'S SAND

The long brackish lake I hurried by a few pages back is the remains of an inlet of the sea. At high tide small boats used to be able to sail across the bar at its mouth to anchor at its head, in Poll na bPortán, the bay of the crabs, while hookers could be hauled with ropes to a safe winter anchorage there. At low tide the bar was dry enough to make a shortcut across the mouth of the inlet—hence the name Loch an Chara, the lake of the ford. The building up of this ford into a causeway carrying a road was the work of the Reverend William Kilbride, who was the Protestant Minister of Cill Rónáin during the bitter years of the Land War in the 1880s. As spiritual leader of a very small and perhaps spiritually undemanding community of constables and coastguards, he had time for archaeological investigations and for farming. His contributions to knowledge are to be found in a couple of papers

in antiquarian journals and provide a few clues to certain stones I
will puzzle over in their places. His role in the economic exploitation of the islanders and in the profiteering in souls, the offering of
soup and salvation together, based on the misery consequent upon
that exploitation, has won him a rank second only to that of the
wicked agent Thompson in the demonology of Aran. I shall return
to his missionary work in *Labyrinth* when I reassemble the characters of old Cill Rónáin, all stiffened and shrunk into a puppet-
show by the passage of a century.

It is Kilbride's piece-by-piece acquisition of a useful farm of
land during that time of evictions that is principally remembered
against him today. A story I have heard several times about a field
by the head of the pier which Kilbride wished to incorporate into
his farm shows the islanders' tendency to place all the blame for
their oppressions on the agent and the local Protestant establishment, leaving the ultimate profiteers, the landowners, in lofty irre-
proachability, far away in the nimbus of a fairytale. This field was
part of the small-holding of a man called Dirrane, and one day he
saw Thompson and "someone else" looking about the field.
(Sometimes this "someone else" is identified as Kilbride and sometimes left anonymous, perhaps in deference to my feelings, for
since I am not a Catholic it seems to follow that I must be a
Protestant.) Dirrane seized his spade and ran down to warn them
off, and as they jumped over the wall of the field to escape him he
made a swing at them with the spade and sliced the heel off
Thompson's shoe. His neighbours were very alarmed about this
and told him he would surely be evicted, but Dirrane decided to
lay his case before Lady Digby herself. So he walked to Dublin—
perhaps it took him a month—and called on Her Ladyship. After
hearing his story Lady Digby asked, "Are there many intelligent
men like you in Aran? I had always heard they were savages!" She
opened a chest and showed him five guineas. "That's all the
money I ever got from Aran," she said. "And now go home and
tell the agent you can keep your land."

How Kilbride created that part of his farm around Loch an

Chara, starting from the basis of a few rocky islands in the lake, is told by Pat Mullen in his book *Man of Aran*:

As a first step he managed to get the owner of the little islands a reduction in rent for the rest of his property, and then by giving a couple of pounds for luck, he became the owner of them.

Aran men never want to part with a sod or a rock of their few acres, but at this time they were very poor and had very little say about any of the laws that were in force. Kilbride could have taken these islands at this time, had he so wished, and have given no compensation whatever to the owner. And if the owner had objected to the selling, he would have got a notice to quit his little holding entirely. Such things had been done many times before, but not by Kilbride.

Kilbride went ahead with his work. He began by hiring men for tenpence or a shilling a day, and women for about sixpence or eightpence, to dig the mud at low tides, in the dry summer weather, and pile it up on the islands; then he had stones hauled from the adjoining crags and filled in the places where the mud had been dug from, until they were level with the islands. A layer of stones, broken small, was spread on top and then the mud placed over all, which, when mixed with seaweed, made a fine rich soil. Finally, after some years of work, the farm was made. A few drains ran through it to the shore, at which end they were covered by iron plates backed by heavy stones. These were removed everyday at half ebb tide, when the water ran from the drains into the sea, till half flood time came when the iron plates were put up again to cover the openings and to prevent the tide from getting in as it grew higher and flooding the land. A wild, powerful workman was employed to do this work, and to look after the farm.

Despite Pat Mullen's rather equivocal testimonial it does seem that Kilbride cannot be acquitted of "land-grabbing." The accusation of profiting from the evictions of smallholders was made against him even in the House of Commons when a question was asked on behalf of the member for Galway, about the misdeeds of the notorious Thompson, and today the folk memory is unanimous against him.

The "wild, powerful workman" in charge of Kilbride's drains was later superseded by automatic devices, large stone tanks in which the pressure of the rising tide itself shut the sluices; but as the land changed hands after Kilbride's time the outlets became blocked with sand, and now the lake reclaims much of the surrounding pasture every winter. The remains of one of the tanks can be seen where one of the old drainage channels stops against the causeway along the shore.

Pat Mullen's little history of Kilbride's farm is a preliminary to a long account of an incident from his own childhood concerning the beach on the outside of this causeway. Before the building of the road and sea-wall there, the local people had been accustomed to take sand from that shore for "making land," but Kilbride forbade them to do this and had a few of them fined for trying to do so, on the grounds that the sand was a necessary protection for his causeway and his farm against the high seas of winter. So the sand accumulated year after year, and when it blew onto the road Kilbride's workmen would shovel it inside where it built up into a solid backing to the causeway. "While this arrangement was satisfactory for Kilbride," writes Pat Mullen, "*we* had to live too. Our family was increasing, and we had to make more gardens." Pat was the fourth of eleven children growing up in their little cottage in Cill Rónáin. His father, Johnny Mullen, was a small truculent man, an island "character" of whom many tales are still current (he was the first person Robert Flaherty the film-maker noticed on his arrival at Cill Rónáin pier. "The dignity of a Dook!" was Flaherty's comment, but in fact Johnny had a higher opinion of his status and called himself the King of the island). Johnny owned a bit of crag near this beach, "a waste of rock on which nothing grew except, here and there, a white thorn bush that had found root in the deep fissures," and he decided to make fields out of it with the aid of about "five or six hundred tons" of the forbidden sand. (There is an Aran Factor of numerical exaggeration at work in nearly all writing on these islands; in Pat Mullen's books it usually stands at around a hundred per cent, but in this instance surely it rises a good deal higher.) The expropriation of the expropriator was carried out over a number of dark winter nights. Pat and the other children would scout around the boreens of the area beforehand to check where the neighbours' donkeys were grazing and where their wooden straddles and baskets had been left lying in the shelter of field-walls, and then when the village was asleep the donkeys and their gear would be assembled and the whole family would work furiously bringing up loads of sand from the beach to the Mullen crag. Before dawn the donkeys would be back in the boreens, the baskets rinsed out and replaced, and Johnny, backtracking all the way with a shovel, would have smoothed out the beach and removed every trace of the work and of the donkeys. As the winter progressed people began to remark on the way in which stones were beginning to show through the sand of the beach, but one of the easterly gales that always produce an undertow sweeping sand off that shore came opportunely to divert suspicion from the Mullens. Later Johnny spread a few currach-loads of seaweed from Straw Island on the crag and the new gardens were ready for the spring planting of potatoes. The causeway did not suffer, and "all these five little gardens are now, through endless improvements, very rich and can grow all kinds of vegetables and root crops as well; and when in grass they can be mown for hay if the summer happens to be showery."

Not long after I had read this raw little creation-myth I happened upon an image from the other end of the spectrum of human dreams. It was a photograph by Cecil Beaton, a carefully confected essence of sophistication; it showed a bar in, I suppose, Manhattan (an island about the same size and shape as Aran on the other edge of the Atlantic), with, in the centre, Audrey Hepburn exquisitely reclined across several barstools; on the right S. J. Perelman proffers a silent New-Yorkerism, while on the left is an elegant couple in evening dress, tête-à-tête: an actor whose name I forget—and Johnny Mullen's daughter. How infinitely odd, how endlessly productive of more than root-crops and hay the world is! And yet, how inevitable all its transformations.

In 1905, at the age of nineteen, Pat Mullen left Aran like so many for whom no amount of sand and seaweed could provide a living, and he went to America. After years of rambling and labouring he married a Connemara woman, took to making moonshine, and had two daughters and a son. In 1921 Johnny wrote to say that if he didn't come back soon the old home and the little holding of land they had worked so hard to create would be sold off. Pat returned to Aran with his little son, P.J., leaving the rest of the family to run the shebeen. The younger daughter, Barbara, escaped from a Cinderella existence there by winning prizes for Irish stepdancing, and by working in a New York store. At the age of twenty-one she too came to Aran. Robert Flaherty was there at the time making *Man of Aran*, and Pat was his facto-tum. Barbara met and married the young camera-man John Taylor, and went to England with him. Her career thenceforth is part of film history—which means, I am afraid, that I do not know it, but it can be looked up in books; I only remember her in her later years, as the housekeeper Janet in the TV series *Dr. Finlay's Casebook*, a refined and deeply feminine character we have since found re-embodied, to a hallucinatory degree of resem-blance, in certain Aran ladies.

Barbara Mullen died in 1979 and is buried in Tír an Fhia where her mother came from. The bungalow she had built as a summer home is just south of Loch an Chara, and the gardens around it are those made from the minister's sand.

THE GENERATIONS

Each one of these homes, the bungalows rather recently scattered like a handful of dice over the green fields around Loch an Chara, the cottages and two-storied houses clustered on the rise to the south-west, has its own continuing history, and since this is an introspective community dependent upon its own doings for dramatic entertainment, we know all these histories, or think we do. But to avoid gossiping about the neighbours, or, even worse, generalizing about them, I will approach the subject of Cill Rónáin and its pocketful of fortunes obliquely, by way of the fine shingle beach that lies on the left of the road (on the right are the broad fields in which the races are held) from Loch an Chara to the first buildings of the harbour.

This shingle beach is Trá na bhFrancach or Frenchmen's Strand, from the drowned sailors washed ashore here when a French sloop was wrecked off the island, nobody knows how long ago. They are buried in a field by the shore road and on the north of a sideroad running inland from it called Bóithrín na Leachtaí, the boreen of the cairns, from the little heaps of stone that mark their graves. Frenchmen's Strand makes a perfect, shallowly concave curve of a quarter mile of coast; its profile is an elegant shallow concave too, emerging from the waves and sweeping up to the sea-wall. Its stones have been graded by size, from small boulders at the northern end to tiny pebbles where it stops against a rocky point at the south, for the tendency of the waves that strike southwards along this shore is always to shift smaller stones farther than bigger ones. Theoretically, stones endlessly rattled together will be ground into perfect ellipsoids, but this mathematical destiny is constantly forestalled by chance breakages, leaving oddly shaped bits to the further workings of the sea. So one can imagine a family tree, stemming from any one boulder, of pebbles scattered along the beach at various stages of their randomly interrupted journey, with its recurrent aspirations to roundedness and (in theory, and were it not for the headland that puts a stop to the pattern and process of the shore) to pinhead size and then ultimate dissolution. Since much of the limestone outcrop from which this shingle originated has branches of fossilized corals running through it, many of the pebbles have round white spots on their surfaces, and towards the southern end of the shore look more and more like dice half melted by the fury of the game.

On passing the rocky end-stop of Frenchmen's Strand the road leaves these allegorical mutterings of surf on stones and makes a turn to the west, by an old storehouse for nets which now holds the hundreds of bicycles hired out to tourists by the great-grandsons of Johnny Mullen. (On the day that I wrote this, the 2nd of September 1983, as I heard later, their father P.J., brought up by Pat Mullen in the spirit of his novel *Hero Breed*, died in his house back near the lake, after many months of constant and courageous wrestling with an invisible, tireless opponent, Parkinson's Disease. Two generations of visitors to whom he was boatman and oracle will remember this difficult and rewarding man.) From this point, whence the pier runs out to the left and the road continues around the sandy shore of the harbour bay, one sees Cill Rónáin whole for the first time, at least in its marine aspect, on the land sloping down to the waterfront opposite.

If one may read its architectural expression from this angle the sole vocation of the little town is to watch whatever, if anything, is going on in the harbour. Its most characteristic and intriguing feature is a narrow road rising steeply from the waterfront and immediately twisting out of sight between oddly angled gable-ends. Motionless figures lean over its curved retaining wall and survey the scene as if from an opera box; from a distance they are exactly the same people as appear in a photograph of this view taken at the turn of the century. On the right of this *carcair* (to use the local word for a steep way) is a flat-roofed, two-storied public house, Joseph McDonagh's according to the faded gilt lettering across its grey frontage, although even his daughters had long retired from the business when we first came to Aran. Behind it and above the roofs of cottages it obscures appear the snowy walls and many windows of the parish priest's residence, relaxed and spreading in discreet triumphalism on the rise of the land, and behind that again the long slated roof of the nineteenth-century coastguard station. On the left at the foot of the *carcair* is an old stone-built kelp-store, now fitted with glass doors and intermittently functioning as a café. Then farther round the curve of the waterfront the rest of the town comes down boldly led by Bay View Guesthouse, newly extended and announcing itself in several European languages, to greet the tourists disembarked by the motorboats plying from Connemara at An tSean-chéibh, the old quay. Opposite the old quay itself, which ends the harbour perimeter, is a crafts shop, white-washed and bright with the coloured woven things hung across the walls of its little forecourt, that sells Aran sweaters, sheepskin rugs, pottery, postcards and (most importantly from the point of view of our survival) my map of Aran.

Attached to the crafts shop on the right is a more retiring segment of the row of old two-storied buildings, that gives little impression of being inhabited but was once the Atlantic Hotel, landfall for all visitors to the islands in the period of their literary rediscovery. Here in 1898 J. M. Synge wrote the words "I am in Aranmor, sitting over a turf fire, listening to a murmur of Gaelic that is rising from a little public-house under my room," so beginning the account of his quietly imperious courtship of the islands. It was Yeats who, he claimed, had first turned Synge in the direction of Aran when they met in Paris in 1896, but in fact Synge had a prior connection with the islands as his uncle had been the Protestant minister here in the 1850s. An old man had spotted the family look on Synge's first arrival: "I was standing under the pier-wall mending nets," he said, "when you came off the steamer, and I said to myself in that moment, if there is a man of the name of Synge left walking the world, it is that man yonder will be he."

Synge only stayed a fortnight in Cill Rónáin before going on to Inis Meáin, which was to be his spiritual summer home for the next few years; Cill Rónáin, he felt, "has been so much changed by the fishing industry, developed there by the C.D. Board, that it has now very little to distinguish it from any other fishing village on the west coast of Ireland." The man who oversaw this change in Cill Rónáin from magical penury to mundane profitability has his memorial nearby, the handsome high cross overlooking the harbour from the top of an irregular plot of ground reaches up from the old quay between the grey and defunct hotel and the gleaming guesthouse. He was Father Michael O'Donohue, parish priest of Aran from 1881 to 1892, and he is said to have sent a momentous telegram to Dublin Castle in 1886:

SEND US BOATS OR SEND US COFFINS

—an act which, if not so miraculously or electrically causative of the C.D. Board's intervention as oral history would have it, is the perfect emblem of his dedicated representation of his flock in the face of governmental delay and the agent's rapacity.

The cross itself, of a single block of limestone ten feet tall, carved in a sturdy Victorian-Celtic style with a rational allowance of the irrational, the panels of the front being filled with plaited snakes and those on the back left blank, is the work of James Pearse of Dublin (stonecarver, socialist, and father of the hero of 1916), and it is remembered that old men used to remember him enjoying a pint in the pub here after his long hours of work on the cross, and urging the fishermen to form themselves into a cooperative to defend themselves against the outside buyers who would otherwise surely rob them. The stepped plinth of the cross and the worn grassy plot below it (what would a Mediterranean fishing village make out of this inconsequential triangle loitering down to the quayside between oddly disposed and pleasingly various buildings?) are the visitors' favoured resting-places from which to observe the business of the harbour, as opposed to the *carcair* which, with its row of faces as impassive and weatherbeaten as the gargoyles of a cathedral's eaves, declares itself quite forbiddingly as the Aran-man's preserve.

Somehow one returns to this *carcair* as the most abiding feature of Cill Rónáin's harbour-watching face. It is noticeable that very few of the newly arrived coming round from the pier turn up this way; it has the appearance of leading too abruptly into more private parts of the town, and instinctively they wander on to make their way up into the centre of things through the ambling, holidaying space around the cross. But in winter that space is a mere wind-gap to be hurried across, while the *carcair* has gable walls and corners one can peer round while waiting for the steamer or the trawlers to berth, whether or not their coming is of any personal relevance. Its full name is Carcair Joe Andy, from the erstwhile owner of the pub beside it; but in Pat Mullen's *Hero Breed*, which is set in the end of the last century, when a stick-fight breaks out on the quay, men come running from "Andy John's Hill" to watch it, and this Andy (son of John) would have been the father of Joe Andy. Several Aran placenames go through a genealogy of their own in this way, lagging slightly on that of some notable family of the vicinity. Nowadays the younger generation call the hill Carcair Katy Joe after the last of Joe's daughters to withdraw from the scene.

The taciturn watchers on this hill, the chronically or temporarily idle (whether through force of character or feebleness of circumstance), seem still to be waiting for the next thing to happen after that stick-fight of Pat Mullen's, but in the meantime they have made another appearance in literature, in one of the most likeable of books on Aran, *Úll i mBarr an Ghéagáin* by Risteard de Paor (*Apple on the Treetop* by Richard Power in its later English version). He describes the "lives of quiet desperation" of *lucht an charcair*, the hill-folk, of a generation ago with wry sympathy and perhaps some self-recognition. But he gives them one quiet laugh, to see them through the years:

A Welsh professor spent his vacation lecturing the people like a missioner with Self-help Smiles as his text instead of the Bible. A very tall man he was, in short pants, stalking through the islands like the Industrial Revolution. . . . He'd head for the hill and its inhabitants, his stick in hand, his boots knocking sparks out of the road.

"Is this a holiday?" he'd ask them.

They'd gaze at him one after the other. They wouldn't know if he had spoken or if he hadn't. He'd have to repeat the question.

They'd think a while. One of them would shrug a shoulder.

"How would we know?" another would ask.

"I have always worked hard," he'd respond, emotionally banging his stick, "and I've earned my vacation. I've worked hard since I was a young man. And look at me now."

Bug-eyed, they'd look at him, from top to toe.

"What's to stop us having holidays at the same time as yourself?" a voice would ask peevishly.

This answer would put a sudden halt to his gallop. Off with him then, his stick still threatening, his short pants flapping in the wind with the passion of his stride. They wouldn't manifest even the joy of victory. They'd gaze after him for a while.

Then they'd shift the eyes to the horizon once more.

When he was about to go home, however, they paid him a compliment that they wouldn't offer to just anybody. They left the hilltop and went down in a cluster to the quayside. They assembled round him and they shook hands with him, one after the other. As he was boarding, they promised him they'd declare a special holiday the first day he returned.

DESTRUCTION AND RECONSTRUCTION

The names of places have an explosive power, as any researcher of lost space-time knows. An old man leaning on the parapet of the *carcair* tells me that An tSean-chéibh, the old quay, used to be called Céibh na Móna, the quay of the turf—and unwittingly he has effected a mighty demolition. Three-quarters of the old quay has gone, leaving a stub scarcely bigger than the turf-quays of any of the other villages; Cill Rónáin has contracted into a cluster of cottages beside it; and of course since the name of the old quay implies the existence of the new one, whose three hundred yards of stone, steel and concrete constitute the eastern side of the harbour basin, that has evaporated too, and the view from the *carcair* is open right across Cill Éinne bay to Straw Island, which has simultaneously lost its little white lighthouse. A hooker from Connemara is sailing towards us across this sudden tide of space, and other tan sails are moving slowly against the golden-green sandhills of the farther side of the bay, heading for Cill Éinne.

Cill Éinne was the chief harbour of the islands from the days of the saints, if not before, down to the early nineteenth century. But its approaches are narrow and shallow at low water, and only limited developments were ever undertaken there. When the distresses of the mid-nineteenth century at last moved the government to put money into Irish fisheries, which had been left to rot in favour of their Scottish rivals since the Act of Union, the bay was re-examined, and it was concluded that a point just east of the old turf-quay of the hamlet of Cill Rónáin was the only place from which a pier could be put out into sufficiently deep water. So the decisions were taken that made this little recess of the bay into the islands' principal harbour, summoned the coastguard station, the barracks, the shops and churches to take their places on the rise behind it, and left Cill Éinne to sink into the direst poverty.

If, trying to reconstitute the "new" pier stage by stage, one paces it out and pries into the now all-too-obvious disjunctions between the original part and the later extensions, a history of decline is revealed—and the older trawler owners overseeing the repair of nets or the repainting of boats there will gladly join with one in praising the past and decrying modern slackness. The first hundred and fifty yards of the pier are of blocks that the builders of the pyramids would not have despised, three- and four-foot cuboids that fit together precisely, taken from a certain stratum of limestone of suitable thickness that outcrops on the other side of the bay, where they were split from the bedrock with lines of wedges, dressed with hammer and cold chisel, hauled to the shore and loaded by a hand-operated winch onto rafts to be floated across.

This great work of the year 1853, the definitive foundation of Cill Rónáin's history, cost £2407, of which the landlord, the Reverend John Digby, contributed a third, under the provisions of an Act of 1846. Céibh Ganly it was called, after the master-builder Thomas Ganly who came to Aran to oversee both the pier and the Earragh lighthouse that was being built at the same time, and stayed to marry a widow with a bit of land in Mainistir, and contributed to the Aran stock a bold, genial and light-hearted strain which, as will appear, figures repeatedly and for the good in the island's subsequent history. Thomas Ganly himself is revered by those crusty trawler captains sitting on the stone bollards he provided and grumbling about their work-shy crews. Ganly was the man who knew how to make Aran lads work! To which it must be added that necessity was on his side, for his pier was a relief work of the years just after the Famine, and the titans who manhandled these blocks into position so neatly must often have been faint with hunger before they had earned their feed of Indian meal.

After Ganly's cyclopean masonry and megalithic bollards come about thirty-six yards of concrete pier with iron bollards, the extension built by the Congested Districts Board in 1901–1902. The older trawler owners have a certain surly regard for the C.D.B. and for the works of "the British" in general, which, having lived through the bleak years after Independence, they like to contrast with the torpor of their successors. In fact the reign of the C.D.B. was comparatively energetic. By the time of its foundation in 1891, the local sailing fleet was smaller than it had been at the time of the Famine, having shrunk to just two boats of the sort called a *púcán*, a small version of the hooker. Bigger and safer boats were needed especially for the winter herring season, and the C.D.B. was anxious to explore the possibilities of a spring mackerel fishery. In 1892 the Board offered bounties of £40 to fishermen from Arklow to bring their boats and work out of Aran for a season, so that the Aran men could learn from them. Pat Mullen saw the response:

> One day in early Spring, there came sailing down Gregory's Sound the first of the fine fleet of fishing boats that had sailed from Arklow (Co. Wicklow) to begin Spring mackerel fishing in the waters around Aran—boats with beautiful names and manned by hardy men: *Mystical Rose, St. Veronica, The True Light, The Frigate Bird, The Rover's Bride,* and so on. How the sight of those boats used to thrill us. It was the beginning of better days for Aran.

A thrice-weekly steamer service had been inaugurated the previous year, which could carry the catch to Galway, and now a telegraph link was established to keep Aran in touch with its markets. The experiment was a success, and the next year the Arklow men came back without the persuasion of a bounty. Thanks to loans from the C.D.B. there were now five Aran vessels to join with them. For a few seasons thereafter the fishing industry prospered, and Cill Rónáin shop- and bar-keepers began to build themselves the two-storied, slate-roofed houses that hide the old thatched village from the harbour.

In 1900 the C.D.B. set up a boat-yard at Frenchmen's Strand under a young craftsman from Frazerburg in Scotland, James Sim. It built boats of two designs imported into western waters by the Board, the Manx nobbie and the Scottish zulu, both double-ended, two-masted boats rather larger than the local, single-masted hookers. Sim oversaw the production of four nobbies and seven zulus before his early death in 1907. (His grave is in the Protestant churchyard; he died of T.B., I am told.) The yard did not reopen after his death, as it seems his boats had always been more expensive than Scottish ones, because of the cost of importing wood. Hardly a trace of it now remains—just a long step-like foundation to the field-wall by the road, near the graves of the drowned Frenchmen, and a gap in the sea-wall opposite, through which the boats used to be launched.

The rapid growth of the fleet in the 1890s had made Céibh Ganly quite inadequate; not even a small hooker could come alongside it at low water, and as the water beyond the end of it was not much deeper, a C.D.B. report of 1893 had recommended that a new pier be built a little farther to the east. But when, eight years later, the Board set about improving the harbour, the inertia of what already exists decided them on extension rather than replacement—and to this day the pier is groping out farther and farther in search of depth for ever-larger boats. However, even as the pier was being extended the fishery entered a troubled phase; the weather was bad and the catch poor in 1902, in 1905 many boats were badly damaged in a storm, by 1908 competition from foreign steam drifters became overwhelming. Loans could not be repaid, and two Aran boats were confiscated.

Then came the years of war-time prosperity, when the foreign trawlers were absent and prices were high. The success story of the Aran Fisheries Co-operative Society has already been told, apropos of its birthplace in Cill Mhuirbhigh. The Cill Rónáin fishermen soon joined the Society as its prices were so much higher than those the outside buyers were offering. The best memorial of this period is the handsome pier-building of cut stone with which the C.D.B. had by then replaced an earlier single-storied row of stores on Ganly's pier. This sensible and solid building, with its four arched double doorways into the storage areas for fishing gear, and its long raftered chamber for net-mending above them, is still in use and in good condition—or at least that part of it standing on the sound foundation of Ganly's masonry, for the farther end of it is one the concrete of the C.D.B.'s extension, which has come adrift from the earlier stonework, so that the gable-end of the pier-building is cracked and sagging. There is a hatch in this gable which belonged to a coffeeshop, something notably lacking on the pier today. In those days, the trawler-men tell me with awe, there were even flush toilets on the pier! (Now we have only a urinal, the stink of which appals the four winds that blow through it.) Another addition of that era is the "slip" at the base of the pier, now only used for corralling cattle awaiting shipment on the steamer; this was where the business of filleting and barrelling the spring mackerel catch was done. Girls from Scotland and Donegal came to do this work, passing on their skills to Aran women.

These flush days ended soon after the war. The Society went bust, and with the return of the English and Scottish steam drifters, and then the disruption of markets throughout the years of the "Troubles," the Aran fisheries almost vanished yet again—though it was left to the Free State government to repossess the boats that could not be paid for, at least one of which lay rotting in Galway harbour for years.

After the Aran fleet had declined to a mere couple of boats by the end of the Twenties, the slow recovery towards today's fleet of diesel-engined trawlers and half-deckers began. In the Fifties the pier responded by paddling out a bit farther to the south-west, and then turning at right-angles for a similar distance to the south-east. Now, while the C.D.B.'s concrete was inferior to Ganly's stone, it did at least provide a sound surface for boats to moor against; but the contribution of the Irish Office of Public Works (and here the embittered Aran skipper will hold you with glittering eye and skinny hand while making you lean over the edge to examine its underpinnings) is carried on great drums made by planting circles of girders in the seabed and then filling them with concrete, and its frontage below is of narrow pillars with deep recesses of surging water between them, so that fenders cannot save the smaller boats from being bumped and scraped against the uprights and the continuous rim of the roadway above.

Even this contribution has been outgrown by the fleet now; at weekends the trawlers are moored five deep along it, and the latest acquisitions, the 83-foot *Colmcille* and the *Westward Isle* which arrived in 1982 (belated last-fruits of the boom of the early Seventies, before the oil crisis, when catches were good and markets high), cannot approach the pier except at high water. For this reason and because of the lack of other facilities many Aran boats are now working out of Ros a' Mhíl and their owners are building themselves homes on the mainland, deserting the opulent bungalows that sprang up here in the fat years. And of course the steamers from Galway often have to moor in the bay until the rising tide lets them come in to the pier. I remember once arriving here in company with a crowd of tourists who lined the rail as the steamer neared the harbour; progress was halted a yard or two short of our destination, and the captain appeared on the bridge and in his customary polite whisper asked us all to walk across to the other rail, which manoeuvre somehow saved an inch of draught and let the boat sidle up to the pier.

So yet another extension is now (in 1983) in hand, to my eye at least the most unsatisfying of them all. For some time now dozens of concrete boxes, each as big as a small room, have been complicating the traffic-jam on the pierhead that greets the arrival of the steamers, and now these boxes are being lowered into the sea and filled with more concrete. An inelegant approach; one hopes that it will be the solution of our problems, but I have met none among the grumblers on the pier who believe so.

POINT OF ARRIVAL

I am no disinterested historian; I study the past only to amplify my greedy awareness of the present. The foregoing account of the pier's stage-by-stage construction, with the brief history of the Aran fleet I have moored alongside it, is designed to lead me out to the pierhead, the place of arrivals and departures, as the past continually conducts one to the present, the moment of perpetual arrival and departure. What is it like to see Aran for the first time?

I wonder, watching the comings and goings. What is it like to see Aran for the last time? The latter question I will face some other time, I tell myself, if time does not catch me unawares in the meantime. The former question I can never answer for myself; my first impressions of Aran are as withered and insignificant now among the later ones as some scrap of holiness in an ornate reliquary. Therefore I find myself eyeing new arrivals coming off the steamer with a twinge of envy, and I have to remind myself that the holiness and innocency of first sight is a myth. At disembarkation, that transition from ship-board lethargy to the freedom of an islandful of choices, anxiety about mislaying physical luggage leaves one more than usually fettered to the luggage of the mind. Nevertheless I try to catch in the eyes of those coming down the gangway some reflection that might enhance my carefully built-up mosaic of perceptions, replacing the lost or faded tesserae of my own first steps on Aran.

Summer arrivals are the least productive. For those who come every year it is a moment of unreflective expansion; rucksacks are shrugged off gratefully in the quay, because these *habitués* know that there is no further need to hurry; there are knowing scraps of Irish to be flung to those islanders generally reckoned to be "great characters," and reminiscential laughs to be exchanged with other veterans of last year's "great crack." For first-timers, and especially for foreign tourists, the steps down the awkward gangplank are anxious ones. Even while the steamer was yet some yards from berthing they have been picked out, sized up and apportioned by a number of almost ominous pillar-like figures standing a little apart from one another in the forefront of the crowd on the pier: the "jarveys" or drivers of jaunting cars for hire. Their wide-legged trousers and dark jackets of stiff tweed make them monumental, their caps pulled down to the bridge of the nose give them a lofty and inscrutable demeanour. (The hardy islander, one's ideals and preconceptions agree, is impervious to winter gales, but, in fact, it is summer heat that has no effect on these well-insulated traditionalists.) As "the strangers" struggle down the narrow gangway with their bags they are solicited by the more forward of the jarveys, who thrust their rigid sun-cured masks close to them from either side with incomprehensible whispers. Those who accept out of free-will or out of bewilderment the offer of "a ride to the Dún" are jealously shepherded through the tangle of minibuses and taxis waiting on the pier with open doors as if trawling for custom, to a line of traps and side-cars along the harbour road, where the Connemara ponies stolidly waiting in the shafts with occasional twitches and snorts have been filling the air with the green tang of their dung.

The rest of the visitors, having shaken off the last of their importunate shadows, press on around the harbour, free now to look around themselves. The things they notice are probably just the ones I omitted from my panorama of the sea-front, for instance the small monument of blue limestone half-way round the curve of the sea-wall, the plaque of which has been wrenched off. This commemorates, or dumbly fails to commemorate, the landfall here on the dark rainy evening of September the 3rd, 1966, of the first men to row the Atlantic, John Ridgeway and Chay Blyth, two English paratroopers. (Whether the plaque was stolen by our Cill Rónáin vandals or by "a crowd from the North" as I have heard, the monument might as well be left blank until all soldiers on Irish soil are as harmlessly employed and as welcome as these two heroes were made upon their unexpected arrival.) A little farther on, perhaps the visitors will stop to read the notice by the lifeboat-house door listing vessels assisted and lives saved by the famous Aran lifeboat, which itself is always at the ready, anchored out beyond the harbour mouth. (I would have written about the lifeboat if all my acquaintance with it had not been at least second-hand. I did once stand looking out at it for a long time waiting for inspiration on the topic, noting its low, alert, hare-like crouch, and the way the mirror-smooth water reflected blue-white-orange, its neat orange, white and blue paintwork. Eventually a dim sense of *déjà-vu* stirred. What did it remind me of? Nothing more exciting, I realized with a sigh, than the familiar R.N.L.I. collecting-box in the

shape of a lifeboat, sitting on the glass counter in a shop. Fortunately, like the Ridgeway-and-Blyth epic, the Aran lifeboat service
has been copiously written-up by more seaworthy hands than
mine.)

Then, on passing the lifeboat-house and reaching the foot of
the *carcair*, a botanist among the visitors would notice a swag of
delicate floral forms on the curve of its retaining wall, enhancing
its absurd likeness to a megalithic opera-box, and might go over to
identify it, braving the impassive gazes of *lucht an charcair* above.
The ivy-leaved toadflax it is, an exquisite little purple-flowered
wallplant, very common around Galway docks but only recently
come here, no doubt on the heels of some visitor, and so far restricted to this its point of arrival (though, most mysteriously, it is
well established in fissures of the crags of Inis Meáin some way
from any houses).

Meanwhile the botanist's companions will have gone on impatiently, and are wandering out onto the old quay to watch the
messing about in boats that goes on there or are queuing at the
information-caravan parked nearby, or making their way up into
the town past the tall Celtic cross—where I will not follow them
because of the vow or *geasa* this book is under, to complete the circuit of the coast before broaching the interior.

These great shoals of tourists, a hundred or two or even three at
a time, day-trippers most of them, come on the *Galway Bay*,
which sails between Galway and Cill Rónáin every day of the
week except Wednesdays, from the beginning of June to the middle of September. In fact the sight of her snowy upperworks sliding towards us out of the pale trough of heat-haze between the
limestone-blue of Clare and the purple-brown of Connemara is
the very emblem of summer itself for us, that brief and profitable
season of charming, irritating novelty. The other steamer, a little
green-painted freighter called the *Naomh Éanna* (which is Irish for
Saint Enda), comes all the year round on Wednesdays and Saturdays, weather permitting, as the timetable says. And very often
the weather does not permit, especially around the spring and au-

tumn equinoxes, so that the shops may run out of bread and the pubs run dry of porter. Or there may be a gale warning on Tuesday evening so that the sailing is cancelled, and then the gale does not materialize and the only possible sailing-day of a turbulent fortnight is lost. Sometimes if the weather is worsening the steamer may only stay at the pier for long enough to fling the mailbags ashore before turning and running. It has happened that having come within yards of the pier the captain has decided not to risk being damaged against it, and has returned to Galway with his groaning passengers. (I remember hearing about an Aran man who was bringing a bull into the island once; the steamer turned back from the pier because of the weather, and delivered him and his bull back onto the rainy streets of Galway late on a Saturday evening. What he did then I do not know, fortunately, as the episode has the makings of an all-too-Irish short story.)

Passengers other than islanders are very rare in the winter months, but if I happen to be on the pier (awaiting delivery of some timber for more bookshelves, perhaps; for we all have to be on hand to collect our own freight when the *Naomh Éanna* berths) and I catch sight of a stranger half hiding in the cabin door from the blast as the steamer makes her cautious crabwise approach, then I have hopes of someone with an eye committed to seeing, who though perhaps half-effaced with weariness (as the voyage may have started at six or seven in the morning and taken six or even ten hours, with long waits on the heaving seas off the two other islands on the way) will relish the wildness of the scene on the pier, having come with something of that in mind. The rain-squall that has lashed the grey-faced town comes pelting across the harbour and blackens the backs of the men trundling gas-cylinders and beer-kegs out of the way as pallet after pallet of them is winched up from the hold and swung ashore. The shopkeepers shelter in their vans, hoping the rain will stop before the cartons of groceries and wicker bread-hampers they are waiting for are dumped on the pier. Sacks of cement, drums of petrol, stacks of drainpipes, Mrs. Dirrane's TV set back from the repairers, accumulate among mountains of miscellanea, through which we all go hunting for our own packages (and I am left cursing because my shelving hasn't turned up, for the third time). Then round the corner of the pier come running a dozen bullocks, whacked through the maze of vehicles by men with sticks, to be penned between a wall of coalsacks and a heap of chipboard until the captain gives the word to begin loading and one of the beasts is grabbed by six or eight men holding onto all its natural handles; the sling is passed under its belly, and it suddenly becomes an inert black sack against the sky, lofted, swung out, and dropped into the hold. If a horse is being shipped in the same way, everyone leaps back out of range of its lashing hooves as it pendulums overhead. The men sending the empty gas-cylinders and beer-kegs rumbling across the concrete and hefting them on board work on doggedly, hunched against the rain. The captain and the sky in glowering collusion advance the time of departure, for the gale is rising and it is time to run for Galway, however much still lies unloaded on the pier.

Meanwhile the stranger has slipped (not unnoticed though) through the turmoil at the pierhead, and is trying to decipher the names of the trawlers at their uneasy berths one outside another, all along the body of the pier. The *Arkin Castle* (we shall come to the origin of that name), the *Fort Aengus*, the *Carraig Éanna* (I painted that name, I want the stranger to know; it has been repainted since, and half-scuffed off against the pier, but that is still in part my hand, my sole contact with the beyond-the-horizon life of the herring-fishermen, those fabulous compounds of ancient virtues and modern skills, the hunter-technicians, who will be flashing impressive wads of notes in the pubs this Saturday night, who will stagger down to sleep in the boat after the Sunday-night *céilí*, and will be off into the grey drizzle some hours before I stir on Monday morning. And that name has been a lucky one, the owner tells me, it has brought good catches; so that once when I passed by on the pier he shouted out "Do you want a feed of fish?" and sent a lad below to fetch a ray the size of a tablecloth, which he rolled up around half-a-dozen mackerel for good measure, clamping the whole slithery impossible parcel onto the carrier of my bike...but that was in the middle Seventies when fish were plentiful and prices high and the fisherlads were the envy of the shorebound; luck was in the air and on the waves in those days.) Then comes the *Rose d'Ivoire* (pronounced "rose divoyer"), bought second-hand in Brittany many years ago. And then this abandoned wreck (if you must know, stranger), taking up valuable space by the pierside as those irascible old trawlermen will readily point out, is the *Asco*, a little cargo-vessel bought very cheaply and ill-advisedly in Stornoway by our island co-operative. It was nursed through the Caledonian canal and round the coast to Aran with only one major breakdown, but since that epic and funereal voyage has well merited the nickname some pessimist wit (not I) gave it, the *Fiasco*.

So, having loitered along the pier in the rain, the stranger, whose reading of these names I cannot read, since I cannot un-learn their little histories, jumps down onto the scruffy beach around the head of the harbour and tramps across it, kicking at clumps of driftwood, plastic bottles and dead dogfish, to the lifeboat slip opposite, and disappears up the *carcair* with a nod to the one or two figures maintaining their dogged harbour-watch from the rain-shadow of the pub's gable-end.

Stranger (I find myself using the familiar Aran term, *stráinséir*, which carries no charge of exclusiveness): one who arrives and departs, to whom time here is strange. Is it only the stranger who can hope to be met by winter and summer on the pierhead of a single moment? Or is there a way of inhabiting a moment, rather, of knowing all its bays and headlands intimately and lovingly, without that familiarity making one half-blind?

THE BAY OF DOUBT

Cill Rónáin's waterfront comes to a dead end to the south, after the old quay, the crafts shop and one or two fishermen's store-houses, and sometimes it is my pleasure to jump over the low sea-wall onto the rocky foreshore and sneak out of town behind the backs of the houses instead of going up through the busy parts, for after some months of life in Fearann an Choirce even Cill Rónáin seems to buzz with illicit distractions and tiresome obligations.

Once over the wall, the moody sea reasserts itself even while the town is still lagging alongside. The first point of rock beyond the end of the waterfront is Spur Cháit, but of the woman Cáit I can learn only that she had a little cottage on it and was perforce at home to high spring tides. Such anomalies are not tolerated now; the town keeps well back from high water mark, and even where the road running around the bay towards Cill Éinne follows the curve of the shore closely, it is separated from it by a concrete wall the waves slop across only when a spring tide coincides with a northerly gale. Nevertheless a very high tide is psychologically disturbing to those who live nearby, especially when it comes in stillness and silence. I remember a young woman coming out to stand in the doorway of her shop in the part of Cill Rónáin that looks out this way, and murmuring more to herself than to me, "The tide's very high today"—and there at the end of the street was the bay, much nearer than one had remembered, brimming, gleaming, pressing on some nerve in the town's subconscious.

But then the waters withdraw so far across the shallows here, exposing the luminous acres of sand called Cockle Strand, that this vast neighbouring mutability seems purely benignant towards the town, giving it a pleasure-ground for half a day at a time. The old Cill Rónáin people tell me how when they were children they would look for the tiny plump cowrie-shells they call "pigs" here, for let's-pretend farms, and an almost salivary gleam comes into their eyes when they speak of the delicious cockles from which the strand is named. Far out on it among the rocks near low water lies a rusty boiler from some forgotten wreck, which children used to put bait in to catch the occasional foolish lobster that couldn't find the way out of it. The young lads of the town still sometimes go hunting razorfish here, the molluscs with long curved shells like old-fashioned barbers' razors, which can dig themselves deep into the sand very quickly and have to be prodded for with long skewers or made to come out of their burrows with a pinch of salt.

Cockle Strand is the delight of summer visitors, who come here to bathe or paddle, or to sunbathe on the rocky steps and slopes along the roadside. For me, though, when I walk or cycle by, there is usually an inkling of unease about the place, a rawness of the adjustment between its vaguely open oval of unemphatic naturalness and its patchily socialized rim, which I think antedates the new houses so crudely sited above scarps to the south of the road. The sun-cultists sprawled on their awkward rocks look uncomfortable, and even the vegetation of this shoreline is somehow dispiriting. At the Cill Rónáin end of the curve there is almost a low hedge along the concrete wall of an odd conjunction of species, both with coarse and ragged leaves and flowering in a barbarous dissonance of colours, the creamy yellow of sea-radish and the pinkish purple of common mallow; while at the other end of the beach where broad sheets of rock interrupt the sand, the principal growth is a four-inch forest of glasswort, like a miniature translucent cactus, and seablite, a dull rubbery-green dwarf. The slight tedium I feel sometimes along this shore has been replaced on occasion by a more positively disquieting atmosphere. About half a mile from the town there is a little cabbage-plot on the shore side of the road called Garraí na Taoille, the garden of the tide, because a high enough tide makes a little promontory of it. I remember watching the still waters come creeping up around this garden one stifling day when there were muttering fog-banks offshore and lighting punching down into the sea; the mullet, big grey fish that visit muddy shallows in summer, were making sudden rushes to and fro, ripping the glassy surface. It was a sinister hour, that dispersed with the turning of the tide.

Sometimes I like to go and poke about a small lake over the road from the shore a little farther on, although it is not now a peaceful spot, as the generators supplying our electricity grumble and throb in a slovenly enclosure nearby; nor is it attractive at the first glance, for the waters are often covered by a green slime and seem to lie inertly among grey sheets of limestone pavement. One of these expanses of unfissured rock is so broad and smooth that it has been made into the floor of a handball alley, little used nowadays, the great blank wall of which (built, it used to be said, with the money from some nineteenth-century relief scheme) seems to mirror the ambience of dereliction. This sullen water is Loch an tSáile, the lake of the brine (for although it is a hundred yards from high tide mark the sea infects it through fissures running under the road), and its name, anglicized as Lough Atalia, recurs in many of the botanical reports on the island written by generation after generation of visiting scientists. Its fascination is primarily the extraordinary interpenetration of diverse habitats around its margins, giving rise to a species list that might make one think a botanist had muddled together field-notes taken in a variety of different places, and secondarily, the anomalies in some of those botanical reports, which successive investigators come here hoping to resolve, so generating further reports and making for a self-perpetuating cult of Lough Atalia.

For instance, the earliest attempt at a comprehensive listing of the Aran flora was made by Dr. E. P. Wright, Professor of Zoology in Trinity College, Dublin, in 1866, and he includes among his finds at Lough Atalia *Ranunculus lingua*, the greater spearwort, a large and rather uncommon buttercup of fens and marshes, not to be expected in Aran. The next important investigator was H. C. Hart in 1869; he searched the lake and found the lesser spearwort, which is common, but not the greater. He also noted here a rare horsetail, *Equisetum variagatum*; Robert Lloyd Praeger, most ubiquitous and comprehensive of Irish naturalists, confirmed this find in 1895, but since then nobody else has been able to do so. During the intensive combing of the islands and the critical re-examination of old records undertaken in the preparation of the most recent and definitive work on the subject, Professor D. A. Webb's article, "The Flora of the Aran Islands," of 1980, the lake was closely scrutinized by amateurs and experts, but neither of the missing plants was found. The conclusion was that Wright must have mistaken a particularly hearty specimen of the lesser spearwort for the greater (after all, he did describe his sufferings in the Atlantic Hotel, working at his specimens in the evenings, when the only choice of light was between "a farthing dip of the worst description—i.e. with the thickest possible wick and the smallest amount of tallow—and a slender cotton thread lying in a saucer of fish-oil"). The rare horsetail is accepted as a reality, however, and may yet turn up in the anomalous margins of Loch an tSáile.

Coming on the scene after these illustrious discomfitures, it would give me a slightly improper pleasure to find either of these plants, and so I turn off the road here now and again and make a circuit of the lake, trying to tune out of my mind the buzz of the generator, the egoistic discovery-ethic, and other fragmenting influences on the consciousness. Laying aside the search for rarities, it is marvellous to see how a single crevice running into the surrounding rock from the edge of the lake contains a summary of Aran's flora, from the seaweeds of the middle shore like *Ascophyllum* (the knotted wrack, which only grows in the inmost parts of Cill Éinne bay, as it needs quiet water), and those of the upper shore like channelled wrack and spiral wrack; then the flowers of shinglebanks and rocky foreshores like thrift, sea campion, pellitory, and the sea spleenwort fern that one finds in fissures on the clifftops; and only a few feet away from them all of the usual cragplants, wall-pepper, hemp agrimony, thyme, and dozens of others; while a muddy hollow nearby will hold a miniature saltmarsh of glasswort and seablite, then sea-aster, and farther back where the freshwater springs feeding the lake from under the scarp south of it make themselves felt, the plants of Aran's turloughs such as marsh pennywort, loosestrife, watermint, bog pimpernel, etcetera. These ecological sentences (all multicoloured punctuation and no sense) lead me back to the seductive tangles of the scarp itself, with its sweet-smelling hawthorns and dog roses sheltering rank garlic mustard, delicate wood sorrel and hidden gardens of violets and primroses in spring, and thence to the open hillside above, luring me away from the puzzles of the shore, to which I must now return.

Beyond the lake and the ball alley the road climbs the scarp and leaves the coast, which here stretches out a low headland into the bay, dividing it into two lobes. This flat area of crag, thicket, little fields of rough grazing and low stony shore, has a name that remains indeterminate however often I hear it: Carraig an Bhanbháin, Carraig an Mharbháin, the rock of the something-or-other; its consonants seem to hesitate between *b*'s and *v*'s and *w*'s, *r*'s and *n*'s, and everyone is ready to make wildly various senses of it: the rock of the little piglet, of the corpse, of the white woman, of the sultry weather.... I record another of these guesses out of respect for deathbed testimony, for an old man of the locality who died a few years ago used one of his last breaths, no one knows why, to explain to those around his bedside that this shore is really Carraig na Mara Báine, the rock of the white sea. Unlikely, I am afraid; but it does make me think of a night I have heard of when the sea was white with foam along this normally sheltered shore. It was on the evening of the 28th of December, 1899, and a number of fishermen were sleeping in their boats moored offshore in readiness for an early start the next morning, when a storm struck suddenly into the bay. One man was by himself in a nobbie and managed to lower the mainmast single-handed, reducing the wind's purchase and saving the anchor from dragging. Five other boats were driven against the rocky shore and three of them were utterly smashed. The seas were so fierce that those on land could do nothing to help; four men were drowned, and the corpse of one of them never recovered. It was a terrible blow for Aran's new fishing-fleet. Synge heard of the tragedy when he visited Inis Meáin the next summer:

"Ah!" said the man that told me the story, "I'm thinking it will be a long time before men will go out again on a holy day. That was the only storm that reached into the harbour the whole winter, and I'm thinking there was something in it."

The name of the headland, like this event, remains uninterpretable for now, but the low rockface the boats were smashed on is Aill na mBád, the cliff of the boats, and it was baptized by this disaster.

There are slight traces of a ruinous stone quay there, for the blocks used in the building of Cill Rónáin pier in the 1850s were quarried close by and rafted across the bay from this point. Later on, the stone for Kilmurvey House came from here too, and there is a big block with a curved face lying not far away which looks as if it had been intended for one of the lighthouses. A field near the old quay is still called Garraí na Craeneach, the garden of the crane, from the winch used in loading the blocks. Evidently these massive pieces of stone were split out of the bedrock by tapping wedges into rectangular slots, for rows of these slots can be seen here and there in what remains of the original limestone pavement surface. The interior of this headland always seems to promise archaeological discoveries, in the way the lake nearby promises botanical rarities, which do not materialize, for it is a neglected corner of the island and very overgrown, but the intriguing hummocks of stone half-hidden in brambles all derive from nineteenth-century quarrying, so far as I can tell.

Disappointed, I return to Aill na mBád, the site of the disaster. What exactly did Synge's islander think was "in it"? What significance did he see in its happening on a holy day? And what art have I been exercising on this bay through the epithets I have associated with it (moody, disturbing, uneasy, raw, dispiriting, tedious, ominous, sinister, slovenly, derelict, anomalous, indeterminate, uninterpretable, disappointing)? I become anxiously aware of a convergence between these two questions as I walk on towards the turn of the headland, mentally reviewing what I have written. (And what a peculiar shore this is, beyond Aill na mBád, confirming me in my choice of adjectives: dreary rock-flats patched with an extraordinary black-and-white strand made up of limpet-shells and wave-worn lumps of coke, perhaps from the same wreck as the rusty boiler stuck out there in the tide.) The islander did not have in mind any such comparatively modern and well-formulated concept as that of a jealous Old-Testament God snatching up a storm to smite those who slight his feasts. Similarly I would not impute to this bay a devious, recalcitrant, inconsistent personality, nor indeed a human characteristic of any kind. The islander's thought moves in a vague and ancient terrain around a craggy idol only half-worked into a human face: Luck. On the one hand luck is merely the interplay of the random; on the other it is a force influencing the outcome, if not absolutely fixing the game then at least improving the odds. Observing the feast-days, whether they be Christian in origin or Celtic or even neolithic, is lucky; skimping their observance is unlucky. I worship Art, another half-humanized boulder lying on unprofitable ground. Calling Nature names is only my way of claiming a relationship deeper than blood. Observe the rites and obey; observe the facts and describe; otherwise, it is hard to know what to do for the best, for survival, in this improbable, probabilistic world. We are not all as hard-headed as that other native of Inis Meáin who told Synge, "A man who is not afraid of the sea will soon be drownded, for he will be going out on a day he shouldn't. But we do be afraid of the sea, and we do only be drownded now and again." Under the fey charm worked by Irish grammar on English speech, this is a classic statement of the facts of life in a chancy universe, in which anything can happen at any moment. . . .

But at this moment I hear strange voices from beyond the turn of the headland; it sounds like a row. I leave my puzzling and hurry on, full of curiosity.

THE FIELD OF THE CLOAK

A crowd of hairy-chinned, bald-pated men in dingy robes make a frieze against the sky along a low clifftop. Their eyes are focused on a scene being played out on the shore below; their gestures express awe, embarrassment, edification, glee, etcetera. The protagonists are a gaunt, implacable elder and a fervent youth, both skeletal but hardy, both illuminated by their passion for God in the first place and for Aran in a very close second; saints, evidently. Enda, founder of the towers of learning I can see rising from the hillside beyond, has just refused his pupil Columba or Colm Cille, a small share of Aran by which to be remembered. Colm takes off his cloak and flings it on the ground. Mastering his anger he says between his teeth, "Give me the width of my cloak thereof." Enda can hardly refuse the modest request, but his eyes are very wary. And indeed the cloak is already spreading miraculously; it has gobbled up an acre before Enda recovers from his astonishment, snatches it up and shakes it back to its normal size. He rears up in outrage at this use of God-given powers against his own God-given authority over Aran of the Saints. He grabs the younger man, swings him high and dashes him down against the rocks. As Colm Cille crawls into the surf, a hand to his ribs, Enda raises his arm to the horizon and pronounces immediate banishment. No currach will be provided either; let the ambitious neophyte take himself off by another of his miracles. Colm Cille wades out a little way and then turns, raises both fists and curses the place he loved too greedily:

> The isle shall be the worse therefore, for if thou hadst suffered me to bless it, there had come thereto no ship save a ship that came with pilgrims, and there had been no port where a ship might come to, save one port only, in that place that is called Acaill. And one man might have defended it against ships of the men of the world. And no stranger nor foreigner had come there ever. And he that had

done shame or evil there, his two soles should have stuck to
the soil of the island, so that he might not have taken one
step until he made good that shame. And it had been a
burying ground for the hosts of the Western World. And
there had been a throng of birds of paradise singing there
each day. And there had been no sickness nor distemper
upon the folk there save the sickness of death. And the taste
of its water had been mixed with honey, and its fields and
harvests without sowing or plowing and labour from them
save the labour of harvest. And the folk of this island had
had no need of kine save one cow for each house. And they
had had from her their fill of milk and the fill of their
guests. And the bells had struck themselves at the hour of
the masses and of the hours, and the candles been enlu-
mined of themselves at the mass and in the midst of the
night when the saints were saying their hours. And there
had been no lack of turf for laying a fire again forever in that
place. And since I have not left my blessing, belike there
shall be every want thereon whereof we have made mention.

Then he strikes out for the open sea, and is last seen heading for
Kerry with a powerful dog-paddle. The other revenants dissolve
into thin air, crossing themselves. I advance to investigate the site
of this divine knockabout.

To this day, it is said, the mark of St. Colm Cille's ribs are to be
seen on the stone. I have never been able to find them, but perhaps they are represented by the fissures of a sheet of rock near low
tide mark, opposite a curious embayment of the coastal field-wall
around a bare patch of land. This piece, visibly excerpted from the
rest of Aran, is Gort an Chochaill, the field of the cloak. Very high
tides claim it and relinquish it. A hundred yards to the south-east
on a little bluff below the line of small cliffs that continues the
shore east-wards, is an altar of rough stone blocks with an old
stone cross. On the saint's day, the 9th of June, many islanders
come to visit Altóir Cholm Cille and make their "rounds," repeat-

ing the Creed and the Ave Maria, for if the island lies under the cloak of any saint nowadays it is that of Colm Cille, while Enda's own well on the hillside above Cill Éinne is little attended. The altar has a sink-like hollow in its upper surface in which are a number of pebbles, and the practice is to take seven of these pebbles and throw one back after each round of the *turas*. The awkward little path thus tramped out scrambles (sunwise, of course) around the slopes of the bluff, close above the sea. There is no real well but people take a few drops from the seepage under the cliff as holy water. The cross is a strange one, shaped out of a comparatively thin slab, with a broad octagonal central area and very short, wide arms and uprights. There is a rather spindly outline cross inscribed on its face with the letters IHS above and (of later date) the words "St. Collum Kill" written in a slanting line of cursive script below. An old photograph shows the cross standing on top of the altar, but now it is propped up in the hollow that holds the pebbles, and one of its arms is missing; presumably it was wind or wave that knocked it down. Flowers are sometimes left on the altar, so the pebbles in the hollow are usually mixed with bits of broken jamjars, which I pick out now and again, and withered stalks, which I leave.

St. Colm Cille is supposed to have come to Aran after his early studies at Clonard and before founding his own monasteries at Durrow, Derry and Iona, and undertaking his great work, the "Conversion of the Picts." But since he left Ireland for Iona in 563 and Enda is said to have founded his monastery here in 483, it does not seem likely that they met. The tale of their coming to blows over Aran is already a monkish concoction of the ridiculous and the sublime; my version merely stirs in a pinch of today's deplorable levity, together with the naïve realism of Aran's fireside tales and the Latinate sonority of Manus O'Donnell's *Betha Coluimb Chille* of 1532 as translated by a Celtic philologist in 1914; we tellers of the tale all come long after the event, if event there ever was, that imprinted this otherwise nondescript patch of shore with so much remarkability.

But to undo the effect both of mediaeval curse and modern frivolity I will add here Colm Cille's love-poem to Aran. It is an apocryphal work, which O'Donovan dates to the ninth or tenth century. My version merely condenses his, abandoning the four-line verse structure of the original Irish:

Farewell from me to Aran, a sad farewell I think; I must go east to Iona, separated since the Flood.

A farewell from me to Aran; it torments my heart not to be in the west by her billows, among throngs of heaven's saints.

A farewell from me to Aran, a sad farewell it is; Aran full of fair angels; not even a servant with me in my currach.

The Son of God, oh it is the Son of God who sends me to Iona and gives Enda (what prosperity!) Aran, the Rome of pilgrims.

Aran, Sun, oh Aran, Sun! my love stays with her in the west. It is the same, being within sound of her bells, and being in heaven.

Aran, Sun, oh Aran, Sun! my love stays with her in the west. Whoever lies under her pure earth will never be seen by the devil's eye.

Saintly Aran, oh saintly Aran! Woe to him who is her foe, for angels come from heaven to visit her every day of the week.

Gabriel comes each Sunday, for Christ has so ordered, and fifty angels (no feeble power!) to bless her Masses.

Every Monday, oh every Monday, Michael comes (a great advantage), and thirty angels (their habit is good) to bless her churches.

Every Tuesday, oh every Tuesday, Raphael comes, of mysterious power, to bless the houses serving her guests.

On hard Wednesday, oh hard Wednesday, Urial comes (a great advantage), and three times blesses her high angelic cemeteries.

On every Thursday, oh every Thursday, Sarial comes (a great treasure), that God's beneficence be poured from heaven onto her bare stones that day.

On Friday, oh on Friday, comes Ramiel and his host, that every eye be filled with the sight of truly bright beauteous angels. Mary, Mother of God's Son, and her train comes too with angels among the host, to bless Aran on a Saturday.

If there were no life in Aran but listening to her angels, it would be better than any other life under heaven, to hear their celebrations.

CILL ÉINNE: THE VILLAGE

The shoreline backed by little cliffs that leads on from the saints' battleground to the harbour of Cill Éinne is the only Aran coast on which rats are common. It was not always so, on this holy island. In about 1185 a Welsh cleric, Giraldus Cambrensis, wrote a description of Ireland for his master, King John, in which he had two remarkable things to say about Aran:

> Here human bodies are neither buried, nor do they putrefy, but, lying on the surface and exposed to the open air, they remain uncorrupted; and man may thus behold and recognize their grandfathers and great-grandfathers. Another thing remarkable is that, although all Ireland abounds with rats, this island is free from any, for should that reptile be brought thither, it either leapeth into the sea, or being prevented, instantly dies.

But by the time Roderic O'Flaherty was writing almost exactly five centuries later, either some of the virtue had gone out of the soil of Aran or incredulity was on the increase:

Giraldus Cambrensis was misinformed to say that...human carcasses need no buriall in it, as free from putrefaction; which last was attributed to Inisgluaire on the sea of Irrosdownan, and there itself it is by experience found false. But what he alledges, that it did not breed rats, and that by chance, thither transported, they immediately dyed, I believe was true in his time; for that is the nature of all the rest of the territorie, except the districts of Galway town.

So it is in the vicinity of the two ports of his "territory" of west Connacht, Galway and Cill Éinne, that rats became known in O'Flaherty's time (for the big brown rat is an immigrant and in Irish it used to be called *luch fhrancach*, French mouse, and today it is simply the *francach*). Rats haunt all the villages of Aran now, but this is the only village with a cliff just at the bottom of its back-gardens, and a lot of rubbish comes sailing over this convenient provision of Nature; so that it is only a coincidence that I am reminded of the purity of St. Enda's Aran by some minute monkish things rummaging among the pebbles as I approach Cill Éinne, the church of Enda itself. Farther on, the beach is largely made up of broken glass from the pub above and is in any case impassable when the tide is in, so it is better to go up the path through a little break in the cliffs two hundred yards beyond St. Colm Cille's altar and follow the main road through the village itself.

Cill Éinne is a *sráidbhaile*, a street-village, like most of Aran's villages. A mixture of recent bungalows, one or two mobile homes, a few well-set-up two-storey houses from the 1950s, cottages built by the Congested Districts Board for fishermen earlier in the century, and the remains of the hovels these last replaced, line a mile or so of roadside, with casual interruptions of little stone-walled fields. The pub, called "Fitz's" from its former owner Tommy Fitzpatrick (it was also known as "Licensed to Sell," for that was the rather cryptic legend over its door) is on the left, the sea-side of the road. The two attractive and distinctive features it possessed in the days of Fitzpatrick have been swept away by the younger generation: a fine pair of cypresses, unique in this wind-shorn island, and an impressive piece of country signwriting from the days of Tommy's father, displaying his name in the resounding Irish form:

Pádraig Mac Giolla Pádraic

hand-lettered in a majestic Gaelic script, with extra ovals in the loops of the letters P, giving them the look of a pair of wide-set eyes. (In return for these losses, the new interior, a little lounge-bar that could be anywhere in Ireland, is preferable to the chilly bare room furnished only with a few benches and beer-barrels and a dartboard that preceded it.)

Opposite the pub begins a line of buildings, only two of them inhabited, set back a little from the road, called *An Ró Nua*, the new row, incorporating the derelict remains of a long row of tiny attached cottages that was new some time early in the last century, and whose inhabitants were rehoused in the C.D.B. cottages farther on. I once asked an islander how many rooms these old dwellings had had, and he replied that he didn't think they had a room at all—which puzzled me until I remembered that the traditional farm cottage of the west of Ireland has a kitchen and a room off it to the west called simply *an seomra*, the room; these long rows of fishermen's cottages had no such amenities.

The Ró Nua is a memory of that dreadful Cill Éinne of a hundred years ago, the village of landless fishermen who had no boats for fishing, which drew a certain amount of horrified attention from the outside world. In 1880 the Duke of Edinburgh was in Galway, interesting himself in the distribution of Indian meal to the starving of Connemara, and enjoying some remarkably fine salmon fishing on the Corrib, according to the reporters covering the visit. In April he was conducted around Cill Éinne by a member of the Mansion House Committee, a Dublin charity engaged in famine-relief.

In all the huts the Prince visited he saw no food, no fuel, no
bed clothing, no furniture, but the most abject and squalid
poverty prevailing—to such an extent that the Prince won-
dered how they were able to live.

A girl was born into that Cille Éinne during his visit. When informed of the happy event by the parish priest, His Royal
Highness requested that she be named Marie, after his Duchess,
and later sent a cheque. What happened to this Marie? Did she escape the fevers, did she gather armfuls of nettles for dinner like the
other village children, did her parents save the money to pay her
passage to America? The parish records of the period are lost; I
have not been able to trace her history, if she had one.

The very first Cill Éinne, that of St. Enda's abbatical successors,
looks down on this mingling of decayed nineteenth-century and
revived twentieth-century Cill Éinne from the hillside inland, in
the shape of a stump of a round tower and a tiny oratory perched
as neatly as a robin on the skyline. Another Cill Éinne, the stronghold that was of such military importance in Elizabethan and
Cromwellian times, obtrudes its broken bones among the houses
and gardens on the coastal side of the road opposite the Ró Nua.
Then comes a T-junction; a side-road runs inland to the monastic
sites and to Killeany Lodge, which I shall visit in the sequel to this
book, while the main road turns sharp left to the coast. The old
fort, Arkyn Castle, occupied this angle, but the road turns right
again so immediately that one could miss the remaining lengths of
curtain-wall and the little square tower by the sea, because one's
eye is caught by the sudden vistas of the bay and the sand dunes
beyond. Here is the harbour, down a slight scarp at one's feet, with
just one or two small trawlers and none of the appurtenances of a
port.

A small quay was built here in 1826 as a famine-relief project,
with the aid of a grant from the Fishery Board; it was called Céibh
an "Rice" because the labourers were paid in rice rather than in
cash. The Cill Éinne fleet of those days included thirty-eight

hookers employed in fishing and drawing kelp to Galway, as well as many currachs. By the 1890s it had been reduced to just one sailing vessel, and the village was in the state I have described. The C.D. Board when it came to the rescue put most of its efforts into developing the already superior harbour at Cill Rónáin, but here in 1912–13 it provided some cottages to replace the squalid rows of hovels, and some pier-buildings, now vanished; the big square limekiln by the quay dates from this phase of construction. The quay has since been extended, most recently in 1977, but the bigger trawlers of Aran's modern fleet cannot reach it as the approaches are too shallow. For the smaller boats it is a useful harbour of refuge, as Cill Rónáin is vulnerable to south-easterly gales.

The C.D.B.'s row of semi-detached cottages, each with its tiny garden in front, its sentry-box of an outside lavatory behind, and a strip of land running back to a line of cliffs three hundred yards inland, brings Cill Éinne to an end within another quarter of a mile. From there I turn back now, to look more closely at the obscure remains of the castle, around which I will hang a history of its eventful centuries.

AIRCÍN: THE CASTLE

When, therefore, St. Endeus was serving God faithfully in his Monastery with holy college, it seemed troublesome to his monks that they had not a level passage to the sea. The man of God, therefore, coming to the harbour of the sea, signed with his staff that very hard rock which offered to ships an impediment to approaching the monastery, and afterwards returned home. But on the following night an angel of the Lord holding a flaming knife in his hand, cut that very hard rock into two parts, making a wide passage through the middle, which even to this day affords a level passage and without impediment to those entering this island.

Although the Cill Éinne trawler-owners of today probably wish that the angel had cut deeper while he was at it, the results of these initial harbour-works of faith (as described in the mediaeval *Life of St. Enda*) are very striking at low water, when the sea-way between the level sheets of rock on either side is revealed to be marvellously straight and parallel-sided. Here the underlying rectangularity of Aran's rock-structure appears in the guise of miracle. The rising tide obscures all this, and there are five beacons (three fine old masonry beehives and two angular concrete replacements) to define the passage.

This is Aran's first port, Aircín, anglicized to Arkin, Arkyn, Ardkin etcetera. in old documents. Some islanders will tell you that Arkin must have been the Elizabethan settler who built the fort here, which indeed figures as Arkin's Castle in some naïve works on Aran including my own first and premature attempt at a map. But with the dawn of scholarship I had to consign this man Arkin, this notional sea-dog of Merrie England, to the depths of nonentity ("Arkin, art tha sleepin' thar below?"). For although the word has dropped out of Aran Irish, *aircín* is extremely common as a placename element on the Connemara coast where it means simply a place where the sea breaks into the land, a little natural harbour; in fact there is another place called Aircín in Aran too, on the east coast of An tOileán Iarthach.

The history of Aircín begins long before the Elizabethans, for even in the days of saints and angels there was a secular power in Aran, a warrior band occupying it as sword-land. They were of the Eóganachta, a Munster people whose record slowly crystallizes into history out of legend in the early Middle Ages. They rose to control Cashel and the kingship of the province, and by the fifth century had conquered what is now Clare from the rulers of Connacht, and installed there a vassal people later to be known as the Dal gCais. One group of the Eóganachta held Aran at some early period and have left their name upon the western third of the island, Eóghanacht. By the tenth century the Eóganachta were in decline and the Dal gCais began to replace them. Their leader

Brian Bóromha (the famous Brian Boru of nationalistic legend) became first the king of Munster, and then in 1002 the High King of Ireland. For the next hundred years his descendants, the Uí Briain or O'Briens, were powerful contestants of the high-kingship, and have dominated the history of Clare ever since. A sept of the Uí Briain held the Aran Islands by the thirteenth century; they were known as the Clann Thaidhg, the descendents of Tadhg, who himself was the son of a Munster king and the great-great-grandson of Brian Bóromha. Tadhg's own (great-?) grandson, Diarmaid Mór, Lord of the Aran Islands, had a stronghold at Tromra on the Clare coast, from whence his ships controlled the approaches to Galway Bay, so that the merchants of the rising town of Galway used to pay him a tribute of twelve tuns of wine a year for keeping these vital waterways free of pirates. The "portolan" charts of the Irish coast made and used by Italians at this period show Aran but not Galway, and it is possible that Aircín was then the depot at which foreign traders would discharge their goods, which the O'Briens would convey to the town in their boats.

Galway had been founded in the thirteenth century by Norman settlers, the de Burgos, but its destinies later separated from theirs. In 1333 the de Burgos cast off their allegiance to the English Crown, adopted Gaelic ways, and seized the province of Connacht. Galway's ties with trade kept it loyal to England and in enmity with the surrounding territories of the Burkes (as the de Burgos now called themselves). Aran followed Galway in this, no doubt because it was a link in the chain of trade, and when, as an exception to their settled policy due to some discontent with trade legislations, the Galway merchants briefly joined the rebels in 1388, Aran was implicated too. One of the Galway burgesses who refused to join the rebels went to England and together with some Bristol merchants petitioned the king for permission to mount an expedition against the Aran Islands, which, they claimed, "always lie full of galleys to ensnare, capture and plunder our liege English." However, both town and islands returned to their allegiance before the Bristol ships got under way, and nothing came of the scheme.

Presumably the main O'Brien harbour in Aran was at Aircín, but if anything remains of their stronghold it is untraceably buried in the foundations of later fortifications. Nevertheless one can reasonably assume that it included a tower-house similar to their many surviving "castles" in Clare; that is, three or four large rooms one above another, linked by a spiral staircase in a corner, having slit windows and probably a thatched gable roof. There is an O'Brien tower-house which is thought to date from the fourteenth century in Inis Oírr, built within the walls of a Celtic hill-fort perhaps a thousand years older. In Árainn itself, in the townland of Eoghanacht, there are low ruinous traces of what was evidently a square building the size of a tower-house, known as An Seanchaisleán, the old castle, which some old folk of the neighbourhood tell me was called Caisleán Uí Bhriain.

From the end of the fourteenth century to the middle of the sixteenth century successive royal charters had given Galway increasing freedom from the interference of the Burkes, and confirmed it as a bastion of English influence amid seas of Irishry. One of the provisions of the charter of 1545 was that the Corporation should control the port of Galway and the seaway from thence to Aran. Exemption from tolls for all ships entering this way made Galway, now at the peak of its prosperity, virtually a free port. The Clann Thaidhg O'Briens of Aran were no longer such important allies. Perhaps symptomatically of their decline, the *Annals of the Four Masters* give us this, the first written record of the placename Aircín, in connection with a deed of treachery and murder, for the year 1565:

> Mahon, the son of Turlough Mantach, son of Donough, son of Donnell, son of Turlough Meith [i.e. the fat] was treacherously slain in his own town of Aircin, in Aran, by his own associates and relations. When the chief men of Galway heard of this, they set out to revenge this misdeed

upon the treacherous perpetrators, so that they compelled them to fly, and they went into a boat and put to sea; and where they landed was in the harbour of Ross [i.e. Kilrush in Co. Clare]. Donnell, the son of Conor O'Brien, having heard of this, hastened to meet them with all the speed he could exert; and he made prisoners of the greater number of them and carried them in close fetters to Maigh Glae [near Doolin, on the Clare coast], in order that their sorrow and anguish might be the greater for being in view of the place where they had perpetrated the crime; he hanged some of them and burned others, according as their evil practices deserved.

These events seem to presage the end of the O'Briens in Aran. Perhaps it is an amplified and distorted echo of the same story that one hears in an Aran tradition of a battle near Port Mhuirbhigh in which the O'Briens are said to have slaughtered each other almost to extinction at a place later to be called Fearann na gCeann, the quarter of the heads, from the number of skulls found in its soil. Whatever the details of these divisions among the O'Briens, there were other interests ready to take advantage of them, and the Clann Thaidhg was not to hold Aran for much longer.

In the intensely complex and dynamic politics of the Elizabethan age there were three powers, apart from the O'Briens, concerned with the islands: Galway city, the O'Flahertys of Connemara, and the Crown itself. Galway, like other and greater Renaissance cities, was a mercantile oligarchy, and its councils were dominated by the fourteen families later to be known as the Tribes of Galway, among whom the Lynches were pre-eminent. Wealth rather than the sword was Galway's weapon. While the Clann Thaidhg was a sea-power Galway could buy its protection with tuns of wine, and when the Clann Thaidhg fell on hard times Galway could accommodate it with mortgages. By 1575 the Clann was trying to ransom Aran back from James Lynch

FitzAmbrose to whom their leader Murchadh had mortgaged it. They came to town on this business, claiming ancient rights of hospitality, and Galway had to pass a by-law limiting these rights:

> Mem. the 14th day of July, one Morchowe Mac Tirriligh Mac Donill, chief of his nacion, called *Clanteige of Aron*, appeared before the mayor, bailiffs and com-brethren, claimage to have the ancient custom of *Connowe and Meales* due to him and his ancestors within the town, to say, for two days and two nights, and the mayor, etc., calling before them auncient old credible persons, they declared upon their oaths that they never heard of their parence, or saw the said sept have no more within this town but only two meales. It was thereupon ordered that said sept shall have no more but that two, they being always bound to serve, attend and wait upon us and in our service, as their auncestors hath bene; also the said sept is bound to give the accustomed *Meales and Cannowe* to all the commecn of Galway when they shall repair to the isles of *Aron*: and the mayor, etc., did grant and promise to be aydors, helpers, mayntainers and assisters of said Clanteige against all persons that would lay siege, spoille or raise the said islands or castwell of *Aron*, or otherwise wrong the said Morchowe sept.

One gets the impression, despite their promises of support, that the Galway notables found the Clann Thaidhg somewhat antiquated at this date. Within a couple of generations those notables would have profited well out of lending money on the security of Aran to the troubled clansmen. It had been agreed within the clan that whatever its chief could ransom back would be his and his heirs forever, but that if the Clann Thaidhg died out the islands would be the Lynches'. Later this was amended to make the Galway Commons and Corporation their heirs in the event of the extinction of the clan. However, the intervention of the O'Flahertys at this juncture made the question academic.

Centuries earlier the O'Flahertys had been lords of lands east of Lough Corrib. Then the Norman de Burgos had driven them westwards into the fastnesses of Connemara, where they had continued to rule according to the old Gaelic ways, which were anathema to both the modern citizens of Galway and the statesmen of England. To the Galway merchants the O'Flahertys were a wild tribe of pirates preying on their trading vessels, and legend has it that they wrote up over the city's west gate the prayer "From the ferocious O'Flahertys, O Lord deliver us." English statecraft aimed at neutralizing the O'Flahertys and other chieftains (whether Gaels or Normans gone Gaelic like the Burkes) by displays of force and by the bribery of titles. Every now and then a Lord Deputy would come as dangerously far west as Galway and require the chieftains of Connacht to come in and "submit," and sometimes various chieftains found it prudent to do so and then went back to their mountains and carried on as before. Submission and the acquisition of a spurious title which could be repudiated when convenient, a spell of alliance with or rebellion against the English forces, were all so many tactical options in their interminable feuds, for Ireland, as a cause, had yet to be invented. In 1569 Queen Elizabeth had recognized a Murchadh na dTua, Murrough of the battleaxes, as head of the O'Flahertys in place of Dónal Crón, the legitimate chief under Gaelic law, which opened another round of cousinly murders. Murchadh must have seized the Aran Islands soon after this, as it is recorded that the Lynches held the castles of Aircín, Inis Meáin and Inis Oírr from him in 1574. Aran tradition is rather precise, where book-history is vague, about this ousting of the O'Briens by the O'Flahertys. Murchadh and the main body of his followers are said to have landed at Port Mhuirbhigh and driven the O'Briens eastwards, while a smaller party came ashore near Mainistir or Cill Rónáin and attacked them in the rear. The O'Briens were routed and fled to the rocks above Cill Éinne where all but one of them, who escaped by boat or hid in a cave, were slaughtered. Their corpses were buried by the shore half-a-mile east of Aircín; the place is called Poll na Marbh, the hole of the dead, and bones are still turned up there.

In 1581 an "Inquisition" or enquiry into ownership was held on the subject of Aran, and came to the conclusion that the islands belonged neither to the O'Briens nor the O'Flahertys but to the Queen. A veneer of legality was given to this decision by the argument that the islands had been monastic lands and were therefore confiscate, the monasteries having been dissolved. So when in the following year Murchadh "submitted" and was granted all his other lands under English law, the Queen was able to give him the "fee-farm" of Aran too. However, three months later she took it back and granted the islands to a Robert Harrison. This is the first English name to appear in the history of Aran's ownership, and the most significant condition of his and subsequent leases was that a force of twenty English foot-soldiers was to be maintained at Aircín. At this time of course England was engaged in the religious, political and military conflicts through which Europe was being reshaped, and in the grand strategies of Protestant England against Catholic Spain, Ireland and therefore Galway, and therefore Aran, were factors of a certain weight, and even the last was too important to be left any longer in the hands of such creatures of another age as the O'Flahertys. Perhaps the Elizabethan castle was begun at this time, but Harrison can hardly have done much towards it as within two years he had forfeited the lease through failure to pay the rent, and in 1584 the islands were granted to a more considerable personage, Sir Thomas Lestrange, who was one of the commissioners of Connaught under Sir Richard Bingham, and had distinguished himself by a valiant defence of the castle at Loughrea against the Burkes a few years earlier.

In this same year of 1584, the O'Flaherty feud spilled over into Aran, and there was a battle that ended for some in graves at Log na Marbh, the hollow of the dead, near Cill Rónáin, where I shall tell the complicated tale, the history of Aircín, like that of England in Ireland, being unaffected by it. Aircín was now a Queen's Manor, and when the comprehensive settlement called

The Composition of Connaught was drawn up in 1585, under which the Gaelic lords were confirmed in their estates with feudal rights of succession instead of the old Brehon law of elective leadership and clan ownership of its territory, Murchadh na dTua, now Sir Murrough O'Flaherty, and the other chieftains of West Connacht, received their lands from the Queen "by knights' service as of her castle or mannor of Ardkine in the greater iland of Arren, with suit and service to the Courte barron and lete of the said mannor."

Lestrange in this year replaced Bingham as governor of Connacht for a while, and probably re-fortified and garrisoned Aircín during that period. In March 1588 the Corporation of Galway belatedly petitioned the Queen on behalf of the Clann Thaidhg, and were ignored. But Lestrange too had failed to pay the rent, and the islands were granted to a Sir John Rawson of Athlone, who is described in a State document of the times as "an industrious discoverer of lands for the Queen"—that is, an expert in detecting flaws in titles leading to expropriation in the name of the Crown. He only lasted three months and then the islands were acquired by the Earl of Ormonde, one of the most powerful Anglo-Irish lords. Lestrange was still in Aran and stayed on as Ormonde's tenant.

The background to these property-wrangles was the tragic procession of Spanish galleons beating their way around the coast like gorgeous moths helpless against the windowpane, after the defeat of the Armada by the English fleet and the storms of the English Channel. Two galleons were wrecked on the Connemara coast, and although at first the O'Flahertys sheltered the survivors, later they found it politic to hand them over to the ferocious Bingham, who hanged nearly three hundred of them. Another ship was blown onto the Clare coast, and the chief of that territory, Boetius MacClancy, who had accepted the post of Sheriff of the County, outdid his new masters in the bloodthirstiness of his treatment of the wretches that struggled ashore. He also wrote to the authorities that two more galleons could be seen around Aran and others farther out to the west, but all these ships struggled on southwards, and although Aran folklore is rich in pots of Spanish gold awaiting discovery, it seems no landings were made on the islands.

The Mayo branches of the Burkes rose in rebellion against the much-hated Bingham late in 1588, and Murchadh na dTua came out with them, largely from discontent over his loss of the islands. Allied with Murchadh on this occasion was Gráinne Ní Mháille or Grace O'Malley, the sea-queen of the Mayo coast, whom the English administrators described as "a most famous feminine sea captain... a notorious woman in all the coast of Ireland," and as "a woman that hath impudently passed the part of womanhood and been a spoiler, and chief commander and director of thieves and murderers at sea." Gráinne's son-in-law Richard Burke, known to the English as the Devil's Hook, was among the rebels too. By the beginning of 1589 Bingham had crushed the rebellion on land and forced the Burkes to sue for peace. Richard Burke gave guarantees for his mother-in-law's good behaviour, but whether or no she knew of the treaty, Gráinne continued to harry the coast with her galleys. In April Bingham had to inform the Queen's secretary, Sir Thomas Walsingham, that:

> Immediately after the peace was concluded, Grana O'Malley, with two or three baggage boats full of knaves, not knowing that the peace was made, committed some spoil in the island of Arran upon two or three of Sir Thomas le Strange's men, to the value of 20 marks, which she did by persuasion of some of the O'Flahertys.... Richard Burke, the Devil's Hook, hath Grana O'Malley in hand till she restore the spoils and repair the harms.

This characteristically hawkish intervention seems to be Gráinne's only entrance in Aran's history, but in the folklore she has a larger role. In fact her first husband, an O'Flaherty known as Dónal an Chogaidh, Dónal of the war, is often said to have died in the O'Flahertys' battle against the O'Briens and to be buried in the old church at Mainistir; however, this tale seems to be based on a misreading of a novel called *Grania Waile*, which was read in Aran two or three generations ago. (Nowadays there exists a hybrid of folklore and literary culture, circulating in both oral and written channels, and having its own character, so far unexplored.)

Sir Thomas Lestrange had died shortly before Gráinne's raid, and in the succeeding brief years of local peace after the scattering of the Armada and settlement of the Burkes' rebellion, the records only give one tantalizing glimpse of the history of Aircín: a Captain Fildew was murdered there by his own soldiers in 1595 and his galley stolen; why, we do not know. While Connacht was again devastated by rebellion, and a Spanish invasion in support of O'Neill was daily expected in Galway, ownership of the islands passed from hand to hand in obscure and involved transactions, and little or nothing was done about refortifying Aircín. In 1599 the industrious John Rawson had been given a second lease; later in the same year a Robert Rothe of Kilkenny appears as the lessee; in 1598 a Sir John Peyton, Knight of the Tower of London, was complaining that his tenants in Aran had been plundered by the captain of the English garrison at Galway, and in 1607 there was a legal action in progress involving one Smyth, the tenant of Aran, the Earl of Ormonde and Rothe as agent of the latter.

With the suppression of the rebellion, the initiation of a peaceful settlement with Spain and the death of the Queen in 1603, the defences of Galway became a less pressing matter, but within a few years Spain was an enemy once again. In 1614 Sir Oliver St. John, Master of the Ordnance in Ireland, noted the fact that an enemy possessing Gregory's Sound between the islands would be master of both Aran and Galway Bay:

It may be secured by building a fort in the Great Island and be of great use and importance. It was hithertofore projected and the late queen gave a liberal allowance of land etc. for the building of it, but according to the usual fate of this Kingdom it was not looked after and so cast away.

During the rather more peaceful times of James I, the Lynches of Galway began to predominate in Aran's history. Henry Lynch had inherited his claim from the James Lynch to whom the Clann Thaidhg had mortgaged the islands long before, and he now held half the estate, while the rest belonged to a William Anderson, the heir of Lestrange. In 1618 Lynch assigned his moiety to Anderson, "excepting great trees, mines, minerals and great hawks." By the time of the Ulster Rising in 1641, the islands were in the hands of the Lynches again. The Clann Thaidhg of the O'Briens was reasserting its claim too and plotting with Boetius Clancy (the son of the notorious sheriff of Clare who hanged the Armada men) to seize the islands. The Earl of Clanricarde, who was governor of Galway and concerned for its security, heard of it and wrote to the Earl of Thomond to have the scheme stopped:

> Amongst all (places) I find none more necessary to be preserved than the Isles of Arran. These are in possession and inheritance of Sir Roebuck Lynch son to Sir Henry. I am now informed that Boetius Clancy the younger and the Clan-Teige of Thomond under pretence of some antiquated claim intend to invade it, and request that you take steps to prevent it.

The Earl of Thomond must have exerted his authority as the senior O'Brien, for that is the last one hears of the Clann Thaidhg and their "antiquated claim." But Sir Roebuck Lynch's tenure was disturbed again the next year, by the captain of the English fort outside Galway city, as the mayor of Galway reported:

> Some of Captain Willoughby's ships have plundered and spoiled the Isles of Arann, which belong to Sir Roebuck Lynch, whereby he lost the profits of the Island which amount to £400 per annum.

This episode was a premonitory flash from the coming storm which would leave the whole country in ruination. For as the echoes of the struggle between King and Parliament in England reached the west, Galway itself fell into a state of civil war, with the English garrison in their fort becoming more and more openly Parliamentarian, the townsfolk increasingly committed to the cause of the "Confederate Government" then campaigning in Ulster, and the governor, Clanricarde, less and less able to impose his will in the name of a State divided against itself. The town had besieged the fort, and the governor had besieged the town and would have impressed peace upon both parties had not the wild young Willoughby persisted in his murderous plundering expeditions into the surrounding countryside. By this time King and Parliament were at open war in England, and when the captain of an English ship supplying the fort appeared on its ramparts and shouted across to the townsfolk on their walls, "A new king, you rogues and traitors; your king is run away; you shall have a new king shortly, you rogues," then (in the dry words of Hardiman's *History of Galway*) "It was at length concluded that the fort was no longer in his majesty's obedience, but entirely at the disposal of the parliament." The Confederates appointed a Colonel Burke as lieutenant-general of Connacht, and on his arrival in Galway he set about the extirpation of this wasps'-nest of parliamentarianism. In April of the next year Sir Roebuck Lynch had the satisfaction of being among the gentry led by Colonel Burke against the fort. Willoughby surrendered after a month or so of siege and was allowed to take himself off by boat, leaving the fort to be demolished by the Confederate Catholics.

During these internal convulsions Galway had imprudently called to its aid thirteen or fourteen hundred "wild Irish" from Iar-Chonnacht under various O'Flahertys, including another Murchadh na dTua, great-grandson of his namesake who had briefly held the Aran Islands, and Colonel Edmund O'Flaherty of Bunowen Castle in the west of Connemara. After terrorizing the English inhabitants of the town for a while, Edmund and a hundred of his men went to Aran, but after a fortnight the inhabitants began to complain of the burden of these guests, so he sailed for Tromra in

Clare and besieged a castle there (he claimed afterwards he had no idea who lived in it, but it was held by an Englishman at the time). After a few days the castle fell, its inhabitants were slaughtered, and the raiders retired to Straw Island off Cill Éinne to divide their spoil, the wind preventing them from sailing home to Connemara. One of the party was a drummer from Inis Oírr called John Browne; he had not wanted to accompany them, or so he claimed when the matter came to trial years later, but Edmund had had him carried into the boat. Browne asked for a silver cup from the looted castle, which Edmund refused him. And in later years after the total defeat of the Confederate cause by the Cromwellians it was Browne who laid information against Edmund, so that a party of soldiers was sent into Connemara to arrest him. They were led by the croaking of ravens to his hiding-place under a rock where they found him and his wife "pyned awaye for want of foode, and altogether ghastly with fear." Edmund was brought to Galway, tried and hanged.

After the ejection of the Parliamentarians from Galway and while the Civil War raged in England, the Confederate Catholics prospered, but they were always divided among themselves between the extreme clerical party, led by the Papal Nuncio Rinuccini, and more cautious heads who cared less for the cause of Catholicism in Europe and more for the fate of Ireland. When the lay Confederates at length united with the King's other supporters in Ireland, Galway offered the Nuncio a refuge although many of its notables (including Sir Roebuck) were opposed to him, and in 1648 the town was once again besieged by its governor Clanricarde in the name of the King. The Nuncio's most vigorous supporter in Connacht was a German convertite known as John Vangyrish, a cavalry officer who had come to Ireland to serve the Confederate cause. Having captured a castle of Clanricarde's near Galway, he led a force to Aran and occupied it, to the annoyance of Sir Roebuck Lynch and his son Sir Robert. But Vangyrish soon left in search of aid, first from Prince Rupert, who would have sent ships to Aran had the Parliamentarians not prevented him, and then to the Vatican, which promised nothing. Meanwhile Clanricarde forced the expulsion of the Nuncio from Galway in February of 1649.

By then the King's English army and the Confederate army had been united under the Marquis of Ormonde by the Treaty of Kilkenny, but the King himself was dead, beheaded by the Parliamentarians, and his successor, Charles II, was in exile in Jersey. The government of the new "Commonwealth" now concentrated its attention on Ireland, and this most horrific period in the history of the country began with the landing at Dublin of Oliver Cromwell and his Puritan army. Ormonde and other Royalist notables took ship in little ports of Galway Bay and slipped away to France in December of 1650, leaving Clanricarde, now a Marquis, as the new Lord Deputy. Clanricarde, struggling to hold demoralized forces together, tried to negotiate support from the Duke of Lorraine and eventually arranged an advance of £20,000 on the security of the cities of Galway and Limerick. The fortification of Aran, as a base for receiving the promised aid, was part of the agreement:

> ...And we are further pleased that two hundred musketeers, with officers and a gunner, under the command of Sir Robert Lynch, be forthwith sent to the isles of Arran, with a reasonable proportion of ammunition and three pieces of ordnance with necessaries; and that three months means be provided them out of the said twenty thousand pounds to be received, deducting so much as the contribution of the islands comes unto, according to their divident for that time. The said ammunition to be provided by the publick; and the said town of Galway to furnish the three pieces of ordnance, for which the said corporation is to be paid by the publick, out of the next supplies: and after the expiration of the said two months the said two hundred men and officers to be there maintained at the public charge, as the rest of the standing forces of the county of Galway.

While Clanricarde was wrestling with the supply problem the Cromwellians were overwhelming the country, and by the time some help from Lorraine began to reach Aran and that other island-fortress off the Connemara coast, Inishbofin, it was too late. The Irish commander, General Preston, was driven back into Galway and besieged there by Sir Charles Coote. Limerick surrendered in October 1651, but Galway held out through the winter despite Preston's flight by sea to France. Two vessels bringing corn into the starving, over-crowded city at this time were pursued by Parliamentary frigates; one was taken and the other driven onto the rocks off Aran and its cargo lost. Galway surrendered to Coote in April 1652, on terms that included the surrender of Aran.

Famine, plague and massacre followed. Aran perhaps escaped the worst of it, but Galway fell into desolation, and much of the countryside was almost depopulated. Fearing the intervention of Spain on behalf of Charles II, the Cromwellian forces emptied the town of its Catholic inhabitants, and began to improve and re-build the fort at Aircín, quarrying the churches of the nearby monastery for the purpose. Inishbofin still held out, under a Colonel Synnot who had landed there with aid from Lorraine in the previous year. In December of 1652 the Commonwealth's Commissioners in Ireland had a reverse to report to the Council of State, for which they were hard put to it to find excuses:

Since our last we have received intelligence of a sudden surprisal that hath been made by the enemy upon a garrison of yours in the Isle of Aran...near the two fastnesses of Ir-Connaught and Inisboffin, from whence the enemy landing (as we are informed) 600 men, and with the assistance of the inhabitants of that island, they have possessed themselves of it. In the attempt of which also, the enemy had advantage from the weakness of the works, which were not altogether finished; but principally by reason of the want of shipping and vessels in that harbour, either to relieve the garrison or to make an assault upon the enemy at their landing. The ships appointed to attend that place, and which had directions not to depart that harbour until the works were finished, contrary to their orders leaving it, and putting out to sea, in whose absence this attempt was made by the enemy.

Feeling that the Lord had manifested some displeasure against them in allowing a vanquished and dispersed enemy to prevail in this way, the commissioners recommended that December the 30th be observed by fast, humiliation and prayers. They also took more practical steps. Three or four ships were ordered round the coast from Kinsale to carry an invasion force, bringing provisions as none were to be had in Galway. In January thirteen hundred foot-soldiers and a battering-piece were shipped to Aran, while a further body of six hundred marched out along the coast to be shipped from Connemara if necessary. Aircín capitulated within a few days. The articles of surrender were concluded between Commissary-General Reynolds of the Commonwealth force, and Colonel Oliver Synnot, commander of the fort:

1. It is concluded that and agreed, that all the officers and soldiers both belonging to sea and land, shall have quarters, as also all others, the clergymen, and all other persons within the fort.

2. That they shall have six weeks for their transportation into Spain, or any other place in amity with the state of England; and that hostages be given by colonel Synnot for the punctual performance of these articles.

3. That colonel Synnot shall deliver up the fort, with all necessaries of war, by three o'clock this instant, 15th January, 1653, before which time all officers and soldiers belonging to the said fort shall march, with drums beating, to the church near Ardkyn, and there lay down their arms.

4. That colonel Synnot and the captains, eight in number, shall have liberty to carry their swords; the other officers and soldiers to lay down their arms; that commissary

Reynolds shall nominate four officers of the fort hostages.

5. That colonel Synnot, with the rest of the officers and soldiers and all other persons in the fort, shall, upon delivering their arms and delivering their hostages, be protected from the violence of the soldiers, and with the first conveniency be sent to the county of Galway; there to remain in quarters for six weeks, in which time they are to be transported, as aforesaid: Provided that no person whatsoever, belonging to the fort of Ardkyn, and found guilty of murder, be included or comprised in these articles, or have any benefit thereby.

Thus ended the fort's days of high drama, to the beating of drums. Although its defences were now to be completed (to the ruination of the monasteries at hand), and although it was armed and manned by fifty or a hundred soldiers during the lifetime of the Commonwealth and for a while after the restoration of Charles II, its future was to be one of petty intrigues, neglect and eventual abandonment, to be itself a quarry for the building of cottages.

AIRCÍN: THE PAWN

The Commonwealth's grand scheme for Ireland was to dispossess the Catholic landowners east of the Shannon and replace them by Protestants. Those Catholics who had not been involved in the "rebellion" were to be given equivalent areas of land beyond the Shannon, in Connacht and Clare, though a strip of territory (called "the Line") along the coast was to be preserved for Protestants here too, for reasons of security. (Later on, in 1655, as some of the Line had not been taken up, this rule was relaxed, but it was still illegal for "popish recusants" to live within a mile of certain garrisons, including Aircín and Inishbofin.) Sir Robert Lynch had of course been active with the Confederate forces, so he was deemed a "forfeiting traitor" and his lands confiscated. Cromwell's expedition had been financed by loans adventured on security of lands it would conquer, and now Ireland was being parcelled out among the financial "Adventurers," and among the soldiers, in lieu of pay. Aran and other territories around the cities of Galway and Athlone, and in Sligo, Tipperary and Antrim, were assigned to a London alderman, Erasmus Smith, who had done well for himself as an army contractor and had purchased a vast number of land debentures from both Adventurers and soldiers. However, under the Cromwellian scheme of things a Protestant should not have been in possession of lands in Connacht, so Smith wisely assigned these lands to a trust for the setting up of grammar schools. His intention was to educate the children of his tenants "in the feare of God and good literature," it being his opinion that

> most of the sins which in former times have raigned in this nation have proceeded chiefly of lacke of the bringinge up of the youthe of this realme either in publique or in private schools, whereby through goode discipline they might be principled in literature and good manners, and soe learn to loath these haynous and manifold offences which, when they did come to years, they did dayly perpetrate and committe.

His schools would prepare such of the tenants' children as were fit for Trinity College in Dublin, and the poor were to be educated free. Of course as most of his tenants were Catholics not many could take up this magnanimous offer of the man who had financed the slaughter of their co-religionists. However, Erasmus Smith's Free School was the principal educational foundation in Galway for over a century, at least for the Protestant ascendancy.

In that year of Smith's benevolent Deed it was decreed that

Aran and Inishbofin would be holding-camps for fifty or more of the Catholic clergy whom the Cromwellians had been rounding up. The governor of Aircín, a Major John Allen, was allowed sixpence a head for their keep, including twopence per day for their food, on which rations they nearly starved, until rescued some time after the collapse of the Commonwealth and the recall of Charles II in 1660.

The Restoration aroused high hopes among the dispossessed Catholics, but although Charles smiled on Catholicism he was too dependent on the government that had brought him back from exile to be able to alter the Cromwellian settlements to any large extent. Erasmus Smith continued to own Aran, at least for a while, and Major Allen took up cattle-farming on land rented from him. In May 1662 a new governor of the fort arrived, a Robert Deey, mayor of Dublin; the King had settled a foot company in the new Standing Army on him, "as a reward for his loyal assistance in our restoration." It seems that the Cromwellian soldiery of Aran and Inishbofin were absorbed into his command without recriminations.

This Restoration period of the fort's history is copiously documented and it is possible to follow developments—very humdrum, after what had gone before—almost month by month. In August Deey's company was allowed three months' advance of pay for the purchase of winter provisions. In March of the following year Deey reported that the advance had all been spent on beef, butter and oatmeal, the islands being so remote as to be supplied with difficulty. As the inhabitants had already trusted the soldiers beyond their means, he requested the allowance of an extra month's pay for them from time to time, and this too was agreed. Deey was replaced in September by a Captain Bayly, who owed his promotion to the King's recommendation and the Ormondes' patronage in recognition of the fact that "he has been under sequestration for his loyalty and actings for the King for these seven years past to the ruin of himself, his wife and children."

Bayly certainly made up for lost time in Aran. His stream of requests for more guns, powder and shot, more soldiers and advances of pay for them, a frigate and a boat to bring in turf, captains for these boats, muskets, swords, drums and drumsticks, give an impression of great energy in military matters, but he was determined to become the tenant of the islands too, using the confused state of property legislation of the times to oust John Allen. The confiscated lands in four counties including Galway had been set aside as security for the claims of officers who had served the King loyally in the years before 1649 and had not been paid for it. (Charles' lavish promises to both Catholics and Protestants had led the Earl of Ormonde, now Lord Lieutenant, to observe: "There must be new discoveries made of a new Ireland, for the old will not serve to satisfy these engagements!") Now Bayly claimed Aran on these grounds, and when Allen refused to pay his rent to him, distrained his cattle. Allen, so far as he understood, was the tenant of Erasmus Smith. However, Ormonde's younger son, Richard Butler, had been recently created a peer, taking the title "Earl of Arran" since his grandfather was the Ormonde who had had estates there sixty years earlier, and he now wished to acquire the land to go with the title. He came to a settlement with the trustees of the '49 soldiers as they were called, in this same year of 1663, and so Allen decided to pay the rent to him rather than to Erasmus Smith. But while he was away in Dublin doing this, Bayly's second-in-command, Sergeant John Browne, climbed into Allen's house with drawn sword, swearing to kill the first person he met, and turned his pregnant wife and her children out of doors, and set soldiers to guard it. (Could this fell sergeant be the drummer, John Browne, who unwillingly assisted at the sack of Tromra twenty years earlier, promoted perhaps for having betrayed Edmund O'Flaherty to the Cromwellian soldiers?) Then, when a hearing convened at Loughrea to settle the conflicting claims decided that the islands still were Erasmus Smith's, and the deputy sheriff of Galway came out with Allen to put the ruling into effect, Sergeant Browne met them with a file of musketeers and kept the official a prisoner for three days, and

Allen had the annoyance of seeing his own corn being brought into the fort by Bayly's soldiers. Allen applied to Ormonde for relief (the above details are taken from his petition), and at Ormonde's command Bayly gave his version of events; that the court's judgement in favour of Erasmus Smith had been unfairly procured and had in fact since been reversed; that he himself had always acted as the Earl of Arran's loyal tenant and never as a claimant in his own rights; that in fact he had only become tenant the better to serve the Earl's interests; that Allen's wife had seldom been acquainted with such civility as she met with when desired to leave her home and move into the fort—and so on, interminably and implausibly. However, the two Earls backed Bayly again as they had done in the past, and Allen disappears from the history of Aran.

Bayly, though, continues to figure as Arran's supporter, if not his parasite, in the Ormonde correspondence. In April 1681 he is in London on business and resolved to return to Ireland the next week; in September he is still in London and asking leave to stay till Christmas, "by which time he will have dispatched his affairs; if not, he will be undone." In October he orders a cast of hawks from Aran to be delivered to the Earl; and then asks him to obtain permission from Ormonde to sell his company, being too busy to attend to it. Ormonde grants the permission, and in November Arran writes to tell him that Bayly has sold the company to one Amyas Bushe, who has never borne arms before; nevertheless Arran is pleased because it means that Bayly will be able to pay him the £200 of rent he owes. Two years later Bayly asks Arran to find a place for his son, and the lad is made an ensign. After another five years Bayly writes to Ormonde reminding him that it is now thirty years since he was first introduced to him in Brussels by Lord Clanricarde, and that he has served him for many years in Ireland, and would the Earl please let him have credit for £10 to keep him at Windsor, where he hopes to get something? His wife's and children's bread is at stake as at present he has no other way to live…and so Bayly too fades out of Aran's history into reduced circumstances.

And that really concludes the history of the fort at Aircín, for according to Hardiman when a company was sent to Aran in 1691 after the victory of King William in the Jacobite war, a barracks was built for them. Certainly in 1710 the fort was in disrepair and Aran was only garrisoned in summer. The owner of the islands then was Sir Stephen Fox, a former Paymaster of the Forces and a Commissioner of the Treasury, who had purchased them from the Earl of Arran. He petitioned Queen Anne in that year for bedding and other necessaries for lodging a company in Aran and for repairing the fort, which he said had been neglected in time of peace. The soldiers stationed there had been withdrawn each winter, and their bedding had always been spoiled or embezzled by the time they returned in the spring. French privateers had been infesting the coast and plundering his tenants, to whom he had had to grant abatements of rent. However, it seems that nothing was done to help him, and in 1713 he sold out to his tenants, the Fitzpatricks of Galway, and to a representative of the Digbys, who were to be Aran's masters for many of its saddest years thereafter. The age of the barracks, of rack-renting and absentee landlords was coming, and the old fort with its strategic grip on the *aircín* lapsed into anachronism.

CROMWELL'S WALLS

Can the foregoing account, compiled from variously remote texts, be appropriated into the immediacy of this book? My principle has been to find among the stones of Aran the touchstone of admissibility appropriate to each sort of material; here I must search among the stones of Arkin Castle.

Many of these stones are missing. The landward walls, especially to the south and west, have been nibbled away by the teeming cottages that invaded the castle yard in the last century. The cottages themselves have gone now, or have declined into sheds and barns for the one or two more recent dwellings that constitute a part of Cill Éinne still known as An Bábhún, the bawn or courtyard.

On the east the roadside wall incorporates some rags of ancient masonry, while on the north along the shoreline forty yards or so of curtain wall still stands tall, looming over the back gardens of the houses. At the north-east angle is a small, square, parapeted tower, standing forward of the rest on a natural bastion of rock over the shore. These fragments are known as Ballaí Chromaill, Cromwell's walls, after the man whose ogre memory has gobbled up all history but his own.

From landward, glimpsed between the houses, the sea-defences appear as an abnormally high back-garden wall. Shadowy outlines on the masonry indicate the cottages once built against it. Towards the east is a row of six small musket loops, horizontal rectangular openings splayed both within and without to give a wider field of fire. In summer potato stalks reach up towards their sills. To view the wall from the other side one can scramble down the little cliff around the foot of the tower, if the tide is out, onto the flat rock-sheets of the shore under the castle's dank frontage. Among the boulders littering this shore, low water reveals one with a mediaeval, ecclesiastical look, a five-foot length of pillar with a square base and octagonal shaft; I gather that it probably came from an archway in the east wall, now blocked by a shed, through which the road used to enter An Bábhún. The sea-wall appears to rise directly from the shore, but in fact its first ten feet must be merely a cladding of the cliff; above that it rises another eighteen or twenty feet. Towards its western end there is a round-headed arch at sea level which gave access by steps up a tunnel or a cranny of the cliff to the courtyard within. Above the archway is one of those projecting structures called machicolations, like a balcony on two stout corbels with an open floor through which discouragement could be rained on unwelcome callers below.

Nowadays the repellant substances come sluicing down through the archway itself, which has been half walled up and converted into a drain for some disused pigsties above, and still serves as a rubbish chute; I had to jump back smartly to avoid a nasty soaking once when investigating the defences.

Cycling through Cill Éinne one autumn day, I caught an antique sight here that seemed to close up the whole history of the castle like a book not worth reading. Perched high on the ragged skyline of the great wall an old man was threshing rye, whipping each fistful of stems down across a wooden bench so that the grain fell onto a spread sheet and the chaff went glimmering downwind. History and harvest are antitheses, the chaff seemed to say, and the elders of Cill Éinne might agree. Certainly for them the stories of those vanished cottages shadowed forth by the castle wall and their magical inhabitants of not-so-long-ago out-talk the centuries of the history books. Here, says garrulous old tradition, lived a man who had a pet seal. Every day it went down to the sea through the arch. If the man was fishing on the Glasson Rocks he would see it swimming out of the Sound, going south. One night it came home with a spear in its back, and it died. The spear was put up on the rafters, and a long time afterwards a visitor to the house recognized it as his; he was a bailiff from the salmon fisheries at Foynes on the Shannon. And here lived two brothers who could recite the alphabet backwards as fast as anyone else could forward. They were weather-glasses too; they had the gift from their grandmother, Nell-an-Tower. But if we let tradition start on tales of Nell-an-Tower we'll be here for chapters. She was a *bean feasa*, a woman of knowledge. Once she was attending a woman in childbirth in Gort na gCapall when a man came to fetch her to his wife in Iaráirne. He offered to take her behind him on his horse but she said, "Let you be going on ahead now, and I'll follow." So off he went on his horse, but when he reached the Carcair Mhór in Cill Éinne he saw her going up it before him! Of course, he'd come past all the pubs and shebeens, and perhaps he'd stopped for a souse of *poitín*. But you wouldn't know; there's a lot of stories about her travelling fast like that. She knew about herbs too. They say she could take a disease of a person and put it on a beast, or another person. Once she was picking the herb to cure someone and she happened to look out to sea. There was a currach there, and the man in it died. She was very sorry about that, but she couldn't help it. The castle used to have a round tower—it's gone long ago—and her cottage was built against it; that's why she was called Nell-an-Tower. Once she was going by some men making a coffin and she said.... And in that little boreen east of the houses—it's still called Bóithrín an Bhábhúin—a lad made a very smart reply to the priest, at the time of the Saucepans. But the Saucepans is another chapter too...

Wall-rue, wall-pepper, wall-pennywort, pellitory-of-the-wall; the old wall, backdrop of these tales, has itself abandoned chronology to vegetate in perennial recurrence. The rusty-backed fern likes its ancient mortar, escaped veronica bushes have taken to it, and high up on it grow tree-mallows, as on the real cliffs. The wall has become the stony, untilled margin of the plots at its foot. But then, as one's eye browses over this crannied acreage, a shadowy form, a slight depression in a smoother stone, comes suddenly into focus: a Latin cross carved on the lintel of the easternmost musket loop. A church was pulled down to build a fort! And if that is true, so is the rest: the O'Briens were defeated by the O'Flahertys, the Lynches foreclosed on the mortgage, the thirteen hundred foot-soldiers of the Puritan army came with their battering piece, the drums beat for the surrendering Irish, the priests starved on twopence a day. The whole story from St. Enda's angel with his blazing knife down to the embezzled bedding of good Queen Anne's neglectful reign, all happened, all is attested to by this cross. And now, being reasonably persuaded of its authenticity, I can append my clerkly note: History, unlettered thresher, its mark.

AER ÁRANN

The word *maoil* in Irish means among other things a hillock with a flattish top; it is cognate with dozens of others denoting things blunt, bald, roofless, or low-topped in some way. The eastern end of Cill Éinne, beyond the harbour, is An Maoilín, the small flat height. Elderly folk taking the sun on a strip of waste land between the road and the sea, opposite the line of cottages, have a fifteen-foot cliff at their heels, and below it a shallow annex of Cill Éinne bay called Poll na dTarbh, the inlet of the bulls. Beyond that expands a blonde low-land of sandy beaches, pasturage almost as sandy, and dunes crested with marram grass: An Rinn Mhéith, the fertile point. Here our local airline, Aer Árann, has its little terminal building and its crossed runways marked out on the grass by lines of white-painted tyres. The comings and goings of its Islander aircraft give the old fellows on the *maoilín*, and myself when I join them there, something not over-exciting to comment upon, with long intervals of silent contemplation. An arrival is announced by a faint buzzing in the north-eastern sector of the huge sky around the airport, and soon a little cream-coloured fleck appears between two puffs of cumulus. Is she going to one of the other islands first? Yes, she sags away in the direction of Inis Meáin and disappears; silence rejoins us, relaxing its limbs on the *maoilín*. Now she's revving up again over there, now she's taking off—and here she is already, skimming in over the great oval strand to the east, touching down with a bounce as soon as her wheels have cleared the rocks of the shore, as if there were not twice as much runway as she needs in the width of the headland. She slows almost to a halt, turns, and trundles back towards us. A brisk figure emerges from the terminal to meet her: Colie Hernon; we know him well, his horizon-blue eyes, his jaw of officer-material, his backbone straight as a flag-staff. As soon as the propellers are stilled he ducks under the high wings, opens up the pregnant-cow bulk of the fuselage, and with the brusqueness of a vet delivers the nine passengers, their suitcases and the bundle of today's newspapers onto the soil of Aran. His is the first, and quite untypical, face of the Man of Aran these visitors see. (An Inis Meáin man once said to me, as to a kindred spirit, "If you or me was walking down the road now, and we saw some strangers coming up, we might turn aside into the boreen so as not to have to meet them. But not Colie! He'd just go marching ahead!") And for years Colm Ó hIarnáin, to give him the Irish form of his name, has been the island's grizzled interface with the outside and official world. In his younger days, we on the *maoilín* can remember, he was cox of the lifeboat, and then he was a prime mover of the cooperative set up to bring electricity to our houses.

The history of Aer Árann is said to begin with his letter to *The Irish Press* in 1969, stating the islands' need for an air link with the mainland to prevent their further depopulation. Some Galway businessmen scented a proposition, and Aer Árann came into being the following year. Its periods of growth and recession since then, profits and losses, grants from the Gaeltacht authority to subsidize islanders' tickets, its services, proposed, inaugurated or abandoned, to Shannon, Dublin, London, its charter flights to Britain or Europe, are all beyond the horizon, as seen from An Maoilín. We hear that ferrying businessmen to Hamburg and such places is now the most lucrative of its operations, and we feel vaguely aggrieved, no longer having the delusion of earlier years that we own an airline. But Colie is still here as a guarantor of Aer Árann's continued commitment to the islands. And his son Michael is a familiar component of the scene, driving the minibus that distributes and collects Aer Árann passengers up and down the island. In the old days Michael used to have to chase the donkeys off the airstrip before the first flight of each morning; now An Rinn Mhéith is fenced and gated, and rabbit-holes are the only obstacles to a smooth landing. Michael has a fund of Aran lore at the service of visitors, on the stone walls for example, which I hear him say would stretch from here to Boston; and if he overhears me talking to the person next to me in the bus and imparting some scrap that could be added to his repertoire he will have a word with me afterwards: "What was that about the angel with the blazing knife? That would be something new to tell the Yanks!"

Among the pilots we oldsters know only the first of them, Bill Wallace, and entrust ourselves to any of his successors with a twinge of misgiving. "We'll be all right with Bill Wallace," I once heard a slightly drunken voice behind me in the plane intoning repetitively: "We'll be all right with Bill. He used to bring bombers back from over Germany on one engine; that's flying for you! We'll be all right with Bill." Bill Wallace's feeling for the island is probably unspoken, but to me his relaxed and joyous flying expressed that first delighted discovery of Aran from the air, a *maoilín* set in the giant interference patterns of Atlantic rollers coming through the various sea-ways. At the hint of a wish Bill would tilt the whole island up for us so that we could look more closely at our own rooftop and into our backyard. But those days of caressing Aran's outlines with our wingtips in impromptu circuitings are gone; the oil crisis made us mindful of how much it costs per minute to keep the plane in the air. Bill Wallace has retired (though he often comes back to fish from the Glasson Rocks and drink in Fitz's), and now we have to learn the names of young, smartly uniformed pilots, who weigh us and our baggage before each flight and allot us seats after a computation of balances, who look tense about the nape of the neck as they come into land, and who call the islands More, Maan and Eer.

St. Enda, as I have told, sailed to Aran on a stone; we, when we can afford the thrill, fly in a cubby-hole of metal and plastic, and feel miracle has not died out of the world. The Saint's Boat, Bád na Naomh, a limestone block that looks like a beached currach, lies on the shore near the west end of the runway, and often the plane starts its take-off from near it. Having taxied out and turned to face into the wind it pauses there while we all make what preparations we can for the moment of disconnection with the earth. The pilot flicks various switches on and off, the islanders cross themselves. I make no gesture to technology or religion, but I keep my eyes fixed on St. Enda's boat, the paradoxical foundation-stone of the Aran I am about to leave. Neither the Galway businessmen nor the dozers on the *maoilín* know what figurations of first and last things they preside over.

BONES IN THE SAND

Beyond the last of the cottages the road makes a long slow bend around An Trá Mhór, the big strand. Half way between Cill Éinne and the last of Aran's villages, Iaráirne, is the graveyard, standing over the beach on a sandy bluff. In a steep hollow perpetually threatened by sand-slides in the middle of the graveyard is a ruined church, roofless, its gable peaks on a level with the surrounding tombstones. This is Teallach Éinne; the word *teallach* means a household or domestic establishment, which may be a monastic one, as here: St. Enda's "familia."

The church, which I shall describe in detail when I visit the rest of the monastic remains inland of Cill Éinne, is in part very early; it has the huge rough masonry, the narrow round-topped east window and other features of eighth-century work. But it is by no means as early as some allegedly historical events indirectly associated with St. Enda, whose own dates are not recorded. (According to the mediaeval account published in Colgan's *Acta Sanctorum Hiberniae*, St. Enda was granted the island by a certain king, who, say the Four Masters, died in AD 489.) The saint is said to be buried to the north-east of the church—this seems to be a traditional site for a founder's grave—but his tomb is deeply covered in sand, along with no fewer than a hundred and twenty other graves "in which none but saints are buried," if Colgan's *Acta Sanctorum* and Michael Hernon the minibus driver are to be believed.

In fact it is not necessary to believe that there actually was a St. Enda in order to venerate him properly; the case of the miracle worker runs parallel to that of the miracle, already discussed in connection with stone boats. By the probable date of the earliest written references to him, monks and hermits may well have been inhabiting Aran for many lifetimes. The blown sand was perhaps already heaping up among their predecessors' tombstones when they began to build the church here. Marram grass grew up through the sand and stabilized it; the legend of the founding father grew up through these strange celibate and therefore radically disjunct generations of monks, giving them a continuous identity, a "family." The earliest burials, marked by unlettered boulders or slabs inscribed only with a cross, were reburied again and again as newer gravestones caught more sand and the indefeasible grass forced its way up through it; there was no going back to check dates or cross-examine witnesses of earlier days. As the monastery grew, adding a round tower to itself, a dormitory, a refectory, other cells and churches, giving rise to sister houses in other parts of Aran, so the retrospective glory of St. Enda grew, while perhaps the sand was already lapping at the sills of his chapel in the graveyard. There may even have been a calendar-custom of digging it out every year, just as today the similarly beduned chapel of St. Caomhàn in Inis Oírr is rescued from the year's burial on the saint's day. Similarly, St. Enda's *Life* was being rescued from the slippage of memory, written down, copied, annotated, translated, in distant seats of learning. By the time the *Life* was printed the monastery had long been dead, for O'Flaherty's *West Connaught* of 1684, on what evidences is unknown, states that the last abbot of St. Enda's flourished in 1400. Meanwhile sand continued to wrap around the old church, perhaps helping to shelter it from the turbulent centuries of Elizabeth and Cromwell that saw the utter ruination of the rest of the monastery.

The graveyard seems to have acted as an endstop for the running battle of the O'Briens and the O'Flahertys in the 1560s; at least, tradition has it that the slain are buried by the shore just west of it. There are no stones to fix the spot; probably the O'Brien corpses were hastily shovelled into the dunes, any survivors who might have marked their resting-place having fled, and

it not being in the interest of the usurpers to memorialize the former lords of the islands. Bones occasionally drop out of the sandy
brink around the shoreline here, which is called Poll na Marbh,
the bay or hollow of the dead. In 1984 a man digging a pit for a
cattle-grid by the roadside opposite came across parts of skeletons.
The *garda* came in haste, took one look, and put away his notebook saying disappointedly, "Those have been there hundreds of
years!"—decay's merciful Statute of Limitation precluding any
definite assertion that these were O'Brien bones and that the
name of their killers was O'Flaherty.

In the middle of this field of the fallen is a little hollow, between the road and the shore and about a hundred yards north-
west of the consecrated graveyard, traditionally used as an infants'
burial ground. Limbo, that neutral domain between the bliss of
Heaven and the pains of Hell, invented by theologians to accommodate the afterlife of those who had not had life enough either
to sin or to be saved, was until a couple of generations ago thought
to be the portion of the stillborn or of babes who died unbaptized.
Their bodies were discreetly buried in places that seem to answer
to their spiritual abode: on boundaries between townlands, under
mearing walls between holdings, on the no-man's-land of the
seashore, in the ancient earthworks and ring-walls popularly associated with the non-Christian otherworld, or on the margins of
consecrated ground.

"Strangers" washed up on the shore, of whom no one could tell
if they had been believers or not, were also buried here at Poll na
Marbh, a place not consecrated by the Church but not completely
secular either, for any long-continued custom is to a degree conse-
cration. But this uncharitable exclusion of human sea-wrack from
the blessed soil of the graveyard has been gradually relaxed. Two
corpses from the sinking of the *Lusitania* off Kinsale in 1915 ("E.
V. Woolden and L. C. C." is all the plaque of their little monument can tell of them) are buried in a secluded and peripheral hollow but nevertheless within the cemetery walls, while one of the

prime sites along the walk from the cemetery gates to the church is occupied by a florid high cross with an inscription in Basque to a sailor lost off a Greek ship in the last war.

Even an atheist is lurking in here somewhere, according to old gossip. Johnny Mullen, father of Pat, was considered such a social and religious heretic that it seemed doubtful if Father Killeen, the parish priest of the day, would permit his burial in God's ground. Pat's attitude to his Da was ambivalent; he both hated and relished the old man, the self-styled king of the island. "If we can't bury him we'll pickle him!" Pat is said to have said, but instead they forestalled the priest by bringing the corpse here and burying it secretly, replacing the sods, erecting no cross, but taking "marks" for the spot—currachmen themselves, they were in the habit of using alignments of onshore features to guide them on the sea—so that none but they would be able to find it.

Celtic crosses and upright slices of shiny black or white marble ordered from monumental masons in Galway are the graveware of twentieth-century Aran, while the nineteenth century sleeps under recumbent limestone slabs, ponderous, grey and very dignified, carved by local craftsmen. These rectangles of stone, so reminiscent of the sheets of bare rock from which they were prized with crowbars, used to be shaped, decorated and lettered out on their native crags, and only then carried to the graveyard. Many of them are four or five feet long by three across, and six or eight inches thick, and moving them was a strenuous and even a dangerous business, especially when a quart of *poitín* was provided to fuel the teamwork; here and there in Aran one can find finished specimens that have been dropped and broken in transport. No Araner joins with me in preferring them to the imported novelties, largely because of the physical effort they used to exact from the family of the deceased. It is also true that the rain smoothes away their inscriptions and their simple embellishments (usually restricted to rayed quarter-circles in the corners, rows of zigzags or lozenges along the edges, and the IHS monogram) within a century or so; but that merely makes their noble proportions the plainer, and at the last they lie on the ground like the conclusive card of our great game, the Nought of Blanks.

Contrary to what one might expect, the Irish language does not occur in these old slabs. English, old Aran's sole means of intercourse with all official powers, also did for payment of the last debt and submission to the ultimate judgement. It took the Gaelic League, emanating from Dublin towards the end of the century, to tell rural Ireland that its language could and should be written down. Kilbride, the Protestant minister, was an early member of the Aran branch of the League, and so it comes about, ironically enough, that Aran's earliest funerary inscription in Irish is on Mrs. Kilbride's gravestone in Cill Rónáin.

All the graves in this cemetery face east to greet the dawn of the Last Day, except that of a Father Francis O'Flaherty, who will rise facing his flock. Father Francis is said to have been Aran's first parish priest, and he died in 1825. The O'Flaherty insignia on the foot of his box-like tomb of big slabs, just south of the church, had been long lost to sight when it was disinterred from the rising sand in the course of repairs to the tomb next door, that of his relatives by marriage, the Gills of Cill Rónáin. The digging and tending of graves is a family matter in Aran; there are no undertakers or sextons here to interpose their practised suavity between the bereaved and the physical future of "the remains." And as the graveyards are ancient, piled and packed with generations, among which it is often difficult to make room for newcomers, there is a general familiarity with bones, coffins and tombs and their processes of collapse, which may find relief in grim jests. Pat Mullen again, describing a rabbit-hunt here, in his novel *Hero Breed*:

> They arrived at the graveyard. It was built of sand and the bones of the dead, and was riddled with rabbit burrows.
>
> "Let us stay in this corner of it," said Steve. "Larry, look at that tombstone and tell me who's under it."
>
> "Mary Costelloe," read the boy. "Shall I put the ferret in?"

"No! No!" cried Steve hastily. "She was your great-grandmother, and a decenter woman or a better neighbour never lived in Aran, according to what the old people say about her. Let her spirit rest in peace."

"Michael Fallon is under this one," sang out Larry.

"Ha!" said Steve excitedly. "He was a bailiff. Many's the poor family he evicted in the bad times, the scoundrel. In with your ferret!" he shouted. "The devil has no landlord to back him now and we shall have satisfaction at last. No mercy now!" he warned. "Let the first man that can, flatten him."

Giraldus Cambrensis, as I have mentioned, reported of Aran that here bodies do not putrefy but are left exposed, so that one may recognize one's grandfathers and great-grandfathers. Were it so, by now we would be pressed against Heaven by the stacks of ancestors underfoot. Instead, the island uses the weight of sand and the lightness of the breeze to compress its human detritus into this slowly rising knoll, transmuting in its depths hermits into legend and bailiffs into rabbits.

By chance, the only interment I have attended here was that of Tiger King, the Man of Aran of the film, so once again he will be called upon to fill the role of representative islander. He died in a London nursing home, and his coffined corpse came back to Aran on the steamer, accompanied by mourners and day-trippers. A tractor carried him to the chapel in Cill Rónáin, and after the service we all followed him around the bay in an informal procession of cars, traps and bicycles. It was one of the best sort of Aran days, dazzling and gusty, boisterously generous to the eyes and lungs. At the graveyard the mourners dispersed for a while, following various worn sandy tracks between the stones to go and pray beside their own dead. Then the Tiger's coffin was lowered into the new grave to a few wind-scattered decades of the rosary. I admired the competence of the younger male relatives who quickly filled the grave, patted the mound into neatness with the backs of their spades, and arranged a rim of stones around it. We shook hands with the elder bereaved, using the simple formula "*Ní maith liom do thrioblóid*," "I'm sorry for your trouble," to which the response was, as always, a hasty, muttered, repeated "*Tá 'fhios a'am*," "I know, I know." Many of the mourners were already hurrying to catch the departing steamer. Along the sea horizon a march-past of tall rain-showers concluded the ceremony.

SANDS IN THE WIND

The great strand, An Trá Mhór, presided over by St. Enda's bones, is at high tide a broad oval of shallow water held between two promontories—that on the west carrying the airstrip, the other on the east a similar low duneland—and a sandspit extending westwards from the latter towards the former, leaving only a narrow gap for the sea's exits and entrances. As the tide falls it gathers itself into a sinuous channel around the southern and western perimeter of the strand, passing close under the cemetery knoll and then winding river-like around the sandspit to flow out into the wider reaches of Cill Éinne bay. The bed of sand it leaves behind to dry is deep and soft in places, but with caution one can walk the lesser, quarter-mile, axis of the oval from the cemetery to the spit, though not without leaving an incriminatory trail of footprints across the delicate patterns of the sandwaves.

There are a few patches of marram grass off the point of the spit with incipient dunes swelling up around them, and local people have the impression that the spit itself is longer than it was, and that high tides driven by northerly gales break across it less frequently than formerly. If so, it may not be very long before the bay is completely enclosed and turned into an extension of the sandy grasslands around it. On the other hand the neck joining the eastern promontory to the general shoreline is said to be narrowing as winter storms coming up Gregory's Sound eat into Port Daibhche on the other side of it, so perhaps another gap will open up here in the south-east to replace the one now closing in the north-west of the bay. Certainly there have been some drastic changes in the geographical past of this corner of Aran. While the Ordnance Survey map of 1899 shows things much as they are to-day, on that of 1839 the spit is only a quarter of its present length and lies much closer to the southern shore of the strand. According to the Reverend William Kilbride, the Protestant pastor, writing in 1868, within the previous twenty or thirty years a ten or fifteen-foot depth of sand had been swept by winds into the sea from off the plains around the south and east of the strand, leaving them bare rock. Today they are plentifully sanded again, but rock shows through here and there.

This stripping away of the sand a century and a half ago revealed evidence of much earlier changes in the relationship of land and sea here, as will become apparent in the course of a walk around the bay. Kilbride can be our guide, as his observations on shifting sands were preliminary to an account of "several objects of antiquarian interest" exposed by the denudation of the rock, which he contributed to the *Journal of the Historical and Antiquarian Association of Ireland.*

The first of these objects, going eastwards around the bay from the cemetery, seems to have disappeared long ago, perhaps reburied by sand, so it is impossible to be definite about its nature. Kilbride termed it, rather warily, a "flag cell." His text locates it "on the western brink of Traighmhór, about forty or fifty yards south of the mortuary chapel of St. Endeus," but clearly his mental compass was almost ninety degrees out, for the sketch-map accompanying his article marks it about five hundred yards east-south-east of the chapel, close to the southern shore of the strand, and this is where some Iaráirne people vaguely remember it, on the plain directly below their village. It was (or is; who knows?)

about nine feet long, enclosed on three sides. The ends face south and north, which is open on that end; the west side is formed of one entire flag, rather thin for its size, and is nine feet long; the south end is also of one flag; but the east side is formed of two, whose tops have evidently been broken off, as it is somewhat lower than the western one. The horizontal capping stones are wanting, and not to be seen near the place, however they cannot be removed far, and may yet be found under the sand close by.

Again the map shows that one should read "east" for "south" in this account, and "west" for "north." Kilbride also says that the villagers who remembered its gradual emergence from the sands recognized its likeness to certain other structures of flagstones that occur here and there in the islands, and called it as they did these others *Leaba Dhiarmada agus Ghráinne*, Diarmaid and Gráinne's bed. The ancient Celtic legend of Gráinne's elopement with Diarmaid, and Fionn Mac Cumhal's pursuit of them throughout Ireland, is well known to countryfolk, and various odd configurations of stone, some natural and some artificial, used to be explained as being the beds the couple built for themselves, in a different place each night. Kilbride followed tradition in ascribing such "beds" to Diarmaid and Gráinne, whom he regarded as having actually existed, in the second or third century AD:

> From the legends associated with them...it would appear that some change or development had been effected by them, or in their age, in the ancient Celtic religion. Their disenchanting powers, their expertness and ready ability in transforming individuals at will, by magic, into animals of various kinds, would lead us to suppose that they, if not the actual introducers, yet helped to propagate and extend a belief in the metempsychosis.

Kilbride himself was of evangelical persuasions, and it seems more likely that he has endowed his Celtic forerunners with a little of his own temperament than that he re-embodied theirs.

However, since his day all theories based on the existence of the heroes of ancient days have been dissipated by the winds of scepticism; Diarmaid and Gráinne have been expelled from history into mythology, where they shine as deities, while many of their "beds" are known to be megalithic tombs, very much earlier than the coming of the Celts to Ireland. In particular the two island specimens that I shall be visiting in *Labyrinth* are identified as "wedge-graves" (so called from the fact that they are narrower towards one end), and date from the beginnings of the Bronze Age, about three or four thousand years ago. Kilbride's "flag cell" may well have been a tomb of this type; they are usually aligned east-west (which is why I mentioned the corrections necessary to Kilbride's compass-points) and often have the dimensions he recorded. But, whatever it was, the sand has swallowed it again.

There remains something to be seen yet of Kilbride's second object, a set of ruinous field-walls irregularly netting the plain below the village and parts of the promontory east of the great strand. I have slightly abbreviated his description of them as they were in 1868 not long after their exposure:

Some are double, a few single, and extremely well built. They are without cement, and the stones are of limestone, but none similar to the partially worn down ones now visible on the shore. The fields partitioned off were of good size, but the soil must have been very shallow as the walls rest upon the solid rock. We find the fences, some altogether denuded of sands, others with only a foot or perhaps a few inches exposed; following these, we find them receding under the sand until they are finally lost to view; when digging down a foot or so we again come upon them. Some appear to have passed through the Traghmhór, thus indicating that this tidal lake was not in existence at the period of their erection. Others ran out apparently under the sea; at least they are traceable to low water mark, thus showing the sea has encroached in this quarter upon the land.

A few years later Kilbride wrote that these walls had become "a delapidated wreck, no longer a delight for the enquiring mind," but how this had happened he did not specify. Many of the walls he records are still traceable and no doubt the rest could be found by probing the sand; certainly the scattered remains visible at low tide of the walls running out into the basin of An Trá Mhór for two or three hundred yards are still enough to delight the enquiring mind.

In other parts of the country, notably Mayo and more recently Connemara, old field-walls have come to light through the cutting away of peat bog for turf. Since it is thought that the bogs started to form about three and a half thousand years ago these walls represent the agriculture of the late Stone Age, and some of them are associated with megalithic tombs. Whether Kilbride's walls are contemporary with his "flag cell" or not could only be established by a proper "dig"; but it is noteworthy that in many places on the Connemara coast the blanket bog that covered the old field-walls as well as a few megaliths extends down to low water mark or beyond, showing that there has been a rise in relative sea level since the beginning of bog formation; similarly here in Aran the sea now flows in over the sand covering the old walls.

The changes in sea level since the Ice Ages have been extremely complex, but it has been concluded from a wide range of evidence that the sea was a good deal lower relative to the land than it is today for a period starting about four thousand years ago and ending about one thousand years ago. These fluctuations were long-delayed aftereffects of the last Ice Age. The great thaw topped up the oceans with melt-water, but as the sea rose, so did the land, for as they were freed from the weight of ice the plates constituting the earth's surface rode higher on the "mantle," the layer of slightly more fluid material supporting them below. The post-glacial history of relative sea-levels is the outcome of the race between these two processes, which themselves varied from place to place and time to time. Here at An Trá Mhór the building-up and breaking-down of sandbars may have further complicated the history, so that the most one can deduce from the fact that

Kilbride's fences run down into the tide is that they are "very old." In fact one could imagine that, should the bay ever be totally occluded by the spit's growing across its outlet, it would grass over and become a soggy hollow pasturage, whereupon the old fences might be repaired. The nature of Aran is such that it can never quite forget the Stone Age. If the Neolithic is the era in which these fences were built, and should they ever be renewed, it would be only one of the many instances in which the farmer of today works shoulder to shoulder with the earliest farmers of Aran, manhandling the same stones between them into whatever configurations suit the times.

The third and last of Kilbride's "objects of antiquarian interest" lies on the peninsula that embraces the eastern and north-eastern sectors of the oval strand. The peninsula is wide, but its attachment to the mainland is only a hundred yards or so across. (In disturbing fact, at this point I am within a few minutes' walk of the starting-point of this book and finishing-point of this volume, should I choose to cut across the base rather than persist in tramping out to the ultimate footstep of this last complication of my course—which is why I am proceeding in such an orderly and composed way, under the Vicar's guidance.) The site I am making for is a pair of stony hummocks close to the eastern shore of the headland, and half a mile from its base. Let Kilbride describe them:

> At a little distance they appear like two large mounds of loose, disjointed stones, half buried in sand; but on a nearer survey something like order, though of a very rugged and rude character, begins to be perceived, but it is not until we really stand upon the summit of the one nearest the Sound that it could be identified as one of those ancient structures denominated clocháns. The rounded or beehive-shaped roof then becomes apparent. When the writer first saw it a few years ago, the greater part of this building was embedded in the sand, nothing of it being visible except a few of the topmost courses of light flags forming part of the roof, and the

horizontal ones stretched across the top, and covering all in.... The second clochán is only distant a few yards from the first.... Externally it only presents a mass of ruins imbedded in sand with loose stones scattered over it. On the top, in the centre, lies a heavy slab of limestone...used to point out where some lone stranger found his last resting-place. Around about this mound several small headstones are apparently observable. On the south-east side are two smaller ones of that description, placed, one at the head and the other at the foot of a grave.

Such beehive-roofed huts (for which the Irish word *clochán* has been adopted by English-speaking Ireland) are well known in Aran and in other parts of the country. Most of them are of early Christian or mediaeval date, but given the conservatism of build-ing techniques in remote areas some could be earlier and others later even than that broad range of time.

The eastern clochán, Kilbride goes on to tell, was excavated in 1867 by the land-agent Mr. Thompson and a visitor, Captain Rowan of Tralee. Men were employed to dig out the sand filling it, whereupon part of the roof collapsed. The interior proved to be just over eight feet square, the walls rising vertically to about four feet and then being corbelled inwards to form the roof, the total interior height being eight feet. The doorway, on the east, was only one foot seven inches wide, and from it an open passageway extended east-wards (for about eighteen feet, judging by the plan Captain Rowan made of it for Kilbride's paper) between walls three foot six high, ending with six steps leading up to the same height. Kilbride speculates that this was to protect the doorway from drifting sand.

Behind or on the west of this clochán is an oval area seventy-two feet long enclosed by a wall or bank of loose stone that abuts onto the north and south sides of the clochán, and the second clochán lies within this enclosure, near its western end. Kilbride explains why it is more ruinous than the other:

It was related to the writer by a villager of Iarárna about fifty years of age, who stated that he often heard his father (who died upwards of eighty years of age) mentioning it as a tradition received from his father, and often spoken of amongst them as having happened before his time; so that the occurrence to which it refers may date, perhaps, from one hundred to one hundred and fifty years back, and is as follows: A Spanish (some say a French) ship was driven into Cala-na-luinge (whether from stress of weather, or any other cause, is not remembered), and all on board were lost. The bodies were washed ashore; but the islanders have been, it seems, ever averse to inter strangers, and especially shipwrecked ones, in their own burial grounds. Being, however, unwilling to deny them the rite of sepulture, they resolved to bury them in the great sand plain around them, and for this purpose opened the graves accidentally over the spot where the clochán lay entombed beneath the sand. They never imagined for an instant that a building of any description lay underneath; for the sand plain was at the time several feet higher than the tops of the clocháns. In digging down they, however, disturbed the roof, which must have fallen inwards, and also the side walls, from which cause the building when the sand was drifted by the wind from it about fifteen years ago, was found to be in ruins, a mere mass of loose stone imbedded in sand.

That this tradition is in the main correct there is now little or no room for doubt. Captain Rowan, while investigating the place, collected several detached human bones; and in the spot marked by the two upright stones already mentioned discovered an entire skeleton.

The place Kilbride recorded as "Cala-na-luinge" (i.e. Caladh na Loinge, harbour of the ship) is the shore nearest to the clocháns. The ship in question is said to be the one whose sailors' bones were found here, but if so it found no harbour for its landfall, as the correct name of the place, a trustworthy Iaráirne man tells me, is Cara na Loinge, and a *cara*, in Aran usage at least, can be just such a stretch of shallow stony shore as this.

The tombstone still lies on the top of the western clochán, but if, from that little eminence, I survey the wide spaces all around, I can hardly believe that the islanders chose this spot in which to dig a grave by chance. However, only a professional excavation could establish whether or not these mounds represent, perhaps, an early religious site with a burial place, some memory of which may have lingered on long after it had been deserted and drowned in sand.

Now that sand has refilled the clochán unroofed by Captain Rowan's dig, both look much as they did to Kilbride, "large mounds of loose, dislocated stone, half buried in sand." In search of a word to describe the setting of this final object-lesson in the Minister's discourse on relics of the past, "dislocated" is the one that comes back to me, initiating a redirection, or a retranslation, of the antiquarian enquiry through which he has led me to this viewpoint. Sitting on the tombstone and looking around me, I see to the east the featureless *cara*, the usually troubled waters of the Sound, and the relentless stony profile of Inis Meáin. To the north, south and west is a flat wasteland rimmed by dunes, its smooth sheets of glaciated rock showing here and there through a sward worn thin by overgrazing. Nothing grazes here now except the countless rabbits that burrow in the dunes. I never meet any-one here, though an occasional patch of *carraigín* spread to dry on a bare area, looking like a forgotten picnic rug, tells me that at least one villager still derives something from this shore. I seem to have visited this remote corner of Aran only on days made comfortless by needling winds or overbearing sun, that made the half mile of heavy going over the dunes back to the end of the road, and then the long cycle home, a prospect scarcely preferable to staying where I was, on this tombstone, which, being blank, could as well be mine as any other dislocated voyager's. "Vanity of vanities, saith the Preacher, vanity, all is vanity," and in his latter-day, antiquarianizing embodiment as the Reverend William Kilbride, expounds his text thus: sand comes with the wind and goes again, exhuming and reburying our scattered works and bones; the bay opens and closes like an eye troubled by flying grit; the Earth itself shudders from Ice Age to Ice Age; and so on. Some such sermon can be read into Kilbride's "Notes of Some Antiquities on Aranmore" by a certain mood. Preachers induce such moods, the better to peddle their teleological pick-me-ups. If one declines these, the only cure is to walk on, out of the state in which nothing matters into its mirror image, more vivid like all such, in which everything matters.

I walk on now, to the last corner of Aran.

STRAW ISLAND

This last corner, the tip of the arrow-shaped peninsula beyond the great strand, has a superfluity of names attached to it. First, it is Ceann an Duine, the person's head, and second, it is Ceann an Mhadra, the dog's head. Colie Hernon, with seamanlike precision, once laid it down for me that the first name refers to the point from high water mark down to half water, and the second to its extension from half to low water mark. The "person's head" is said to derive from some skull-like appearance of the tip of the peninsula as seen from out at sea, but I have never been able to catch the likeness. Nor do I know the reason for the "dog" name, which has been at Aran's heels for centuries: Speed's map of 1610 marks "Ye Dogge" as an islet (which does not exist in fact) in the sound between Árainn and Inis Meáin.

Five hundred yards off the tip of the peninsula, like the dot of an "i," is Oileán na Tuí or Straw Island, a mere plateful of sandhills, carrying on its northern rim a small lighthouse by which vessels steer into Cill Éinne bay. The "straw" is that of the marram grass which grows on the dunes, and it used to be important enough to have figured in a legal document; in 1717 when Edmund Fitzpatrick, then Aran's landlord, demised Inis Oírr to an Andrew French, it was stipulated in the lease that French could cut enough straw from Straw Island and the headland to thatch all the houses of Inis Oírr.

Finally, the headland itself is Barr na Coise, the point of the foot, and An Chois, the foot, is the seaway between it and the islet. But this last name demands a deeper consideration from me (in fact it precipitates a crisis for this book), which I will defer for a while.

Straw Island has never been inhabited so far as is known, except by lighthousemen for the period between the establishment of the light in 1878 and its automation in 1926. Recently it was electrified, and a little windcharger has been set up beside it; from Cill Rónáin we can see its blades flickering away in any opportune wind. A man goes out by currach now and again to tend the light, and in 1976 I accompanied him together with some botanists who wanted to see what Straw Island could contribute to the *Flora of Connemara and the Burren*, then in preparation.

We launched the currach from Trá na bhFrancach north of Cill Rónáin. While Bobbie Gill, the light-keeper, mounted the outboard engine and the currach was idling on the lucid water, the botanists were exclaiming over the dense beds of eel-grass lying in lank green festoons below us. *Maolscannach* was the local name Bobbie supplied for it, which seems to derive (at least to the satisfaction of my do-it-yourself etymology) from words implying its prostrate, filmy nature. (Later I was able to look at it more closely when a spring ebb exposed it on the muddy sand in the mouth of Cill Rónáin harbour—it is a pulpy, waterlogged, grass-like plant a few feet long—and an old shoreman there told me that sixty years ago he saw it gathered and hung over walls to dry for use in stuffing armchairs.)

Then the engine started and we headed a devious arrow of

wake across the calm bay, Bobbie in the bows signalling the course to his son at the tiller as we snaked between the buoys marking lobsterpots. The lighthouse, which from Cill Rónáin appears like a small, whitewashed gate-pillar out there by the wide exit of the bay, never quite ceased to look like a scale-model of a lighthouse even when our boat was nuzzling into the beach close by it, such is the diameter of the waters the bay opens into. There were lines of otters' pawprints on the damp sand where we stepped ashore. I followed Bobbie through the narrow, high-walled yard of the lighthouse, past the chill stone vacancies of the old living-quarters and up the stairs to the glass octagonal room housing the lamp. The acetylene flame at its heart seemed insignificant. Bobbie explained the clockwork mechanism on which the two lenses rotated about it, sweeping its beams around the horizon, and pointed out the two slatted panels that had been added to the merry-go-round to eliminate a reflection of the lamp off the windows of the octagon (in which it seems they are not entirely successful, the light still being known up and down the coast as the one with the double flash). The botanists had fanned out to quarter the island's eleven acres, and now and again as I attended to these matters, I caught sight of a bent head or rounded back among the marram crests of the dunes. Soon I went out to join the searchers.

The great prize would have been to re-find the sea stock, *Matthiola sinuata*, now extremely rare if not extinct in Ireland. It was discovered on Straw Island by J. T. Mackay before 1805 and seen once or twice in the next thirty years; it has also been recorded from dunes in Clare and Wexford a few times, but it is many years since the botanical establishment had word of it, nor did it make itself known on this occasion. Indeed to my eyes the island offered little of floral interest; this was, after all, in September, after a summer-long drought, and apart from the indestructible marram grass and a few dull foreshore species, everything had been reduced to brownish withered scraps. However, as one of the party sternly remarked, one cannot restrict botanizing to the flowering season, and they diligently searched out forty-five species, a total I found impressive. The find I chiefly remember from that day, with horror, is the carcass of a donkey that someone had left to foal here, which had dutifully done so, and then died of thirst together with its child. Another, I was told, had saved itself by swimming across An Chois.

THE STEP

Of course I returned to Cill Rónáin with the others, but for the purposes of this book I remain on Straw Island to contemplate the gap, the step necessary to complete this volume, which I have not taken, between the islet and the headland stretching out towards it.

The Ordnance Survey map of 1839 shows a sandbar, drying at low tide, linking the islet with the headland. It never dries nowadays, I believe, although one can wade across it with a spring ebb, that is, at low water of one of the extreme tides that occur for a few days after a full or new moon. Hence the name, An Chois, the foot, transferred by the act of walking or wading, from the body to the ground. An Iaráirne man once said to me, making nothing of it but leaving the notion to make its own way in my mind, that Easter Sunday is a good day for wading out to Straw Island. A celestial logic underlies the observation. The tides are the oceans' swinging to and fro in their beds under the influence of the moon and the sun, and it is necessary to think through these influences in some detail to appreciate this logic of An Chois.

Consider first the moon. The gravitational attraction between any two objects is greater the closer they are together. Thus the force the moon exerts on a unit mass of the waters on the face of the earth near to it is greater than that it exerts on a unit mass of the solid globe as a whole, while the force per unit mass exerted on the waters of the farther face of the earth is smaller than that exerted on the globe itself. It is these differential forces that produce the tides, and if the surface of the earth were all one ocean it would have a high tide at the point nearest to the moon and another at the point opposite to that, with low tides at the points of the globe halfway between them.

The sun also would produce a pair of tides, but since it is so much farther away its effect is only about two-fifths that of the moon. Because of the daily rotation of the earth each point of this idealized ocean would experience a small solar high tide every twelve hours, at midday and midnight (or a little later, making allowance for friction), and a large lunar tide every twelve and a half hours (the difference in period being due to the moon's own rotation about the earth). These solar and lunar tides would coincide and reinforce one another whenever sun, moon and earth were in line. At full moon the earth is approximately between the sun and moon; that is why we, from earth, see the moon's illuminated face full on. When the moon is new, it is between the earth and the sun, so that we see only a narrow margin at most of its illuminated face. Therefore it is at full and new moon that an idealized ocean would have its highest tides.

The sun's contribution to the tides varies with the season of the year because the earth's axis is tilted with respect to its orbit about the sun. In summer our days are long because the sun is north of the equatorial plane, in winter the nights are long because the sun has gone south, while day equals night when the sun is over the equator; and it is at these times of symmetry, the spring and autumn equinoxes, that the sun's tidal influence is at its greatest.

The various oceans of our real world, however, are far from being of ideal simplicity in their behaviour. Their individual tidal responses to the periodic influences of sun and moon are determined, in an incalculably complex way, by their boundaries, depths and interconnections. Just as the water in a cup or a bath will slosh to and fro with a particular frequency when disturbed, so the body of water in an ocean bed has its natural periods of oscillation, and will respond most fully to stimuli of similar periods. Some oceans only manage one tide a day, but as it happens the

Atlantic at our latitudes is sensitive to the approximately twice daily pull of the moon, giving us a high tide every twelve and a half hours, with large variations due to the sun. Adding together the twice-daily, twice lunar-monthly and twice-yearly variations in the combined effect of sun and moon, therefore, Aran, like most west European coasts, should expect two roughly equal high tides a day, these being rather larger around the times of full and new moon, and especially large near the equinoxes. And with these extremely high tides come extremely low ebbs.

Now, Easter is in origin the festival of the risen year, celebrating the day's winning out against the night, and when, fifteen hundred years ago, Christianity was undertaking the ordering of our relationship to the cosmos, the Council of Nicaea laid it down that Easter Sunday was to be the one after the full moon following upon the spring equinox. And although every link in the above chain of statements is weakened by qualifications—for winds and atmospheric pressures influence the tides as well as the sun and moon, there are perturbations and precessions and nutations to complicate the geometry of the solar system, and the modern way of calculating Easter does not always agree with the Nicaean formula—nevertheless there remains a correlation strong enough for Iaráirne to have noticed and blessed the fact that Easter Sunday usually provides the entertainment, when work is tabooed, of walking out to Straw Island. The fact is, I imagine, accepted with the same wondering but incurious good grace as that other fact pointed out to me by an Oatquarter man, that on every shore of Aran is a boulder marking the half tide level: such slight perquisites are only what is due to us, the constant servants of the shore.

As it happens, I have always been elsewhere on Easter Sunday, and have never crossed An Chois. But since this is a step at least approximately blessed by such an august configuration of Sun, Moon and Earth, I will adopt it into the structure of this book as a moment of questioning of what I am about, as I did the bad step, An Troigh Mhairbh, that invitation to death on Aran's other coast. What connotations has my ruling image, the step, picked up in this circuit of the island-world, now so nearly closed? Listening to this book as it has formed itself thus far in my mind, here and there I catch the hollow footfall of the museum attendant, for instance, and elsewhere the breathy creeping of the Peeping Tom. Among the echoes of all these steps—rash or wary, ritualistic or whimsical, processional or jiggish, trespassory or proprietorial—it is impossible to isolate the particular resonance I had hoped to amplify further, that of the good step, the one equal to the ground it covers. And while I have taken care to distance this book from that imaginary work of art preparatory to the taking of such a step—just as the architect of the tower of Babel no doubt preferred to watch its progress from a hillock not too close at hand—nevertheless I cannot quite evade the shockwaves of that project's inevitable collapse. Having now acted out to the best of my capacity the impossibility of interweaving more than two or three at a time of the millions of modes of relating to a place, I can feel in the tiredness of my feet what any sensible thinker would have gathered from a moment's exercise of the brain, that the good step is inconceivable. And this book in its oblique and evasive way had undertaken the conceiving of what I knew to be inconceivable.

Well, a book that is committed to failure may allow itself an interlude of rueful celebration of its success, so I will sit down by the waters of An Chois, bathe my bruised soles, and listen to the voices that say, "How foolish an enterprise! Surely everyone knows that you cannot estimate the height of the sky by climbing ever higher mountains, or get a sense of numerical infinity by wasting years in counting? The correct ways of contacting the depths of reality are just two: either to throw yourself over the cliff into your choice of mysticisms, or to do your time in one of the cultural armies, scientific or artistic. Otherwise your contribution is not even a dot of confetti at the wedding of humanity and the world!"

Perhaps so. These are mighty abstractions, humanity and the

world, and I repent my presumption before them. But here I am,
as one always is, faced with the next step, and to bridge An Chois
and so move on to a resting-point in my work, I need some definition of my purpose, even if it is only provisional, which will give
my progress a touch of that unity the dolphin achieves so
thoughtlessly. All that lies to hand (man of straw, marooned on
Straw Island!) is the wreckage of an ideal. The notion of a momentary congruence between the culture one bears and the
ground that bears one has shattered against reality into uncountable fragments, the endless variety of steps that are more or less
good enough for one or two aspects of the here and now. These
splinters might be put together into some more serviceable whole
by paying more heed to their cumulative nature, to the step's re-
peatability, variability, reversability and expendability. The step, so
mobile, so labile, so nimbly coupling place and person, mood and
matter, occasion and purpose, begins to emerge as a metaphor of a
certain way of living on this earth. It is a momentary proposition
put by the individual to the non-individual, an instant of trust
which may not be well-founded, a not-quite-infallible catching of
oneself in the act of falling. Stateless, the step claims a foot-long
nationality every second. Having endlessly variable grounds, it
needs no faith. The idea of freedom is associated in dozens of
turns of speech with that of the step. To the footloose all boundaries, whether academic or national, are mere administrative im-
pertinences. With this freebooter's licence there goes every
likelihood of superficiality, restlessness, fickleness and transgres-
sion—and so, by contraries, goes the possibility of recurrency, of
frequentation, of a deep, an ever-deeper, dwelling in and on a place,
a sum of whims and fancies totalling a constancy as of stone.

In all this the step is to be distinguished, maximally, from those
metaphorical appendages of humanity, the need for which is
much cried up by so many well-wishers of the species: roots—a
concept which, though obviously deep, is to me unacceptably vegetable.

This will do for now: the adequate step will be one light and sure enough to carry such explosive significances across tricky ground. This will do; this will get me across An Chois.

EASY GOING

The way to the end of this stage of my walk has eluded me for a long time. But now, having dreamed of crossing An Chois—dry-foot, on a sandbank of words, the accumulated dust on my heels—perhaps I can let the impetus of that dream float me smoothly past what remains to be described: the headland of Barr na Coise, because I did not do it justice before, Port Daibhche, the bay almost severing it from the rest of Aran, and the half-mile of shore leading south from it back to my starting-point.

It is not true that I have only explored Barr na Coise on difficult days. Reviewing my memories of it from the disadvantage-point of that tombstone on which the Reverend Kilbride left me stranded, I lost sight of certain hours, scattered through the years, that were as rich in life as the richest Book of Hours, but with their own Atlantic astringency. Once or twice interweaving showers and sun have laid a fine tweed carpet over this bare floor for me, a tough, close-knit sward minutely flecked with blossom—scarlet pimpernel, the mauve common storksbill, wild yellow pansies with afterthoughts of violet—that celebrated each step with a bounce and a puff of many-scented ozone. One year, I remember, the yellow wall-pepper flowered here so abundantly that when I climbed up the dune-cliffs of Port Daibhche onto the headland I found a Land of Cockaigne in which every hollow was brimming with custard. And in 1975, on a day of clouded blue, I saw a clouded yellow butterfly here. That was one of those rare years that bring an influx of these migrants from the Continent to the southern parts of Britain and Ireland; unusually favouring breezes must have floated this one so far north, for the species had never been recorded from Aran before.

Generations of rabbits following each other along lines of least resistance through the ankle-high maquis of Barr na Coise have worn neat tracks radiating from every burrow and triangulating a terrain that is shapeless to us. Certain plants find an ease of growth on these paths freed from the wirier species. In summer the yellow-wort raises its star-like flower on straight stems a foot high, like lampposts along these ways. The common daisy here attains to a glory of a mention in *Flora of Connemara and the Burren*:

> *Bellis perennis....* On the sand dunes and sandy pastures at Killeany the daisy becomes dominant on rabbit-tracks, which are visible as white streaks at a distance of over a kilometre.

Along the white avenues of this garden city of rabbits, stoats deliver swift death, and in between times lark about. I watched a couple of them playing Pop Goes the Weasel here once. They began by facing each other, a dozen yards apart, tensely upright on their hind legs with their front paws neatly folded against their white chests. Then as if at a signal they bounded forward a short way and vanished down separate burrows. An instant later they shot up from other burrows, one here, the other there, whirled around to locate each other, and began the game again.

If Barr na Coise is only now and again a dreamworld, a fairyland or a playground, Port Daibhche is more settled in benignity. Facing eastwards, with the great wall of Inis Meáin opposite, it is sheltered from the most prevalent gales, and has gathered into itself shelving sands on which the currachs of Iaráirne can run ashore softly, while among the dunes around it are deep hollows in which they can lie safe from all winds. These dunes hug the beach with soft sandcliffs, the matted overhangs of which are tressed with the rare sea bindweed, flowering in June with flared bells striped in pink and white. Another and even rarer plant is frequent here, the purple milk-vetch, *Astragalus*. In describing the clifftops west of Dún Aonghasa I stated that it flourishes there "because of rather than despite the adjacent gulf," but one year since writing that harangue I found it so abundant as to produce a colourful haze on the sandy pasturage inland of Port Daibhche, where it was luxuriating in one of Aran's kinder environments and declining the stern metaphoric role I had chosen for it on the edge of the abyss.

Legends of peace and promise are harboured by Port Daibhche. Near the beginning of this book I told how the corpse of St. Gregory, the hermit of Inis Meáin, was set adrift in a barrel, and as a sign of the forgiveness of his sins found landfall here, on the holy shores of St. Enda's Aran; hence, it is said, the name: Port Daibhche, the harbour of the barrel. Kilbride suggests that the name may in fact have been Port Duimhche, the harbour of the sand-plain, but in any case long usage has smoothed all the consonants out of the second element of the name, so that many islanders hear and understand it as "Port Aodha" (in which the "dh" goes for nothing), Hugh's harbour, and wonder who Hugh was. However, the derivation from *dabhach*, a barrel, is very ancient, for the mediaeval *Life of St. Enda* contains another legendary justification for it. When Enda arrived in Aran (by stone boat from Connemara, as I have told), he found a pagan called Corban in possession. Corban was soon persuaded by various miracles to withdraw to Corcomroe (in what is now County Clare) for a trial period until God's will for the island should be made manifest:

But Corbanus ordered a large barrell to be made, which filling with the seed of corn, he said; if the God whom Endeus preaches, wishes that he should possess that island, let him send this barrell full of corn to him dwelling in the island. Wonderful to be said... for the consolation of that Endeus, the Lord by the ministry of Angels transmitted this barrell of corn. And, as the skilled relate, the seed of corn, this kind of, is had on the island, even to the present. They, moreover, assert that the trace of that barrell appears in the sea, as to the serenity of the sea, so that the sea does not become disturbed by waves in the way through which the barrell passed, but a calm always remains there. The place where it was miraculously brought to the island is called Portus Dolii [the harbour of the barrel] even to the present day. But Corbanus, seeing so great a miracle, coming himself to the man of God, gave the island to him, and to God for ever.

And now, may that serene and luminous current float me on from Port Daibhche to a calm conclusion.

UPON THIS ROCK

Just one placename and one place and the mystery of their conjunction remain to be considered. The southern rim of Port Daibhche is a shinglebank that gives way to a level terrace of rock where the coast turns due south again; about three hundred yards beyond this corner there is a seepage of fresh water onto the terrace from a spring under the stony ledges above it, and a few rough steps, more than half natural, by which one could bring water from the spring to cattle in the fields inland of it. This is the place. The name is Teampall na mBráthar, the church of the brothers, that is, the friars. But the Franciscan monastery founded by the O'Briens had its church in Cill Éinne, so far as is known, until the Cromwellians took its stones for their fortifications, and no other friars are recorded in Aran. There is no mark of foundations in the fields or on the shore here, and since this is a comparatively sheltered coastline of solid rock it is unlikely that a church-site has been lost through erosion. Neither have I heard or read any suggestion, except for that made by the name itself, of there ever having been a church here.

So, since this is still dreamtime, or some illicit after-hours of it, and there is no rationale of the name to inhibit me, I could build a church here and call it Teampall na mBráthar, or let the name float free and spread like a sea-mist over Aran as a whole: the Temple of the Brothers. Would such a foundation do as a half-way house for my meaning? Somewhere I have read of a temple built around a footprint of the Buddha, and, looking back, I see that it was a god's all-comprehending step I had in mind when I set out. But that footprint (is it in Ceylon?) is, I believe, the last, the take-off point for transcendence, and the next one, which would complete a step, does not exist; whereas in fact the earth and its powers of healing and wounding, of affirming and contradicting, of supporting and tripping you up, can never be finished with. And the idea of brotherhood, even leavened with sisterhood, has only a limited application to the dense thorny thickets of interrelatedness I have been skirting around. When I review the cast I have gathered in this round of Aran of the Saints and Stones—myself the walker, you the reader, they the farmers and fishermen, landlords and bailiffs, rabbits and stoats, gulls, cormorants, dolphins, plants, fossils; the gamut from saint to stone—I realize that the idea of a temple of brotherhood is born out of loneliness, that it soon recoils before the bitterness of sibling politics, and that it subsides at last into cosy tautology. Better to let the obscuring name evaporate. There remains the bare stone, upon which, having completed this circuit of the island, we can now pace to and fro, marginally better informed as to its provenances and properties, its relationships to those other horizons of stone to the north and east, its usefulness as a sea-mark to Mikey going by there in his boat piled high with lobsterpots; this ordinary stone of Aran, of which we can scarcely dream now that its virtues could all be caught together into a moment of vision, having peered a little farther down the bottomless cliff of its reality.

From this point, Teampall na mBráthar, looking south I see once again the ruined watch tower perched high above the Sound, marking the resting-place of St. Gregory of the Golden Mouth. It suggests the possibility of going round the island once again, looking at everything in more detail, or in others of the infinity of ways of looking. Perhaps a second circuit would be more rewarding now that my pace has been chastened by so many miles, my breath deepened by so many words. But for a book to stand like an island out of the sea of the unwritten it must acknowledge its own bounds, and turn inward from them, and look into the labyrinth.

SOURCES

ABBREVIATIONS

Jn.H.A.A.I. Journal of the Historical and Antiquarian Association of
  Ireland

R.D.S. Royal Dublin Society

R.I.A.Proc. Proceedings of the Royal Irish Academy

R.I.A.Trans. Transactions of the Royal Irish Academy

R.S.A.I.Jn. Journal of the Royal Society of Antiquaries of Ireland

T.C.D. Trinity College, Dublin

Trans.Dub.Soc. Transactions of the Dublin Society

TIMESCAPE WITH SIGNPOST

8 Éamonn de hÓir, Ordnance Survey Office (personal communication).

8 T. S. Ó Máille, "*Ára* mar áitainm," *Galvia*, Iml. IV (1957).

9 Rev. Denis Murphy, "On two sepulchral urns found, in June 1885,
   in the South Island of Arran," *R.I.A.Proc.* Ser. 2, Vol. II (1879–80).

10 *Life of St. Kieran*, quoted in Roderic O'Flaherty, *West or H-Iar
    Connaught* (written in 1684, first published 1846, ed. James
    Hardiman, reprinted Galway, 1978).

10 Antoine Powell, *Oileáin Árann* (Dublin, 1984).

11 Oliver J. Burke, *The South Isles of Aran* (London, 1887).

13 Censuses, 1841, 1871 and 1981.

14 John T. O'Flaherty, "A sketch of the history and antiquities of the
    Southern Islands of Aran," *R.I.A.Trans.* Vol. XIV, Antiquities
    (1821–25).

14 William Stokes, *The Life and Labours in Art and Archaeology of
    George Petrie* (London, 1868).

15 John O'Donovan, *Ordnance Survey Letters* (ms., written Galway,
    1839).

15   Martin Haverty, *Ethnological Excursion to the Aran Islands* (Dublin, 1859).

15   John M. Synge, *The Aran Islands* (London and Dublin, 1907).

18   Tim Robinson, *Oileáin Árann, a map of the Aran Islands* (Cill Rónáin, 1975).

18   Tim Robinson, *Oileáin Árann, a map and guide* (Cill Rónáin, 1980).

I. SOUTH

BEFORE BEGINNING

25   Thomas J. Westropp, "The North Isle of Aran," *R.S.A.I.Jn.* Vol. 25 (1895); reprinted in *The Aran Islands* (Dublin, 1971).

26   Conor MacDermot, Geological Survey of Ireland (personal communication).

CONNOISSEURS OF WILDERNESS

31   O'Donovan, *op. cit.*

31   R. O'Flaherty, *op. cit.*

THIS VALE OF TEARS

33   *Dublin University Magazine* (April 1853).

SIGNATURES

45   C. MacDermot (personal communication).

46   Lady A. Gregory, *Visions and Beliefs in the West of Ireland* (New York, 1920).

NINE FATHOMS

46   Liam Ó Flaithearta, "An Scathán," in *Dúil* (Dublin, 1953).

46   C. MacDermot (personal communication).

48   Hardiman's appendices to R. O'Flaherty, *op. cit.*

49   Tom O'Flaherty, *Aranmen All* (Dublin, 1934).

DÚCHATHAIR

50   George Petrie, *Military Architecture of Ireland* (ms., R.I.A.).

51   J. O'Donovan, *op. cit.*

51   T. J. Westropp, "A study of the early forts and stone huts in Inish-more, Aran Islands, Galway Bay," *R.I.A.Proc.* Vol. XXVIII, Sect. C (1910).

51   T. J. Westropp, "The ancient forts of Ireland," *R.I.A. Trans.* Vol. 31 (1902).

54   Dr. John Waddell (personal communication).

STYLES OF FLIGHT

55   Tony Whilde, *Birds of Galway and Mayo* (Galway, 1977).

ARGUMENTS FROM WEAKNESS

59   A Connemara version of this story is recorded in *Peadar Chois Fhairrge*, ed. Seán Mac Giollarnáth (Dublin, 1934).

THE CLIFFMAN'S KINGDOM

65   R. O'Flaherty, *op. cit.*

65   J. T. O'Flaherty, *op. cit.*

65   Tadhg Ó Ceallaigh, "Ailleadoireacht i nÁrainn," *An Stoc* (April 1929).

70   Tom O'Flaherty, *Cliffmen of the West* (London, 1935).

72   Seán Póil (Baile na Creige, Arainn, personal communication).

THE WORM AND THE ROOT

84   T. O'Flaherty, *Aranmen All.*

DÚN AONGHASA: A LEGENDARY PERSPECTIVE

86   R. O'Flaherty, *op. cit.*

87   *Lebor Gabála Érenn*, ed. and trans. by R. A. S. Macalister (Dublin, 1938).

POSTHUMOUS CAREER OF THE FIR BOLG

96 M. Haverty, *op. cit.*

98 T. J. Westropp, *op. cit.* (1902).

101 T. F. O'Rahilly, *Early Irish History and Mythology* (Dublin, 1946).

102 Giraldus Cambrensis, *Topographia Hiberniae*, read publicly at Oxford in 1188. Translated by John O'Meara as *The History and Topography of Ireland* (Dundalk, 1951; revised ed. Dublin and Harmondsworth, 1982).

102 Thomas J. Westropp, "Prehistoric remains in north-western Clare," *R.S.A.I.Jn.* Vol. XI, Ser. 5 (1901).

DÚN AONGHASA: A CLOSER LOOK

106 T. J. Westropp, *op. cit.* (1902).

106 J. O'Donovan, *op. cit.*

107 T. J. Westropp, *op. cit.* (1895).

107 T. J. Westropp, *op. cit.* (1902).

108 H. O'N. Hencken, *Cahercommaun* (Dublin, 1938).

108 E. Rynne, "The Early Iron Age in Co. Clare," *North Munster Antiquarian Journal* Vol. 24 (1982).

109 E. Œ. Somerville and M. Ross, *Some Irish Yesterdays* (London, 1906).

TIDES OF THE OTHER WORLD

116 Pádraig Ó Flaithbheartaigh (Inis Córthaigh, personal communication).

LIFE ON THE BRINK

117 Liam O'Flaherty, "Two Dogs" in *The Short Stories of Liam O'Flaherty* (London, 1937).

DIVISIONS OF THE LAND

120 James G. Barry, "Aran of the Saints," *R.S.A.I.Jn.* Ser. 2, Vol. VII (1885–86).

AN "AGRARIAN OUTRAGE"

124 Robert Kee, *The Green Flag*, Vol. II (London, 1976).
125 A. Powell, *op. cit.*

FEAR OF FALLING, FEAR OF FAILING

129 T. O'Flaherty, *Aranmen All.*
129 Pádraig Mac Piarais (Patrick Pearse), "Poll an Phíobaire," *An Claidheamh Soluis* (March 1905).
129 P. Ó Flaithbheartaigh (personal communication).
132 Seán Mac Giollarnáth ed., *Peadar Chois Fhairrge* (Dublin, 1944).

LOOKING BACK

134 C. MacDermot (personal communication).
135 Richard Kirwan, "Essay on the primitive state of the globe," quoted in James Hardiman, *The History of Galway* (Dublin, 1820).

II. EXCURSION

152 R. O'Flaherty, *op. cit.*
152 T. J. Westropp, *op. cit.* (1895).

III. NORTH

A DIFFICULT MILE

171 D. A. Webb and Mary J. Scannell, *Flora of Connemara and the Burren* (Cambridge, 1983).

ON THE SHORES OF THE PAST

176 Máirtín Ó Direáin, *Dánta* 1939–79 (Dublin, 1980).
177 M. Ó Direáin, *Feamainn Bhealtaine* (Dublin, 1961).
178 L. O'Flaherty, *op. cit.* (1937).

SHORE DIVISIONS

180 Pat Mullen, *Man of Aran* (New York, 1935).
181 Conchúr Ó Síocháin, *Seanchas Chléire* (Dublin, 1940).

WOMEN'S WORK

187 Máirtín Ó Cadhain, "An Taoille Tuile" in *An Braon Broghach* (Dublin, 1948).

POETS ON THE SHORE

189 M. Ó Direáin, *op. cit.* (1961).

THE KELP AGE

195 A. and N. L. Clow, *The Chemical Revolution* (London, 1952).
196 *Freeman's Journal* (3 October 1884).
197 *Report on the Aran Islands* (Congested Districts Board, 1893).
199 Colm Ó Gaora, *Obair Is Luadhainn* (Dublin, 1937).

SMOKE AND ASH

200 Mícheál King (Fearann an Choirce) and Peadar Ó Fatharta (Sruthán) (personal communications).
201 T. O'Flaherty, *Aranmen All.*
204 J. M. Synge, "The Kelp Makers," *Manchester Guardian* (July 1905), reprinted in *The Works of John M. Synge*, Vol. 4 (Dublin, 1910).

AFTERIMAGES, AFTERTHOUGHTS

206 Elizabeth Rivers, *Stranger in Aran* (Dublin, 1946).
207 A. C. Haddon and C. R. Browne, "The ethnography of the Aran Islands," *R.I.A.Proc.* Vol. II, Ser. 3 (1891–93).
207 Thomas H. Mason, *The Islands of Ireland* (London, 1936).

MAN OF ARAN

212 Arthur Calder Marshall, *The Innocent Eye* (London, 1963).
214 Pat Mullen, *Man of Aran.*
215 George Stoney, *How the Myth Was Made* (film distributed by Museum of Modern Art, New York, 1978).
216 Robert Flaherty, *Oidhche Sheanchais or The Story Teller* (film, 1934).
217 Máire Bn. Uí Conghaile (Cill Mhuirbhigh, personal communication).

HISTORY OF A STRANGER

223 E. Rivers, *op. cit.*

223 C. C. Vyvyan, *On Timeless Shores* (London, 1957).

223 Risteard de Paor, *Úll i mBarr an Ghéagáin* (Dublin, 1959).

224 Breandán Ó hEithir, "An sagairt a d'fhógair cath ar mná treabhsair," *Irish Times* (June 1977).

FISHERMEN OF CILL MHUIRBHIGH

227 W. L. Micks, *History of the Congested Districts Board* (Dublin, 1925).

WRITING ON THE BEACH

232 D. A. Webb, "The flora of the Aran Islands," *Journal of Life Sciences, R.D.S.* Vol. II (1980).

THE LUCK OF THE SHORE

237 T. O'Flaherty, *Aranmen All.*

THE IRISH IODINE & MARINE SALTS MFG. CO. LTD.

240 References to contemporary newspaper reports are given in Antoine Powell, *op. cit.*

242 *Freeman's Journal* (3 October 1884).

SAILING ON A STONE

246 Dr. M. D. Max, Geological Survey of Ireland (personal communication).

247 M. D. Max et al., *Preliminary Report on the Geology of the North-West Approaches to Galway Bay*, Geological Survey of Ireland RS 75/3.

247 P. D. Ryan, M. D. Max, and T. Kelly, "The petrochemistry of the basic volcanic rocks of the South Connemara Group (Ordovician), Western Ireland," *Geological Magazine* Vol. CXX, Ser. 2 (1983).

249 Dr. M. D. Max (personal communication).

249 Tim Robinson, *Mapping South Connemara*, Parts 1–29 (Roundstone, 1985).

251 Magradin's *Vita S. Endei*, in John Colgan's *Acta Sanctorum Hiberniae*

(Louvain, 1645; facs. reprint Dublin, 1947).

252 R. O'Flaherty, *West or H-Iar Connaught.*

253 O'Donovan, *Ordnance Survey Letters.*

DIFFERENCES BETWEEN LIMESTONE AND GRANITE

262 C. R. Browne, "The ethnography of Garumna and Lettermullen," *R.I.A.Proc.* Vol. V, Ser. 3 (1899).

262 Colm P. Ó hIarnáin, "Ábhar na Bó" in *Gleann an Chuain* (Dublin, 1978).

263 Colm P. Ó hIarnáin, "An Bádoir Santach" in *Gleann an Chuain.*

264 Hal Sisk, "Dutch influence on Irish small craft," *Cultura Maritima* (Autumn 1974).

THE FEAST OF SAINTS PETER AND PAUL

270 *Béaloideas* Vol. XXVII–XXVIII (1959–60).

THE MINISTER'S SAND

279 Barbara Mullen, *Life Is My Adventure* (London, 1937).

THE GENERATIONS

282 J. M. Synge, *The Aran Islands.*

284 Pat Mullen, *Hero Breed* (London, 1936).

284 Risteard de Paor, *Úll i mBarr an Ghéagáin* (Dublin, 1959; translated by Victor Power as *Apple on the Treetop*, Swords, 1980).

DESTRUCTION AND RECONSTRUCTION

286 John de Courcy Ireland, *Ireland's Sea Fisheries* (Dublin, 1981).

287 A. Powell, *op. cit.*

287 Leo Daly, *Oileáin Árann* (Swinford, 1975).

288 Pat Mullen, *Man of Aran.*

288 Richard J. Scott, *The Galway Hooker* (Swords, 1983).

POINT OF ARRIVAL

292 John Ridgeway and Chay Blyth, *A Fighting Chance* (London, 1966).

292 Leo Daly, *op. cit.*

THE BAY OF DOUBT

300 E. P. Wright, "Notes on the flora of the Islands of Arran," *Proc. Nat. Hist. Soc. of Dublin* Vol. V (1866).

300 H. C. Hart, *A List of Plants found in the Islands of Aran* (Dublin, 1875).

300 Robert Ll. Praeger, "Report of Conference and Excursion held at Galway, 1895," *Irish Naturalist* Vol. IV (1895).

300 D. A. Webb, "Flora of the Aran Islands," *Journal of Life Sciences, Royal Dublin Society*, Vol. II (1980).

302 A. Powell, *Oileáin Árann*.

303 J. M. Synge, *The Aran Islands*.

THE FIELD OF THE CLOAK

305 Manus O'Donnell, *Betha Coluimb Chille*, 1532 trans. and ed. A. O'Kelleher and G. Schoepperle (Illinois, 1918); this section trans. by Richard Henebry in *Zeitschrift für Celtische Philologie* Vol. X (1914).

CILL ÉINNE: THE VILLAGE

309 Giraldus Cambrensis, *Topographia Hiberniae*.

310 R. O'Flaherty, *West or H-Iar Connaught*.

311 *Galway Vindicator* (17 April 1880).

AIRCÍN: THE CASTLE

313 Magradin, *Vita S. Endei*, quoted in translation in O'Donovan, *Ordnance Survey Letters*.

314 Gearóid Mac Niocaill, *Ireland Before the Vikings* (Dublin, 1972).

315 Hardiman, *History of Galway*.

319 E. W. Lynam, "The O'Flaherty Country," *Studies* (June 1914).

320 Tomás Ó Cillín (former parish priest in Aran), *Short Annals of Aran* (ms. in Archiepiscopal Library, Tuam; this gives many detailed references to State Papers etc.).

320 Hardiman's appendix to R. O'Flaherty, *West or H-Iar Connaught*.

320 T. P. Kilfeather, *Ireland, Graveyard of the Spanish Armada* (Dublin, 1967).

322 Anne Chambers, *Granuaile, the Life and Times of Grace O'Malley* (Dublin, 1983).

322 "Fulmar Petrel," *Grania Waile* (London, 1895).

324 M. D. O'Sullivan, *Old Galway* (Galway, 1983).

324 T. V. O'Brien, *History of the Aran Islands* (ms. 1945, copies in T.C.D. and the London Library; this gives detailed references to State Papers, the Ormonde ms. and other sources).

325 Rev. Seán O'Riordan, "Rinuccini in Galway," *Galway Arch. and Hist. Soc. Journal* Vol. XXIII (1948).

328 R. Dunlop, *Ireland under the Commonwealth* (Manchester, 1913).

328 Hardiman, *History of Galway*.

AIRCÍN: THE PAWN

330 Peter Beresford Ellis, *Hell or Connaught! The Cromwellian Colonisation of Ireland 1652–1660* (London, 1975).

333 T. V. O'Brien, *op. cit.*

BONES IN THE SAND

346 Pat Mullen, *Hero Breed*.

SANDS IN THE WIND

348 Rev. William Kilbride, "Notes on some Antiquities on Aranmore; Part 1, Iararna," *Jn.H.A.A.I.* Vol. I, Ser. 3 (1868).

352 Frank Mitchell, *The Irish Landscape* (London, 1976).

STRAW ISLAND

357 Oliver J. Burke, *The South Islands of Aran* (London, 1887).

359 J. T. Mackay, "A systematic catalogue of rare plants found in Ireland," *Trans.Dub.Soc.* Vol. V (1805).

EASY GOING

367 Magradin, *op. cit.*

THE ARAN ISLANDS AND
NEIGHBOURING COASTS

1	Roundstone	7	*Camas*
2	Skerd Rocks	8	*Leitir Móir*
3	Cashel	9	*Garomna*
4	*Cill Chiaráin*	10	*Leitir Mealláin*
5	*Cnoc Mordáin*	11	*An Cheathrú Rua*
6	*Ros Muc*	12	*Casla*

Inishbofin

The
Joyce Country

The
Twelve Bens

Clifden

CONNEMARA

Lough
Corrib

C O U N T Y   G A L W A Y

Slyne Head

GALWAY

Ros a' Mhíl

Cois Fharraige

Golam Head

Na hOileáin

GALWAY BAY

Black Head

Kinvara

Ballyvaughan

ÁRAINN

INIS MEÁIN

THE

BURREN

INIS OÍRR

OILEÁIN ÁRANN

Doolin

Cliffs of
Moher

C O U N T Y

C L A R E

Ennis

≡	limestone
╲╲	granite
⫽	mainly meta-
	morphic rocks
⦀	shales and
	flagstones
▓	South Connemara
	group
⌒	cliffs

The Shannon

0   10   20

miles

ÁRAINN

N

43 Port an Choma
44 An Coirnéal
45 Scrios na gCapall
46 An Scrios Mór
47 Loch Dearg
48 An Chora Dhubh Thiar
49 An Seanchaisleán
50 Na Seacht dTeampaill
   (The Seven Churches)
51 An Chora Dhubh Thoir

52 An Creachoileán
53 Cora Scaití Ciúin
54 An Uaimh Mhór
55 Buaile Ghaeil
56 Teach an Smáil
57 An Corradán
58 Fearann na Bacaí
59 Poll na Loinge
60 Balla na Sáibhéarachta

An tOileán Iarthach
lighthouse

An Gleannachán
46
45
47 51 Port Chonnla
52
Creig an Chéirín
53
44
49 50 54
42
41 43 Srutbán 55
40 Eoghanacht
39 38 37 Bun Gabhla 56 57
Oileán Dá Bhranóg
35 Dún Port Sheánla
36 EOGHANACHT Eoghanachta
33 58 Port Mhuir-
An Gríóir 34 bhigh
32 Cill 59 60
Binn an tSléibhe Mhóir 30 27 Mhuírbhígh
31 28 26 CILL
29 MHUÍRBHÍGH
An Sraoilleán 24 Dún Aonghasa
Gort na gCapall
An Sunda Caoch
Poll na bPéist
Port Bhéal 22
an Dúin 21

33 An Carnán
34 Binn an Iarainn
35 Ulán na gCrosán
36 An Creachoileán Mór
37 Cladach Bhun Gabhla
38 An Gob Thoir
39 An Gob Thiar
40 An Caladh
41 An Bodach Crom
42 Leic na Creathnaí

26 Barr an Leath-chartúir
27 An Turlach Mór
28 Binn an Turlaigh
29 Leic an Chlochair
30 Scailp na bPlátaí
31 An Poll Dubh
32 An Troigh Mhairbh

21 An Aill Bhriste
22 Poll Uí Néadáin
23 Carraig an Smáil
24 Leac an tSalainn
25 Binn an Ghlais

sand high ground

shingle low ground

shading shows the orientation
of the principal set of fissures

rocks exposed
at low water

townland
boundaries

townlands: E O C H A I L L

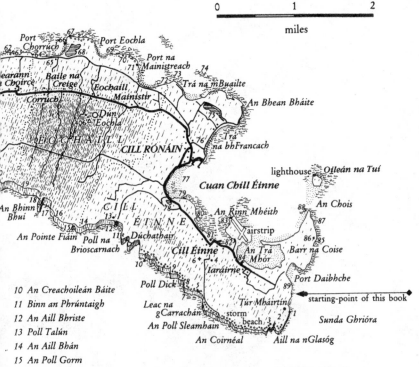

INDEX

TITLES IN SERIES

For a complete list of titles, visit www.nyrb.com or write to:
Catalog Requests, NYRB, 435 Hudson Street, New York, NY 10014